Study Guide

*Volume 2: From 1300*

# A HISTORY OF WORLD SOCIETIES

Study Guide

*Volume 2: From 1300*


# A HISTORY OF WORLD SOCIETIES

*Second Edition*


James A. Schmiechen
Central Michigan University, Mt. Pleasant

John P. McKay
University of Illinois at Urbana-Champaign

**HOUGHTON MIFFLIN COMPANY** • **BOSTON**

Dallas     Geneva, Illinois     Palo Alto     Princeton

Library of Congress Catalog Card Number: 87-81264

ISBN: 0-395-46503-6

ABCDEFGHIJ-H-8987

# CONTENTS

v

# TO THE STUDENT

## HOW TO STUDY HISTORY AND PREPARE FOR EXAMS

The study of history can be rewarding but also perplexing. Most history courses require you to read and understand large bodies of detailed information. The history student is expected to perform many tasks—memorize information, study the reasons for change, analyze the accomplishments and failures of various societies, understand new ideas, identify historical periods, pick out broad themes and generalizations in history, and so forth. These jobs often present difficulties. This guide will make your study easier and increase your efficiency. It has been developed to help you read, study, and review *A History of World Societies*, and regular and systematic use of it will improve your grade in this course. You may use the guide in a variety of ways, but for best results you might choose the following approach:

1. *Preview the entire chapter* by reading the chapter objectives and synopsis; then quickly read through the study outline, noting the reading with understanding exercises. All of this will take only a few minutes but is an important first step in reading. It is called *previewing*. By pointing out what the chapter is about and what to look for, previewing will make your reading easier and improve your reading comprehension.

2. *Now read your assignment in the textbook*. Pay attention to features that reveal the scope and major emphasis of a chapter or section, such as the chapter title, chapter and section introductions, questions, headings, conclusions, and illustrative material (e.g., maps and photographs). Note study hint 3 on page xi about underlining.

3. After reading, *review what you have read* and check your comprehension by going over the chapter outline once again—but this time make sure that you understand

all the points and subpoints. If you do not fully understand a particular point or subpoint, then you need to return to the text and reread. It is not at all uncommon to need to read the text at least twice.

4. Continue your review. *Answer the review questions* that follow the study outline. It is best to write out or outline your answer on a sheet of paper or a note card. Be sure to include the supporting facts. Reread your answers periodically. This process will help you build a storehouse of information and understanding to use at the time of the exam.

5. Now work on the definitions, identifications, and explanations in the study-review exercises provided in each chapter of the *Study Guide*. This will help you to understand and recall both concepts and specific facts. Know not just who or what, but also why the term is significant. Does it illustrate or represent some fundamental change or process? Note that if a particular term appears in the text *and* in your lecture notes, it is of special importance. Do the geography exercises found in all appropriate chapters. This is important because they will enable you to visualize the subject matter and thus remember it better. It will take a few minutes, but the payoff is considerable.

6. Last, *complete the multiple-choice and fill-in exercises* for each *Study Guide* chapter. Some of these questions look for basic facts, while others test your understanding and ability to synthesize material. *The answers are at the end of the Guide.* If you miss more than two or three, you need to restudy the text or spend more time working on the *Guide*.

## ADDITIONAL STUDY HINTS*

1. *Organize your study time effectively*. Many students fail to do well in courses because they do not organize their time effectively. In college, students are expected to read the material before class, review, and do the homework on their own. Many history teachers give only two or three tests during the semester; therefore, assuming personal responsibility for learning the material is vital. Mark up a semester calendar to show scheduled test dates, when term projects are due, and blocks of time to be set aside for exam study and paper writing. Then, at the beginning of each week, check the calendar and your course outlines and notes to see what specific preparation is

---

*For a complete text and workbook written to meet the needs of students who want to do their best in college, see James F. Shepherd, *RSVP, The Houghton Mifflin Reading, Study, and Vocabulary Program*, Third Edition (1988).

necessary for the coming week, and plan your time accordingly. Look at all the reading with understanding exercises in this *Study Guide* and try to estimate how much time you will need to master study skills. Set aside a block of time each day or once every several days for reading your text or studying your lecture notes and working in the *Study Guide*. Despite what one observes on college campuses, studying is not done most effectively late at night or with background music. Find a quiet place to study alone, one where you can tune out the world and tune into the past.

2. *Take good lecture notes.* Good notes are readable, clear, and above all reviewable. Write down as much of the lecture as you can without letting your pen get too far behind the lecturer. Use abbreviations and jot down key words. Leave spaces where appropriate and then go back and add to your notes as soon after the lecture as possible. You may find it helpful to leave a wide margin on the left side for writing in subject headings, important points, and questions, as well as for adding information and cross-references to the text and other readings. One way to use your notes effectively is by *reciting*. Reciting is the act of asking a question and then repeating the answer silently or aloud until you can recall it easily. Above all, do not wait until the night before an exam to use lecture notes you have not looked at for weeks or months. Review your lecture notes often and see how they complement and help you interpret your reading.

3. *Underline.* Too often students mark almost everything they read and end up with little else than an entire book highlighted in yellow. Underlining can be extremely helpful or simply a waste of time in preparing for exams; the key is to be selective in what you underline. Here are some suggestions:

a. Underline major concepts, ideas, and conclusions. You will be expected to interpret and analyze the material you have read. In many cases the textbook authors themselves have done this, so you need to pinpoint their comments as you read. Is the author making a point of interpretation or coming to a conclusion? If so, underline the key part. Remember, learning to generalize is very important, for it is the process of making history make sense. The author does it and you must learn to identify his or her interpretation as well as conflicting interpretations; then to make your own. Here is where your study of history can pay big rewards. The historian, like a good detective, not only gathers facts but also analyzes, synthesizes, and generalizes from that basic information. This is the process of *historical interpretation*, which you must seek to master.

b. Underline basic facts. You will be expected to know basic facts (names, events, dates, places) so that you can reconstruct the larger picture and back up your analysis and interpretations. Each chapter of this guide includes several lists of important items. Look over these lists before you begin to read, and then underline these words as you read.

c. Look at the review questions in the *Study Guide*—they will point to the major themes and questions to be answered. Then, as you read, underline the material that answers these questions. Making marginal notations can often complement your underlining.

4. *Work on your vocabulary.* The course lectures and each chapter in the text will probably include words that you do not know. Some of these will be historical terms or special concepts, such as *polis, feudalism,* or *bourgeoisie*—words that are not often used in ordinary American speech. Others are simply new to you but important for understanding readings and discussion. If you cannot determine the meaning of the word from the context in which it appears or from its word structure, then you will need to use a dictionary. *Keep a list of words* in your lecture notebook or use the pages in the back of this guide. Improving your historical and general vocabulary is an important part of reading history as well as furthering your college career. Most graduate-school entrance exams and many job applications, for instance, have sections to test vocabulary and reading comprehension.

5. *Benefit from taking essay exams.* Here is your chance to practice your skills in historical interpretation and synthesis. Essay exams demand that you express yourself through ideas, concepts, and generalizations as well as by reciting the bare facts. The key to taking an essay exam is preparation. Follow these suggestions:

a. *Try to anticipate the questions on the exam.* As you read the text, your notes, and this guide, jot down what seem to be logical essay questions. This will become easier as the course continues, partly because you will be familiar with the type of question your instructor asks. Some questions are fairly broad, such as the chapter-objective questions at the beginning of each chapter in this guide; others have a more specific focus, such as the review questions. Take a good look at your lecture notes. Most professors organize their daily lectures around a particular theme or stage in history. You should be able to invent a question or two from each lecture. Then answer the question. Do the same with the textbook, using the *Study Guide* for direction. Remember, professors are often impressed when students include in their essay textbook material not covered in class.

b. *Aim for good content and organization.* Be prepared to answer questions that require historical interpretation and analysis of a particular event, series of events, movement, process, person's life, and so forth. You must also be prepared to provide specific information to back up and support your analysis. In some cases you will be expected to give either a chronological narrative of events or a topical narrative (for example, explaining a historical movement in terms of its social, political, and economic features). Historians often approach problems in terms of cause and effect, so spend some time thinking about events in these terms. Remember, not all causes are of equal importance, so you must be ready to make distinctions—and to back up these distinctions with evidence. This is all part of showing your skill at historical interpretation.

When organizing your essay, you will usually want to sketch out your general thesis (argument) or point of interpretation first, in an introductory sentence or two. Next move to the substance. Here you will illustrate and develop your argument by weighing the evidence and marshaling reasons and factual data. After you have completed this stage (writing the body of your essay), go on to your conclusion, which most likely will be a restatement of your original thesis. It is often helpful to outline your major points before you begin to write. Be sure you answer all parts of the question. Write clearly and directly. All of this is hard to do, but you will get better at it as the course moves along.

6. *Enhance your understanding* of important historical questions by undertaking additional reading and/or a research project as suggested in the "Understanding History Through Reading and the Arts" and "Problems for Further Investigation" sections in the *Study Guide*. Note also that each textbook chapter has an excellent bibliography. Many of the books suggested are available in paperback editions, and all of the music suggested is available in most record-lending libraries and record stores.

7. *Know why you are studying history.* Nothing is worse than having to study a subject that appears to have no practical value. And indeed, it is unlikely that by itself this history course will land you a job. What, then, is its value, and how can it enrich your life? Although many students like history simply because it is interesting, there are a number of solid, old-fashioned reasons for studying it. It is often said that we need to understand our past in order to live in the present and build the future. This is true on a number of levels. On the psychological level, identification with the past gives us a badly needed sense of continuity and order in the face of ever more rapid change. We see how change has occurred in the past and are therefore better prepared to deal with it in our own lives. On another level, it is important for us to know how differing political, economic, and social systems work and what benefits and disadvantages accrue from them. As the good craftsperson uses a lifetime of experience to make a masterpiece, so an understanding of the accumulated experiences of the past enables us to construct a better society. Further, we need to understand how the historical experiences of peoples and nations have differed, and how these differences have shaped their respective visions. Only then can we come to understand how others view the world differently from the ways in which we do. Thus, history breaks down the barriers erected by provincialism and ignorance.

The strongest argument for the study of history, though, is that it re-creates the big picture at a time when it is fashionable and seemingly prudent to be highly specialized and narrowly focused. We live in the Age of Specialization. Even our universities often appear as giant trade schools, where we are asked to learn a lot about a little. As a result, it is easy to miss what is happening to the forest because we have become obsessed with a few of the trees. While specialization has undeniable benefits, both societies and individuals also need the generalist perspective and the ability to see how the entire system works. History is the queen of the generalist disciplines. Looking at change over time, history shows us how to take all the parts of the puzzle—politics, war, science, economics, architecture, sex, demography, music, philosophy, and much more—and put them together so that we can understand the whole. It is through a study of the interrelationships of the parts over a long expanse of time that we can develop a vision of society. By promoting the generalist perspective, history plays an important part on today's college campus.

Finally, the study of history has a more personal and surprisingly practical application. It is becoming increasingly apparent to many employers and educators that neglect of the liberal arts and humanities by well-meaning students has left them unable to think and reason analytically and to write and speak effectively. Overspecialized, narrowly focused education has left these students seriously deficient in basic verbal skills, placing them at a serious disadvantage in the job market. Here is where this course can help. It is universally recognized that studying history is an excellent way to develop the ability to reason and write. And the moving pageant of centuries of human experience you are about to witness will surely spark your interest and develop your aptitude if you give it the chance.

## ACKNOWLEDGMENTS

The authors are indebted to Professors Gabriel Chin, Patricia Ramft, John Robertson, Nina Robertson, and James Dealing, all of Central Michigan University, for their suggestions in the preparation of the "Understanding History Through Reading and the Arts" and "Problems for Further Investigation" sections of this guide; to Annette Davis and Ardith Jones for their help in the preparation of the manuscript; and to Chris Uganski for his assistance in the preparation of the test sections.

# CHAPTER 15

## THE CRISIS OF THE
## LATER MIDDLE AGES

## CHAPTER OBJECTIVES

After reading and studying this chapter you should be able to answer the following questions:

Q-1.   What were the causes and the effects of the fourteenth-century disasters in Europe — namely, plague, war, social upheaval, crime, and violence?
Q-2.   Was war a catalyst for change?
Q-3.   What provoked the division in the church in the fourteenth century?

## CHAPTER SYNOPSIS

The fourteenth century was a time of disease, war, crime, and violence. The art and literature of the period are full of the portrayal of death, just as the historical accounts are full of tales of conflict and violence. There were several major causes for this century of human suffering. Natural disasters — including changes in climate and horrible new diseases — attacked Europe. A long series of wars between France and England not only brought death and economic ruin but increased personal violence and crime as well. In addition, a serious shortage of labor, created by the bubonic plague, resulted in intense social conflict between landlords and peasants. Economic crisis during the century also resulted in a bitter struggle between urban workers and their guild masters.

   Amid such violence the church lost power and prestige, partly because of the religious disillusionment that accompanied the plague. In short, the institutional church failed to fill the spiritual vacuum left by the series of disasters. A more immediate reason for the decline of the church's influence and prestige was the Babylonian captivity and the Great Schism. The call for reform, often in the form

1

of the conciliar movement, by people such as Marsiglio of Padua and John Wyclif, was a signal of things to come in the sixteenth-century Reformation.

But the century of disaster was also a century of change, some of it for the good of ordinary people. It is in this light that the chapter examines some important changes in marriage practices, family relations, and the life of the people. The decline in population meant that those who survived had better food and higher wages. Peasants in western Europe used the labor-shortage problem to demand higher wages and freedom from serfdom. These demands often resulted in conflict with their lords. The disillusionment with the organized church also led to greater lay independence and, ultimately, ideas of social and political equality. The wars actually fostered the development of constitutionalism in England. All in all, it was a period of disaster but of disaster that brought with it important changes.

## STUDY OUTLINE

I.   Death and disease in the fourteenth century
  A.  Prelude to disaster
    1.  Climate changes and inflation caused economic decline
    2.  Diseases killed many people and animals
    3.  The population was undernourished, and population growth came to a halt
    4.  Weak governments were unable to deal with these problems
  B.  The Black Death
    1.  Genoese ships brought the plague — the Black Death — to Europe in 1347
    2.  This bubonic bacillus lived in fleas that infested black rats
    3.  Unsanitary and overcrowded cities were ideal breeding grounds for the black rats
    4.  Most people had no rational explanation for the disease, and out of ignorance and fear many blamed it on Jews
    5.  The disease, which killed millions, recurred often and as late as 1700
  C.  The social and psychological consequences of the Black Death
    1.  The plague hit the poor harder than the rich, but all classes suffered
    2.  The decline in population meant labor shortages; thus wages went up and social mobility increased
    3.  The psychological consequences of the plague were enormous: depression, gross sensuality, flagellantism, and obsession with death
II.  The Hundred Years' War (ca 1337–1453)
  A.  The causes of the war
    1.  Edward III of England, the grandson of the French king Philip the Fair, claimed the French crown, and French barons used Edward's claim as a way to check their king

      2. Flemish wool merchants supported the English claim to the crown
      3. Both the French and the English saw military adventure as an excuse to avoid domestic problems
      4. The French barons passed the crown to Philip Valois and not Edward III
      5. Royal propaganda for war and plunder was strong on both sides
  B. The Indian summer of medieval chivalry during the Hundred Years' War
      1. Chivalry was a code of conduct for the knightly class
         a. Knights were supposed to be brave, loyal, courteous, and generous
         b. Chivalry and feudal society glorified war
      2. Chivalry enjoyed its final days of glory during the war
  C. The course of the war to 1419
      1. The battles took place in France and the Low Countries
      2. At the battle of Crécy (1346), the English disregarded the chivalric code and used new military tactics: the longbow and cannon
  D. Joan of Arc and France's victory
      1. Joan of Arc's campaigns meant a turning point and victory for France
      2. Joan was turned over to the English, and a French church court burned her as a heretic
  E. Costs and consequences
      1. The war meant economic and population decline for France and England
      2. War financing caused a slump in the English wool trade
      3. In England, returning soldiers caused social problems
      4. The war encouraged the growth of parliamentary government, particularly in England
      5. The war generated feelings of nationalism in England and France
III. Vernacular literature
  A. The emergence of national consciousness is seen in the rise of literature written in national languages — the vernacular
  B. Three literary masterpieces manifest this new national pride
      1. Dante's *Divine Comedy*, a symbolic pilgrimage to the City of God, embodies the psychological tensions of the age and contains bitter criticism of some church authorities
      2. Chaucer, in his *Canterbury Tales*, uses a religious setting to depict the materialistic and worldly interests of a variety of English people in the fourteenth century
      3. Villon used the language of the lower classes to talk about the reality, beauty, and hardships of life here on earth
IV. The decline of the church's prestige
  A. The Babylonian Captivity (1309–1377)
      1. The pope had lived at Avignon since the reign of King Philip the Fair of France and thus was subject to French control

        2.   This Babylonian Captivity damaged papal power and prestige

        3.   Pope Gregory XI brought the papacy back to Rome in 1377, but then a split occurred when the newly elected Urban VI alienated the church hierarchy in his zeal to reform the church

        4.   A new pope, Clement VII, was elected, and the two popes both claimed to be legitimate (the Great Schism)

   B.  The Great Schism lasted until 1417

        1.   England and Germany recognized Pope Urban VI

        2.   France and others recognized Pope Clement VII

   C.  The conciliar movement was based on the idea of reform through a council of church leaders

        1.   Marsiglio of Padua claimed that authority within the church should rest with a church council and not the pope

        2.   The English teacher John Wyclif and his "Lollard" followers attacked papal authority and called for even more radical reform of the church

        3.   Wyclif's ideas were spread to Bohemia by John Hus

        4.   Finally, the council at Constance (1414–1418) ended the schism with the election of Pope Martin V and condemned Hus to death

V.  The life of the people in the fourteenth and fifteenth centuries

   A.  Marriage and the family

        1.   Economic factors, rather than romantic love, usually governed the decision to marry

        2.   Marriage usually came very early for women and later for men; divorce did not exist

        3.   Many people, however, did not observe church regulations and married without a church ceremony

   B.  Life in the parish

        1.   The land and the religion were the centers of life

        2.   Mobility within guilds declined in the fourteenth century, and strikes and riots within guilds became frequent

        3.   Cruel sports, such as bullbaiting, and drunkenness reflect the violence and frustrations of the age

        4.   Lay people increasingly participated in church management

   C.  Peasants' revolts

        1.   Peasants revolted in France in 1358 and in England in 1381

        2.   One cause was the lords' attempt to freeze wages

        3.   In general, the revolts were due to rising expectations

        4.   The 1381 revolt in England began as a protest against taxes

        5.   As in England, workers in Italy, Germany, and Spain revolted

   D.  Conclusion: catalysts for change

        1.   The crises and wars of the fourteenth and fifteenth centuries altered traditional ways of life

2. Rising social consciousness, changes in government, and advances in technology were some of the changes brought by the events of the times

## REVIEW QUESTIONS

Q-1.   What were the causes of the European population decline that began in the early fourteenth century?

Q-2.   What was the source of the bubonic plague, and why did it spread so rapidly in Europe?

Q-3.   How did the plague affect wages and the demand for labor? Can you guess what happened to land values?

Q-4.   Describe the psychological effects of the plague. How did people explain this disaster?

Q-5.   What were the immediate and other causes of the Hundred Years' War?

Q-6.   In your opinion, did feudalism tend to encourage or prevent war? Explain.

Q-7.   What were the results of the Hundred Years' War? Who were the winners and losers within both countries?

Q-8.   Why did a national representative assembly emerge in England?

Q-9.   Drawing on the writings of Dante, Chaucer, and Villon, describe vernacular literature in terms of its form and subject matter. What makes it "modern"?

Q-10.   The Babylonian Captivity greatly weakened the power and prestige of the church. Explain.

Q-11.   In 1409 there were three popes. Why? Who were they, and how and why did this situation occur?

Q-12.   What was the conciliar movement, and who were its advocates? Was this a revolutionary idea?

Q-13.   Why was Wyclif a threat to the institutional church? Even many powerful and rich lords feared the Lollards. Why?

Q-14.   Did peasant conditions improve or deteriorate in the fourteenth and fifteenth centuries? Explain.

Q-15.   What were the reasons for the French *Jacquerie* of 1358 and the English Peasants' Revolt of 1381?

Q-16.   Who was Joan of Arc, and how did she affect French history?

Q-17.   Describe the marriage patterns of late medieval people in terms of when and why people married and the influence that the Church had on marriage.

Q-18.   What is meant by the idea of the Indian summer of medieval chivalry?

## STUDY-REVIEW EXERCISES

*Define* each of the following key concepts and terms.

English Statute of Labourers

conciliar movement

*Pasteurella pestis*

vernacular

craft guild

*Identify* each of the following and give its significance.

Marsiglio of Padua

Battle of Crécy (1346)

Martin V

Joan of Arc

Babylonian Captivity

Margaret Paston

Lollards

Edward III

John Hus

John Wyclif

*Jacquerie*

*Explain the importance of each of the following concepts in late medieval life and describe what changes it was subject to in this period.*

pluralism

marriage and womanhood

feudal chivalry

individual Christian faith

leisure time

nationalism

*Provide approximate dates for the following important events.*

1. The first instance of the bubonic plague in Europe

2. The Babylonian Captivity

3. The Hundred Years' War

4. The Council of Constance

5. The battle of Crécy

6. The French *Jacquerie* revolt

7. Dante's *Divine Comedy*

*Test your understanding of the chapter by answering the following questions.*

1. In reaction to the calls for reform in the fourteenth century, the church *did/ did not* enter into a period of reform and rejuvenation.
2. Prior to the plague in 1348, Europe experienced a period of unusually *good/bad* harvests.

3. The Hundred Years' War was between the kings of _____

   and _____.

4. The followers of the English theologian Wyclif were called _____ .
5. Up to the nineteenth century, *economic/romantic* factors usually determined whom and when a person married.
6. For the most part, job mobility within the late medieval guilds tended to *increase/decrease.*


## MULTIPLE-CHOICE QUESTIONS

1. The conciliar movement was a (an)
   a. effort to give the pope the power to use councils to wipe out heresy.
   b. effort by the French lords to establish a parliament.
   c. new monastic order vowing poverty.
   d. attempt to place ultimate church authority in a general council.

2. The plague was probably brought into Europe by
   a. Chinese soldiers.
   b. Spanish warriors returning from South America.
   c. English soldiers pushing into France.
   d. Genoese ships from the Crimea.

3. In general, farm laborers who survived the bubonic plague faced
   a. higher wages.
   b. food shortages.
   c. the need to migrate.
   d. excommunication from the church.

4. Most people in the fourteenth century believed that the plague (Black Death) was caused by
   a. bad air.
   b. poor sanitation and housing.
   c. a bacillus living in fleas.
   d. black rats.

5. One reason for peasant-landlord conflict in the fourteenth century was
   a. peasants' opposition to declining wages and inflation.
   b. landlords' attempts to legislate wages.
   c. land scarcity.
   d. peasants' refusal to be drafted for war service.

6. The author of *Defensor Pacis* and proponent of the idea that authority in the Christian church rested in a general council rather than in the papacy was
   a. Cardinal Robert of Geneva.

    b. Pope Urban V.
    c. John Wyclif.
    d. Marsiglio of Padua.

7. After 1347, the Black Death generally moved from
    a. north to south.
    b. west to east.
    c. south to north.
    d. east to west.

8. Initially the Hundred Years' War was fought over
    a. Aquitaine.
    b. King Edward III's claim to the French crown.
    c. the control of the Flemish wool trade.
    d. religion.

9. English military innovation(s) during the Hundred Years' War included
    a. the crossbow.
    b. the cannon and the longbow.
    c. cavalry.
    d. the pike.

10. Who of the following was not a writer of vernacular literature?
    a. Dante
    b. Villon
    c. Clement VII
    d. Chaucer

11. For the French, the turning point of the Hundred Years' War was the
    a. relief of Paris.
    b. defeat of the English fleet in the English Channel.
    c. relief of Orleans.
    d. battle of Poitiers.

12. The condition(s) that made Europeans susceptible to the Black Death included
    a. devastating weather.
    b. crop failure.
    c. typhoid epidemic.
    d. all of the above.

13. The chivalric code applied to
    a. knights.
    b. peasants.

c.   infantry.
d.   all of the above.

14.   The majority of the battles in the Hundred Years' War were fought in
a.   France and the Low Countries.
b.   England.
c.   Germany.
d.   Ireland.

15.   The greatest gain made by England from the Hundred Years' War was
a.   Aquitaine.
b.   the growth of parliamentary power.
c.   Normandy.
d.   royal absolutism.

16.   Of the following social groups, which probably had the highest mortality rate
as a result of the plague?
a.   Knights
b.   Doctors
c.   Clergy
d.   Merchants

17.   The reason many men fought for England against France was
a.   national honor and hatred of the French.
b.   the opportunity provided them to display knightly virtue and the chivalric
code.
c.   the chance provided them to collect the spoils of war.
d.   all of the above.

18.   Which of the following statements about the fourteenth century is true?
a.   The population increased.
b.   The standard of living fell drastically.
c.   The power of the church declined.
d.   War between England and France was infrequent.

19.   Generally, the plague disaster of the fourteenth century resulted in which of
the following?
a.   Higher wages for most workers
b.   A sharp increase in the number of German clergymen
c.   A decline in flagellantism
d.   Little concern about death

20. The Hundred Years' War had which of the following effects on English society?
    a. It encouraged representative government.
    b. It caused nationalism to decline.
    c. It increased the amount of arable land in England.
    d. It created a manpower surplus.

21. Which of the following was a social consequence of the agricultural catastrophes of the fourteenth century?
    a. Earlier marriage
    b. Full employment
    c. Decrease in crime
    d. Increased serfdom

22. Which of the following statements characterizes marriage during the Middle Ages?
    a. Marriages were never made privately.
    b. Women tended to marry in their late twenties.
    c. Divorce did not exist.
    d. Marriages were determined by romantic love.

23. Which of the following was true of Joan of Arc?
    a. She was unpatriotic.
    b. The English king was her greatest supporter.
    c. She was accused of being a heretic and burned.
    d. She was from an aristocratic family.

24. Which of the following statements about the Babylonian Captivity is true?
    a. The papacy was moved to Paris.
    b. The papacy lost its prestige.
    c. The papacy concentrated only on spiritual matters.
    d. Rome experienced an economic boom.

25. Which of the following was a major point expressed by Marsiglio of Padua in his *Defensor Pacis*?
    .a. The church should acquire more property.
    b. The church was subordinate to the state.
    c. The pope's authority could not be overruled.
    d. The Scriptures should be the only basis of Christian belief and practice.

26. Which of the following had become the main purpose of craft guilds in the fourteenth century?
    a. To supply entertainment to members

b.   To maintain a monopoly on its product
c.   To ensure high standards for products
d.   To greatly increase membership

27.  The English Statute of Labourers unsuccessfully tried to address the problem of
a.   poor working conditions.
b.   the manpower surplus.
c.   high wages.
d.   declining workmanship.

28.  Whose vision was the most "modern" of the medieval vernacularists?
a.   Chaucer
b.   Dante
c.   Villon
d.   St. Augustine

## GEOGRAPHY

A.   Using Map 15.2 in the text
1.   Locate the extent of the English possessions in France from about 1337 to 1453. What were the origins of English claims to French land?

2.   Why was it unlikely that England could have held these territories permanently?

B.   Using Map 15.3 in the text
1.   Locate the main centers of popular revolt in France and England.
2.   Why were so many of the English revolts in the highly populated and advanced areas of the country?

## UNDERSTANDING HISTORY THROUGH READING AND THE ARTS

One of the results of the Black Death was a revival of Christian mysticism — a search for meaning in life through a personal relationship with God. One of the most popular books of this movement was *The Imitation of Christ\** by Thomas à Kempis.

An excellent introduction to the music of this period is a recording, *Instruments of the Middle Ages and Renaissance*, with an accompanying illustrated book by David Munro (Angel recording number SB2-3810 [1976] ), and for the French chansons and the English Madrigals listen to the recording titled *The King's Singers Sing of Courtly Pleasures*, which includes text and translations (Angel recording number s-37025 [1974] ).

Students interested in the history of disease in general or in the plague in particular should check the chapter bibliography. Three interesting accounts of the subject are G. C. Coulton, *The Black Death* (1929); P. Zeigler, *The Black Death* (1960); and W. McNeill, *Plagues and Peoples* (1976). E. Perroy, *The Hundred Years' War\** (1951), is a good start for anyone interested in that subject. Boccaccio's *Decameron* is a series of bawdy tales told by a group of Florentine men and women who fled to the countryside to escape the plague.

## PROBLEMS FOR FURTHER INVESTIGATION

What was the cause of the conflict between Philip the Fair of France and the pope? Was the French king out to destroy the power of the papacy? These and other questions are debated by a number of historians in C. T. Wood, ed., *Philip the Fair and Boniface VIII\** (1967).

What were the causes and results of the English peasants' revolt? Begin your investigation with R. Hilton, *Bond Men Made Free: The Medieval Peasant Movements and the English Rising of 1381* (1973).

\*Available in paperback.

## READING WITH UNDERSTANDING
## EXERCISE 1

## LEARNING HOW TO UNDERLINE OR HIGHLIGHT THE MAJOR POINTS

Underlining (or highlighting with a felt-tipped pen, as many students prefer) plays an important part in the learning process in college courses. Underlining provides you with a permanent record of what you want to learn. It helps you in your efforts to master the material and prepare for exams.

The introductory essay (pp. vii-xii) provides some good guidelines for learning how to underline effectively, and you should review it carefully before continuing.

**Further Suggestions**

1. In addition to underlining selectively, *consider numbering the main points* to help you remember them. Numbering helps make the main points stand out clearly, which is a major purpose of all underlining or highlighting.

2. *Read an entire section through before you underline or highlight it.* Then, as you read it a second time, you will be better able to pick out and underline key facts, main points, and sentences or paragraphs that summarize and interpret the information.

3. *Avoid false economies.* Some students do not mark their books because they are afraid that the bookstores will not buy them back. This is a foolish way to try to save money for two reasons. First, students must of necessity invest a great deal of time and money in their college education. By refusing to mark their books, they are reducing their chances of doing their best and thus endangering their whole college investment. Probably the only alternative to marking your books is making detailed written notes, which is more difficult and much more time consuming.

Second, carefully underlined books are *a permanent yet personal record of what you study and learn*. Such books become valuable reference works, helping you recall important learning experiences and forming the core of your library in future years.

### Exercise

Read the following passage once as a whole. Read it a second time to underline or highlight it. Consider numbering the points. On completion, compare your underlining with the model on the next page, which is an example of reasonable and useful underlining. Finally, compare the underlined section with the chapter outline in the *Study Guide*. You will see how the outline summary is an aid in learning how to underline major points.

## EGYPT, THE LAND OF THE PHARAOHS
## (3100-1200 B.C.)

The Greek historian and traveler Herodotus in the fifth century
B.C. called Egypt the "gift of the Nile." No other single geographical factor had such a fundamental and profound impact on
the shaping of Egyptian life, society, and history as the Nile. Unlike the rivers of Mesopotamia it rarely brought death and destruction. The river was primarily a creative force. The Egyptians
never feared the relatively calm Nile in the way the Mesopotamians feared their rivers. Instead they sang its praises:

> Hail to thee, O Nile, that issues from the earth and comes to
>    keep Egypt alive! . . .
> He that waters the meadows which Re created,
> He that makes to drink the desert . . .
> He who makes barley and brings emmer [wheat] into being . . .
> He who brings grass into being for the cattle.
> He who makes every beloved tree to grow . . .
> O Nile, verdant art thou, who makest man and cattle to live.[15]

In the minds of the Egyptians, the Nile was the supreme fertilizer
and renewer of the land. Each September the Nile floods its valley, transforming it into a huge area of marsh or lagoon. By the
end of November the water retreats, leaving behind a thin covering of fertile mud ready to be planted with crops.

The annual flood made the growing of abundant crops almost
effortless, especially in southern Egypt. Herodotus, used to the
rigors of Greek agriculture, was amazed by the ease with which
the Egyptians raised their crops:

> For indeed without trouble they obtain crops from the land
> more easily than all other men. . . . They do not labor to dig
> furrows with the plough or hoe or do the work which other
> men do to raise grain. But when the river by itself inundates
> the fields and the water recedes, then each man, having sown
> his field, sends pigs into it. When the pigs trample down the

seed, he waits for the harvest. Then when the pigs thresh the grain, he gets his crop.[16]

As late as 1822, John Burckhardt, an English traveler, watched nomads sowing grain by digging large holes in the mud and throwing in seeds. The extraordinary fertility of the Nile valley made it easy to produce an annual agricultural surplus, which in turn sustained a growing and prosperous population.

Whereas the Tigris and Euphrates and their many tributaries carved up Mesopotamia into isolated areas, the Nile served to unify Egypt. The river was the principal highway and promoted easy communication throughout the valley. As individual bands of settlers moved into the Nile valley, they created stable agricultural communities. By about 3100 B.C. there were some forty of these communities in constant contact with one another. This contact, encouraged and facilitated by the Nile, virtually ensured the early political unification of the country.

Egypt was fortunate in that it was nearly self-sufficient. Besides the fertility of its soil, Egypt possessed enormous quantities of stone, which served as the raw material of architecture and sculpture. Abundant clay was available for pottery, as was gold for jewelry and ornaments. The raw materials that Egypt lacked were close at hand. The Egyptians could obtain copper from Sinai and timber from Lebanon. They had little cause to look to the outside world for their essential needs, which helps to explain the insular quality of Egyptian life.

Geography further encouraged isolation by closing Egypt off from the outside world. To the east and west of the Nile valley stretch grim deserts. The Nubian Desert and the cataracts of the Nile discourage penetration from the south. Only in the north did the Mediterranean Sea leave Egypt exposed. Thus, geography shielded Egypt from invasion and from extensive immigration. Unlike the Mesopotamians, the Egyptians enjoyed centuries of peace and tranquillity, during which they could devote most of their resources to peaceful development of their distinctive civilization.

Yet Egypt was not completely sealed off. As early as 3250 B.C. Mesopotamian influences, notably architectural techniques and materials and perhaps even writing, made themselves felt in Egyptian life. Still later, from 1680 to 1580 B.C., northern Egypt was ruled by foreign invaders, the Hyksos. Infrequent though they were, such periods of foreign influence fertilized Egyptian culture without changing it in any fundamental way.

**The God-King of Egypt**

The geographic unity of Egypt quickly gave rise to political unification of the country under the authority of a king whom the Egyptians called "pharaoh." The details of this process have been lost. The Egyptians themselves told of a great king, Menes, who united Egypt into a single kingdom around 3100 B.C. Thereafter the Egyptians divided their history into *dynasties*, or families of kings. For modern historical purposes, however, it is more useful to divide Egyptian history into periods. The political unification of Egypt ushered in the period known as the Old Kingdom, an era remarkable for its prosperity and artistic flowering, and for the evolution of religious beliefs.

## EGYPT, THE LAND OF THE PHARAOHS
## (3100-1200 B.C.)

**Geography**

The Greek historian and traveler Herodotus in the fifth century B.C. called Egypt the "gift of the Nile." No other single geographical factor had such a fundamental and profound impact on the shaping of Egyptian life, society, and history as the Nile. Unlike the rivers of Mesopotamia it rarely brought death and destruction. The river was primarily a creative force. The Egyptians never feared the relatively calm Nile in the way the Mesopotamians feared their rivers. Instead they sang its praises:

**1**

> Hail to thee, O Nile, that issues from the earth and comes to
>     keep Egypt alive! . . .
> He that waters the meadows which Re created,
> He that makes to drink the desert . . .
> He who makes barley and brings emmer [wheat] into being . . .
> He who brings grass into being for the cattle.
> He who makes every beloved tree to grow . . .
> O Nile, verdant art thou, who makest man and cattle to live.[15]

In the minds of the Egyptians, the Nile was the supreme fertilizer and renewer of the land. Each September the Nile floods its valley, transforming it into a huge area of marsh or lagoon. By the end of November the water retreats, leaving behind a thin covering of fertile mud ready to be planted with crops.

**1a**

The annual flood made the growing of abundant crops almost effortless, especially in southern Egypt. Herodotus, used to the rigors of Greek agriculture, was amazed by the ease with which the Egyptians raised their crops:

> For indeed without trouble they obtain crops from the land
> more easily than all other men. . . . They do not labor to dig
> furrows with the plough or hoe or do the work which other
> men do to raise grain. But when the river by itself inundates
> the fields and the water recedes, then each man, having sown
> his field, sends pigs into it. When the pigs trample down the

seed, he waits for the harvest. Then when the pigs thresh the grain, he gets his crop.[16]

As late as 1822, John Burckhardt, an English traveler, watched nomads sowing grain by digging large holes in the mud and throwing in seeds. The extraordinary fertility of the Nile valley made it easy to produce an annual agricultural surplus, which in turn sustained a growing and prosperous population.

2  Whereas the Tigris and Euphrates and their many tributaries carved up Mesopotamia into isolated areas, the Nile served to unify Egypt. The river was the principal highway and promoted easy communication throughout the valley. As individual bands of settlers moved into the Nile valley, they created stable agricultural communities. By about 3100 B.C. there were some forty of these communities in constant contact with one another. This contact, encouraged and facilitated by the Nile, virtually ensured the early political unification of the country.

3  Egypt was fortunate in that it was nearly self-sufficient. Besides the fertility of its soil, Egypt possessed enormous quantities of stone, which served as the raw material of architecture and sculpture. Abundant clay was available for pottery, as was gold for jewelry and ornaments. The raw materials that Egypt lacked were close at hand. The Egyptians could obtain copper from Sinai and timber from Lebanon. They had little cause to look to the outside world for their essential needs, which helps to explain the insular quality of Egyptian life.

4  Geography further encouraged isolation by closing Egypt off from the outside world. To the east and west of the Nile valley stretch grim deserts. The Nubian Desert and the cataracts of the Nile discourage penetration from the south. Only in the north did the Mediterranean Sea leave Egypt exposed. Thus, geography shielded Egypt from invasion and from extensive immigration. Unlike the Mesopotamians, the Egyptians enjoyed centuries of peace and tranquillity, during which they could devote most of their resources to peaceful development of their distinctive civilization.

5    Yet Egypt was not completely sealed off. As early as 3250 B.C. Mesopotamian influences, notably architectural techniques and materials and perhaps even writing, made themselves felt in Egyptian life. Still later, from 1680 to 1580 B.C., northern Egypt was ruled by foreign invaders, the Hyksos. Infrequent though
6    they were, such periods of foreign influence fertilized Egyptian culture without changing it in any fundamental way.

### The God-King of Egypt

The geographic unity of Egypt quickly gave rise to political unification of the country under the authority of a king whom the Egyptians called "pharaoh." The details of this process have been lost. The Egyptians themselves told of a great king, Menes, who united Egypt into a single kingdom around 3100 B.C. Thereafter the Egyptians divided their history into *dynasties*, or families of kings. For modern historical purposes, however, it is more useful to divide Egyptian history into periods. The political unification of Egypt ushered in the period known as the Old Kingdom, an era remarkable for its prosperity and artistic flowering, and for the evolution of religious beliefs.

# CHAPTER 16

## AFRICA AND THE AMERICAS
## BEFORE EUROPEAN INTRUSION,
## CA 400–1500

## CHAPTER OBJECTIVES

After reading and studying this chapter you should be able to answer the following questions:

Q-1.  What sources of information help us to understand Africa in history?
Q-2.  What patterns of social and political organization prevailed among the peoples of Africa and Central and South America?
Q-3.  What types of agriculture and commerce did African and American peoples engage in?
Q-4.  What values do their art, architecture, and religion express?
Q-5.  What internal difficulties among American and African peoples contributed to their conquest by Europeans?

## CHAPTER SYNOPSIS

The social and political organization of medieval Africa and pre-Columbian America has received little attention from historians. Until recently we knew virtually nothing about the history of the interior of Africa — and thus held an incomplete picture of the beginning of agricultural civilization. By 1500 Africa, the second-largest continent in the world, supported a variety of very different societies and civilizations. A network of caravan routes connected the Mediterranean coast with the Sudan, bringing Islam to West Africa and stimulating gold mining, trade in slaves, and urbanization. It was the kingdom of Ghana that emerged as one of Africa's richest and most powerful states. By controlling the southern end of the caravan route, the semidivine Ghanaian king and the Ghanaian farmers built an agricultural and gold-rich state with its capital at Kumbi. Likewise, Mali had for centuries carried on a brisk trade in salt,

15

gold, and slaves; significantly, as in much of Africa, this trade introduced the Africans to Islam, which in turn led to the conversion of rulers to Islam, the growth of intellectual centers such as Timbuktu, and the strong influence of Muslim *ulemas*. The city-states of the East African coast conducted complicated mercantile activities with the Muslim Middle East, India, and China. By far, the most important foreign influence was Islam. In Ethiopia the city of Axum became the capital of an important civilization that held to a special brand of Christianity, that of Coptic Christianity, and in South Africa a society evolved that was based on new farming techniques gained from Bantu peoples and the mining of gold.

In America before European intrusion the Aztec, Maya, and Inca societies provide us with several of the most interesting (and puzzling) chapters in human history. By 1500 these cultures had passed their intellectual peaks, as their history became chapters in the history of European imperialism. The Aztec built a unified civilization based heavily on their Toltec heritage and distinguished by sophisticated achievements in engineering, sculpture, and architecture and a military-religious system that demanded enormous human sacrifice. The Inca state revealed a genius for organization — being unique at the time in assuming responsibility for the social welfare of all its people. The Maya used agricultural advancement to support a large population and invented a calendar, writing, and mathematics. After setting forth a variety of possible explanations, the author argues that the primary reason for the failure of the Incas to meet the Spanish challenge was political weakness and inferior military skills.

## STUDY OUTLINE

I. The land and peoples of Africa
    A. The geography of Africa
        1. Five geographical zones divide this continent, which covers 20 percent of the earth's land surface
            a. The Mediterranean and southwestern coasts have fertile land, good rainfall, and dense vegetation
            b. The dry steppe country of the inland, the Sahel, in the north has little plant life
            c. From here stretch the great deserts — the Sahara in the north and the Namib and Kalahari in the south
            d. The equatorial regions of central Africa have dense, humid, tropical rain forest
            e. The savanna lands that extend from west to east across the widest part of Africa make up one of the richest habitats in the world
            f. Each of these ecological zones has encouraged different economic activity

      2. The climate of Africa is tropical; rainfall is seasonal and is sparse in the desert and semidesert areas

      3. Five peoples inhabited Africa by 3000 B.C.

        a. The Berbers inhabited North Africa

        b. The Egyptians were a cultural rather than a racial group

        c. Black Africans inhabited the region south of the Sahara

        d. Pygmies inhabited the equatorial rain forests

        e. The Khoisans lived south of the equatorial rain forests

  B. Early African societies

      1. Africa was one of the sites of the beginning of agriculture

        a. It spread south from Ethiopia

        b. Agricultural development led to strong extended-family life

        c. Ironworking was introduced by 1000 B.C.

        d. The Bantu moved to Central Africa, where they grew as a result of their agricultural life

        e. Thin topsoil and scarcity of water led to migratory agriculture — that is, the shift of cultivation from place to place

      2. The western Sudan

        a. The Sudan is the area bounded by Egypt, the Red Sea, Ethiopia, Uganda, Zaire, Chad, and Libya

        b. Here a series of kingdoms emerged

        c. The Marde and Chadic peoples of western Sudan grew and prospered as a result of settled agriculture

        d. Religions were largely animistic and centered around family ritual cults

      3. The trans-Saharan trade

        a. The introduction of the camel had a profound economic and social impact in West Africa

          (1) Between A.D. 200 and A.D. 700, a network of caravan trade routes developed between the Mediterranean and the Sudan

          (2) Manufactured goods and foods were exchanged for raw materials and slaves

          (3) Caravan trade stimulated gold mining, slavery, and the slave trade

      4. Export of slaves was largely to Muslim societies

      5. Urban centers grew and Muslim culture, law, and religion became important

      6. Because of Islam, West Africa advanced in the fields of culture, government, and construction

II. African kingdoms and empires

  A. The medieval kingdom of Ghana, ca 900–1100, was a wealthy state

      1. The Soninke people called their ruler *ghana*, or war chief

      2.  Ghana's farms supported a large population

      3.  The war chief captured the southern portion of the caravan route in 992

      4.  The king was considered semisacred, his power was absolute, and he attained the crown through matrilineal heredity

B.  The court, influenced by Muslim ideas and run by a bureaucracy, was situated at Kumbi — which contained two sections

      1.  Muslims lived in their own quarter, or "town" — with their own religious-political authority

      2.  The king resided in another "town"

      3.  The royal court was extravagant and rich

C.  Ghana's juridical system was based on appeal to the supernatural — but the king could also be appealed to

D.  The royal estates, the tribute from chiefs, gold mining, and trade duties enabled the king to support a lavish court

E.  Ghanaian society consisted of several ranks

      1.  The governing aristocracy (king, court, officials) occupied the highest rank

      2.  Next were merchants, followed by the middle classes: farmers, miners, craftsmen, and weavers

      3.  At the bottom was a small slave class

      4.  Apart from these classes was the army

F.  The kingdom of Mali, ca 1200–1450

      1.  The kingdom of Ghana split into smaller kingdoms — one of which was Kangaba, which became Mali

          a.  Mali owed its greatness to its agriculture and its two great military rulers: Sundiata and Mansa Musa

          b.  The Mandinke people were successful at agriculture, and they profited from the West African salt and gold trade

      2.  Sundiata encouraged trade and expanded the Mali state

          a.  He transformed his capital, Niani, into an important financial and trading center

          b.  He conquered the former Ghana territories in addition to Gao, Jenne, and Walata

      3.  The Mansa, or emperor, Musa continued these expansionist policies

          a.  He extended his influence northward to Berber cities in the Sahara, east to Timbuktu and Gao, and west to the Atlantic

          b.  Royal control over the trans-Saharan trade brought great wealth; the empire grew to 8 million people

          c.  Musa appointed members of the royal family as governors to rule provinces and dependent kingdoms

          d.  He turned from animism to the Muslim religion, and Islamic practices and influence multiplied

   e. Musa's visit to Egypt illustrated his great wealth, but his spending and gifts caused inflation

   f. His pilgrimage to Mecca furthered relations among Mali, the Mediterranean states, and Islamic culture

   g. Timbuktu was transformed into a commercial, intellectual, and artistic center, to become known as the Queen of the Sudan

  4. The mix between Arabic trade, Muslim culture, and African peoples encouraged a high degree of cosmopolitanism and racial toleration

G. The East African city-states

  1. Commercial activity fostered the establishment of great city-states along the East African coast

   a. Many of the natives were called "Ethiopian," or black

   b. The relationship between Arab traders and native black people is unclear — although Islam did not overtake African religions

   c. Asian, African, and Islamic characteristics were established by the intermarriage of Arabs, Persians, and blacks

   d. This culture was called Swahili — a Bantu language

   e. Ibn-Battuta, a traveler, has left a written account of the great cities of Mombasa, Pemba, Kilwa, and Mogadishu

   f. The city of Kilwa was large and elegant, and the farmland produced rich yields

  2. By 1300 a ruler, or *sheikh*, had arisen, and Kilwa was the most powerful city on the coast

   a. Kilwa's prosperity rested on the gold trade and on the export of animal products

   b. Swahili cities traded these products for goods from China, India

  3. Slaves were bought for military, agricultural, maritime, and other purposes — including domestic work

H. Ethiopia: the Christian Kingdom of Axum

  1. The Kingdom of Ethiopia had close ties with the early Christian rulers of Nobatia, a Nubian state, and the Roman and Byzantine worlds

   a. The Ethiopian city of Axum, the center of this civilization, adopted Monophysite Christianity, which held that Christ was divine only, not divine and human

   b. Axum was the major military and political power in East Africa

   c. Economic contact with the Muslim world, along with the Abyssinian mountain range, caused Axum to sever ties with the Byzantine Empire

   d. The special brand of Christianity (Coptic Christianity) that developed here is the most striking feature of Ethiopia between 500 and 1500

I. South Africa

  1. This region is bordered on the northeast by the Zambesi River (see

Map 16.2), has a Mediterranean-type climate, and the land varies from desert to temperate grasslands

    2.  Until the arrival of the Portuguese (late 15th century) South Africa, unlike the rest of Africa, remained isolated from the outside

        a.  Only the Bantu ironworking and farming skills reached South Africa — this occurred by the year 1000 A.D. in what is now Zimbabwe, Orange Free State, and the Transvaal, and by 1500 in the western coastal region

        b.  In the west were Khosian-speaking farmers and in the east Bantu-speaking farmers who practiced polygamy

        c.  The city of Great Zimbabwe, built entirely of granite between the eleventh and fifteenth centuries, was over sixty acres in area, with great decoration, a temple, and an encircling wall

           (1)  This city was the capital of a vast empire consisting of the Zambezi-Limpopo region, and its wealth rested largely on gold mining

           (2)  Great Zimbabwe declined in the fifteenth century and a new empire, also based on gold trade, was built in the Mazoe Valley under the Mwene Mutapa rulers

  J.  All early African societies were stateless societies — in that their social and political organization was an outgrowth of clan bonds

  K.  The eastern region of Africa (East Africa) and the western region (the western Sudan) were similar in that they were shore cultures that had in common some word roots, cross-cultural interaction with the Muslim world, and a slave trade

III.  The geography and peoples of the Americas

  A.  The concept of the "New World" was a European invention that had no basis in European thought

  B.  The name "America" applies to the entire continent

    1.  It is about 9,000 miles in length, with a mountain range from Alaska to the tip of South America that crosses Central America from northwest to southwest

    2.  Mexico is dominated by high plateaus bounded by coastal plains: The plateau regions are "Cold Lands," whereas the valleys are "Temperate Lands" and the coasts are "Hot Lands"

    3.  The Central American coast is characterized by jungle, heavy rainfall, and heat; the uplands are better for agriculture and habitation

    4.  South America contains twelve nations and is a continent of extremely varied terrain

        a.  The western coast is edged by the Andes Mountains

        b.  On the east coast is the range called the Brazilian highlands

        c.  Three-quarters of the continent is plains

      d.   The Amazon River bisects the north-central part of the continent and creates dense and humid jungle lands

   5.   Immigrants — including Amurians and Mongoloids — crossed the Bering Straits as long as 20,000 years ago

      a.   Amerinds, or the American Indians, were a hybrid of these two groups

      b.   They practiced migratory agriculture, but some settled in villages

      c.   These newcomers spread out to make diverse linguistic and cultural groups

      d.   By about 2500 B.C. they had learned how to domesticate plants

   6.   The Mexicans built *chinampas*, whereas the land was terraced in Peru

IV.   Mesoamerican civilizations from the Olmec to the Toltec

   A.   The Olmec civilization (ca 1500 B.C. to A.D. 300) was the first Mesoamerican civilization

      1.   All subsequent Mesoamerican cultures have rested on the Olmec

         a.   Olmec society revolved around groups of large stone buildings that housed the political and religious elite

         b.   Peasants inhabited the surrounding countryside

         c.   A hereditary elite governed the mass of workers

         d.   Around 900 B.C. power shifted from San Lorenzo to LaVenta

      2.   The Great Pyramid at LaVenta was the center of the Olmec religious cult

      3.   When LaVenta fell around 300 B.C., Tres Zapotes became the leading Olmec site

   B.   The Maya of Central America

      1.   Between A.D. 300 and 900 the Maya of Central America built one of the world's highest cultures

         a.   The first Maya emigrated from North America

            (1)   The Cholan-speaking Maya apparently created the Maya culture

            (2)   Its economic base was agriculture, which supported a large population, and trade between cities evolved

         b.   Sharply defined social classes characterize the Maya culture

            (1)   No distinct mercantile class existed

            (2)   The hereditary nobility possessed the land and acted as warriors, merchants, and priests

            (3)   The rest were free workers, serfs, and slaves

         c.   Maya hieroglyphic writing has been deciphered, allowing us to understand the history and art of the Maya

         d.   The Maya invented a calendar and devised systems of mathematics and writing

   C.   Teotihuacan and Toltec civilizations lasted from about A.D. 300 to A.D. 900 and were the "Classic Period"

1. New people from the Mexico Valley built the city of Teotihuacan, which reached a population of over 200,000
   a. Its inhabitants were stratified into the powerful elite and ordinary workers
   b. It was the center for Mesoamerican trade and culture as well as its ceremonial center
   c. At its center were the Pyramids of the Sun and Moon, while other gods were worshipped at lesser temples
2. In the valley of Oaxaca, the Zapotecan peoples established a great religious center
3. Teotihuacan society collapsed before invaders around A.D. 700
4. This was followed by "the Time of Troubles" — a period of disorder, militarism, and emphasis on militant gods and warriors

D. The Toltec confederation rose up during "the Time of Troubles"
   1. The Toltecs assimilated into the Teotihuacan culture
   2. Under Toliptzin, or Quetzalcoatl, the Toltecs came to control most of central Mexico from coast to coast
   3. According to legend, the rich and powerful Quetzalcoatl went into exile when the god Tezcatlipoca won the battle over sacrifice
      a. The promise of Quetzalcoatl to return confused the emperor Montezuma and the Mexicans when the Spanish conquerors arrived
      b. Drought, weak rulers, and northern invasions brought trouble to the Toltecs
      c. In 1224 the Chichimec peoples of the north captured the Toltec capital of Tula
      d. The last of these Chichimec were the Aztecs, who absorbed the Olmec-Teotihuacan-Toltec culture

V. Aztec society: religion and war
   A. The early Aztecs founded a poor city on the swamps of Lake Texcoco in 1325
      1. By the time of Cortes in 1520, the Aztecs had risen to control all of central Mexico
      2. The Aztecs attributed their success to their god Huitzilopochtli and to their own will power; equally important, the Aztec state was geared for war
   B. War and human sacrifice in Aztec society
      1. War was the dominant cultural institution in Aztec society
         a. The Aztecs believed that the sun needed human blood as its fuel
         b. Victim-gladiators were sacrificed to the sun god
         c. At times thousands of victims were sacrificed, then eaten
      2. Anthropologists have proposed a variety of explanations for these practices

      a.  Human sacrifice served to regulate population growth

      b.  Protein deficiency turned the Aztecs to cannibalism

      c.  State terrorism used human sacrifice to control the people

C.  The life of the people

    1.  The early Aztecs made no sharp social distinctions

    2.  By 1500 a stratified social structure existed

      a.  Legend claims that the first king, a Toltec, fathered a noble class

      b.  By 1500 warriors dominated the state

      c.  The highest generals were great lords, or *tecuhtli*

      d.  Provincial governors functioned much like the feudal lords in medieval Europe

      e.  Beneath the nobility of soldiers were the common warriors

      f.  Male children were instructed in the art of war and sought to become *tequiua* (nobility)

    3.  A *maceualti*, or working class, made up the backbone of society

      a.  Members of this class were assigned work, but some of them enjoyed certain rights

    4.  The lowest class was the *thalmaitl*, which was made up of the landless workers or serfs

      a.  They were bound to the soil

      b.  They had some rights and often performed military service

    5.  Alongside all of these were the temple priests, who performed the sacrifice rituals and predicted the future

    6.  At the very top was the emperor, who was selected by a small group of priests, warriors, and officials

      a.  He lived in great luxury and ceremony

      b.  He was expected to be a great warrior and the lord of men (*tlacatecuhtli*)

D.  The cities of the Aztecs

    1.  Tenochtitlan, or Mexico City, was one of the largest and greatest cities in the world at the time of Diaz

      a.  Built on salt marshes and connected to the mainland by four highways, it had a population of half a million

      b.  Streets and canals crisscrossed the city and were lined with stucco houses

      c.  The Spanish marveled at the city's aqueduct, public squares, and marketplace with its variety of goods

      d.  The pyramid-temple of Huitzilopochtli dominated the city's skyline and was surrounded by a wall and many towers

      e.  In spite of their paganism, Cortes found these people remarkable in their accomplishments

VI.  The Incas of Peru

  A.  The Inca civilization was established in the six fertile valleys of Peru

    1.  Its culture rested on agriculture based on hill farming and guano fertilizing
        a.  By the fifteenth century, the farms could support a large number of warriors and industrial workers

B.  Inca imperialism
    1.  The Incas ascribed divine origin to their earliest king, Manco Capac
    2.  The king Pachacuti Inca and his son Topa Inca launched the imperialistic phase of Incan civilization
        a.  He extended Incan rule north to modern Ecuador and Colombia and to the Maule river in the South
        b.  Pachacuti made Quechua the official language
        c.  By imperial colonization (*mitima*) — language, religion, politics, and communication — the Incas controlled their subjects

C.  Incan society
    1.  The *ayllu*, or clan, was the central unit of early Incan society
        a.  The chief, or *curacau*, of the clan was used by kings Pachacuti and Topa to unify society
        b.  Eventually a new noble class was created by the king-emperors
        c.  Peasants were required to work for the nobility and the state
    2.  Marriage was required of all and was often decided by the state; polygamy was common
    3.  Daily life was regimented but all people were cared for
        a.  Although it had some socialist appearances, society was not based on equal distribution of wealth
        b.  The great nobility, the ones called big ears, and the lesser nobility were exempt from work

D.  The fall of the Incas
    1.  The Incan empire, with the emperor as a benevolent despot, fell easily to the Spanish under Pizarro
        a.  Isolation and legendary beliefs — such as the return of the legendary god Virocha — kept the Incas from taking prompt action
        b.  Pizarro came at a time of civil war
        c.  Pizarro wisely captured the emperor, Atahualpa

## REVIEW QUESTIONS

Q-1.  Name and briefly describe the five groups of people who had inhabited Africa by 8000 B.C.

Q-2.  What have been the sources of our knowledge of Africa?

Q-3.  Describe the Bantu agricultural achievements. Why did the Bantu adopt the practice of migratory agriculture?

Q-4.   What were the cultural and religious features of life in the western Sudan and how did the introduction of the camel affect West African life?

Q-5.   What was the economic base of the Ghanaian state and what sort of political organization did it exhibit?

Q-6.   Describe the reigns of Sundiata and Mansa Musa in Mali. What did they accomplish?

Q-7.   Discussing the economic, intellectual, and artistic features of the East African states, explain why this area can be described as highly cosmopolitan, rich, and racially tolerant.

Q-8.   Where was the location of the Kingdom of Axum, and in what way did its form of Christianity differ from that of the orthodox West?

Q-9.   Why was South Africa "far removed" from the outside world, and how was it influenced by Bantu-speaking peoples?

Q-10.   Describe the city of Great Zimbabwe. What was its economic base?

Q-11.   Early African societies are described as stateless societies. Explain.

Q-12.   What role did religion play in the Olmec civilization? How did architecture complement this?

Q-13.   Describe Teotihuacan-Toltec civilization in terms of its class structure and religion.

Q-14.   What was the legend of Quetzalcoatl's exile, and what role may it have played in later Mexican history?

Q-15.   To what features of Aztec culture do you attribute its success in building a great empire?

Q-16.   Why was human blood sacrifice an integral part of Aztec culture? What explanation is most plausible to you?

Q-17.   Describe the social structure of Aztec society. Who were the *tecuhtl*, the *maceualti*, and the *thalmaitl*? Who was the *tlacatecuhtli*?

Q-18.   Who were the Mayans and how was their society organized?

Q-19.   What did the Mayans accomplish?

Q-20.   Compare and contrast the agricultural-economic system and the political system of the Mayans and the Incas.

Q-21.   The Incan emperor has been described as a benevolent despot. Explain. Was Incan society an early socialist state?

Q-22.   Explain why the Inca civilization fell so easily to the Spanish under Pizarro.

Q-23.   Compare and contrast the Mayan and Aztec military systems and their methods of warfare.

## STUDY-REVIEW EXERCISES

*Define* the following key concepts and terms.

trans-Saharan trade

*ulemas*

*ghana*

Swahili

"New World"

*chinampas*

Mesoamerican

*tecuhtl*

Incan policy of *mitima*

*ayllu*

*sheikh*

stateless societies

*Identify* each of the following and give its significance.

Tenochtitlan

Amerigo Vespucci

Mansa Musa

Timbuktu

Ibn-Battuta

Kingdom of Axum

Kilwa

Toliptzin-Quetzalcoatl

Huitzilopochtli

Francisco Pizarro

Atahualpa

Pachacuti Inca and Topa Inca

the *Periplus*

*Ras Assir*

Manco Capac

Montezuma II

Hernando Cortes

Aztec "gladiator"

*Explain* the main features and characteristics (social, political, economic, and religious) of the following civilizations.

Olmec

Teotihuacan-Toltec

Aztec

Incan

Mayan

Ghanaian

Mali

early South Africa

*Test your understanding of the chapter by answering the following questions.*

1.  The great Mali emperor whose lavish spending during a visit to Egypt caused terrible inflation as well as world recognition was _____.

2.  The Soninke people of Africa called their ruler _____, meaning war chief.

3.  The most powerful city of the East-African city-states was _____.

4.  Bantu agricultural achievements rested on (a) settled agriculture, (b) migratory agriculture. _____

5.  The early Aztecs founded their city _____

    on the swamps of _____ in 1325.

6.  The secret of the Incan imperial system seems to be its (a) military terrorism, (b) benevolent despotism. _____

7.  The great pyramid-temple that dominated the Tenochtitlan city was the temple

    of _____

8.  In early times, the term *Ethiopian* referred to _____.

## MULTIPLE-CHOICE QUESTIONS

1.  The Berbers inhabited
    a.  South Africa.
    b.  the Congo region.
    c.  North Africa.
    d.  the Gold Coast.

2.  Most of Africa's interior was not explored by Europeans until the
    a.  1800s.
    b.  1700s.
    c.  1500s.
    d.  1900s.

3.  The Bantu people originally inhabited
    a.  South Africa.

    b.  Rhodesia.
    c.  Nigeria.
    d.  Ethiopia.

4.  By A.D. 400, the Western Sudan's population had increased dramatically as the
    result of
    a.  changes in climate.
    b.  increased concern for hygiene.
    c.  increase in food production.
    d.  the practice of polygamy.

5.  The religious beliefs of animism center on the
    a.  worship of animals.
    b.  sacredness of cows.
    c.  idea that *anima*, or spirits, reside in almost everything.
    d.  idea that the gods assume animal forms.

6.  Trans-Saharan trade was made possible by
    a.  the canteen.
    b.  the camel.
    c.  coined money.
    d.  caravans.

7.  The slave population of West Africa was composed of
    a.  those guilty of civil or religious offenses.
    b.  persons of certain ethnic groups.
    c.  peoples captured in war.
    d.  debtors who sold themselves into slavery.

8.  The line of succession in the kingdom of Ghana was
    a.  elective.
    b.  matrilineal.
    c.  patrilineal.
    d.  none of the above

9.  The Ghanaian king's top officials were
    a.  eunuchs.
    b.  Muslims.
    c.  Europeans.
    d.  Arabs.

10. Mansa Musa created a stir in Egypt with his
    a.  enormous armies.

    b.   generosity.
    c.   fabulous wealth in gold.
    d.   both b and c

11.  At its peak, Timbuktu was
    a.   a trade center.
    b.   an intellectual center.
    c.   a cosmopolitan, tolerant city.
    d.   all of the above.

12.  The Swahili language blends both Bantu and
    a.   Indonesian.
    b.   Mali.
    c.   Malagasy.
    d.   Arabic.

13.  Arab influence in eastern Africa
    a.   extended deep into the interior.
    b.   spelled the end for animist religion.
    c.   was mostly confined to coastal ports.
    d.   left few permanent traces.

14.  The Indians of Mexico used *chinampas* in
    a.   human sacrifice.
    b.   the growing of corn.
    c.   military campaigns.
    d.   religious observances.

15.  The potato originated in
    a.   West Africa.
    b.   South America.
    c.   eastern Europe.
    d.   India.

16.  The earliest American civilization was the
    a.   Aztec.
    b.   Incan.
    c.   Mayan.
    d.   Olmec.

17.  The central institution of the Aztec state was the
    a.   priesthood.
    b.   army.

c.   peasantry.
d.   great landed estates.

18.   The Aztecs believed that without human sacrifice the
a.   corn would not grow.
b.   rain would cease.
c.   gods would take revenge.
d.   sun's orbit would stop.

19.   The text suggests that the social purpose of human sacrifice and cannibalism
was to
a.   control population.
b.   alleviate a scarcity of meat.
c.   terrorize and subdue the population.
d.   control bloodthirsty impulses.

20.   The Mayans were most advanced in their
a.   mathematics.
b.   literature.
c.   agriculture.
d.   architecture.

21.   In the Inca empire, *mitima* was the
a.   colonization of conquered areas.
b.   paying of tribute to the King.
c.   cult of the sun-god.
d.   system of roads.

22.   An Inca man "courted" a girl by
a.   sending her gifts.
b.   getting permission from the governor to marry.
c.   hanging around her house and sharing in the work.
d.   formally asking her father for permission to marry.

23.   The Incas had been weakened previous to Pizarro's arrival by a (an)
a.   civil war.
b.   terrible epidemic.
c.   earthquake.
d.   provincial rebellion.

24.   *Tuaregs*, the caravan's greatest enemy, were
a.   hallucinations caused by heat and glare.

    b.   sandstorms.
    c.   poisoned wells.
    d.   nomadic robbers.

25. Muslim law regarding slaves decreed that
    a.   children of slaves be freed.
    b.   slaves be freed on their master's death.
    c.   slaves be treated humanely at all times.
    d.   runaway slaves be severely punished.

26. Bananas were introduced into Africa from
    a.   Europe.
    b.   the Middle East.
    c.   South and Central America.
    d.   Southeast Asia.

27. Between the eleventh and fifteenth centuries, the gold trade wealth of the
    Zambezi-Limpopo region was centered at the city of
    a.   Axum.
    b.   Great Zimbabwe.
    c.   Sofala.
    d.   Meroe.

28. The Teotihuacan civilization inhabited
    a.   central Mexico.
    b.   the Panamanian isthmus.
    c.   southern Florida.
    d.   Peru.

## GEOGRAPHY

A.  Using the outline map provided and referring to the text Map 16.1 as your guide:
    1.  Indicate the geographic features that define the five distinct geographical zones that divide Africa. In the space below describe the climatic features of these zones, and explain how geography has shaped the lives of African peoples.

2.  Indicate the location and chief characteristics of the following early African societies:

Kingdom of Ghana

Western Sudan

Kingdom of Mali

East African city-states

Kingdom of Axum

South Africa

3.  Indicate the location of the trans-Saharan trade routes. What was the importance of these routes to the history of Africa?

B.  Using Maps 16.4 and 16.5 in the text on pages 476 and 484 as a guide, answer the following questions about South America.
    1.  Identify the major South American mountain range and river.
    2.  Describe the geography of Incan Peru in terms of (1) its impact on Incan contact with the outside world, (2) its agriculture, and (3) the Incan imperial road system.
    3.  Describe the variety of Central American geography. In which of these areas did the Aztec and Mayan civilizations evolve?

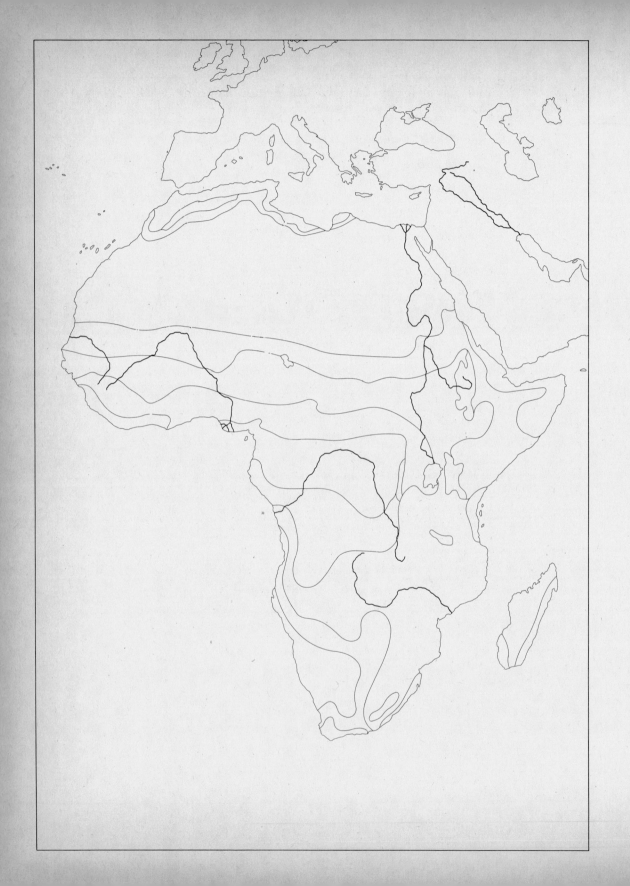

## UNDERSTANDING HISTORY THROUGH READING AND THE ARTS

For untold centuries before the Spanish conquest of Central America, the peoples of Central America developed an art and architecture of their own, particularly in ceramics, gold work, and city building. How and why were the fabled cities of the Aztecs and Incas built? Begin your investigation with Leopoldo Castedo's *A History of Latin American Art and Architecture* (1969).

## PROBLEMS FOR FURTHER INVESTIGATION

This chapter describes the bloody rituals of human sacrifice practiced by the Aztecs. For further investigation into why the Aztec society was based on war and human sacrifice, see G. Vaillant, *Aztecs of Mexico* (1979), as an initial source.

Why was Islam the major intellectual force in much of Africa in its earlier history? How did Islam help shape African society? Begin your research with J. Trimingham, *A History of Islam in West Africa* (1970) and *Islam in East Africa* (1974).

# CHAPTER 17

# EUROPEAN SOCIETY IN THE AGE OF THE
# RENAISSANCE AND REFORMATION

## CHAPTER OBJECTIVES

After reading and studying this chapter you should be able to answer the following questions:

Q-1.   What does the term *Renaissance* mean?
Q-2.   How did the Renaissance influence politics, government, and social organization in Europe?
Q-3.   Why did Luther's ideas trigger political, social, and economic reactions, and how did the Catholic church respond to these changes?

## CHAPTER SYNOPSIS

The Renaissance is difficult to define but usually is regarded as an era of intellectual and artistic brilliance unsurpassed in European history. Many educated people in this era saw themselves living in an age more akin to that of the bright and creative ancient world than that of the recent dark and gloomy Middle Ages. Although many of the supposedly "new" Renaissance ideas are actually found in the Middle Ages, scholars generally agree that the Renaissance was characterized by a number of distinctive ideas about life and humanity — individualism, secularism, humanism, materialism, and hedonism.

The Renaissance began in Florence, Italy, in the fourteenth century. It subsequently spread to the rest of Italy — particularly Rome — and then to northern Europe, where it developed somewhat differently. The best-known manifestations of the bold new Renaissance spirit can be seen in the painting, sculpture, and architecture of the period. But new attitudes were also found in education, politics, and philosophy and in northern Europe in ideas of social reform. Although the

Renaissance brought some benefits to the masses of people, such as the printing press, it was basically an elitist movement. One negative feature of the age was a deterioration in the power and position of women in society.

The political side of the Renaissance expressed itself in an approach to power and the state that historians often call the theory and practice of "new monarchies." The best known theoretician of this school was Niccolo Machiavelli. Its most able practitioners are the fifteenth- and sixteenth-century monarchs of France, England, and Spain. In Italy, the city-state system led to wealthy and independent cities that were marvelously creative but also vulnerable to invasion and control from the outside by powerful Spanish and French kings.

A great religious upheaval called the Protestant Reformation ended the centuries-long religious unity of Europe and resulted in a number of important political changes. Cries for reform were nothing new, but in the sixteenth century they resulted in revolution. There were a number of signs pointing to the need for moral and administrative reform. For example, it was the granting of indulgences (remissions from the penalties for sin) that propelled Martin Luther into the movement for doctrinal change in the church. Luther had come to the conclusion that salvation could not come by good works or indulgences, but only through faith. This was to be one of the fundamental tenets of Protestantism and one of the ideas that pushed Luther and the German nobility to revolt against not only Rome but Rome's secular ally, the Holy Roman Emperor.

Luther's challenge to the authority of the church and to Catholic unity in Europe invited and supported an attack on the emperor by the German nobility. The pope and the emperor, as separate powers and allies, represented religious and political unity and conformity in Germany. Thus, the victory of Luther and the nobility was a victory for decentralized authority; it meant the collapse of Germany as a unified power in Europe. This is one reason that Catholic France usually supported the German Protestants in their quarrel with Rome.

Outside of Germany the Protestant reformer Calvin's harsh and dogmatic religion spread from Geneva into northern Europe, England, and Scotland. It was England, in fact, that eventually became the political center of Protestantism. Initiated by Henry VIII, the English Protestant Reformation was at first motivated by the personal and political interests of the king himself. The type of Protestantism eventually adopted by the Church of England was much more moderate — and closer to Catholicism — than that of Scotland.

With the Council of Trent of 1545–1563, the Catholic church launched a massive and somewhat successful Counterreformation to convince dissidents to return to the church.

**STUDY OUTLINE**

I. The evolution of the Italian Renaissance
   A. The "Renaissance" was a period of cultural achievement in two phases —
      from 1050 to 1300 and from 1300 to about 1600
      1. The wealth of the northern Italian cities was a cause of the Renais-
         sance; it was an artistic and intellectual movement sustained by urban
         wealth
      2. Florence, the first city of the Renaissance, was a banking and manu-
         facturing center
   B. Communes and republics
      1. In the Italian cities of Milan, Florence, Genoa, Siena, and Pisa the
         feudal nobility and the commercial aristocracy merged and ruled
         a. The *popolo*, or middle class, was excluded from power
         b. Popolo-led republican governments failed — which led to the rule
            of despots or oligarchies
         c. In the fifteenth century, the princely courts of the rulers were
            centers of wealth and art
   C. The balance of power among the Italian city-states
      1. Italy had no political unity; it was divided into city-states such as
         Milan, Venice, and Florence, a papal area, and a kingdom of Naples in
         the south (see map 17.1)
      2. The political and economic competition among the city-states was
         damaging and weakened Italy
      3. After 1494 a divided Italy became a European battleground, beginning
         with an invasion by Charles VIII of France
II. Intellectual hallmarks of the Renaissance
   A. Many, like the poet and humanist Petrarch, saw the fourteenth century
      as a new age and a revival of ancient Roman culture
   B. Individualism stressed personality, genius, and uniqueness
   C. The revival of antiquity was one important feature of the Renaissance and
      led to humanism
      1. Italians copied the ancient Roman lifestyle
      2. The study of the classics led to humanism, or an emphasis on human
         beings
         a. Humanists sought to understand human nature through a study of
            pagan antiquity *and* Christian thought
         b. The humanist writer Pico della Mirandola believed that there were
            no limits to what human beings could accomplish
      3. Ancient Latin style was considered superior to medieval Latin
   D. Secular spirit
      1. *Secularism* means a concern with materialism rather than religion

2. Unlike medieval people, Renaissance people were most concerned about money and the accumulation of wealth
3. They were also interested in pleasure and the enjoyment of life on earth
4. The church did little to combat secularism; in fact, many popes were Renaissance patrons and participants

III. Art and the artist
  A. The *quattrocento* and the *cinquecento* saw great artistic activity as the center of activity shifted from Florence to Rome
  B. Art and power
    1. Art served a social function during the Renaissance
      a. It was patronized by corporate groups such as guilds and religious bodies and by rich individuals
      b. It was a means of glorifying politicians and rich families
    2. The purpose and style of art changed in the fifteenth century
      a. It became more secular
      b. Painting and sculpture became more naturalistic and realistic
      c. The human body was glorified in art — for example, by Michelangelo
      d. A new "international style" emphasized color, decoration, and curvilinear rhythms
  C. The status of the artist
    1. The status of the artist improved during the Renaissance; most work was done by commission from a prince
    2. The creative genius of the artist was recognized
    3. The Renaissance was an elitist movement that cared little for ordinary people and thus maintained the gulf between the educated few and the multitude

IV. Social change
  A. Education and political thought
    1. Vergerio's humanism represents the Renaissance concern for education
    2. The Renaissance man was well rounded
    3. Castiglione's *The Courtier* describes the model Renaissance gentleman as a man of many talents, including intellectual and artistic skills
    4. Machiavelli's *The Prince* describes how to acquire political power
      a. Machiavelli believed that the politician may use any means to gain power
      b. He viewed the state not as a utopia but as an amoral force
  B. The printed word
    1. The invention of movable type by Gutenberg, Fust, and Schöffer — all at Mainz, Germany — revolutionized life
    2. Printing brought about new possibilities for propaganda, encouraged wider "common identity," and improved literacy

        3. It meant the spread of ideas — ideas that were often critical of the existing order

   C. Women in Renaissance society

        1. The status of upper-class women declined during the Renaissance

        2. Nevertheless, the Renaissance meant improved educational opportunities for women

        3. Women's position declined with regard to sex and love

        4. The rape of women by upper-class men was frequent and not considered serious

        5. Infanticide and abandonment of children was frequent and eventually led to the establishment of foundling hospitals

   D. Blacks in Renaissance society

        1. Beginning in the fifteenth century, black slaves were brought into Europe in large numbers

        2. Black slaves filled a variety of positions, from laborers to dancers and musicians

        3. The Europeans perceived blacks from both positive and negative religious perspectives

V. The Renaissance in the north of Europe

   A. The Renaissance in the north began about 1475 and was more Christian than the Renaissance in Italy; it stressed social reform based on Christian ideals

   B. Christian humanists sought to create a more perfect world

        1. Humanists like Lefèvre believed that the use of the Bible by common people would bring about social improvement

        2. Thomas More, the author of *Utopia*, set forth the new idea that society, not people, needed improving

        3. The Dutch monk Erasmus best represents Christian humanism in his emphasis on education and inner Christianity

   C. French humanist writers were more secular; Rabelais satirized social institutions and behavior while he promoted individual instinct and enjoyment of life

   D. Northern art and architecture were more religious than in Italy and less influenced by classical themes and motifs

        1. Van Eyck painted realist works based on human themes

        2. Bosch used religion and folk legends as themes

VI. Politics and the state in the Renaissance (ca 1450–1521)

   A. The "new" monarchs

        1. The fifteenth century saw the rise of many powerful and ruthless rulers interested in the centralization of power and the elimination of disorder and violence

        2. Many of them seemed to be acting according to Machiavelli's principles

      3.  The ideas of the new monarchs were not entirely original — some of them had their roots in the Middle Ages

  B.  France after the Hundred Years' War

      1.  Charles VII ushered in an age of recovery of the monarchy

      2.  He ended civil war, established a royal army, and made the church subject to the state

      3.  Louis XI, the "Spider King," expanded the French state and laid the foundations of later French absolutism

  C.  England

      1.  Feudal lords controlled England in the fifteenth century, leading to the Wars of the Roses

      2.  Edward IV and his successors began to restore royal power

      3.  The English Parliament had become a power center for the aristocracy but was manipulated by Henry VII (Tudor) into becoming a tool of the king

         a.  Henry VII used the royal council and the Court of Star Chamber to check aristocratic power

         b.  He rebuilt the monarchy and restored the economy — relying on middle class support and the local justices of the peace

  D.  Spain

      1.  The marriage of Ferdinand and Isabella united Spain into a loose confederation

      2.  They used the *hermandades*, or local police forces, to administer royal justice

      3.  The royal council checked aristocratic power

      4.  The church was used to strengthen royal authority

      5.  Ferdinand and Isabella completed the *reconquista* — the expulsion or conversion of Arabs and Jews

      6.  Anti-Semitic riots were frequent

  E.  Germany and the rise of the Habsburg dynasty

      1.  In the Holy Roman Empire (the German states) the Golden Bull of 1356 gave each of the seven Electors virtual sovereignty

         a.  This form of localism gave the nobility the power to strengthen their territories

         b.  Chronic disorder also helped the nobility

      2.  The rise of the Habsburgs, particularly with the marriage of Maximilian I of Austria and Mary of Burgundy in 1477, gave unity to much of Europe

         a.  Charles V, their grandson, dominated Europe

         b.  He was committed to the idea of its religious and political unity

VII.  The condition of the church (ca 1400–1517)

  A.  The declining prestige of the Church was due to the Great Schism, while

the Humanists satirized and denounced moral corruption within the
Church

B.  Signs of disorder in the early sixteenth century
1.  Critics wanted moral and administrative reform in three areas
    a.  Clerical immorality created a scandal among the faithful
    b.  The lack of education of the clergy was condemned by Christian
        humanists
    c.  The absenteeism, pluralism (holding of several *benefices*, or
        offices), and wealth of the greater clergy bore little resemblance
        to Christian gospel
2.  The prelates and popes of the period lived like secular princes; they
    did not set a good example

C.  Signs of vitality in the late fifteenth and early sixteenth centuries
1.  Sixteenth-century Europe remained deeply religious
2.  New organizations were formed to educate and minister to the poor
3.  Thomas à Kempis and the Brethren of the Common Life urged ordi-
    nary people to achieve spiritual perfection by means of the simple life
4.  The Italian Oratorians devoted themselves to ministering to society
5.  Pope Julius II summoned an ecumenical council on reform in the
    church called the Lateran Council (1512–1527)

VIII.  Martin Luther and the birth of Protestantism

A.  Luther was a German miner's son trained as a monk and a professor of
    religion; he concluded that faith was central to Christianity and the only
    means to salvation

B.  Luther's Ninety-five Theses (October 1517)
1.  Luther's opposition to the sale of indulgences (remissions of penalties
    for sin) prompted his fight with Rome
2.  His Ninety-five Theses, or propositions on indulgences, raised many
    theological issues and initiated a long period of debate in Europe
3.  Luther was excommunicated by the pope and declared an outlaw by
    Charles V at Worms in 1521

C.  Protestant thought (1520–1530)
1.  Protestant thought was set forth in the Confession of Augsburg, in
    which Luther raised four basic theological issues
    a.  He believed that salvation derived through faith alone
    b.  He stated that religious authority rests with the Bible, not the pope
    c.  He believed that the church consists of the entire community of
        Christian believers
    d.  And he believed that all work is sacred and everyone should serve
        God in his or her individual vocation
2.  Protestantism, therefore, was a reformulation of Christian beliefs and
    practices

D. The social impact of Luther's beliefs
  1. By 1521 Luther's religious ideas had a vast following among all social classes and eventually led to social revolt
     a. Luther's ideas were popular because of popular resentment of clerical wealth
     b. Prosperous burghers encouraged preaching of sermons while peasants found in Luther a reason to demand land
     c. In the end Luther did not support them; he believed in obedience to civil authority
     d. Widespread peasant revolts were brutally crushed but some land was returned to common use
     e. Luther's greatest weapon was his mastery of the language, and his words were spread by the advent of printing
        (1) Zwingli and Calvin were greatly influenced by his writings
        (2) The publication of Luther's translation of the New Testament in 1523 democratized religion
  2. Luther held enlightened views on sex and marriage — although he claimed that women should be no more than efficient housewives
  3. The political impact of Luther's beliefs
     a. The Protestant Reformation stirred nationalistic feelings in Germany against the wealthy Italian papacy
     b. Luther's appeal to patriotism earned him the support of the princes, who used religion as a means of gaining more political independence
     c. Thus, Luther's teachings prevailed, despite his condemnation by the pope and the Holy Roman Emperor
     d. Charles V did not understand or take any interest in the Luther issue
        (1) The Turkish threat blocked Charles V's position in Germany
        (2) He was also involved in numerous wars against France, which kept Germany a divided and weakened royal power
     e. By the Peace of Augsburg of 1555, Charles recognized Lutheranism as a legal religion
IX. The growth of the Protestant Reformation
  A. Calvinism
     1. Calvin believed that God selects certain people to do His work and that he was selected to reform the city of Geneva
     2. Under Calvin, Geneva became a theocracy, in which the state was subordinate to the church
     3. Calvin's central idea was his belief in the omnipotence of God and the insignificance of humanity
        a. People lacked free will

        b.   God decided ahead of time who would be saved (the doctrine of predestination)

    4.   Austere living and intolerance characterized Calvin's Geneva

    5.   The city was the model for international Protestantism, and Calvinism became the most dynamic and influential form of Protestantism

B.  The Anabaptists

    1.   This Protestant sect believed in adult baptism, revelation, and the separation of church and state

    2.   Their beliefs and practices were humane but too radical for the times, and they were bitterly persecuted

C.  The English Reformation

    1.   As early as the fourteenth century the English Lollards stressed the idea of a direct relationship between the individual and God

    2.   Wolsey's career represents corruption in the English church

    3.   Henry VIII desired a divorce from his queen, Catherine, daughter of Ferdinand and Isabella of Spain

    4.   Pope Clement VII and emperor Charles V blocked the divorce

    5.   The pro-Protestant Archbishop Cranmer engineered an annulment

    6.   The result was the nationalization of the English church and a break with Rome as Henry used Parliament to legalize the Reformation

        a.   Henry needed money so he dissolved the monasteries and confiscated their lands

        b.   Some traditional Catholic practices, such as confession and the doctrine of transubstantiation, were maintained, however

        c.   Nationalization of the church led to a new form of government

    7.   Under Edward VI, Henry's heir, England shifted closer to Protestantism

    8.   Mary Tudor attempted to bring Catholicism back to England

    9.   Under Elizabeth I a religious settlement — mainly Protestant — was made

D.  The establishment of the Church of Scotland

    1.   Scotland was an extreme case of church abuse

    2.   John Knox brought Calvinism to Scotland from Geneva

    3.   The Presbyterian Church became the national church of Scotland

E.  Protestantism in Ireland

    1.   The English ruling class in Ireland adopted Protestantism

    2.   The Irish people defiantly remained Catholic

F.  Lutheranism in Scandinavia

    1.   In Sweden, Norway, and Denmark the monarchy led the religious reformation

    2.   The result was Lutheran state churches

X.  The Catholic and counterreformations

A.  The slowness of institutional reform

       1.  Too often the popes were preoccupied with politics and material pleasures

       2.  Also, popes feared conciliarism because it would limit their authority, so they resisted calls for reform councils

  B.  The Council of Trent

       1.  Pope Paul III called the Council of Trent, which met from 1545 to 1563

          a.  An attempt to reconcile with the Protestants was made, but it failed

          b.  International politics hindered the theological debates and the attempts at reconciliation

  C.  New religious orders within the Catholic Church

       1.  The Ursuline order was dedicated to combating heresy

       2.  The Jesuits, under Loyola, sought to fight heresy and reform the Church

  D.  The Sacred Congregation of the Holy Office

       1.  The Roman Inquisition — founded in 1542 by Pope Paul III — was an arm of the Counterreformation empowered to combat heresy

       2.  Under the direction of religious fanatics, it had the power to arrest, imprison, and execute

       3.  Its influence was confined to Italy

# REVIEW QUESTIONS

**Q-1.**  How do Valla and Boccaccio illustrate and represent what Renaissance people were like?

**Q-2.**  Do you believe that it is possible, through education, to perfect mankind? What did the Renaissance thinkers believe the keys to this process to be?

**Q-3.**  According to Vergerio, what is the purpose of education? Was he a humanist?

**Q-4.**  How does Castiglione's *The Courtier* define the "perfect Renaissance man"? How does this book represent the philosophy of humanism?

**Q-5.**  In what ways does Machiavelli represent a Renaissance thinker? What were his suggestions for and philosophy of the acquisition and meaning of political power?

**Q-6.**  Explain why the invention of movable type revolutionized European life.

**Q-7.**  What were the similarities and differences between the Renaissance in northern Europe and that of Italy?

**Q-8.**  Discuss Christian humanism by describing the works and ideas of Thomas More and Desiderius Erasmus.

**Q-9.**  Describe the make-up of the Italian city-state political system. How well did it work?

**Q-10.**  "After 1494, Italy became a battleground for the European superpowers." Explain.

Q-11.   What were the obstacles to royal authority faced by the kings of France in the fifteenth century? How did Charles VII and his successors strengthen the French monarchy?

Q-12.   What devices did Henry VII of England use to check the power of the aristocracy and strengthen the monarchy?

Q-13.   The reign of Ferdinand and Isabella is one of the most important in Spanish history. Why? What were their achievements in the areas of national power and national expansion?

Q-14.   Why were blacks valued in Renaissance society? What roles did they play in the economic and social life of the times?

Q-15.   What were some of the signs of disorder within the early sixteenth-century church? How did church wealth affect the condition of the church?

Q-16.   What were some of the signs of religious vitality in fifteenth- and early sixteenth-century society?

Q-17.   Describe the circumstances that prompted Luther to post his Ninety-five Theses.

Q-18.   Describe the practice of indulgence selling. What authority did Luther question, and on what argument did he base his position?

Q-19.   What were Luther's answers, as delineated in the Confession of Augsburg, to the four basic theological issues?

Q-20.   What effect did Luther's concept of state authority over church authority have on German society and German history?

Q-21.   Calvin's Geneva was called "the city that was a church." Explain. What is a theocracy?

Q-22.   In what ways were the Anabaptists radical for their time? Why did many of their beliefs cause them to be bitterly persecuted?

Q-23.   Explain the causes and results of the English Reformation. What was the Elizabethan Settlement?

Q-24.   Compare and contrast the religious settlements made in Scotland and Ireland. Why was Protestantism in one place a source of national strength and in the other a source of national weakness?

Q-25.   What were the repercussions of the marriage of Maximilian and Mary? How did this marriage affect France?

Q-26.   Charles V has been considered a medieval emperor. In what respects is this true? What were the origins of his empire?

Q-27.   Why was the condemnation of Luther in 1521 at Worms not enforced by the German nobility? What was the result?

Q-28.   What were the goals and methods of the Ursuline order and the Society of Jesus?

Q-29.   Why was reform within the Catholic church often unwelcome and slow in coming?

Q-30.   What were the achievements of the Council of Trent? What circumstances surrounding the calling of the council made its task difficult and its goal of reconciliation with Protestantism unattainable?

## STUDY-REVIEW EXERCISES

*Define the following key concepts and terms.*

oligarchies

*signori*

Brethren of the Common Life

John Knox

Pope Paul III

Archbishop Cranmer

Martin Luther

Henry VIII

Charles V

Mary Tudor

Pope Alexander VI

Council of Trent

Elizabethan Settlement

Act of Restraint of Appeals

pluralism

benefices

Peace of Augsburg

Ninety-five Theses

Spanish *conversos*

communes

*reconquista*

Renaissance

humanism

secularism

individualism

materialism

"Machiavellian"

<u>Explain</u> *the importance of each of the following.*

English Royal Council and Court of Star Chamber

Habsburg-Valois wars

Brunelleschi's Foundling Hospital in Florence

Spanish anti-Semitic riots of the fourteenth century

<u>Identify</u> *each of the following people and give his significance.*

Pico della Mirandola

Desiderius Erasmus

Thomas More

Donatello

Baldassare Castiglione

Niccolo Machiavelli

Johann Gutenberg

Jacques Lefèvre d'Etaples

Saint John Chrysostom

François Rabelais


*Explain why each of the following is often considered to be a "new monarch."*

Louis XI of France

Henry VII of England

Ferdinand and Isabella of Spain

Charles VII of France

Cesare Borgia


*Define the basic beliefs of the following Christian religions and churches.*

Roman Catholicism

Lutheranism

Calvinism

Anabaptism

Church of England

Presbyterian Church of Scotland


*Test your understanding of the chapter by answering the following questions.*

  1.  He was the author of a best-selling political critique called *The Prince*.

  _____

2. Renaissance humanists tended to be *more/less* concerned about religion than about people.
3. In the fifteenth century, infanticide *increased/decreased*.
4. He was an important English humanist and the author of *Utopia*.

_____

5. Generally, the legal status of upper-class women *improved/declined* during the Renaissance.
6. It *is/is not* clear that the economic growth and the material wealth of the Italian cities were direct causes of the Renaissance.
7. The Council of Trent *did/did not* reaffirm the seven sacraments, the validity of tradition, and transubstantiation.

8. The English Supremacy Act of 1534 declared the _____ to be the Supreme Head of the Church of England.
9. For the most part, the English Reformation under Henry VIII dealt with *political/theological* issues.
10. He wrote: 'How comes it that we Germans must put up with such robbery and such extortion of our property at the hands of the pope?"

_____

11. This pope's name became a synonym for moral corruption.

_____

12. Mary Tudor, the English queen and daughter of Henry VIII, *was/was not* interested in the restoration of Catholicism in England.
13. In general, Protestantism tended to *strengthen/weaken* Germany as a political unit.
14. During the reign of Elizabeth, the English church moved in a moderately *Protestant/Catholic* direction.

## MULTIPLE-CHOICE QUESTIONS

1. The Renaissance began in
   a. the Low Countries.
   b. Rome.
   c. France.
   d. Florence.

2. The patrons of the Renaissance were mostly
   a. churchmen.

b.   the popes.
c.   the common people.
d.   merchants and bankers.

3.   The king who began French economic and political recovery in the early fifteenth century was
a.   Henry Tudor.
b.   Charles VII.
c.   Philip the Fair.
d.   Louis XI.

4.   It appears that in Renaissance society blacks were
a.   valued as soldiers.
b.   valued as servants and entertainers.
c.   considered undesirable and were not allowed in society.
d.   treated equally with whites.

5.   A major difference between northern and Italian humanism is that northern humanism stressed
a.   economic gain and materialism.
b.   social reform.
c.   pagan virtues.
d.   popular education.

6.   Local groups in Spain that were given royal authority to administer justice were the
a.   *conversos.*
b.   liberals.
c.   *hermandades.*
d.   royal tribunals.

7.   The Court of Star Chamber in England was
a.   a common law court.
b.   under the control of the barons in the House of Lords.
c.   done away with by the powerful Tudors.
d.   used to check aristocratic power.

8.   The superiority of the French monarch over the church was the object of the
a.   Pragmatic Sanction of Bourges.
b.   Habsburg-Valois wars.
c.   Declaration of Calais.
d.   Hundred Years' War.

9.  Most of the northern Renaissance thinkers agreed that
    a.  democracy, not monarchy, was the only workable political system.
    b.  humanity is basically sinful.
    c.  Christianity is unacceptable.
    d.  society is perfectible.

10. The late-fifteenth-century ruler of England who ended the civil war and strengthened the crown was
    a.  John I.
    b.  William III.
    c.  Henry II.
    d.  Henry VII.

11. The High Renaissance masterpiece, the dome of St. Peter's in Rome, is considered to be the greatest work of
    a.  Brunelleschi.
    b.  Donatello.
    c.  Michelangelo.
    d.  Ghiberti.

12. The term *Renaissance* means
    a.  a rise in the average standard of living among the masses.
    b.  a resurgence of art and culture out of a concern for individualism and study of the ancients.
    c.  an increase in the population after the ravaging effects of the "Four Horsemen of the Apocalypse."
    d.  the recovery of the church from economic and moral decline.

13. The financial and military strength of the towns of northern Italy was directly related to
    a.  their wealth, which enabled them to hire mercenary soldiers to protect their commercial interests.
    b.  their contractual and marital alliances with the rural nobility.
    c.  protections provided them by the Holy Roman Emperor.
    d.  their alliance with the papacy.

14. Erasmus advocated
    a.  paganism.
    b.  Christian education for moral and intellectual improvement.
    c.  monastic life of contemplation and divorce from the material world.
    d.  obedience to church doctrine and ritual.

15. The Renaissance artist of talent and ability often lived a life
    a.  of economic desperation.
    b.  of economic security through patronage.
    c.  of luxury, but without social status.
    d.  like that of the masses.

16. The most influential book on Renaissance court life and behavior was
    a.  Castiglione's *The Courtier*.
    b.  Machiavelli's *The Prince*.
    c.  Augustine's *The City of God*.
    d.  Boccaccio's *Decameron*.

17. The Wars of the Roses were
    a.  civil wars between the English ducal houses of York and Lancaster.
    b.  between England and France.
    c.  civil wars between the English king, Henry VI, and the aristocracy.
    d.  minor disputes among English gentry.

18. Just before the advent of Ferdinand and Isabella, the Iberian peninsula could best be described as a
    a.  homogeneous region sharing a common language and cultural tradition.
    b.  heterogeneous region consisting of several ethnic groups with a diversity of linguistic and cultural characteristics.
    c.  culturally poor and backward region.
    d.  region dominated equally by Arabs and Jews in both numbers and political power.

19. Under the Presbyterian form of church government, the church is governed by
    a.  bishops.
    b.  the king of Scotland.
    c.  ministers.
    d.  the people.

20. According to Luther, salvation comes through
    a.  good works.
    b.  faith.
    c.  indulgences.
    d.  a saintly life.

21. The cornerstone of Calvin's theology was his belief in
    a.  predestination.
    b.  indulgences.

    c.  the basic goodness of man.
    d.  religious tolerance and freedom.

22.  John Knox and the Reformation movement in Scotland were most influenced by which of the following theological positions?
    a.  Catholicism
    b.  Calvinism
    c.  Lutheranism
    d.  Church of England

23.  Overall, Henry VIII's religious reformation in England occurred for
    a.  strictly economic reasons.
    b.  religious reasons.
    c.  mostly political reasons.
    d.  mostly diplomatic reasons.

24.  The Reformation in Germany resulted in
    a.  a politically weaker Germany.
    b.  a politically stronger Germany.
    c.  no political changes of importance.
    d.  a victory for imperial centralization.

25.  The great Christian humanists of the fifteenth and sixteenth centuries believed that reform could be achieved through
    a.  the use of violent revolution.
    b.  education and social change.
    c.  mass support of the church hierarchy.
    d.  prayer alone.

26.  Luther tacked his Ninety-five Theses to the door in Wittenberg as a response to the
    a.  sale of indulgences and papal wealth.
    b.  revelation he experienced instructing him to start a new church.
    c.  illiteracy of the clergy.
    d.  oppressive rule of Frederick of Saxony.

27.  By 1555 the Protestant Reformation had spread to all but
    a.  England.
    b.  Scandinavia.
    c.  Spain.
    d.  Scotland.

28. The chief center of the Protestant Reformers in the sixteenth century was
    a. Paris.
    b. Geneva.
    c. Zurich.
    d. Cologne.

29. The Anabaptists appealed to the
    a. nobility.
    b. poor, uneducated, and unemployed.
    c. intellectuals.
    d. merchant classes.

30. Henry VIII dissolved the monasteries largely because
    a. they were corrupt and mismanaged.
    b. they were symbolic of papal authority.
    c. he needed the wealth they would bring.
    d. they were a burden on the state.

31. The Scandinavian countries were most influenced by the religious beliefs of
    a. Martin Luther.
    b. John Knox.
    c. Roger Brown.
    d. the Jesuits.

32. A vow of the Jesuit order making it uniquely different from others was
    a. poverty.
    b. chastity.
    c. obedience to the pope.
    d. pacifism.

## UNDERSTANDING HISTORY THROUGH READING AND THE ARTS

The music of the European Renaissance is introduced in the recordings *From the Renaissance* (STL-150) and *From the Renaissance-Concert* (STL-160) in the Time-Life series *The Story of Great Music* (1967), which includes a book with a good introduction to the period and its musical styles, art, and history. Another good introduction to Renaissance music is H. Brown, *Music in the Renaissance** (1976).

One of the best ways to understand the Renaissance is to read the works of its participants. Three works dealt with in this chapter are Niccolo Machiavelli, *The*

*Available in paperback.

*Prince* (a number of paperback translations are available); Baldassare Castiglione, *The Courtier*, Charles Singleton, trans. (1959); and Thomas More, *Utopia*.

Few men in history have been the subject of more biographies than Martin Luther, the German reformer. One of the most important is a psychological study by E. Erikson entitled *Young Man Luther: A Study in Psychoanalysis and History* (1962). Other books about Luther include R. Bainton, *Here I Stand* (1950); E. Schwiebert, *Luther and His Times* (1952); G. Forel, *Faith Active in Love* (1954); and J. Atkinson, *Martin Luther and the Birth of Protestantism* (1968).

King Henry VIII of England is the subject of a number of interesting biographies. Three of the best are L. B. Smith, *Henry VIII* (1971); A. F. Pollard, *Henry VIII* (1905); and J. Scarisbrick, *Henry VIII* (1968). Henry's marital problems, as seen from his wife's side, are the subject of the fascinating and exciting *Catherine of Aragon* (1941) by G. Mattingly.

## PROBLEMS FOR FURTHER INVESTIGATION

Students interested in women in the Renaissance in Europe should begin with M. Rose et al., *Women in the Middle Ages and the Renaissance: Literary and Historical Perspectives* (1986).

The Swiss historian Jakob Burckhardt called the Renaissance the "mother" of our modern world. Was the Renaissance as important as Burckhardt and others have claimed? Did it dramatically change the way people acted and the direction history was to take? These and other questions are considered in several historical debates on the Renaissance: D. Hay, ed., *The Renaissance Debate* (1965); B. Tierney, et al., *Renaissance Man — Medieval or Modern?* (1959). How did Renaissance thinking affect the arts? Fine illustrations and a discussion of new directions in the arts are woven into a number of interesting essays on the age in D. Hay, *The Renaissance* (1967).

Students interested in further study of the religious revolution of the sixteenth century will find some of the problems of interpretation and investigation relative to that subject set out in L. W. Spitz, ed., *The Reformation* (1972), and K. Sessions, ed., *Reformation and Authority: The Meaning of the Peasants' Revolt* (1968). The relationship between the Protestant religion and economic growth has long interested historians. This historical problem is defined in R. Green, ed., *Protestantism, Capitalism, and Social Science* (1973). Students interested in the Counterreformation should begin with E. M. Burns, *The Counter Reformation* (1964), and those interested in the political implications of Calvinism should see R. Kingdon, *Calvin and Calvinism: Sources of Democracy* (1970).

*Available in paperback.

# CHAPTER 18

## THE AGE OF EUROPEAN EXPANSION
## AND RELIGIOUS WARS

## CHAPTER OBJECTIVES

After reading and studying this chapter you should be able to answer the following questions:

Q-1.   Why and how did Europeans gain control over distant continents?

Q-2.   How did overseas expansion affect Europe and conquered societies?

Q-3.   What were the causes of religious wars in France, the Netherlands, and Germany, and how did the religious wars affect the status of women?

Q-4.   How and why did African slave labor become the dominant form of labor organization in the New World?

Q-5.   What religious and intellectual developments led to the growth of skepticism?

Q-6.   What literary masterpieces did this period produce?

Q-7.   How did the invading Spaniards overcome the powerful Aztec and Incan Empires in America?

## CHAPTER SYNOPSIS

In this chapter we see how the trends in the High Middle Ages in Europe toward centralized nations ruled by powerful kings and toward territorial expansion were revitalized. The growth of royal power and the consolidation of the state in Spain, France, and England accompanied and supported world exploration and a long period of European war.

The Portuguese were the first to push out into the Atlantic, but it was Spain, following close behind, that built a New World empire that provided the economic basis for a period of Spanish supremacy in European affairs. In the short run, Spanish gold and silver from the New World made the Spanish Netherlands the financial and manufacturing center of Europe, and Spain became Europe's greatest military power. In the long run, however, overseas expansion ruined the Spanish economy, created massive European inflation, and brought the end of Spain's empire in Europe.

The fall of the Aztec and Incan nations to the Spanish was due to a variety of reasons — internal struggle, legendary beliefs, and technological and military backwardness are four. The takeover of the Americas led to the first world seaborne empires, first by the Portuguese and the Spanish and then by the Dutch. The Spanish concentrated in the Philippines, the Portuguese in the Indian Ocean, and the Dutch in Indonesia.

The attempts by Catholic monarchs to re-establish European religious unity and by both Catholic and Protestant monarchs to establish strong centralized states led to many wars among the European states. Spain's attempt to keep religious and political unity within her empire led to a long war in the Netherlands — a war that pulled England over to the side of the Protestant Dutch. There was bitter civil war in France, which finally came to an end with the reign of Henry of Navarre and the Edict of Nantes in 1598. The Thirty Years' War in Germany from 1618 to 1648 left that area a political and economic shambles.

The sixteenth century also saw a vast increase in witch-hunting and the emergence of modern racism, sexism, and skepticism. Generally, the power and status of women in this period did not change. Protestantism meant a more positive attitude toward marriage, but the revival of the idea that women were the source of evil and the end of the religious orders for women caused them to become increasingly powerless in society. North American slavery and racism had their origins in the labor problems in America and in Christian and Muslim racial attitudes. Skepticism was an intellectual reaction to the fanaticism of both Protestants and Catholics and a sign of things to come, while the Renaissance tradition was carried on by Shakespeare's work in late sixteenth-century England.

## STUDY OUTLINE

I.  Discovery, reconnaissance, and expansion (1450–1650)
    A.  Overseas exploration and conquest
        1.  The spread of the Ottoman Turks frightened the Europeans and overshadowed their international exploits at first
        2.  Political centralization in Spain, France, and England prepared the way for expansion
        3.  The Portuguese, under the leadership of Prince Henry the Navigator, pushed south from North Africa
            a.  Da Gama, Diaz, and Cabral set routes to India
            b.  The Portuguese gained control of the Indian trade by overpowering Muslim forts in India

4. Spain began to play a leading role in exploration and exploitation
   a. Columbus sailed under the Spanish flag and discovered the Caribbean
   b. Spanish exploitation in the Caribbean led to the destruction of the Indian population
   c. Magellan sailed southwest across the Atlantic for Charles V of Spain, and his expedition circumnavigated the earth
   d. Pizarro crushed the Inca empire in Peru and opened the Potosi mines to Spanish use
   e. New Spain brought great wealth to Spain
5. The Low Countries, particularly the cities of Antwerp and Amsterdam, became the center of European trade
   a. The Dutch East India Company became the major organ of Dutch imperialism
   b. The Dutch West India Company gained control of much of the African and American trade
6. France and England made sporadic efforts at exploration and settlement

B. The explorers' motives
1. The desire to Christianize the Muslims and pagan peoples played a central role in European expansion
2. Limited economic and political opportunity for upper class men in Spain led to emigration
3. Government encouragement was also important
4. Renaissance curiosity caused people to seek out new worlds
5. The economic motive — the quest for material profit — was the basic reason for European exploration and expansion

C. Technological stimuli to exploration
1. The development of the cannon aided European expansion
2. New sailing and navigational developments — such as the caravel ship and the compass — also aided the expansion

D. The conquest of Aztec Mexico and Incan Peru
1. The strange end of the Aztec nation at the hands of the Spanish is one of history's most fascinating events
   a. Cortes gained control of the capital in less than two years
   b. One reason was that the Aztecs were preoccupied with harvesting their crops at the time of invasion
   c. A comet raised the specter of the return of Quetzalcoatl
   d. Many people under Aztec rule welcomed the Spanish as liberators
   e. The emperor Montezuma's vacillation led to his being taken hostage by Cortes
   f. The major reason for the collapse of the empire lies in the Aztec notion of warfare and its low level of technology
2. The Incan empire, with the emperor as a benevolent despot, fell easily to the Spanish under Pizarro

      a.   Isolation and legendary beliefs kept the Incas from taking prompt action
      b.   Pizarro came at a time of civil war
      c.   Pizarro wisely captured the emperor, Atahualpa

E.  The South American Holocaust
  1.  The Spanish settlers in the New World established the *encomiendas* system
      a.   The Spanish needed laborers to work their mines and agricultural estates
      b.   The *encomiendas* system was a legalized form of slavery
      c.   Millions of Indians died as a result of this system
  2.  Scholars have debated the causes of this devastating slump in population
      a.   The long isolation of the Indians made them susceptible to diseases brought from Europe
      b.   Indians in Mexico and Peru fell victim to smallpox
      c.   The Spanish murdered thousands of others
      d.   Missionaries such as Las Casas fought for Indian rights and the end of *encomiendas* abuse
      e.   Some argue that much death was due to mass suicide and infanticide

F.  Colonial administration
  1.  The Spanish monarch divided his new world into four viceroyalties, each with a viceroy and *audiencia*
  2.  Spanish economic policy toward its colonies was that of mercantilism
  3.  Portuguese administration and economic policy was similar

G.  The economic effects of Spain's discoveries in the New World
  1.  Enormous amounts of American gold and silver poured into Spain
  2.  It is probable that population growth and not empire building caused inflation in Spain
  3.  Spanish gold caused European inflation, which hurt the poor the most

H.  Seaborne trading empires
  1.  The first global seaborne trade was the result of the linking of the newly discovered Americas and the Pacific with the rest of the world
      a.   The sea route to India came under Portuguese control — with their major bases at Goa and Malacca
      b.   The Portuguese traded in a variety of goods, including slaves and sugar
      c.   The Spanish built a seaborne empire that stretched across the Pacific, with Manila its center
      d.   Manila became rich from the Spanish silk trade
  2.  In the later seventeenth century the Dutch overtook Spanish dominance in world trade
      a.   The new Dutch East India Company led the Dutch to Indonesia, where it established a huge trading empire

   b. The Dutch, Portuguese, and Spanish all paved the way for the French and the British

II. Politics, religion, and war

 A. The Spanish-French wars ended in 1559 with a Spanish victory, thus leading to a variety of wars centering on religious and national issues

  1. These wars used bigger armies, with gunpowder, and with a need for better financial administration

  2. Governments had to use various propaganda devices, including the printing press, to arouse public opinion

  3. The Peace of Westphalia (1648) ended religious wars but also ended the idea of a unified Christian society

 B. The origins of difficulties in France (1515–1559)

  1. By 1500, France was recovering from plague and disorder, and the nobility began to lose power

  2. The French kings, such as Francis I and Henry II, continued the policies of centralization but spent more money than they raised

  3. The wars between France and Emperor Charles V — the Habsburg-Valois wars — were costly

  4. To raise money, Francis signed the Concordat of Bologna (1516), in which he recognized the supremacy of the papacy in return for the right to appoint French bishops

   a. This settlement established Catholicism as the national religion

   b. It also perpetuated corruption within the French church

   c. The corruption made Calvinism attractive to Christians eager for reform: some clergy and members of the middle and artisan classes

 C. Religious riots and civil war in France (1559–1589)

  1. The French nobility, many of them Calvinist, attempted to regain power

  2. Frequent religious riots symbolized the struggle for power

  3. The Saint Bartholomew's Day massacre of Calvinists led to the War of the Three Henrys, a conflict for secular power

  4. King Henry IV's Edict of Nantes (1598) saved France from further civil war by allowing Protestants to worship

 D. The Netherlands under Charles V

  1. The Low Countries were part of the Habsburg empire and enjoyed relative autonomy

  2. Charles V divided his empire between his brother Ferdinand and his son, King Philip of Spain

 E. The revolt of the Netherlands (1556–1587)

  1. Regent Margaret attempted to destroy Protestantism by establishing the Inquisition in the Netherlands

  2. Popular support for Protestantism led to the destruction of many Catholic churches

       3.  The Duke of Alva and his Spanish troops were sent by Philip II to crush the disturbances in the Low Countries

       4.  Alva's brutal actions only inflamed the religious war, which raged from 1568 to 1578

       5.  The Low Countries were finally split into the Spanish Netherlands in the south and the independent United Provinces of the Netherlands in the north

          a.  The north was Protestant and ruled by the commercial aristocracy

          b.  The south was Catholic and ruled by the landed nobility

       6.  Elizabeth I of England supported the northern, or Protestant, cause as a safeguard against Spain's attacking England

          a.  This was for economic reasons

          b.  She had her rival, Mary Queen of Scots, beheaded

F.  Philip II and the Spanish Armada

       1.  Philip II planned war on England for several reasons

          a.  He wanted to keep England in the Catholic fold

          b.  He believed he would never conquer the Dutch unless he defeated England first

       2.  The failure of the Spanish invasion of England — the armada of 1588 — did not mean the end of the war, but it did prevent Philip from forcibly unifying western Europe

       3.  In 1609, Philip III agreed to a truce, recognizing the independence of the United Provinces

G.  The Thirty Years' War (1618–1648)

       1.  Protestant Bohemian revolt over religious freedom led to war in Germany

       2.  The Bohemian phase was characterized by civil war in Bohemia for religious liberty and political independence from the Habsburgs; the Catholics won

       3.  The Danish phase led to further Catholic victory

       4.  The Swedish phase ended the Habsburg plan to unite Germany

       5.  The French phase ended with a destroyed Germany and an independent Netherlands

H.  Germany after the Thirty Years' War

       1.  The war was economically disastrous for Germany

       2.  The war led to agricultural depression in Germany, which in turn encouraged a return to serfdom for many peasants

III.  Changing attitudes

A.  The status of women

       1.  Literature on women and marriage called for a subservient wife with the household as her first priority and a protective, firm-ruling, and loyal husband

      a.  Catholic marriages could not be dissolved while Protestants held that divorce and remarriage were possible

      b.  Women did not lose their identity or meaningful work, but their subordinate status did not change — although a few women (like Bess of Hardwick) gained wealth and power

  2.  Sexual indulgence was popular and widespread; prostitution was common — as brothels were licensed — but Protestant moralists fought it

  3.  Protestant reformers believed that convents were antifeminist

      a.  They felt that women should be free to marry and enjoy sex

      b.  However, it was understood even by Protestants that religious orders for women provided upper class women with an outlet for their talents

B.  The great European witch-hunt

  1.  Growth in religion and advent of religious struggle led to a rise in the belief in the evil power of witches

  2.  The thousands of people executed as witches represent society's drift toward social and intellectual conformity

  3.  Reasons varied but all in all witch-hunting reflects widespread misogyny

C.  European slavery and the origins of American racism

  1.  Black slavery originated with the end of white slavery (1453) and the widespread need for labor, particularly in the new sugar-producing settlements

  2.  Africans were brought to America to replace the Indians

  3.  A few, like Las Casas, called for the end of slavery

  4.  North American racist ideas originated in Christian and Muslim ideas

D.  The origins of modern skepticism: Michel de Montaigne

  1.  Skeptics doubt whether definitive knowledge is ever attainable

  2.  Montaigne is the best representative of early modern skepticism

      a.  He was a humanist graced with open-mindedness and tolerance

      b.  He believed that the beginning of wisdom lies in the confession of ignorance

  3.  Montaigne's skepticism represents a sharp break with the past; it is a forerunner of modern attitudes

IV.  Elizabethan and Jacobean literature

A.  The golden age of English literature was the late sixteenth and early seventeenth centuries

B.  Shakespeare reflects the Renaissance in that his great plays express national consciousness and human problems

C.  The Authorized Bible of King James I is a masterpiece of English vernacular writing

## REVIEW QUESTIONS

Q-1.    Describe the Portuguese explorations. Who were the participants, and what were their motives?

Q-2.    Describe the American-Spanish-Dutch economic arrangement. How did it work? Who were the winners and who were the losers?

Q-3.    The sixteenth century was a century of money inflation. Why?

Q-4.    What role did technology play in European expansion?

Q-5.    Overall, what do you believe to be the major reasons for European expansion in the fifteenth and sixteenth centuries?

Q-6.    How did Protestantism affect the economic and political development of France? Why is the Edict of Nantes an important event in French history?

Q-7.    What were the causes and consequences of the French civil war of 1559–1589? Was it chiefly a religious or a political event?

Q-8.    Discuss the origins and the outcome of the war between the Netherlands and Spain in the late sixteenth and early seventeenth centuries.

Q-9.    What were the circumstances surrounding Elizabeth's decision to aid the United Netherlands in their war against Spain? What was the Spanish reaction?

Q-10.    Why did Catholic France side with the Protestants in the Thirty Years' War?

Q-11.    What were the political, religious, and economic consequences of the Thirty Years' War in Europe?

Q-12.    Describe the social status of women between 1560 and 1648.

Q-13.    What were the origins of North American racism?

Q-14.    What is skepticism? Why did faith and religious certainty begin to come to an end in the first part of the seventeenth century?

Q-15.    What were the major literary masterpieces of this age? In what ways can the English playwright Shakespeare be regarded as a true Renaissance man?

Q-16.    What do the witch-hunts tell us about social attitudes toward women?

Q-17.    What peoples built the first global seaborne trading empire, and what were the reasons for their success?

Q-18.    What was the function of the Dutch East India Company? How successful were the Dutch in the field of international trade?

Q-19.    Why did the Aztec and Incan empires fall to the Europeans? Which explanation, to you, is the most plausible? Why?

Q-20.    What is meant by the South American holocaust? Discuss it in terms of causes and results.

## STUDY-REVIEW EXERCISES

*Identify* and give the significance of each of the following.

*politiques*

Elizabeth I of England

Huguenots

Philip II of Spain

Prince Henry the Navigator

Michel de Montaigne

Christopher Columbus

Bartholomew Diaz

Portuguese cities of Goa and Malacca

Dutch East India Company

Hernando Cortez

Elizabeth Hardwick

Council of Blood

Habsburg-Valois wars

*quinto*

*audiencia*

*corregidores*

Thirty Years' War

defeat of the Spanish Armada

Concordat of Bologna

Peace of Westphalia

Saint Bartholomew's Day massacre

War of the Three Henrys

Edict of Nantes

Pizarro


*Define the following key concepts and terms.*

*encomiendas*

mercantilism

inflation

sexism

racism

skepticism

misogyny

Spanish American holocaust


*Test your understanding of the chapter by answering the following questions.*

1. The war that brought destruction and ensured division in Germany was

   _____ .

2. The Spanish explorer _____ conquered the Aztecs.
3. The Spanish priest and defender of the American Indians was

   _____ .

4.  The law of 1598 that granted religious freedom to French Protestants was

    _____ .

5.  Spain's golden century was _____ .

6.  King _____ of Sweden intervened in the **Thirty Years'** War.

7.  After 1551, the seven northern provinces of the Netherlands were called

    _____ .

8.  The city of _____ became the financial capital of Europe by 1600.

9.  The monarch of Britain at the time of the Spanish Armada was

    _____ .

10. The idea that nothing is completely knowable is

    _____ .

11. _____ was the emperor who divided the Habsburg empire into two parts.

12. The 1516 compromise between church and state in France was

    _____ .

13. _____ was the first European country to establish sea routes to the east.

## MULTIPLE-CHOICE QUESTIONS

1.  Beginning in 1581, the northern Netherlands revolted against their political overlord,
    a.  France.
    b.  Spain.
    c.  Elizabeth I of England.
    d.  Florence.

2.  North American racist attitudes toward African blacks originated in
    a.  South America.

   b.  Spain.
   c.  France.
   d.  England.

3.  In the Thirty Years' War, France supported
    a.  the German Catholics.
    b.  the Holy Roman Emperor.
    c.  Spain.
    d.  the German Protestants.

4.  The nation that considered itself the international defender of Catholicism was
    a.  France.
    b.  Spain.
    c.  Italy.
    d.  England.

5.  Columbus, like many of his fellow explorers, was principally motivated by
    a.  a desire to discover India.
    b.  a desire to Christianize the Americans.
    c.  the desire of Spain to control the New World.
    d.  the Spanish need to control the Mediterranean.

6.  The earliest known explorers of North America were the
    a.  Spanish.
    b.  Vikings.
    c.  Italians.
    d.  English.

7.  In order to gain control of the spice trade of the Indian Ocean, the Portuguese
    were thrown into direct competition with
    a.  Spain.
    b.  England.
    c.  the Muslims.
    d.  France.

8.  The main contribution of Cortez and Pizarro to Spain was the
    a.  tapping of the rich silver resources of Mexico and Peru.
    b.  Christianizing of the New World peoples.
    c.  further exploration of the Pacific Ocean.
    d.  discovery of South Africa.

9.  France was saved from religious anarchy when religious principles were set aside for political necessity by the new king,
    a.  Henry III.
    b.  Francis I.
    c.  Henry IV of Navarre.
    d.  Charles IX.

10. The vast palace of the Spanish monarchs, built under the direction of Philip II, was called
    a.  Versailles.
    b.  the Escorial.
    c.  Tournai.
    d.  Hampton Court.

11. The Treaty of Westphalia, which ended the Thirty Years' War (1618–1648),
    a.  further strengthened the Holy Roman Empire.
    b.  completely undermined the Holy Roman Empire as a viable state.
    c.  maintained that only Catholicism and Lutheranism were legitimate religions.
    d.  refused to recognize the independence of the United Provinces of the Netherlands.

12. Of the following, the best representative of early modern skepticism is
    a.  Las Casas.
    b.  James I.
    c.  Calvin.
    d.  Montaigne.

13. The Portuguese explorer who first reached India was
    a.  Bartholomew Diaz.
    b.  Prince Henry the Navigator.
    c.  Vasco da Gama.
    d.  Hernando Cortez.

14. The origin of racial attitudes found in North America was
    a.  England.
    b.  Spain.
    c.  Catholic teaching.
    d.  the Dutch.

15. The fundamental driving force of European expansion and exploration was
    a.  religious zeal.
    b.  curiosity stirred up by the Renaissance.

    c.   the desire for wealth and material gain.

    d.   the need for spices that improved the blandness of food.

16.  The Calvinists in the Low Countries initially rebelled against Spanish oppression by

    a.   guerrilla war tactics.

    b.   large military confrontations.

    c.   destroying those images and symbols they considered false.

    d.   attacking the Spanish verbally through political and religious pamphlets.

17.  The defeat of the Spanish Armada in 1588

    a.   brought Spanish power in Europe to an end.

    b.   cut off the supply of gold and silver from the New World.

    c.   kept Philip II from uniting western Europe by force or conquering England.

    d.   resulted in the invasion of Spain by an English fleet.

18.  During the fifteenth century Europe was threatened by the

    a.   Ottoman Empire.

    b.   Chinese Empire.

    c.   Indian Empire.

    d.   Black Death.

19.  Generally, between 1560 and 1648, the status of women

    a.   improved because of new economic opportunities.

    b.   improved only for Protestant women.

    c.   declined because of increased sexism.

    d.   changed little from previous generations.

20.  Although his early life is unknown, Christopher Columbus was originally a

    a.   Portuguese seaman.

    b.   Genoan mariner.

    c.   Florentine banker.

    d.   Venetian merchant.

21.  Columbus always thought that

    a.   he had discovered islands off the coast of India.

    b.   he had discovered a vast new continent.

    c.   he had failed in his quest for a new route to India.

    d.   none of the above.

22.  French Calvinists were called

    a.   Huguenots.

   b.  Conversos.
   c.  Gallicans.
   d.  Jesuits.

23.  The seaborne commercial empires of the Portuguese and the Spanish were succeeded by the
   a.  Ottoman Turks.
   b.  English.
   c.  French.
   d.  Dutch.

24.  What group of people did Pope Pius IV expel from Rome in 1566, only to rescind his order because of the financial depression it caused in the city?
   a.  Prostitutes
   b.  Artisans
   c.  Calvinists
   d.  Jews

25.  Calvinism appealed to the middle classes for which of the following reasons?
   a.  Its emphasis away from morals
   b.  Its stress on leisure and ostentatious living
   c.  Its anti-intellectual emphasis
   d.  Its approval of any job well done, hard work, and success

26.  Which of the following statements is true about the Spanish Armada in 1588?
   a.  It was the end of a long war with England.
   b.  It achieved its objective.
   c.  It prevented Philip II from reimposing unity on Western Europe by force.
   d.  It made possible Spanish conquest of the Netherlands.

27.  Which of the following statements about Protestantism in France is true?
   a.  Its theological source was Luther.
   b.  It attracted many people of the middle class.
   c.  It was universally rejected by the nobility.
   d.  It was particularly appealing to the French peasantry.

28.  Which of the following was true concerning the status of women during the Restoration?
   a.  Women were thought to be clearly equal to men.
   b.  Their primary role was to produce heirs.
   c.  Women from all social classes made their mark in the world.
   d.  Women could obtain a divorce without much difficulty.

## GEOGRAPHY

A.  Using Map 18.1 in the text as a guide:
1.  Show on the outline map the exploration routes of da Gama, Columbus, and Magellan.
2.  Mark the location of the Aztec and Inca empires and locate and label the following places.

| | | | |
|---|---|---|---|
| Ceuta | Cape of Good Hope | Amsterdam | Guinea Coast of Africa |
| Calicut | Cape Horn | London | Lisbon |
| Goa | Antwerp | Mexico City | Moluccas |

3.  Why did the Spanish and Portuguese gain an early lead in European expansion? What were the goals of the early explorers, such as Columbus?

4.  Explain, in geographic and economic terms, the reasons for the growth of the Flemish (Netherland) towns such as Antwerp and Amsterdam.

5.  Explain the important economic relationship that developed among Spain, the Americas, and the Netherlands.

B.   Using Map 18.5 in the text as a reference, list below the areas that were the main sources of African slaves and the main areas of slave importation into the New World. Do the latter areas illustrate the economic origins of the slave trade?

## UNDERSTANDING HISTORY THROUGH READING AND THE ARTS

Those interested in skepticism and the life of its finest representative will want to read M. Lowenthal, ed., *Autobiography of Michel de Montaigne* * (1935). There were a number of extremely important and powerful women of the sixteenth century whose biographies make for fascinating reading: R. Roeder, *Catherine de Medici and the Lost Revolution* * (1937); J. E. Neal, *Queen Elizabeth I* * (1934, 1966); and A. Fraser, *Mary Queen of Scots* * (1969). An interesting seventeenth-century woman is Gustavus Adolphus's daughter, whose life is told in G. Masson, *Queen Christina* (1968); N. Harvey, *The Rose and the Thorn* (1977), is an account of the lives and times of Mary and Margaret Tudor.

## PROBLEMS FOR FURTHER INVESTIGATION

Those interested in doing work in the area of European expansion should begin with D. L. Jensen, ed., *The Expansion of Europe: Motives, Methods, and Meaning* (1967). A discussion of some of the problems faced in studying the religious conflict in France is found in J. H. M. Salmon, *The French Wars of Religion* * (1967), and anyone interested in research on the Thirty Years' War should begin with S. H. Steinberg, *The Thirty Years' War and the Conflict for European Hegemony, 1600–1660* * (1966) and T. K. Rabb, *The Thirty Years' War* * (1964). Those interested in understanding how the vast Spanish Empire worked will want to see C. H. Haring, *The Spanish Empire in America* * (1947, 1963). This book includes an excellent bibliography on the subject.

*Available in paperback.

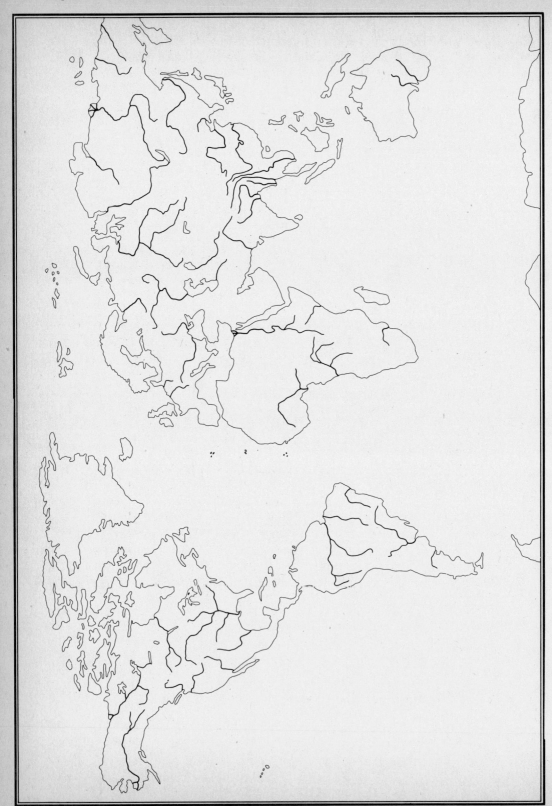

# CHAPTER 19

## ABSOLUTISM AND CONSTITUTIONALISM
## IN WESTERN EUROPE (CA 1589-1715)

## CHAPTER OBJECTIVES

After reading and studying this chapter you should be able to answer the following questions:

Q-1.   In what ways are absolutism and constitutionalism "modern" political systems?

Q-2.   How did absolute monarchy and constitutionalism differ from the feudal and dynastic monarchies of earlier centuries?

Q-3.   Which countries best represent absolutism and constitutionalism?

## CHAPTER SYNOPSIS

This chapter examines how the political system of absolutism succeeded gloriously in France and failed dismally in England in the seventeenth century. Few kings have been as successful in establishing complete monarchial sovereignty as the great Sun King of France, Louis XIV. Louis gave Europe a masterful lesson on how to reduce the power of the class that historically had been a constant competitor of the monarchy, the nobility. He was a superb actor and propagandist, who built on the earlier achievements of Henry IV and Richelieu and used his magnificent palace of Versailles to imprison the French nobility in a beautiful golden cage. He succeeded in expanding France at the expense of the Habsburgs, and his patronage of the arts helped form the great age of French classicism. However, the economic progress he first made was later checked by his policy of revoking religious toleration.

While the France of Louis was the classic model of modern absolutism, Spain was the classic case of imperial decline. By 1600 Spain was in trouble, and by 1700 it was no longer a major European power. Not only did the silver and labor of

America run out, but this great American wealth ruined the Spanish economic and social structure. War with the Dutch, the English, and the French also helped turn Spain into a backwater of Europe.

England and the United Provinces of the Netherlands provide a picture of constitutionalism triumphing over absolutism. For England, the seventeenth century was a long period of political conflict, complete with a bitter civil war and a radical experiment with republicanism. The causes of this era of conflict were varied, but it is clear that by 1689 the English army and Parliament had destroyed the Stuart quest for divine-right absolutism. The period that followed witnessed some important changes in the way the state is managed.

The Netherlands was important not only because it became the financial and commercial center of Europe, but also because it provided the period's third model of political development — a loosely federated, middle-class constitutional state.


## STUDY OUTLINE

I. Absolutism
   A. Absolutism defined
      1. Under absolutism, sovereignty resided in kings — not the nobility or the parliament — who considered themselves responsible to God alone
      2. Absolute kings created new state bureaucracies and armies, and they regulated all the institutions
      3. However, the ambitions of absolute monarchs were limited and not the same as those of leaders of modern totalitarian states
   B. The cornerstone of French absolutism: Louis XIII and Richelieu
      1. Cardinal Richelieu, the ruler of France under King Louis XIII, broke the power of the French nobility
      2. He also brought about administrative reform that helped centralize the state's power
      3. However, his financial actions were unsound and created problems for the future
      4. Richelieu regarded the Protestant Huguenots as a source of aristocratic power
      5. Under Richelieu, France sought to break the Habsburg power
      6. Mazarin's policies gave rise to the *Fronde*, which was a noble movement in opposition to the crown
   C. The absolutism of Louis XIV
      1. Louis the "Sun King" was selfish, an insatiable eater, a great actor, and fearful of the nobility
      2. He made the court at Versailles a fixed institution and used it as a means of preserving royal power and as the center of French absolutism

      a.   Showmanship and the court ceremonials at Versailles were devices to ruin the power of the aristocracy

      b.   The architecture and art of Versailles were means of carrying out state policy

      c.   The French language and culture became the international style

D.  Economic management under Louis XIV: Colbert

   1.   The tax burden fell most heavily on the poor peasants.

   2.   Mercantilism is a collection of governmental policies for the regulation of the economy by the state

   3.   Louis XIV's finance minister, Colbert, tried to achieve a favorable balance of trade and make France self-sufficient so the flow of gold to other countries would be halted

      a.   Colbert encouraged French industry, enacted high tariffs, and created a strong merchant marine

      b.   He hoped to make Canada part of a French empire

      c.   Though France's industries grew, its agricultural economy declined

E.  The revocation of the Edict of Nantes

   1.   In 1685, Louis revoked the Edict of Nantes, which had given religious freedom to French Protestants

   2.   This revocation caused many Protestants to flee the country; but it had little effect on the economy and it caused fear and hatred abroad

F.  Louis XIV's wars

   1.   The French army under Louis XIV was modern because it employed mercenaries rather than nobles

   2.   Louis XIV's foreign policy was expansionist

   3.   The height of French expansion was reached in 1678 with victory over Spain and the Holy Roman Empire

   4.   Louis then fought the new Dutch king of England, William III, and the League of Augsburg

   5.   The War of the Spanish Succession (1701-1713) involved the issue of the succession to the Spanish throne: Louis claimed Spain but was opposed by the Dutch, English, Austrians, and Prussians

      a.   The war was also an attempt to check French economic growth in the world

      b.   The war was concluded by the Peace of Utrecht in 1713, which forbade the union of France and Spain

      c.   The war left France on the brink of bankruptcy with widespread misery

G.  The decline of absolutist Spain in the seventeenth century

   1.   Several factors contributed to Spain's decline

      a.   Fiscal disorder, political incompetence, population decline, intellectual isolation, and psychological malaise contributed to the decline

      b.  The defeat of the "Invincible Armada" in 1588 was a crushing blow to Spain's morale

      c.  Spain's economy began to decline by 1600

        (1)  Royal expenditure increased, but income from the Americas decreased

        (2)  Business and agriculture suffered

      d.  Spanish kings lacked force of character and could not deal with all these problems

      e.  Spain could not escape from her past: military glory, Roman Catholicism, and easy money from America

II.  Constitutionalism in England and the Netherlands

    A.  Constitutionalism defined

      1.  Under constitutionalism, the state must be governed according to law, not royal decree

        a.  It implies a balance between the power of the government and the rights of the subjects

        b.  A nation's constitution may be written or unwritten, but the government must respect it

      2.  Constitutional government is not the same as full democracy because not all of the people have the right to participate

    B.  The decline of royal absolutism in England (1603–1649)

      1.  The Stuart kings of England lacked the political wisdom of Elizabeth I

      2.  James I was devoted to the theory of rule by divine right

      3.  His absolutism ran counter to English belief

      4.  James I faced a new, educated merchant-gentry class that opposed absolutism

      5.  This new class controlled the House of Commons, which the Stuarts attempted to control

      6.  The Protestant or "capitalist ethic" and the problem of religion in England

        a.  Many English people were attracted by the values of hard work, thrift, and self-denial implied by Calvinism; these people were called Puritans

        b.  The Puritans, who were dissatisfied with the Church of England, saw James I as an enemy

        c.  Charles I and his archbishop, Laud, appeared to be pro-Catholic

      7.  The English Civil War (1642–1649)

        a.  Charles I had ruled without Parliament for eleven years

        b.  A revolt in Scotland over the religious issue forced him to call a new Parliament into session to finance an army

          (1)  The Commons passed an act compelling the king to summon Parliament every three years

        (2)   It also impeached Archbishop Laud

        (3)   Religious differences in Ireland led to a revolt there, but Parliament would not trust Charles with an army

    c.   Charles initiated military action against Parliament

        (1)   The Civil War revolved around the issue of whether sovereignty should reside in the king or in Parliament

        (2)   The problem was not resolved, but Charles was beheaded in 1649

  8.  Puritanical absolutism in England: Cromwell and the Protectorate

    a.   Kingship was abolished in 1649 and a commonwealth proclaimed

    b.   In actuality, the army — led by Cromwell — controlled the government

    c.   Cromwell's Protectorate became a military dictatorship, but it ended when Cromwell died in 1658

C.  The restoration of the English monarchy (1660–1688)

  1.  The restoration of the Stuart kings failed to solve the problems of religion and authority in society

  2.  Charles II's Cabal was the forerunner of the cabinet system, and it helped create good relations with the Parliament

  3.  Charles's pro-French policies led to a Catholic scare

  4.  James II violated the Test Act, which prevented Catholics from holding government posts

  5.  Fear of Catholicism led to the expulsion of James II and the *Glorious Revolution*

D.  The Triumph of England's Parliament: Constitutional Monarchy and Cabinet Government

  1.  The Bill of Rights of 1689 stated that sovereignty henceforth resided with Parliament

    a.   Locke argued that all people have natural rights — including that of rebellion

    b.   Locke's ideas served as the foundation of English and American liberalism

  2.  The cabinet system, which developed in the eighteenth century, reflects the victory of aristocratic government over absolutism

E.  The Dutch republic in the seventeenth century

  1.  The Dutch republic emerged from the sixteenth-century struggle against Spain

  2.  Power in the republic resided in the local Estates

    a.   The republic was a confederation: a weak union of strong provinces

    b.   The republic was based on middle-class ideas and values

  3.  Religious toleration fostered economic growth

  4.  The province of Holland became the commercial and financial center of Europe

# REVIEW QUESTIONS

Q-1.   In what way does the French minister Richelieu symbolize absolutism? What were his achievements?

Q-2.   It has been said that the palace of Versailles was a device to ruin the nobility of France. Explain. Was Versailles a palace or a prison?

Q-3.   Define *mercantilism*. What were the mercantilist policies of the French minister Colbert?

Q-4.   The revocation of the Edict of Nantes has been considered a great error on the part of Louis XIV. Why?

Q-5.   What were the reasons for the fall of the Spanish Empire?

Q-6.   Discuss the foreign policy goals of Louis XIV. Was he successful?

Q-7.   Define *absolutism*. How does it differ from totalitarianism?

Q-8.   How did Louis XIV's wars affect the French economy and French society?

Q-9.   What were the causes of the War of the Spanish Succession? How did William III of England affect European events after about 1689?

Q-10.   What was constitutionalism? How does it differ from democratic form of government?

Q-11.   Discuss John Locke's political theory. Why is it said that Locke was the spokesman for the liberal English Revolution of 1689 and for representative government?

Q-12.   What were the attitudes and policies of James I that made him so unpopular with his subjects?

Q-13.   Who were the Puritans? Why did they come into conflict with James I?

Q-14.   What were the immediate and the long-range causes of the English Civil War of 1642–1649? What were the results?

Q-15.   Why did James II flee from England in 1688? What happened to the kingship at this point?

Q-16.   Were the events of 1688–1689 a victory for English democracy? Explain.

Q-17.   Compare and contrast constitutionalism and absolutism. Where does sovereign power reside in each system?

Q-18.   What accounts for the phenomenal economic success and political stability of the Dutch republic?

# STUDY-REVIEW EXERCISES

*Define the following key concepts and terms.*

mercantilism

absolutism

totalitarianism

republicanism

constitutionalism

cabinet government

sovereign power

commonwealth

*Identify* each of the following and give its significance.

Versailles

Dutch Estates General

intendants

Count Olivares of Spain

Spanish Armada of 1588

Peace of Utrecht

Cabal of Charles II

Instrument of Government

Puritans

Long Parliament

Oliver Cromwell

Cardinal Richelieu

Louis XIV of France

James II of England

Glorious Revolution in England

English Bill of Rights

John Churchill

Philip II of Spain

Thomas Hobbes

Richelieu's *Dictionary*

William Laud


*Explain* what each of these men believed about the placement of authority within society.

James I of England

Thomas Hobbes

Louis XIV of France

John Locke


*Explain* what the following events were and why they were important.

revocation of the Edict of Nantes

Scottish revolt of 1640

War of the Spanish Succession

Glorious Revolution

English Civil War of 1642–1649

Treaty of the Pyrenees

<u>Test</u> *your understanding of the chapter by answering the following questions.*

1. The highest executive office of the Dutch republic was _____.

2. Louis XIV's able minister of finance was _____.
3. During the age of economic growth in Spain, a vast number of Spaniards *entered/ left* religious orders.
4. For Louis XIV of France the War of the Spanish Succession was a *success/disaster*.
5. The Englishman who inflicted defeat on Louis XIV at Blenheim was

   _____.

6. The archbishop whose goal was to enforce Anglican unity in England and Scot-

   land was _____.

## MULTIPLE-CHOICE QUESTIONS

1. French Protestants tended to be
   a. poor peasants.
   b. the power behind the throne of Louis XIV.
   c. a financial burden for France.
   d. clever business people.

2. The War of the Spanish Succession began when Charles II of Spain left his territories to
   a. the French heir.
   b. the Spanish heir.
   c. Eugene of Savoy.
   d. the archduke of Austria.

3. This city was the commercial and financial capital of Europe in the seventeenth century.
   a. London
   b. Hamburg
   c. Paris
   d. Amsterdam

4. Of the following, the country most centered on middle-class interests was
   a. England.
   b. Spain.
   c. France.
   d. the Netherlands.

5.  Which of the following Englishmen was a Catholic?
    a.   James II
    b.   Oliver Cromwell
    c.   Archbishop Laud
    d.   William III

6.  Cardinal Richelieu's most notable accomplishment was
    a.   the creation of a strong financial system for France.
    b.   the creation of a highly effective administrative system.
    c.   winning the total support of the Huguenots.
    d.   allying the Catholic church with the government.

7.  The statement "There are no privileges and immunities which can stand against a divinely appointed king" forms the basis of the
    a.   Stuart notion of absolutism.
    b.   Stuart notion of constitutionalism.
    c.   English Parliament's notion of democracy.
    d.   English Parliament's notion of constitutionalism.

8.  The English Long Parliament
    a.   enacted legislation supporting absolutism.
    b.   supported the Catholic tendencies of Charles I.
    c.   supported Charles I as a military leader.
    d.   enacted legislation against absolutism.

9.  Cromwell's government is best described as a
    a.   constitutional state.
    b.   democratic state.
    c.   military dictatorship.
    d.   monarchy.

10. One way in which Louis XIV controlled the French nobility was by
    a.   maintaining standing armies in the countryside to crush noble uprisings.
    b.   requiring the presence of the major noble families at Versailles for at least part of the year.
    c.   periodically visiting the nobility in order to check on their activities.
    d.   none of the above.

11. When Archbishop Laud directed the Presbyterian Scots to accept the Anglican Book of Common Prayer, the Scots
    a.   revolted.
    b.   reluctantly accepted the directive.

c.  ignored the directive.

d.  willingly agreed to the directive.

12. Acting as spokesman for the landowning class and proponent of the idea that the purpose of government is to protect life, liberty, and property was
    a.  Thomas Hobbes.
    b.  William of Orange.
    c.  John Locke.
    d.  Edmund Burke.

13. After the United Provinces of the Netherlands won independence from Spain, their structure of government was a
    a.  strong monarchy.
    b.  centralized parliamentary system.
    c.  weak union of strong provinces.
    d.  democracy.

14. The Dutch economy was based on
    a.  fishing and the merchant marine.
    b.  silver mining in Peru.
    c.  export of textiles.
    d.  copper mining in central America.

15. The decline of Spain in the seventeenth century was caused primarily by
    a.  a strong monarchy that drove Spain to disaster.
    b.  a program of modernization that was too costly.
    c.  economic depression caused by a decrease of bullion coming from the colonies.
    d.  revolts by the aristocracy.

16. Louis XIV's modern standing army consisted largely of
    a.  the bourgeoisie.
    b.  the French peasants.
    c.  foreign mercenaries, many of whom were from Protestant countries.
    d.  the nobility.

17. James I of England believed that royal power
    a.  should be shared with Parliament.
    b.  should be shared with the people.
    c.  was absolute and God-given.
    d.  was given to the monarch by the people.

18. After the long and difficult struggle for independence, the Dutch
    a. were intolerant of religions except for Calvinism.
    b. persecuted all Catholics.
    c. permitted religious freedom.
    d. were wary of all religions.

19. As an economic system, mercantilism
    a. was indistinguishable from militarism.
    b. advocated a favorable balance of trade.
    c. was adopted in France but not elsewhere.
    d. claimed that state power was based on land armies.

20. The Peace of Utrecht in 1713
    a. decreased the size of the British Empire significantly.
    b. reflected the balance of power principle.
    c. began Spain's role as a major power in Europe.
    d. marked the beginning of French expansionist policy.

21. Cardinal Richelieu consolidated the power of the French monarchy by which of the following?
    a. Erecting castles for the nobility
    b. Ruthlessly treating conspirators who threatened the monarchy
    c. Placing nobles in high government offices
    d. Eliminating the "intendant" system of local government

22. By revoking the Edict of Nantes, Louis XIV
    a. granted liberty of conscience to French Huguenots.
    b. provided political rights to French Calvinists.
    c. attempted to achieve religious unity in France.
    d. encouraged religious dissidents to come to France.

23. Which of the following was part of Colbert's mercantile scheme?
    a. A self-sufficient France
    b. Low tariffs
    c. The decolonization of Canada
    d. A large export trade

24. Which of the following is a characteristic of the English House of Commons in the seventeenth century?
    a. The Commons guarded the pocketbook of the nation.
    b. The members were not well educated.
    c. The Commons supported the Stuart monarchy.
    d. The Commons wanted no voice in the expenditure of taxes.

25. Which of the following statements about the Glorious Revolution is true?
    a. It was quite bloody.
    b. It was democratic.
    c. It was initiated by the fear of having a Catholic monarch.
    d. It restored the Stuart monarchy.

26. Who became known as England's first "prime" minister?
    a. Sir Robert Walpole
    b. Oliver Cromwell
    c. William Laud
    d. The duke of Marlborough

27. The independence of the Dutch republic was confirmed in 1648 by the
    a. Glorious Revolution.
    b. Peace of Utrecht.
    c. Edict of Nantes.
    d. Peace of Westphalia.

## GEOGRAPHY

1. Using Map 19.1 in the text as a guide, on the outline map shade in the territory added to France as a result of the wars and foreign policy of King Louis XIV.
2. Explain how each of the territories was acquired and from whom.

3. Louis XIV declared in 1700 that "the Pyrenees no longer exist." What did he mean?

4. What changes in the balance of power came about as a result of the Treaty of
   Utrecht in 1713?

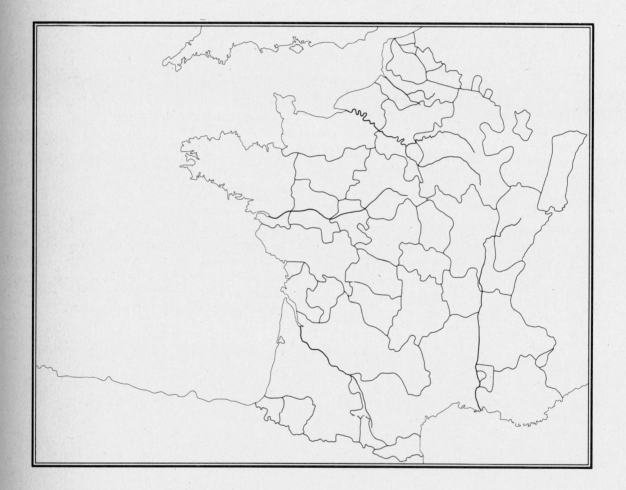

## UNDERSTANDING HISTORY THROUGH READING AND THE ARTS

Louis XIV and the magnificence of his court at Versailles are re-created with color and spirit in W. H. Lewis, *The Splendid Century* * (1953), and a vivid picture of life of the English upper classes — how they ran their estates, entertained, and when possible ran the country — is found in Mark Girouard, *Life in the English Country House: A Social and Architectural History* (1979).

The seventeenth century was a period of architectural splendor in France and in England. Some of the great achievements of this period are discussed in Chapter 7 of N. Pevsner, *An Outline of European Architecture* (7th ed., 1963). The splendor of Versailles and French and British baroque painting and architecture are the subjects of Chapter 7, "The Baroque in France and England," in H. W. Janson, *History of Art* (1962).

Much good reading is found in the literature of the seventeenth century. The great comic writer of the age was Molière, whose *Tartuffe* is still a source of entertainment. LaFontaine's *Fables* are a lively reworking of tales from antiquity and Cervantes's *Don Quixote* continues to inspire its readers. The greatest writer to emerge from the Puritan age in England was John Milton, whose *Paradise Lost* is a classic.

## PROBLEMS FOR FURTHER INVESTIGATION

James Stuart was a successful king in Scotland but a failure in England. Why? See D. Willson, *King James VI and I* * (1956). Was the Glorious Revolution of 1688–1689 in England a victory for modern political democracy or a palace revolution by a group of aristocrats? This and other problems surrounding this political event are discussed in G. M. Straka, ed., *The Revolution of 1688 and the Birth of the English Political Nation* * (rev. ed., 1973). Some of the problems in interpretation of the crucial period 1642 to 1649 in Britain are considered in P. A. M. Taylor, ed., *The Origins of the English Civil War* * (1960), L. Stone, ed., *Social Change and Revolution in England, 1540–1640* * (1965) — and B. Manning deals with popular participation in the wars and revolution in *The English People and the English Revolution* (1976).

Students interested in research on absolutism and Louis XIV in France will want to consider H. G. Judge, ed., *Louis XIV* (1965); William F. Church, ed., *The Greatness of Louis XIV: Myth or Reality?* * (rev. ed., 1972); and R. F. Kierstead, ed., *State and Society in Seventeenth-Century France* * (1975). The best biography of Louis XIV is *Louis XIV* (1968) by J. Wolf.

*Available in paperback.

# CHAPTER 20

## ABSOLUTISM IN EASTERN EUROPE
## TO 1740

### CHAPTER OBJECTIVES

After reading and studying this chapter you should be able to answer the following questions:

Q-1.   Why did the basic structure of society in eastern Europe move away from that in western Europe?

Q-2.   How and why did the rulers of Austria, Prussia, and Russia manage to build more durable absolute monarchies than that of Louis XIV of France?

Q-3.   How did the absolute monarchs' interactions with artists and architects contribute to the achievements of baroque culture?

### CHAPTER SYNOPSIS

This chapter discusses why monarchial absolutism developed with greater lasting strength in eastern Europe than in western Europe. In Russia, Prussia, and Austria monarchs became more powerful as the peasants were pushed back into serfdom. That is, peasants gradually lost the personal and economic freedoms they had built up over several hundred years during the Middle Ages. At the same time that eastern nobles gained greater social and economic control over the enserfed peasants, they lost political power to the rising absolute monarchs. The author concludes that while there were some economic reasons for the re-emergence of serfdom in the east, it was essentially for political reasons that this strong authoritarian tradition emerged. As opposed to western Europe, it was the common people — the peasants — who were the great losers in the power struggle between nobility and monarchy.

Absolutism in Russia, Austria, and Prussia emerged because of war, foreign invasion, and internal struggle. For example, the Austrian monarchs solved the problems arising from external conflicts and a multicultural state by building a strong, central-ized military state. Prussian absolutism — intended to check the power of the nobility — was achieved by the Hohenzollern monarchs, while Russian absolutism was largely the outgrowth of the Mongol conquest and internal power struggles.

Some of the absolute monarchs were enlightened reformers, but their good intentions were often thwarted by internal problems. But if reform from above was not overly effective, the absolute monarchs' use of architecture and urban planning — much of which was in the so-called baroque form — to enhance their images was a noteworthy success. They created buildings and cities that reflected their growing power, and they hired baroque painters and musicians such as Rubens and Bach to glorify them and to fill their palaces with paintings and music.

## STUDY OUTLINE

I. Lords and peasants in eastern Europe
  A. The medieval background (1400-1650)
    1. Personal and economic freedom for peasants increased between 1050 and 1300
    2. Thus, living conditions improved and serfdom was reduced
    3. After 1300, powerful lords in eastern Europe reinstituted serfdom to combat their economic problems
    4. Laws restricted freedom, and labor obligations were increased in eastern Europe
  B. The consolidation of serfdom
    1. The re-establishment of hereditary serfdom took place in Poland, Prussia, and Russia between 1500 and 1650
    2. This was a result of the growth of estate agriculture
      a. Lords seized peasant land for their own estates
      b. They then demanded unpaid serf labor on those estates
  C. Political reasons for changes in serfdom in eastern Europe
    1. Serfdom increased because of political, not economic, reasons
    2. Weak monarchs could not resist the demands of the powerful noble landlords
    3. The absence of the Western concept of sovereignty meant that the king did not think in terms of protecting the people of the nation
    4. Overall, the peasants of the East were weaker than those of the West, and the urban middle class was undermined by the landlords
II. The rise of Austria and Prussia (1650-1750)
  A. Austria and the Ottoman Turks
    1. After the end of the Thirty Years' War in 1648, the Austrian Habsburgs, having failed to destroy Protestantism, turned inward and eastward to unify their holdings

2. Austria became absorbed in a war against the Turks for the conquest of Hungary and Transylvania
3. Under Suleiman the Magnificent the Ottoman Turks built the most powerful empire in the world, which included part of central Europe
4. The Turkish attack on Austria in 1683 was turned back, and the Habsburgs conquered all of Hungary and Transylvania
5. The Habsburg possessions consisted of Austria, Bohemia, and Hungary, which were joined in a fragile union
   a. The Pragmatic Sanction (1713) stated that the possessions should never be divided
   b. The Hungarian nobility resisted accepting Habsburg rule
B. Prussia in the seventeenth century
1. The Hohenzollern family ruled the electorate of Brandenburg but had little real power
2. The Thirty Years' War weakened the representative assemblies of the realm and allowed the Hohenzollerns to consolidate their absolutist rule
3. Frederick William (the Great Elector) used military force and taxation to unify his holdings into a strong state
C. The consolidation of Prussian absolutism
1. Frederick William I encouraged Prussian militarism and created the best army in Europe plus an efficient bureaucracy
2. The nobility — the Junker class — became the military elite
III. The development of Russia
A. The Vikings and the Kievan principality
1. Eastern Slavs moved into Russia between the fifth and ninth centuries
2. Slavic-Viking settlements grew up in the ninth century
3. The Vikings unified the eastern Slavs politically and religiously, creating a ruling dynasty and accepting Eastern Orthodox Christianity for themselves and the Slavs
4. A strong aristocracy (the boyars) and a free peasantry made it difficult to strengthen the state
B. The Mongol yoke and the rise of Moscow
1. The Mongols conquered the Kievan state in the thirteenth century and unified it under their rule
2. The Mongols used Russian aristocrats as their servants
   a. The princes of Moscow served the Mongols well and became the hereditary great princes
   b. Ivan I served the Mongols while using his wealth and power to strengthen the principality of Moscow
   c. Ivan III stopped acknowledging the Mongol Khan and assumed the headship of Orthodox Christianity

C.  Tsar and people to 1689
   1.  By 1505, the prince of Moscow — the tsar — had emerged as the divine-right ruler of all the lands of the eastern Slavs
   2.  The tsars and the boyars struggled over who would rule the state, and the tsars won
   3.  Ivan the Terrible was an autocratic tsar who expanded Muscovy and further reduced the power of the boyars
      a.  He murdered leading boyars and confiscated their estates
      b.  Many peasants fled his rule to the newly conquered territories, forming groups called Cossacks
      c.  Businessmen and artisans were bound to their towns and jobs
   4.  The Time of Troubles (1598–1613) was a period characterized by internal struggles and invasions
      a.  There was no heir
      b.  Cossack bands slaughtered many nobles and officials
      c.  Swedish and Polish armies invaded
   5.  Michael Romanov was elected tsar by the nobles (1613), and he re-established tsarist autocracy
   6.  The Romanovs brought about the total enserfment of the people
   7.  A split in the church over religious reforms led to mass protests by the peasants, and the church became dependent on the state for its authority
D.  The reforms of Peter the Great
   1.  Peter wished to create a strong army for protection and expansion
      a.  He forced the nobility to serve in the army or in the civil service
      b.  He created schools to train technicians for his army
   2.  Army and government became more efficient and powerful as an interlocking military-civilian bureaucracy was created and staffed by talented people
   3.  Russian peasant life under Peter became more harsh
   4.  Modest territorial expansion took place under Peter, and Russia became a European Great Power
   5.  Peter borrowed many western ideas

IV.  Absolutism and the Baroque
A.  Baroque art and music
   1.  Baroque art fulfilled the needs of the Catholic Church and the absolute rulers
   2.  In painting, the baroque is best seen in the work of Rubens; in music it reached its height with Bach
B.  Palaces and power
   1.  Architecture played an important role in politics because it was used by kings to enhance their image and awe their subjects
   2.  The royal palace was the favorite architectural expression of absolutist power

    3.  The dominant artistic style of the age of absolutism was baroque — a dramatic and emotional style

C.  Royal cities

    1.  The new St. Petersburg is an excellent example of the tie among architecture, politics, and urban development

    2.  Peter the Great wanted to create a modern, baroque city from which to rule Russia; the city became a showplace for the tsar, paid for by the Russian nobility and built by the peasants

D.  The growth of St. Petersburg

    1.  During the eighteenth century, St. Petersburg became one of the world's largest and most influential cities

    2.  The new city was modern or "baroque" in its layout and design

    3.  All social groups, including the peasants, paid heavily in the construction of the city

    4.  Tsarina Elizabeth and architect Rastrelli crowned the city with great palaces

## REVIEW QUESTIONS

Q-1.  What were the reasons for the re-emergence of serfdom in eastern Europe in the early modern period (1400–1650)? Build a case for either an economic or political explanation.

Q-2.  In western Europe the conflict between the king and his vassals resulted in gains for the common man. Why did this not happen in eastern Europe?

Q-3.  Why would the reign of the Great Elector be regarded as "the most crucial constitutional struggle in Prussian history for hundreds of years"? What did he do to increase royal authority? Who were the losers?

Q-4.  Prussia has traditionally been considered one of the most militaristic states in Europe. How do you explain this development? Who or what was responsible?

Q-5.  How did war (the Thirty Years' War) and invasion (by the Ottoman Turks) help the Habsburgs consolidate power?

Q-6.  What was the Pragmatic Sanction and why were the Hungarian and Bohemian princes opposed to it?

Q-7.  What role, if any, did war play in the evolution of absolutism in eastern Europe?

Q-8.  Use the following to illustrate the relationship between baroque architecture and European absolutism: St. Petersburg, Karlsruhe, Upper and Lower Belvedere, Schönbrunn. Was it simply that "every fool likes his own hat"? Explain.

Q-9.  It has been said that the common man benefited from the magnificent medieval cathedrals as much as the princes. Can the same be said about the common man and the building projects of the absolute kings and princes? Explain.

Q-10.   Discuss the influence of the Vikings and the Mongols on Russian history.

Q-11.   Why do you think the history of Russia is more a history of servitude than of freedom? How do you account for the enormous amount of violence in Russian history?

Q-12.   Why was territorial expansion "the soul of tsardom"?

Q-13.   Trace the fortunes and political power of the boyar class in Russia from the time of the Kievan state to the death of Peter the Great.

Q-14.   Peter the Great of Russia and Frederick William I of Prussia are often viewed as heroes and "reformers" in the histories of their own countries. How valid is this assessment in terms of the peasants of the early eighteenth century?

## STUDY-REVIEW EXERCISES

*Identify the following people and explain their importance.*

Bartolomeo Rastrelli

Suleiman the Magnificent

Frederick the Great

Charles VI of Austria

Jenghiz Khan

Ivan the Terrible

J. S. Bach

Peter the Great

Frederick William, the Great Elector

Ivan III

Peter Paul Rubens

*Define* the following key concepts and terms.

absolutism

baroque

Prussian Junkers

Hohenzollern

*kholops*

Romanov

boyar

autocracy

Vikings

Habsburg

Mongol yoke

Pragmatic Sanction


*Explain* and describe baroque architecture by referring to the pictures in the textbook.




*Explain* what the following events were, who participated in them, and why they were important.

Building of the Winter Palace of St. Petersburg

Siege of Vienna, 1683

War of the Austrian Succession

Time of Troubles

Battle of Poltava

*Test your understanding of the chapter by answering the following questions.*

1.  The founder of the new Russian city on the coast of the Baltic Sea was

    _____ .

2.  The unsurpassed master of baroque music is _____ .
3.  After 1500, serfdom in eastern Europe *increased/decreased.*
4.  The Ottoman Turkish leader who captured Vienna in 1529 was

    _____ .

5.  In the struggle between the Hungarian aristocrats and the Austrian Habsburgs, the Hungarian aristocrats *maintained/lost* their traditional privileges.
6.  The Prussian monarch who doubled the size of Prussia in 1740 by taking Silesia

    from Austria was _____ .
7.  Number the following events in correct chronological order.

    _____ The election of the first Romanov tsar

    _____ The establishment of the Kievan state

    _____ The Time of Troubles

    _____ Invasion by the Mongols

    _____ The building of St. Petersburg

    _____ The battle of Poltava

8.  The monarchs of eastern Europe in the sixteenth and seventeenth centuries were generally *stronger/weaker* than the kings of western Europe.

## MULTIPLE-CHOICE QUESTIONS

1. The unifiers and first rulers of the Russians were the
   a. Mongols.
   b. Turks.
   c. Romanovs.
   d. Vikings.

2. By the seventeenth century, in Russia commercial activity, manufacturing, and mining were owned or controlled by
   a. rising urban capitalists.
   b. the Cossacks.
   c. the tsar.
   d. foreign investors.

3. The principality called the "sandbox of the Holy Roman Empire" was
   a. Brandenburg-Prussia.
   b. Hungary.
   c. Sweden.
   d. Austria.

4. Ivan the Terrible
   a. failed to conquer Kazan.
   b. was afraid to call himself tsar.
   c. monopolized a great deal of mining and business activity.
   d. abolished the system of compulsory service for noble landlords.

5. The dominant artistic style of the seventeenth and early eighteenth centuries was
   a. Gothic.
   b. Romantic.
   c. impressionistic.
   d. baroque.

6. The noble landowners of Prussia were known as
   a. boyars.
   b. Junkers.
   c. Vikings.
   d. Electors.

7. Apparently the most important reason for the return to serfdom in eastern Europe from about 1500 to 1650 was

a.  political.
b.  economic.
c.  military.
d.  religious.

8.  After the disastrous defeat of the Czech nobility by the Habsburgs at the battle of White Mountain in 1618, the
    a.  old Czech nobility in great numbers accepted Catholicism.
    b.  majority of Czech noble land was given to soldiers who had fought for the Habsburgs.
    c.  conditions of the enserfed peasantry improved.
    d.  Czech nobility continued their struggle effectively for many years.

9.  After the Thirty Years' War and the creation of a large standing army, Austria turned its attention to control of
    a.  northern Italy.
    b.  Prussia.
    c.  Hungary.
    d.  Poland.

10. The result of the Hungarian nobility's struggle against Habsburg oppression was that
    a.  they suffered a fate similar to the Czech nobility.
    b.  they gained a great deal of autonomy compared with the Austrian and Bohemian nobility.
    c.  they won their independence.
    d.  their efforts were inconclusive.

11. In 1742, as a result of the War of Austrian Succession, Maria Theresa
    a.  was forced to abdicate.
    b.  was forced to give up the province of Silesia to Prussia.
    c.  gained Prussian possessions.
    d.  was unable to keep Hungary in the Austrian Empire.

12. The Viking invaders in early Russian history were principally interested in
    a.  controlling vast new lands politically.
    b.  spreading their religion.
    c.  establishing and controlling commercial interests.
    d.  developing cultural exchanges.

13. The Muscovite princes gained their initial power through
    a.  services rendered to the Vikings.

    b.  strategic marriages.

    c.  services rendered to the Mongols.

    d.  a pagan religious cult.

14.  The rise of the Russian monarchy was largely a response to the external threat of the

    a.  French monarchy.

    b.  Asiatic Mongols.

    c.  Prussian monarchy.

    d.  English monarchy.

15.  The Time of Troubles was caused by

    a.  a dispute in the line of succession.

    b.  Turkish invasions.

    c.  Mongol invasions.

    d.  severe crop failures resulting in starvation and disease.

16.  The real losers in the growth of eastern Europe absolutism were the

    a.  peasants.

    b.  peasants and middle classes.

    c.  nobility.

    d.  nobility and the clergy.

17.  A basic social reality on which the absolutist states of eastern Europe rested was

    a.  an oppressed and enserfed peasantry.

    b.  a weak nobility.

    c.  a powerful middle class.

    d.  well-developed urban centers.

18.  Frederick William I was especially fond of

    a.  beautiful women.

    b.  gourmet food.

    c.  the French language.

    d.  tall soldiers.

19.  The greatest obstacle to attempts of the eastern European monarchs to establish absolutism was a (an)

    a.  weak middle class.

    b.  weak nobility.

    c.  oppressed peasantry.

    d.  strong nobility.

20. The first Russian tsar to use an elite corps of service nobility to crush opposition was
    a. Ivan I.
    b. Peter the Great.
    c. Catherine the Great.
    d. Ivan III.

21. Peasants who were drafted into the army of Peter the Great
    a. served a ten-year term.
    b. served for life.
    c. had excellent chances for advancement.
    d. served twenty-five-year terms.

22. The largest empire in the world in the sixteenth century was the
    a. French Empire.
    b. Ottoman Empire.
    c. Spanish Empire.
    d. Habsburg Empire.

23. The eastern European nobility gained power from struggling monarchs during the late Middle Ages because of
    a. a lack of wars during the period.
    b. undisputed royal successions.
    c. aristocratic loyalty to the monarch.
    d. the absence of a well-developed concept of sovereignty.

24. The royal family of Brandenburg-Prussia were the
    a. Hohenzollerns.
    b. Habsburgs.
    c. Hanovers.
    d. Bourbons.

25. Hungarian nobles revolted against the absolute rule of the
    a. Ottoman Turks.
    b. Hohenzollerns.
    c. Habsburgs.
    d. Mongols.

26. The Kievan principality was originally established by
    a. Mongol invaders.
    b. Turkish invaders.
    c. German invaders.
    d. Viking invaders.

27. The reforms of Peter the Great were for the most part
    a. economic and commercial.
    b. political and constitutional.
    c. social and humanitarian.
    d. militaristic and bureaucratic.

28. Which of the following characterizes the peasantry in the sixteenth and seventeenth centuries?
    a. The number of free peasants increased.
    b. Peasants acquired land from their lords.
    c. Peasants became veritable forced laborers.
    d. Peasants gained more freedom of movement.

## GEOGRAPHY

1. Show on the outline map the area covered by the principality of Moscow in 1300. Was the principality of Moscow an important state at that time?

2. Shade in with different colors the territories acquired by the principality of Moscow from 1300 to 1689. How successful was Moscow in expanding before 1689?

3. Shade in the acquisitions of Peter the Great. How do these acquisitions suggest that Russia was becoming more western and European and less eastern and Asiatic during Peter the Great's reign?

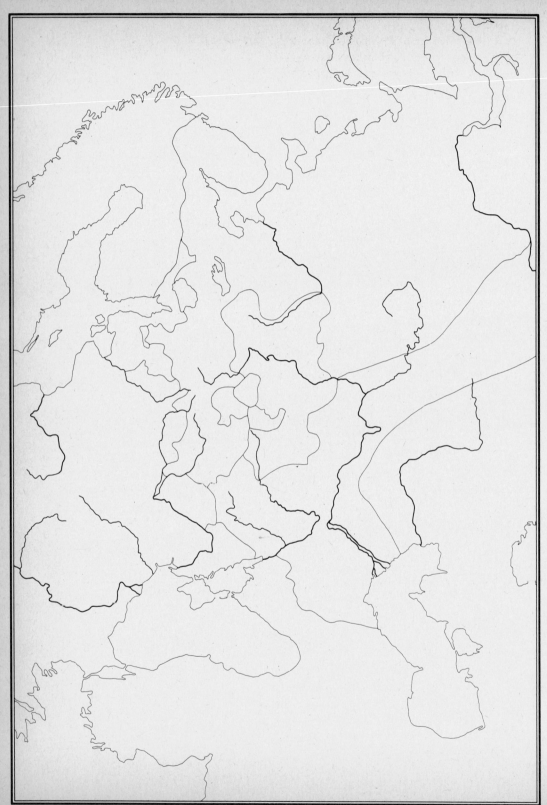

4.  Using your knowledge of Russian geography and the information in the text-book, explain how Russia's history has been influenced by its geography. For example, does Russia's geographic setting contribute to its absolutism?

5.  Looking at Map 20.1 in the text, identify the three territorial parts of the Habsburg (Austrian) state and explain how they came to be united. Do these geographic facts help explain the development of absolutism and militarism in Austria?

## UNDERSTANDING HISTORY THROUGH READING AND THE ARTS

For centuries the Moscow Kremlin was the axis of Russian culture — that is, it was the place where works of great historical and artistic significance were amassed. Many examples of painting and applied art of the Kremlin are discussed and illustrated in *Treasures of the Kremlin** published by the Metropolitan Museum of Art, New York (1979). See also, T. Froncek, ed., *The Horizon Book of the Arts of Russia* (1970), and G. Hamilton, *The Art and Architecture of Russia* (1975).

Baroque music, the dominant musical style in the age of absolutism, was often written for a particular monarch or princely court. The mathematical and harmonic emphasis of baroque music and its aristocratic patronage are illustrated in the six Brandenburg Concertos by Johann Sebastian Bach, written for the margrave of Brandenburg in the early eighteenth century, and in George F. Handel's *Water Music*, written for George I of England at about the same time. Both of these are available on numerous recordings. For the history of baroque music see M. F. Bukofzer, *Music in the Baroque Era* (1947).

*Available in paperback.

## PROBLEMS FOR FURTHER INVESTIGATION

The personality and reign of Tsar Peter the Great have generated considerable controversy for many years. Many ideas for further research can be found in M. Raeff, *Peter the Great* (rev. ed., 1972), and in L. J. Oliva, ed., *Russia and the West from Peter to Khrushchev* (1965).

READING WITH UNDERSTANDING
EXERCISE 2


LEARNING TO IMPROVE YOUR UNDERLINING SKILLS

Read the following paragraphs, in which some words are printed in italic type to
help you find the major points. Read the passage a second time and underline or
highlight one or two sentences in each paragraph that best summarize the paragraph's
major point. Now study and review these points. Finally, close the book and on a
piece of notepaper summarize the major points *with a few words* under the heading
"The Success of Benedictine Monasticism." Compare your summary with that found
at the end of the exercise.

### The Success of Benedictine Monasticism

Why was the Benedictine form of monasticism so successful? Why did it eventually
replace other forms of Western monasticism? The answer lies partly in its *spirit of
flexibility and moderation*, and partly in the *balanced life* it provided. Early Benedictine monks and nuns spent part of the day in prayer, part in study or some other
form of intellectual activity, and part in manual labor. The monastic life as conceived
by Saint Benedict did not lean too heavily in any one direction; it struck a balance
between asceticism and idleness. It thus provided opportunities for persons of en-
tirely different abilities and talents—from mechanics to gardeners to literary scholars.
Benedict's *Rule* contrasts sharply with Cassiodorus's narrow concept of the monastery as a place for aristocratic scholars and bibliophiles.

Benedictine monasticism also *suited the social circumstances of early medieval
society*. The German invasions had fragmented European life: the self-sufficient
rural estate replaced the city as the basic unit of civilization. A monastery too had
to be *economically self-sufficient*. It was supposed to produce from its lands and
properties all that was needed for food, clothing, buildings, and the liturgical service
of the altar. The monastery fit in—indeed, represented—the trend toward localism.

Benedictine monasticism also succeeded partly because it was so *materially successful*. In the seventh and eighth centuries, monasteries pushed back forest and wasteland, drained swamps, and experimented with crop rotation. For example, the abbey of Saint Wandrille, founded in 645 near Rouen in northwestern Gaul, sent squads of monks to clear the forests that surrounded it. Within seventy-five years, the abbey was immensely wealthy. The abbey of Jumièges, also in the diocese of Rouen, followed much the same pattern. Such Benedictine houses made *a significant contribution to the agricultural development* of Europe. The socialistic nature of their organization, whereby property was held in common and profits pooled and reinvested, made this contribution possible.

Finally, *monasteries conducted schools* for local young people. Some learned about prescriptions and herbal remedies and went on to provide medical treatment for their localities. A few copied manuscripts and wrote books. This training did not go unappreciated in a society desperately in need of it. Local and royal governments drew on the services of *the literate men and able administrators* the monasteries produced. This was not what Saint Benedict had intended, but the effectiveness of the institution he designed made it perhaps inevitable.

**ANSWER**

**The Success of Benedictine Monasticism**

1. A flexible and balanced life

2. Economically self-sufficient

3. Economically successful, especially in agriculture

4. Provided education for young and able administrators for governments

# CHAPTER 21

## TOWARD A NEW WORLD-VIEW IN THE WEST

## CHAPTER OBJECTIVES

After reading and studying this chapter you should be able to answer the following questions:

Q-1.  Why did the world-view of the educated classes in Europe change during the seventeenth and eighteenth centuries from a primarily religious one to one that was primarily secular and scientific?
Q-2.  How did this new outlook on life affect Western society and politics?

## CHAPTER SYNOPSIS

This chapter shows how the educated classes in the West moved from a world-view that was basically religious to a world-view that was primarily secular in the course of the seventeenth and eighteenth centuries. The development of scientific knowledge was the key cause of this intellectual change. This change was momentous because it laid the groundwork for both enlightened absolutism and the spirit of revolution.

Until about 1500, Western scientific thought reflected the Aristotelian-medieval world-view, which taught that a motionless earth was at the center of a universe made up of planets and stars in ten crystal spheres. These and many other beliefs showed that science was primarily a branch of religion. Beginning with Copernicus, who taught that the earth revolved around the sun, Europeans slowly began to reject Aristotelian-medieval scientific thought. They developed a new conception of a universe based on natural laws, not on a personal God. Isaac Newton, standing on the shoulders of earlier mathematicians, physicists, and astronomers, formulated the great scientific synthesis: the law of universal gravitation. Newton's work was the culminating point of the scientific revolution.

The chapter examines the causes of the scientific revolution in the West, its relationship to religion, and its impact on nonscientific thought. The new science was more important for intellectual development than for economic activity or everyday life, for above all it promoted critical thinking. Nothing was to be accepted on faith; everything was to be submitted to the rational, scientific way of thinking. This critical examination of everything, from religion and education to war and politics, was the program of the Enlightenment and the accomplishment of the philosophes, a group of thinkers who propagandized the new world-view across Europe and the North American colonies.

The philosophes were reformers, not revolutionaries. Yet reform of European society from the top down — that is, by the absolute monarchs through what is called "enlightened absolutism" — proved to be impossible because the enlightened monarchs could not ignore the demands of their conservative nobilities. In the end, it was revolution, not enlightened absolutism, that changed and reformed Western society.

Enlightened absolutism had its greatest effect in Prussia, Russia, France, and Austria, where new-style monarchs spread the cultural values of the Enlightenment, undertook state-building reforms, and expanded their boundaries. The "Greats" — Frederick of Prussia and Catherine of Russia — best illustrate these movements. Frederick expanded the size and power of Prussia (largely at the expense of Maria Theresa's Austria), while Catherine deposed her husband, adopted Enlightenment ideas and reforms, extended serfdom, and pushed Russia into the West at the expense of Turkey and Poland. In France, Louis XV used Maupeou, his chancellor, to counterattack the growing and well-entrenched aristocracy who had used the Parlement of Paris to check royal power. Louis's efforts came to an end with his death and the succession of the young Louis XVI, who sought popular favor by reinstating the old Parlement of Paris. In Austria, Joseph II continued the state-building of his mother, Maria Theresa (who had limited Church power, strengthened the central government, and reformed serfdom), by granting religious reform and — temporarily — abolishing serfdom.

## STUDY OUTLINE

I. The scientific revolution: the origin of the modern Western world
   A. Historians now recognize that the history of science and the history of society must be brought together
   B. Scientific thought in 1500
      1. Until the early 1500s, European ideas about the universe were based on Aristotelian-medieval ideas

       a.  Central to this view was the belief in a motionless earth fixed at the center of the universe

       b.  Around the earth moved ten crystal spheres

       c.  Beyond the spheres was heaven

   2.  Aristotle's scheme fit into Christianity because it made human beings the center of the universe and established a home for God

C.  The Copernican hypothesis

   1.  Copernicus, a Polish astronomer, claimed that the earth revolved around the sun — that the sun was the center of the universe

   2.  This heliocentric theory was a great departure from the medieval system

   3.  Copernicus's theory created doubts about traditional religion

D.  From Tycho Brahe to Galileo

   1.  Brahe set the stage for the modern study of astronomy by building an observatory and collecting data

   2.  His assistant, Kepler, formulated three laws of planetary motion that described the precise relationship among planets in a sun-centered universe

   3.  Galileo discovered the laws of motion using the experimental method — the cornerstone of modern science

   4.  Galileo was tried by the Inquisition for heresy and forced to recant his views

E.  Newton's synthesis

   1.  Newton integrated the astronomy of Copernicus and Kepler with the physics of Galileo

       a.  He formulated a set of mathematical laws to explain motion and mechanics

       b.  The key feature in his synthesis was the law of universal gravitation

F.  Causes of the scientific revolution

   1.  Medieval European universities provided the framework for the new science

   2.  The Renaissance stimulated science by rediscovering ancient Greek mathematics

   3.  The navigational problems of sea voyages generated scientific research

   4.  New ways of obtaining knowledge improved scientific methods

       a.  Bacon advocated empirical, experimental research

       b.  Descartes stressed mathematics and deductive reasoning

   5.  After the Reformation the Catholic church discouraged science while Protestantism tended to favor it

G.  Some consequences of the scientific revolution in Europe

   1.  There arose a scientific community whose primary goal was the expansion of knowledge

   2.  A modern scientific method arose that rejected traditional knowledge and logic

3. Because the link between pure science and applied technology was weak, the scientific revolution was more an intellectual than material revolution

II. The Enlightenment in the West
   A. Enlightenment ideas
      1. Natural science and reason can explain all aspects of life
      2. The scientific method can explain the laws of human society
      3. It is possible to create better societies and better people
   B. The emergence and results of the Enlightenment
      1. The French philosophes popularized Enlightenment ideas
      2. The Enlightenment and the scientific revolution were directly connected — the former popularized the latter
      3. The Enlightenment encouraged the growth of uncertainty about religious truth, cultural superiority, and the role of experience in learning
   C. The philosophes and their ideas
      1. The philosophes acquainted the elite of western Europe with the ideas of the new world-view
      2. They were committed to the reformation of society and humanity, although they often had to cloak attacks on church and state in satire
         a. Montesquieu used social satire to criticize existing practices
         b. He proposed that power be divided and shared by all classes by adopting the principle that "power checks power"
         c. Voltaire challenged traditional Catholic theology and exhibited a characteristic philosophe belief in a distant God who let human affairs take their own course
         d. Diderot and d'Alembert edited a great encyclopedia that attempted to examine all of human knowledge and to teach people how to think critically and rationally
            (1) The *Encyclopedia* exalted science and knowledge over religion
            (2) As a summary of the Enlightenment world-view it was extremely influential
   D. The later Enlightenment built rigid and dogmatic systems
      1. D'Holbach argued that humans were completely controlled by outside forces
      2. Hume's skepticism argued that the mind can contain only empirical knowledge
      3. Rousseau attacked rationalism and civilization and claimed that children needed to be protected from society
      4. His *Social Contract* centered on the idea of the general will of the people
   E. The social setting of the Enlightenment
      1. Enlightenment ideas were spread by salons of the upper classes

  2. The salons were often presided over by women like the brilliant
     Geoffrin and Deffand
III. The evolution of the "Greats": absolutism
  A. Many believed that "enlightened" reform would come by way of "enlight-
     ened" monarchs
  B. Frederick II and Catherine II of Russia
     1. Frederick II used the War of the Austrian Succession to expand Prussia
        into a Great Power
     2. Renewed conflict in 1756 (the Seven Years' War, 1756–1763) saw
        Prussia aligned against Austria and Russia
     3. Frederick allowed religious freedom and promoted education
     4. He reformed the legal system and bureaucracy and encouraged agricul-
        ture and industry to improve the life of his subjects
     5. Catherine imported Western culture to Russia and corresponded with
        the philosophes
        a. Her ideas about reforming serfdom changed after Pugachev's upris-
           ing in 1773, however, and she restricted the serfs even more
        b. She defeated the Turks
        c. Catherine also succeeded in annexing part of Poland while the rest
           of Poland was taken by Austria and Prussia
  C. Absolutism in France and Austria
     1. With the duke of Orleans and the Parlement of Paris the French nobility
        enjoyed a revival of power following the death of Louis XIV, and the
        monarchy lost the power of taxation
     2. The French minister began the restoration of royal absolutism under
        Louis XV
     3. With the reign of Louis XVI royal absolutism once again declined and
        noble power revived
     4. The Austrian emperor Joseph II was a dedicated reformer who abolished
        serfdom, taxed all his subjects equally, and granted religious freedom
     5. Joseph failed, however, because of aristocratic opposition; his reforms
        were short-lived
  D. An overall evaluation
     1. In France, the rise of judicial and aristocratic opposition combined with
        a public educated in liberalism put absolutism on the defensive
     2. In eastern Europe, however, the results of "enlightened absolutism"
        were modest and therefore absolutism remained entrenched
     3. By combining state-building with the Enlightenment these absolutists
        underscored the long tradition of the dominant role of the state
        in European society

## REVIEW QUESTIONS

Q-1.   Contrast the old Aristotelian-medieval world-view with that of the new science of the sixteenth and seventeenth centuries in the West. What were the contributions of Copernicus, Brahe, Kepler, Galileo, and Newton? What is meant by Newton's "synthesis"?

Q-2.   How did the new scientific theory and discoveries alter the concept of God and religion? Did science, in fact, come to dictate humanity's concept of God?

Q-3.   The author tells us that Copernicus hit on "an old Greek idea being discussed in Renaissance Italy." How does this help explain the origins of the new science?

Q-4.   Discuss the origins and the momentum of the scientific revolution in terms of (a) its own "internal logic" and (b) external and nonscientific causes.

Q-5.   How did Bacon and Descartes contribute to the development of the modern Western scientific method?

Q-6.   Did the Catholic and Protestant churches retard or foster scientific investigation? Explain.

Q-7.   What are the consequences of the rise of modern science?

Q-8.   Were the philosophes interested in popular rule by or the political education of the people? Were their dreams of reform from above utopian?

Q-9.   What was the effect of Catherine's reign on (a) the Russian nobility, (b) the Russian serfs, and (c) the position of Russia in the European balance of power?

Q-10.   Describe the nature of the power struggle in France following the death of Louis XIV in 1715.

Q-11.   Discuss: "Joseph II [of Austria] was a heroic but colossal failure."

Q-12.   Because the enlightened absolutists in the West tried but failed to make life better for common men and women, who were the real enemies of the people? Why was the system of absolutism resistant to change?

## STUDY-REVIEW EXERCISES

*Define the following key concepts and terms.*

deductive reasoning

rationalism

the idea of progress

skepticism

Parlement of Paris

Enlightenment

enlightened absolutism

Aristotelian world-view

empirical method

*Identify* each of the following and give its significance.

Gresham College

Diderot

Bayle

Kepler

Galileo

Partition of Poland

Newton

Montesquieu

Voltaire

Copernicus

Brahe

Catherine the Great

Frederick the Great

Louis XV

Joseph II

philosophes

Bacon

Descartes

D'Holbach


*Explain* the general significance of the following books and indicate how these
works and their authors influenced one another.

*On the Revolutions of the Heavenly Spheres*, Copernicus

*New Astronomy or Celestial Physics*, Kepler

*Two New Sciences*, Galileo

*Principia*, Newton


*Test* your understanding of the chapter by answering the following questions.

1.  According to Aristotle, the sublunar world was made up of four elements: air,

    fire, _____, and _____ .
2.  Copernicus *did/did not* attempt to disprove the existence of God.
3.  Galileo claimed that *motion/rest* is the natural state of all objects.

4.  The key feature in Newton's synthesis was the law of _____ .
5.  In the medieval European universities, science emerged as a branch of

    _____ .

6.  The method of finding latitude came out of study and experimentation in the

    country of _____ .
7.  The idea of progress *was/was not* widespread in the Middle Ages.
8.  In the seventeenth and eighteenth centuries a close link between pure (theoreti-
    cal) science and applied technology *did/did not* exist.

9.  A _____ is one who believes that nothing
    can ever be known beyond all doubt.

10. Voltaire believed that _____ was history's greatest man because he gave humanity truth.

11. Overall, Joseph II of Austria *succeeded/failed* as an enlightened monarch.


## MULTIPLE-CHOICE QUESTIONS

1. "Enlightened" monarchs believed in
   a. reform.
   b. democracy.
   c. urbanization.
   d. all of the above

2. Geoffrin and Deffand were
   a. scientific writers.
   b. religious leaders.
   c. "enlightened" women.
   d. leaders of the serf uprising.

3. The philosophes were
   a. mainly university professors.
   b. generally hostile to monarchial government.
   c. enthusiastic supporters of the Catholic church.
   d. satirist writers who wished to reform society and humanity.

4. The social setting of the Enlightenment
   a. excluded women.
   b. was characterized by poverty and boredom.
   c. was dominated by government officials.
   d. was characterized by witty and intelligent conversation.

5. Catherine the Great
   a. believed the philosophes were dangerous revolutionaries.
   b. freed the serfs to satisfy Diderot.
   c. increased the size of the Russian Empire.
   d. established a strong constitutional monarchy.

6. According to medieval thought, the center of the universe was the
   a. sun.
   b. earth.
   c. moon.
   d. heaven.

7. Copernicus' theory of a sun-centered universe
    a. suggested the universe was small and closed.
    b. challenged the idea that crystal spheres moved the stars around the earth.
    c. ruled out the belief that the worlds of heaven and earth were different.
    d. suggested an enormous and possibly infinite universe.

8. The first astronomer to prove his theories through the use of mathematical equations was
    a. Galileo.
    b. Johannes Kepler.
    c. Tycho Brahe.
    d. Isaac Newton.

9. D'Holbach, Hume, and Rousseau are examples of the later Enlightenment trend toward
    a. rigid systems.
    b. social satire.
    c. religion.
    d. the idea of absolutism.

10. The French philosopher who rejected his contemporaries and whose writings influenced the romantic period was
    a. Rousseau.
    b. Voltaire.
    c. Diderot.
    d. Condorcet.

11. The gathering ground for many who wished to discuss the ideas of the French Enlightenment was the
    a. salon.
    b. lecture hall.
    c. palace at Versailles.
    d. University of Paris.

12. Frederick II was considered an enlightened despot because he
    a. freed the serfs.
    b. wrote poetry, allowed religious freedom, and improved the legal and bureaucratic systems.
    c. kept the Junkers in a dominant position socially and politically.
    d. avoided war.

13. Catherine the Great of Russia hardened her position on serfdom after the _____ rebellion.

a. Pugachev
b. Moscow
c. Polish
d. "Five Year"

14. He used the War of the Austrian Succession to expand Prussia into a great power.
a. Joseph II
b. Frederick II
c. William I
d. Frederick William I

15. The imperialist aggressiveness of Prussia, Austria, and Russia led to the disappearance of this eastern European kingdom from the map after 1795.
a. Hungary
b. Sweden
c. Brandenburg
d. Poland

16. Francis Bacon's great contribution to scientific methodology was
a. the geocentric theory.
b. the notion of logical speculation.
c. the philosophy of empiricism.
d. analytic geometry.

17. This man set the stage for the modern study of astronomy by building an observatory and collecting data.
a. Darwin
b. Hume
c. Newton
d. Brahe

18. Developments in these two sciences were at the heart of the scientific revolution:
a. physics and astronomy
b. chemistry and medicine
c. theology and mathematics
d. biology and politics

19. According to the revised Aristotelian view of the early sixteenth century,
a. the stars revolved around the sun.
b. only the moon and sun revolved around the earth.
c. the earth revolved around the sun.
d. the sun, moon, planets, and stars revolved around the earth.

20. The religion that never discouraged scientific experimentation and writing was
    a. Catholicism.
    b. Protestantism.
    c. Judaism.
    d. Russian Orthodoxy.

21. The Enlightenment thinkers clashed with the established churches because they
    a. renounced their faith in God.
    b. believed it was possible to improve society.
    c. said that theological sources, such as the Bible, should be examined in the light of reason.
    d. wanted to continue the wars of religion.

22. The Enlightenment reached its peak about
    a. 1687.
    b. 1750.
    c. 1810.
    d. 1715.

23. Before Copernicus, people were primarily dependent on the work of the great astronomer of antiquity
    a. Galileo.
    b. Archimedes.
    c. Plato.
    d. Ptolemy.

24. The mathematician who first used controlled experiments to test the movement of objects was
    a. Galileo.
    b. Tycho Brahe.
    c. Copernicus.
    d. Isaac Newton.

25. The French writer who translated the complicated science of his day into entertaining, instructive literature was
    a. Voltaire.
    b. Descartes.
    c. Fontenelle.
    d. Diderot.

26. Generally speaking, the philosophes
    a. concentrated on educating the masses.

b.  distrusted the masses.
c.  believed that democracy was the best road to progress.
d.  held to the doctrines of the Roman Catholic church.

27. In general, the immediate successors of Louis XIV were
    a.  inadequate leaders.
    b.  competent monarchs.
    c.  even more absolute than Louis XIV.
    d.  able to dominate the nobility.

28. Which of the following is true of Joseph II of Austria?
    a.  He abolished serfdom.
    d.  He demanded strict religious conformity.
    c.  He taxed only the nobility.
    d.  He placed education under the control of the Catholic church.

## GEOGRAPHY

Using Map 21.1 in the text as your guide, describe below the "partition of Poland."
Who were the participants, when did it occur, and why did it occur?

## UNDERSTANDING HISTORY THROUGH READING AND THE ARTS

The upsurge of creativity in the arts in Europe in the seventeenth and eighteenth
centuries, which was greatly influenced by the Enlightenment, is known as the age
of the baroque. The meaning of this highly creative and dynamic style and the
achievements of its great artists are discussed in M. Kitson, *The Age of the Baroque*
(1966). See also Chapter 6 in N. Pevsner, *An Outline of European Architecture*
(7th ed., 1963). Few artists captured English life as well as did the painter Hogarth,
whose *Rake's Progress* and *Harlot's Progress* point to the consequences of moral
decay. Hogarth's paintings can be seen and studied in W. Gaunt, *The World of
William Hogarth* (1978), and D. Bindman, *Hogarth\** (1981).

*Available in paperback.

The two greatest philosophes of the age of Enlightenment were Rousseau and Voltaire. Rousseau's ideas on education and natural law are interestingly set forth in his *Emile*, and Voltaire's most-praised work is *Candide*, a funny and sometimes bawdy parody on eighteenth-century life and thought. Much of the new fiction writing of the eighteenth century reflects, often in satire, the spirit of the new world-view — Jonathan Swift, *Gulliver's Travels*; Daniel Defoe, *Moll Flanders*; and Henry Fielding, *Tom Jones*, are just a few. In Germany, the *Sturm und Drang* (storm and stress) movement, which produced works such as Lessing's *Nathan the Wise* which stressed a universal religion, was devoted to the ideas of the Enlightenment and romanticism.

## PROBLEMS FOR FURTHER INVESTIGATION

Those interested in pursuing the topic of the Enlightenment will want to begin with two books that set forth some of the major issues and schools of interpretation on the subject: B. Tierney et al., eds., *Enlightenment — The Age of Reason** (1967), and R. Wines, ed., *Enlightened Despotism** (1967).

Why was it not until the seventeenth century that rational science emerged in the West? What has been the relationship between science and religion in Western society? What ideas did Darwin and modern biology draw from the Scientific Revolution of 1500–1800? These are just a few of the questions asked by scholars of the subject. Begin your investigation with a general reference and bibliography such as G. Sarton, *Introduction to the History of Science* (1927–1948, 5 vols.), and L. Thorndike, *History of Magic and Experimental Science* (1923–1958). On particular figures in science see F. S. Taylor, *Galileo and the Freedom of Thought* (1938), A. Armitage, *Copernicus, the Founder of Modern Astronomy* (1938), M. Casoar, *Johannes Kepler* (1959, trans. C. Hellman), L. T. More, *Isaac Newton* (1934), and I. Cohen, *Franklin and Newton* (1956).

*Available in paperback.

# CHAPTER 22

## THE LIFE OF THE PEOPLE IN EUROPE

## CHAPTER OBJECTIVES

After reading and studying this chapter you should be able to answer the following questions about the peasant masses and the urban poor:

Q-1.   What changes occurred in agriculture and population in eighteenth-century Europe?
Q-2.   Why did traditional marriage and sex practices begin to change in Europe in the late eighteenth century?
Q-3.   What was it like to be a child in European preindustrial society?
Q-4.   How adequate was the diet and health care of eighteenth-century Europeans? Were there any signs of improvement?
Q-5.   What influence did religion hold in everyday life in Europe and what was *pietism*?

## CHAPTER SYNOPSIS

Until recently the aspects of everyday life, such as family relations, sex, marriage, health, and religion, took a secondary place in history. As a result, much of our understanding of these subjects is often based on myth rather than on solid historical research and interpretations.

The chapter begins with three important and interrelated subjects. First, the centuries-old open-field system of agricultural production, a system that was both inefficient and unjust, is described. The second topic is the explosive growth of European population in the eighteenth century. This growth, still imperfectly understood, was probably due largely to the disappearance of the plague and to new and better food, such as the potato. Doctors and organized medicine played a very minor role in the improvements in health. Third, the chapter discusses the movement of manufacturing from urban shops to cottages in the countryside. Rural families worked there as units in the new domestic system, particularly in the textile industry, which provided employment for many in the growing population.

Contrary to early belief, it appears that in western Europe the nuclear family was very common among preindustrial people. Furthermore, preindustrial people did not marry in their early teens, and illegitimacy was not as common as usually thought, and certainly less so than today. The concept of childhood as we know it hardly existed. The author shows that the diet of poor people was probably almost as nutritionally sound as that of rich people — when the poor got enough to eat. As for medical science, it probably did more harm than good in the eighteenth century. Also explained in this chapter are the reasons for a kind of "sexual revolution" beginning in mid-eighteenth-century Europe — with young people engaging in sex at an earlier age and with illegitimacy on the rise.

In the area of religion the West in the eighteenth century witnessed a tug of war between the Enlightenment's attempt to demystify Christianity and place it on a more rational basis and a popular movement to retain traditional ritual, superstition, and religious mysteries. In Protestant and Catholic countries alike, rulers and religious leaders sought to purify religion by eliminating many ritualistic practices. The response to this "reform" by the common people in Catholic countries was a resurgence of religious ritual and mysticism, while in Protestant Germany and England there occurred a popular religious revival based on piety and emotional "conversion." Meanwhile, most of Europe — Catholic and Protestant — saw the state increase its control over the church.


## STUDY OUTLINE

I.  Agriculture and population in eighteenth-century Europe
    A.  Frequent poor harvests and bad weather led to famine and disease and a search for new sources of food and income
    B.  Working the land
        1.  The medieval open-field system divided the land into a few large fields, which were then cut up into long, narrow strips
        2.  The fields were farmed jointly, a portion of the arable land was always left fallow, and output was low
        3.  Common lands were set aside for community use
        4.  The labor and tax system throughout Europe was unjust, but eastern European peasants suffered the most
        5.  By the eighteenth century most peasants in western Europe were free from serfdom and many owned some land
        6.  Crop rotation eliminated the need for fallowing and broke the old cycle of scarcity; more fodder meant more animals, which meant more food

7.   Enclosure of the open fields to permit crop rotation also meant the disappearance of common land

C.  The balance of numbers
1.   The traditional checks on growth were famine, disease, and war
2.   The use of "famine foods" made people weak and susceptible to illness and epidemics
3.   These checks kept Europe's population growth rate fairly low
4.   Quarantine of ports and the victory of the brown rat helped reduce the bubonic plague
5.   The basic cause of population growth was fewer deaths, partly owing to the disappearance of the plague
6.   An increase in the food supply meant fewer famines and epidemics

D.  The growth of cottage industry
1.   Population increase caused the rural poor to take in manufacturing work to supplement their income
2.   This cottage industry challenged the monopoly of the urban craft guilds
3.   It was based on rural workers' producing cloth in their homes for merchant-capitalists, who supplied the raw materials and paid for the finished goods
4.   This system reduced the problem of rural unemployment and provided cheap goods
5.   The textile industry in England was an example of the putting-out system

II.   Marriage and the family in preindustrial European society
A.  Extended and nuclear families
1.   Contrary to popular belief, the extended family was not common in western Europe
2.   Also, early marriage was not common prior to 1750, and many people never married at all
3.   Marriage was commonly delayed because of poverty and/or local law and tradition

B.  Work away from home
1.   Many boys left home to work as craftsmen or laborers
2.   Girls left to work as servants

C.  Premarital sex and birth-control practices
1.   Illegitimate children were not common in preindustrial society
2.   Premarital sex was common, but marriage usually followed
3.   Coitus interruptus was the most common form of birth control

D.  New patterns of marriage and illegitimacy after about 1750
1.   The growth of cottage industry resulted in people marrying earlier — and for love
2.   The explosion of births and the growth of prostitution from about 1750 to 1850 had several causes

        a.  Increasing illegitimacy signified rebellion against laws that limited the right of the poor to marry

        b.  Pregnant servant girls often turned to prostitution, which also increased illegitimacy

  E.  The question of sexual emancipation for women

     1.  Women in cities and factories had limited economic independence

     2.  Poverty kept many people single — leading to premarital sex and illegitimate births

III.  Women and children in preindustrial European society

  A.  Child care and nursing

     1.  Infant mortality was very high

     2.  Breast-feeding of children was common among poor women

     3.  Middle- and upper-class women hired wet nurses

     4.  The occupation of wet-nursing was often exploitative of lower-class women

  B.  Foundlings and infanticide

     1.  "Killing nurses" and infanticide were forms of population control

     2.  Foundling hospitals were established but could not care for all the abandoned babies

  C.  Attitudes toward children

     1.  Attitudes toward children in preindustrial society were different from those of today

         a.  Parents and doctors were generally indifferent to children

         b.  Children were often neglected or treated brutally

     2.  The Enlightenment brought about more humane treatment of children

  D.  Schools and education

     1.  The beginnings of education for common people lie in the seventeenth and eighteenth centuries

     2.  Protestantism encouraged popular education

     3.  Literacy increased, especially in France and Scotland, between 1700 and 1800

IV.  Food and medicine

  A.  The life span of Europeans increased from twenty-five years to thirty-five years between 1700 and 1800 — but why?

  B.  Diet and nutrition

     1.  The major improvements were in the area of prevention, or "preventive medicine"

     2.  The diet of ordinary people improved

         a.  Poor people ate mainly grains and vegetables

         b.  Milk and meat were rarely eaten

     3.  Rich people ate quite differently from the poor

       a.   Their diet was rich in meat and wine
       b.   They avoided fruits and vegetables
  C.  The impact of diet on health
    1.  There were nutritional advantages and disadvantages to the diet of the poor
       a.   Their breads were very nutritious
       b.   Their main problem was not getting enough green vegetables and milk
    2.  The rich often ate too much rich food
  D.  New foods and new knowledge about diet
    1.  The potato substantially improved the diet of the poor
    2.  There was a growth in market gardening and an improvement in food variety in the eighteenth century
    3.  There was some improvement in knowledge about diet, although Europeans did not entirely cast off their myths
    4.  Greater affluence caused many to turn to less nutritious food, such as white bread and sugar
  E.  The medical professionals
    1.  The demonic view of disease was common, and faith healers were used to exorcise the demons
    2.  Pharmacists sold drugs that were often harmful to their patients
    3.  Surgeons often operated without anesthetics and surrounded by dirt
    4.  Physicians frequently bled or purged people to death
  F.  Hospitals and mental illness
    1.  Patients were crowded together, often several to a bed
    2.  There was no fresh air or hygiene
    3.  Mental illness was misunderstood and treated inhumanely
    4.  Some attempts at reform occurred in the late eighteenth century
  G.  Medical experiments and research
    1.  Much medical experimentation was creative quackery
    2.  The conquest of smallpox was the greatest medical triumph of the eighteenth century
       a.   Jenner's vaccination treatment, begun in 1796, was a great medical advance
       b.   Smallpox soon declined drastically in Europe
V.  Religion and Christian churches
  A.  The institutional church
    1.  Despite the critical spirit of the Enlightenment, the local parish church remained important in daily life in Europe
    2.  The Protestant belief in individualism in religion was tempered by increased state control over the church and religion
  B.  Catholic piety
    1.  In Catholic countries the old religious culture of ritual and superstition remained popular

  2. Catholic clergy reluctantly allowed traditional religion to survive

 C. Protestant revival

  1. Pietism stressed religious enthusiasm and individualism

  2. In England, Wesley was troubled by religious corruption, decline, and uncertainty

  3. His "Methodist" movement rejected Calvinism and stressed salvation through faith

  4. Wesley's ministry brought on a religious awakening, particularly among the lower classes

## REVIEW QUESTIONS

Q-1. How did the open-field system work? Why was much of the land left uncultivated while the people sometimes starved?

Q-2. What changes brought the open-field system to an end?

Q-3. Where did the modern agricultural revolution originate? Why?

Q-4. What is meant by "enclosure"? Was this movement a great swindle of the poor by the rich, as some have claimed?

Q-5. It is often believed that the typical preindustrial family in Europe consisted of an extended family. Do you agree? Define extended and nuclear family.

Q-6. In *Romeo and Juliet*, Juliet was just fourteen and Romeo was not too many years older. Is this early marriage typical of preindustrial society? Why did so many people not marry at all?

Q-7. When did the custom of late marriage begin to change? Why?

Q-8. Did preindustrial men and women practice birth control? What methods existed?

Q-9. How do you explain that prior to 1750 there were few illegitimate children but that there was a growth of illegitimacy thereafter?

Q-10. It is often claimed that factory women, as opposed to their rural counterparts, were sexually liberated. Is this claim correct? Explain.

Q-11. How and why did life expectancy improve in the eighteenth century?

Q-12. What were the differences in the diets of the rich and the poor in the eighteenth century? What nutritional deficiencies existed?

Q-13. How important was the potato in the eighteenth century? Is it important enough to merit more attention from historians?

Q-14. How did the "revolution in the animal kingdom" break the force of the deadly bubonic plague?

Q-15. What improvements in the eighteenth century contributed to the decline of disease and famine?

Q-16. How important were the eighteenth-century advances in medical science in extending the life span?

Q-17.  What was the demonic view of disease?

Q-18.  It is said that when it came to medical care, the poor were better off than the rich because they could not afford doctors or hospitals. Why might this have been true?

Q-19.  Why was there so much controversy over the smallpox inoculation? Was it safe? What contribution did Edward Jenner make to the elimination of this disease?

Q-20.  How was mental illness regarded and treated in the eighteenth century?

Q-21.  What effect did changes in church-state relations have on the institutions of the church?

Q-22.  The movement of production from town to country is commonly known as the growth of the domestic, or putting-out, system. Using textile production as an example, explain how the system worked and why it grew.

Q-23.  Describe the forms in which popular religious culture persisted in Catholic Europe.

Q-24.  Define *pietism* and describe how it is reflected in the work and life of John Wesley.


## STUDY-REVIEW EXERCISES

*Define the following key concepts and terms.*

extended family

foundlings

demonic view of disease

nuclear family

illegitimacy explosion

Methodists

famine foods

common land

open-field system

enclosure

cottage industry

putting-out system

purging

"killing nurses"

Jesuits

Pietism

*Identify* each of the following and give his or her significance.

Saint Vincent de Paul

Lady Mary Montague

Edward Jenner

James Graham

Joseph II

John Wesley

*Test your understanding of the chapter by answering the following questions.*

1.  It is apparent that the practice of breast-feeding *increased/limited* the fertility of lower-class European women in the eighteenth century.
2.  The teenage bride *was/was not* the general rule in preindustrial Europe.
3.  Prior to about 1750, premarital sex usually *did/did not* lead to marriage.

4.  In the eighteenth century, the _____ was the primary new food in Europe.
5.  People lived *longer/shorter* lives as the eighteenth century progressed.
6.  The key to Jenner's inoculation discovery was the connection between immunity

    from smallpox and _____ , a mild and not contagious disease.

7. In Catholic countries it was largely *the clergy/the common people* who wished to hold on to traditional religious ritual and superstition.

8. The Englishman who brought religious "enthusiasm" to the common folk of

   England was _____ .

## MULTIPLE-CHOICE QUESTIONS

1. One of the chief deficiencies of the diet of both rich and poor Europeans was the absence of sufficient
   a. meat.
   b. fruit and vegetables.
   c. white bread.
   d. wine.

2. A family in which three or four generations live under the same roof under the direction of a patriarch is known as a (an)
   a. nuclear family.
   b. conjugal family.
   c. industrial household.
   d. extended family.

3. Prior to about 1750 in Europe, marriage between two persons was more often than not
   a. undertaken freely by the couple.
   b. controlled by law and parents.
   c. based on romantic love.
   d. undertaken without economic considerations.

4. The establishment of foundling hospitals in the eighteenth century was an attempt to
   a. prevent the spread of the bubonic plague.
   b. isolate children from smallpox.
   c. prevent willful destruction and abandonment of newborn children.
   d. provide adequate childbirth facilities for rich women.

5. It appears that the role of doctors and hospital care in bringing about improvement in health in the eighteenth century was
   a. very significant.
   b. minor.
   c. helpful only in the area of surgery.
   d. helpful only in the area of ophthalmology.

6. In the seventeenth and early eighteenth centuries European people usually married
   a. surprisingly late.
   b. surprisingly early.
   c. almost never.
   d. with enormous frequency.

7. The overwhelming reason for postponement of marriage was
   a. that people didn't like the institution of marriage.
   b. lack of economic independence.
   c. the stipulation of a legal age.
   d. that young men and women valued the independence of a working life.

8. Which of the following statements best describes the attitude toward children in the first part of the eighteenth century?
   a. They were protected and cherished.
   b. They were never disciplined.
   c. They were treated as they were — children living in a child's world.
   d. They were ignored, often brutalized, and often unloved.

9. Most of the popular education in Europe of the eighteenth century was sponsored by
   a. the church.
   b. the state.
   c. private individuals.
   d. parents, in the home.

10. Which of the following would most likely be found in an eighteenth-century hospital?
    a. Isolation of patients
    b. Sanitary conditions
    c. Uncrowded conditions
    d. Uneducated nurses and poor nursing practices

11. The greatest medical triumph of the eighteenth century was the conquest of
    a. starvation.
    b. smallpox.
    c. scurvy.
    d. cholera.

12. The practice of sending one's newborn baby to be cared for by a poor woman in the countryside was known as

a.  the cottage system.
b.  infanticide.
c.  wet-nursing.
d.  all of the above

13.  It appears that the chief dietary problem of European society was the lack of an adequate supply of
a.  vitamins A and C.
b.  vitamin B complex.
c.  meat.
d.  sugar.

14.  Most probably the best thing an eighteenth-century sick person could do with regard to hospitals would be to
a.  enter only if an operation was suggested by a doctor.
b.  enter only if in need of drugs.
c.  enter only a hospital operating under Galenic theory.
d.  stay away.

15.  The country that led the way in the development of universal education was
a.  Britain.
b.  Prussia.
c.  France.
d.  Italy.

16.  The agricultural improvements of the mid-eighteenth century were based on the elimination of
a.  livestock farming.
b.  the open-field system.
c.  rotation of fields.
d.  nitrogen-producing plants, such as peas and beans.

17.  Which of the following prevented eighteenth-century peasants from making a profit on their land?
a.  The combination of oppressive landlords and poor harvests
b.  The plague
c.  The relatively light taxes imposed on them by landlords
d.  Their reliance on crop rotation

18.  A fair description of population fluctuation figures before 1700 in Europe would be that the
a.  population was remarkably uniform in its growth.

b.   population increased steadily on account of very young marriages and large
     families.

c.   population decreased slightly on account of war, famine, and disease.

d.   population grew slowly and erratically.

19.  Rural workers who participated in the putting-out system
     a.   did so to pass abundant free time.
     b.   became experts in the manufacture of luxury items.
     c.   were highly regulated.
     d.   usually sold their labor for much less than urban workers.

20.  Which of the following is true about preindustrial society's attitudes toward
     children?
     a.   Parents often treated their children with indifference and brutality.
     b.   Children were not allowed to work in the early factories.
     c.   Doctors were the only people interested in the welfare of children.
     d.   Killing of children by parents or nurses became very rare.

21.  The "illegitimacy explosion" of the late eighteenth century in Europe was
     encouraged by which of the following?
     a.   The laws, especially in Germany, concerning the poor's right to marry
     b.   The immobility of young rural workers
     c.   The influence of the French Revolution, which repressed freedom in sexual
          and marital behavior
     d.   The respectful treatment of girls in the servant class

22.  In the second half of the eighteenth century in Europe, the earlier patterns of
     marriage and family life began to change. Which of the following was a result
     of this change?
     a.   Decrease in the number of illegitimate births
     b.   Later marriages
     c.   Weakening of the urban subculture of habitual illegitimacy
     d.   Marriages for love

23.  The diet of the European poor consisted mostly of
     a.   fruit.
     b.   grains and vegetables.
     c.   milk and dairy products.
     d.   meat and eggs.

24.  After the decline of the bubonic plague, the dominant infectious disease in
     Europe was

   a. measles.
   b. tuberculosis.
   c. smallpox.
   d. syphilis.

25. The major health problem linked to the diet of the poor was
   a. constipation.
   b. disorders associated with a deficiency of the vitamin B complex.
   c. scurvy.
   d. gout.

26. The potato first took hold as a dietary staple in
   a. France.
   b. England.
   c. Germany.
   d. Ireland.

27. Which of the following statements best characterizes the medical profession in the eighteenth century?
   a. Medicine played only a very small role in improving the health of the population.
   b. The number of doctors declined steadily.
   c. For the most part, people placed little value on the services of doctors.
   d. The practice of bloodletting was abandoned.

28. Pietism's appeal can be explained by its
   a. isolation of the clergy as agents of God.
   b. emotionalism and enthusiasm.
   c. disdain for "reborn" Christians.
   d. attempt to take religion out of everyday life.


## UNDERSTANDING HISTORY THROUGH READING AND THE ARTS

The relationship between people and agriculture makes for interesting reading. For more on the agricultural life in Britain the reader should start with J. D. Chambers and G. E. Mingay, *The Agricultural Revolution (1750–1880)* (1966). For Europe in general, F. Huggett, *The Land Question and European Society Since 1650** (1975), presents a picture of how agricultural changes have affected the development of European society.

*Available in paperback.

Was the enclosure a blessing or a great swindle for the British farmer? This question has been debated by historians and social commentators since the movement toward business agriculture began in sixteenth-century England. The general argument against enclosure was first set out on the sixteenth century by Sir Thomas More, who claimed (in his book *Utopia*) that it resulted in rural unemployment and rural crime. It is the enclosures between 1750 and 1850, however, that are the most controversial. The best contemporary coverage of the debate is G. E. Mingay, *Enclosure and the Small Farmer in the Age of the Industrial Revolution** (1968), which also contains a useful bibliography.

Painting is one of the major sources of information for the history of childhood. Preindustrial childhood is the subject of *Children's Games*, by Pieter Brueghel the Elder. It is a lively and action-packed painting of over two hundred children engaged in more than seventy different games, and it is the subject of an interesting article by A. Eliot, "Games Children Play," *Sports Illustrated* (January 11, 1971): 48–56.

Tom Jones, eighteenth-century England's most famous foundling, was the fictional hero of Henry Fielding's *Tom Jones* and the subject and title of director Tony Richardson's highly acclaimed, award-winning film version of Fielding's novel. Starring Albert Finney, Susannah York, and Dame Edith Evans, the film re-creates, in amusing and satirical fashion, eighteenth-century English life. A more recent film adaptation is Richardson's *Joseph Andrews*, based on another Fielding novel.

London was the fastest-growing city in the eighteenth century. How people lived in London is the subject of two highly readable and interesting books: M. D. George, *London Life in the Eighteenth Century** (3rd ed., 1951), and R. J. Mitchell and M. D. R. Leys, *A History of London Life** (1963).

Few men in preindustrial society earned enough to support a family. This, in part, explains why and when women married, and why most women worked. The preindustrial woman, therefore, was not in any modern sense a homemaker. The subject of women and the family economy in eighteenth-century France is discussed by O. Hufton in *The Poor of Eighteenth-Century France* (1974).

## PROBLEMS FOR FURTHER INVESTIGATION

Did medical science contribute to an improvement in eighteenth-century life? Until about twenty-five years ago, it was fashionable to believe that the population explosion was due to improvements made by medical science. Although this theory is generally disclaimed today, it appears to be enjoying a slight revival. For both sides, read the following journal articles (which also have bibliographies): T. McKeown and R. G. Brown, "Medical Evidence Related to English Population Change," *Population*

*Available in paperback.

*Studies* 9 (1955); T. McKeown and R. G. Record, "Reasons for the Decline in Mortality in England and Wales During the Nineteenth Century," *Population Studies* 16 (1962); and P. Razzell, "Population Change in Eighteenth-Century England: A Reinterpretation," *Economic History Review*, 2nd series, 18-2 (1965); and on the history of disease see D. Hopkins, *Princes and Peasants: Smallpox in History* (1977).

# CHAPTER 23

# AFRICA, THE MIDDLE EAST, AND INDIA,
## CA 1400–1800

## CHAPTER OBJECTIVES

After reading and studying this chapter you should be able to answer the following questions:

Q-1.   What were the features of Ottoman society and government and those of Safavid Persia? Why did these states decline?
Q-2.   How did Muslim reform and art affect the dominant Hindu population of India?  How and why did the British gain power over India?
Q-3.   How did the slave trade affect African kingdoms?

## CHAPTER SYNOPSIS

By 1500 Africa consisted of a number of kingdoms as well as a number of societies that were held together by family or kinship ties: the Senegambian states on the West African coast, the kingdom of Songhay that dominated much of the Sudan, Kanem-Bornu and Hausa city-states, and the Swahili city-states on the east coast of Africa. This chapter argues that the overall effect of the slave trade was slight. Although French culture influenced the coastal fringes of Senegal, the English maintained factories along the Gold Coast, and the Portuguese held Angola and Mozambique, by 1800 European influence had hardly penetrated the African interior.

The Mughal leader Babur and his successors conquered the Indian subcontinent and Mughal rule inaugurated a period of radical administrative reorganization and the flowering of intellectual and architectural creativity. Babur's grandson, Akbar, gave India one of its greatest periods in history. During this period, India, the prize of European commercial interests, began to experience British political domination. Meanwhile in Turkey another Islamic empire emerged, that of the Ottoman Turks. Stressing the holy war and military organization, the Ottomans established a wealthy empire that stretched from the Balkans in Europe through the Near East and along the West African coast. The reign of Suleiman the Magnificent demonstrated the power and splendid creativity of the Ottomans under the Safavids. Safavid power reached its height under Shah Abbas, whose military achievements — based on the Ottoman model, support for trade and commerce, and endowment of the arts — earned him the title "the Great."


## STUDY OUTLINE

I.   African kingdoms and societies, ca 1500–1800
   A.   Senegambia and Benin
      1.   The Senegambian states of the West African coast possessed a homogeneous culture
         a.   They served as a center in the trade from North Africa and the Middle East
         b.   They became the most important center for the slave trade
      2.   Ghana and Mali controlled much of Senegambia, but other states remained independent
      3.   Senegambian social and political structure
         a.   The three Senegambian states (and language groups) were Wolof, Seere, and Pulaar
         b.   Wolof and Seere culture had defined classes: royalty, nobility, warriors, peasants, artisans, and slaves
         c.   Senegambian slavery was different from Western slavery
         d.   The Wolof nobility elected the king who appointed village chiefs
         e.   In stateless societies, age-grade societies evolved
         f.   The typical Senegambian community was the self-supporting agricultural village made up of family farms
      4.   The forest kingdom of Benin (now southern Nigeria) emerged in the fifteenth and sixteenth centuries
         a.   A balance of power between the king (*oba*) and the nobility had evolved under Ewuare
         b.   Ewuare expanded the state east to the Niger river, west to Yoruba country, and south to the Atlantic
         c.   The capital, Benin City, was large and wealthy
         d.   From 1485 on, the Portuguese and other Europeans tried unsuccessfully to influence Benin
         e.   Reasons for its decline remain a mystery
   B.   The Sudan: Songhay, Kanem-Bornu, and Hausaland

1. Songhay dominated the Niger region of western and central Sudan
   a. Muhammad Toure tried to introduce political centralization and Muslim reforms into Songhay
   b. His death left the country weak and it fell to Moroccan armies
2. Kanem-Bornu thrived under Idris Alooma's leadership
   a. A strong feudal military-feudal state was established
   b. Agriculture and trade with North Africa flourished
   c. Idris Alooma's great feats were described by the historian Ibn Fartua
   d. He introduced Muslim religion and law into Kanem-Bornu
3. The Hausa were agricultural people who lived in city-states
   a. Trade with North Africa resulted in the establishment of Hausa city-states such as Katsina and Kano
   b. Kano and Katsina became Muslim intellectual centers
   c. King Muhammad Rimfa of Kano introduced the practice of wife seclusion and the use of eunuchs

C. Ethiopia
1. The East African Christian kingdom of Ethiopia faced numerous invaders
   a. The state of Adal defeated Emperor Lebna Dengel and then devastated the land and forced many to convert to Islam
   b. The Adal Muslims were defeated by the Portuguese
   c. The Galla peoples occupied parts of Ethiopia and the Ottoman Turks seized Massawa and other coastal cities
2. Portuguese Jesuits tried to replace the Coptic Christian tradition with Roman Catholic Christianity
   a. In spite of these conflicts, the Coptic Christian church remained the cornerstone of Ethiopian national identity
   b. The Jesuits were expelled

D. The Swahili city-states
1. The Swahili city-states prospered until Portuguese intrusion
2. Mogadishu, Mombasa, Kilwa, and Sofala traded ivory, gold, and slaves with Arabian and Persian Gulf ports and the Far East
3. Kilwa dominated the cities, which were cosmopolitan and wealthy
4. In 1498 the Portuguese, under da Gama, conquered the city-states
5. The Swahili people responded by deserting their cities
6. Portugal established a hundred-year East African foothold called Fort Jesus near Mombassa in 1589

E. Africa and the transatlantic slave trade
1. The slave trade began with Spanish and Portuguese exploration
2. Portugal dominated the slave trade from 1493 to 1600; it sent many slaves to Brazil

3.  From 1690 to 1807, England was the leading carrier of African slaves
4.  Most slaves were intended for sugar and coffee plantations
5.  The 400 years of slave trade was a brutal and exploitive process
    a.  At the ports they were treated brutally and given poor food
    b.  They were branded a number of times
    c.  In ships they were packed below deck and received little food
6.  The main sources were downward from the West African coast
    a.  At first the Senegambian coast and the mouth of the Congo River yielded the greatest numbers
    b.  Then the Ivory Coast, the Bight of Benin, and the Gold Coast became large suppliers
    c.  The Portuguese took most of their slaves from Angola
    d.  Most slaves were carried to the sugar and coffee plantations of Latin America
    e.  Luanda and Benguela were the major slave ports to which slaves were brought from the interior
7.  The Portuguese slave trade was dominated by its colony of Brazil
    a.  Ships, capital, and goods for the trade came from Brazil
    b.  Rio de Janeiro commanded the Brazil trade and the slave market with Angola
8.  The British slave trade was dominated by London, Bristol, and Liverpool; the British traded textiles, gunpowder and flint, and liquor for slaves
9.  European traders and African dealers all looked for profits
    a.  The "sorting" was the system of trading goods for slaves
    b.  The Europeans had fort-factories as centers for slave trade
    c.  But the shore method of trading was more popular
10. A northbound trade in slaves went across the Sahara to Algiers, Tripoli, and Cairo — surviving into the twentieth century
11. The economic, social, and political impact of this trade on African societies
    a.  The trade did not lead to the economic development of Africa because slave-trade income was usually spent on luxury and consumer goods or firearms
    b.  The trade encouraged slavery within Africa, encouraged population growth, and resulted in a *métis* or mulatto class
    c.  The *métis* came to exercise considerable economic and social power
    d.  Political and social consequences varied greatly from state to state
12. Although it caused great misery and affected millions, the overall impact of the slave trade on Africa was slight

II.  The Ottoman and Safavid empires
   A.  The Ottoman military state
      1.  The first Ottoman Turkish state expanded out of western Anatolia
      2.  Its rulers were the leaders of the Ghazis, fighters in the holy war
      3.  The principle of *jihad*, or holy war, was central to the Ottoman state
      4.  The Ottomans pushed into the Balkans of Europe, and under Mehmed II they conquered Constantinople
         a.  The conquest of Constantinople inaugurated the imperial phase of the Ottomans
         b.  They threatened Italy and conquered much of the territory surrounding the Mediterranean
         c.  They crushed the Hungarians and attacked Vienna
      5.  Under Suleiman the Magnificent (1520–1566), Ottoman militarism reached classic form
         a.  The military was viewed as the source of the state's existence
         b.  Members of the ruling class held landed estates only for their lifetimes
         c.  Much of the civil service and military was run by slaves loyal to the sultan
         d.  Authority flowed from the sultan to his *pashas*
      6.  Suleiman represents the peak of Ottoman influence and culture
         a.  He used his great wealth to adorn Constantinople with palaces and mosques
         b.  Pasha Sinan's architecture illustrates the creativity and the devotion to Islam that characterized Suleiman's empire
         c.  Following Suleiman, the *janissaries* weakened the sultan's power and became a hereditary feudal class
         d.  Under Muhammad Kuprili the Ottomans' position improved and an aggressive foreign policy was pursued — although their defeat at Vienna (1683) led to their decline in the European Balkan area
   B.  The Persian theocratic state
      1.  Shah Ismail founded the Safavid dynasty and united all of Persia
         a.  He declared the Shi'ite form of religion the state religion
         b.  Shi'ites oppose the traditional, or "Sunni," Islamic branch
         c.  The Shi'ites claim to be descended from Ali and that they alone possess the correct interpretation of the Qur'an
         d.  The Safavid state was a theocratic and puritanical state
      2.  The Safavid state reached its height under Shah Abbas (1587–1629)
         a.  He built an army on the Ottoman model and used it effectively
         b.  He improved trade by encouraging the growth of carpetweaving and tile making
         c.  Isfahan was reconstructed to become a city of active trade and great beauty

        d.  Shah Abbas's successors were inept, and the state fell into the hands of religious leaders — later to be carved up by foreigners

III.  India: from Mughal domination to British domination, ca 1498–1805

    A.  The rule of the Mughals

        1.  Mughal, or Muslim, rule in India began with Babur's conquests

        2.  Babur's grandson, Akbar, gave the Indian Mughal state its form, although his father, Humayun, gave it a strong artistic base

            a.  As *badshah*, the young Akbar was assisted by the military leader Bairam Khan

            b.  Akbar continued Bairam Khan's expansionist policy — adding Mala, Gondwana, Gujarat, and Bengal to the Empire

            c.  Akbar developed an efficient bureaucracy, including a bureau of finance and a royal mint

            d.  He appointed *mansabdars* to administer imperial policy at the local level

        3.  Akbar sought universal religious tolerance, or *sulahkul*

            a.  He worked for the mutual assimilation of Hindus and Muslims

            b.  Under the principle of *sulahkul*, he assumed responsibility for all his subjects

            c.  He abolished taxes (jizya) on non-Muslims, married Hindu women, and employed Hindus in his government

            d.  From his mediation of religious disputes he created the *Din-i-Ilahi*, which was a mix of a number of religions

            e.  With Akbar as the philosopher-king, Din-i-Ilahi created serious Muslim rebellions

            f.  Akbar built a great new city, Fatehpur-Sikri, which combined Muslim and Hindu traditions

            g.  He supported artists and writers

        4.  Akbar was followed by his son Jahangir and his grandson Shah Jahan

            a.  Jahangir consolidated rule in Bengal and supported the arts

            b.  Shah Jahan moved the court to Delhi and built the Peacock Throne and the Taj Mahal — a *pairidaeza*, or walled garden

        5.  The absence of procedure for imperial succession led to Aurangzeb's puritanical rule

            a.  He reimposed laws and taxes against the non-Muslim majority

            b.  His religious policies proved unpopular with the Hindus

            c.  His attempt to conquer the south was only partly successful

            d.  After Aurangzeb's death the provincial governors began to rule independently

            e.  The Marathas revolted and fought the Afghans, who were led by the Persian Nadir Shah

    B.  European rivalry for the Indian trade

1. From their port of Goa, the Portuguese used piracy and terrorism to push the Muslims from the Indian and Arabian oceans and claimed that international law did not apply to non-Westerners
2. The Dutch and British formed East India trading companies
   a. The Dutch East India Company sought profits in the spice trade
   b. Madras and Bombay became British trade centers
   c. The British pushed the Portuguese out of the India trade, while Indonesia came under Dutch control
C. Factory-fort societies
   1. A "factory" was a European trade settlement
      a. At first the British company discouraged involvement in local politics
      b. With local disorder, the company came to exert political control over its factory-forts and surrounding territory
      c. The one-way nature of the trade led to demands in England to prohibit the import of certain goods, particularly Indian cloth
D. The rise of the British East India Company
   1. Colbert's French East India Company established factories in India in the 1670s
   2. Joseph Dupleix advocated use of *sepoys* and alliances with princes to accomplish the French hegemony
      a. India was a battleground in the French-British struggle
      b. British seapower, along with Clive's victory at Plassey, led to British control of India
   3. Hastings implemented the parliamentary legislation that transferred some power from the East India Company to a governor
      a. Hastings laid the foundations for the civil service, instituted reforms, and checked Indian coalition
      b. After his resignation, the British imposed a new property system on India and tightened control over the local princes
   4. At the beginning of the nineteenth century, Britain controlled India through Indian princes, the sepoys, and the civil service

## REVIEW QUESTIONS

Q-1. Describe the Senegambian political and social structure.

Q-2. What was the extent of Benin territory, what was its political structure, and why was it attractive to the Portuguese invaders?

Q-3. What were Muhammad Toure's goals in Songhay, and did he succeed? Explain.

Q-4. Describe Idris Alooma's accomplishments in the state of Kanem-Bornu.

Q-5. Who were the Hausa people, and what was their culture like?

Q-6.   What external threats faced the Ethiopians in the sixteenth century, and what was the outcome?

Q-7.   Describe the conomic basis of the Swahili prosperity. Why did the Swahili city-states crumble?

Q-8.   Describe the African slave trade in terms of its origins, the European countries involved, and the African areas of supply.

Q-9.   Describe the relationship between Portugal, its colony Brazil, and the African slave trade.

Q-10.   What was the economic and demographic impact of the slave trade on African societies?

Q-11.   Describe the role that religion and militarism played in the Ottoman Turkish state.

Q-12.   What were the chief accomplishments of Suleiman the Magnificent? What role did the janissaries play in Turkish history?

Q-13.   Describe the relationship between Shah Abbas and the Shi'ite religion. What were the accomplishments of Abbas?

Q-14.   Trace the religious and political policies and accomplishments of the Mughal Indian state under Akbar. What were the additions and contributions of Jahangir and Shah Jahan?

Q-15.   Why is Aurangzeb's rule described as "puritanical"? What was his attitude toward his grandfather's policies of religious toleration?

Q-16.   Describe the goals, interests, and trade practices of the Dutch and British East India companies.

Q-17.   What were Dupleix's ideas of colonial policy in India? Describe how the British adopted these policies under Hastings.


## STUDY-REVIEW EXERCISES

*Define the following key concepts and terms.*

*métis*

*jihad*

janissaries

*pashas*

factory-forts

*Identify each of the following and give its significance.*

Jesuit missionaries in Latin America

sepoys of India

Las Casas

Benin City

Taj Mahal

Robert Clive

British East India Company

Coptic Christianity

Rio de Janeiro

Battle of Plassey

Dutch East India Company

Warren Hastings

*Explain why each of the following was important.*

*Oba* Ewaure of Benin

Muhammad Toure of Songhay

Idris Alooma of Kanem-Bornu

Mehmed II, the Ottoman Sultan

Shah Abbas of Persia

Akbar, *badshah* of India

Suleiman the Magnificent of Turkey

Shah Jahan of Mughal India

*Test your understanding of the chapter by answering the following questions.*

1.  The Portuguese slave trade was dominated by the Portuguese colony of

    _____.

2.  From 1690 to 1807, the country that led in the slave trade was

    _____.

3.  The principle of *jihad*, meaning _____,
    was the cornerstone of Ottoman political theory and the Ottoman state.

4.  The class of slave recruits in Ottoman Turkey who rose to secure permanent
    military and administrative influence was known as the

    _____ class.

5.  Shah Jahan's most well-known building is the _____.

## MULTIPLE-CHOICE QUESTIONS

1.  In the kingdom of Benin, the *Oba* was the
    a.  clan system.
    b.  king.
    c.  supreme god.
    d.  priesthood.

2.  Benin's political history was marked by struggles between the king and
    a.  European slave traders.
    b.  the nobility.
    c.  Muslim traders.
    d.  the peasants.

3.  In the Sudanese kingdoms, the religion of Islam
    a.  was embraced by the masses.
    b.  was popular primarily with the rulers.
    c.  made deep changes in the legal system.
    d.  was forbidden by royal decree.

4. The Coptic church is an ancient branch of
   a. Hinduism.
   b. Islam.
   c. Christianity.
   d. animism.

5. The nation most deeply involved in the slave trade was
   a. Portugal.
   b. England.
   c. the United States.
   d. Holland.

6. Most Portuguese slave ships were bound for
   a. the United States.
   b. the West Indies.
   c. Brazil.
   d. Argentina.

7. European trade with the Africans
   a. led to technological progress for the Africans.
   b. soaked up the Africans' surplus wealth.
   c. increased the African standard of living.
   d. brought badly needed gold to Europe.

8. The *métis* were
   a. French slave traders.
   b. blacks who spoke French.
   c. mulattoes.
   d. ex-slaves.

9. Which of the following was a consequence of the slave trade?
   a. African kingdoms broke down.
   b. Populations were depleted and economics destroyed.
   c. The trade enriched and strengthened economies.
   d. Consequences varied from place to place.

10. The janissaries were originally
    a. provincial governors.
    b. a slave army.
    c. Ottoman officials.
    d. Muslim monks.

11.  An important point of Akbar's policy was
     a.  religious toleration.
     b.  territorial expansion.
     c.  strong central government.
     d.  suppression of Hinduism.

12.  Sepoys were
     a.  native soldiers.
     b.  Muslim wise men.
     c.  concubines.
     d.  Indian-born Europeans.

13.  Which of the following was *not* a basis for British rule in India?
     a.  Support of the Indian princes
     b.  The British navy
     c.  The sepoys
     d.  The civil service

14.  The source of more New World slaves than any other African region was
     a.  Ghana.
     b.  Mali.
     c.  Sudan.
     d.  Senegambia.

15.  In the fifteenth and sixteenth centuries, a great forest kingdom emerged in what is now southern Nigeria. It is known as the kingdom of
     a.  Senegambia.
     b.  Oba.
     c.  Benin.
     d.  Songhay.

16.  The militaristic king of the Kanem-Bornu who replaced tribal customs with Islamic rule was
     a.  Muhammad Toure.
     b.  Idris Alooma.
     c.  Legna Dengel.
     d.  Ahman ibn Ghazi.

17.  The Swahili city-states were on the
     a.  east coast of Africa.
     b.  north coast of Africa.
     c.  south coast of Africa.
     d.  west coast of Africa.

18. Portuguese merchants in Angola and Brazil sought to keep the flow of slaves at only a trickle from Africa to Brazil because they did not
    a. want to depopulate Angola too quickly.
    b. approve of the slave trade and wanted to eventually stop it for good.
    c. want to depress the American market.
    d. want to pay exorbitant transportation costs.

19. The slave trade that lasted late into the nineteenth century and even into the twentieth century was the
    a. North Atlantic trade.
    b. Angola-Brazil trade.
    c. northbound trade across the Sahara.
    d. eastbound trade via the Indian Ocean.

20. The slave trade produced the greatest demographic losses to the slaving coast of
    a. Angola.
    b. South Africa.
    c. the Gold Coast.
    d. Mali.

21. The Ottomans captured Constantinople during the reign of
    a. Mehmed II.
    b. Suleiman the Magnificent.
    c. Mustafa Naima.
    d. Muhammad Kuprili.

22. The military leader of the Ottoman Empire who tried unsuccessfully to capture Vienna in 1683 was
    a. Suleiman the Magnificent.
    b. Muhammad Kuprili.
    c. Mehmed II.
    d. Kara Mustafa.

23. The founder of the Safavid Dynasty, a Shi'ite state in Persia, was
    a. Shah Abbas.
    b. Shah Ismail.
    c. Babur.
    d. Suleiman II.

24. Babur was a
    a. Mongol.
    b. Safavid.

    c.  Turk.

    d.  Mughal.

25.  Which of the following characterizes Akbar's great empire in India?
    a.  He developed an efficient bureaucracy.
    b.  He employed only Muslim officials.
    c.  He demanded religious conformity.
    d.  He instituted the jizya, a tax on non-Muslim adult males.

26.  The decline of the Mughal state began under Aurangzeb, whose unsuccessful reforms were basically
    a.  economic in nature.
    b.  bureaucratic in nature.
    c.  religious in nature.
    d.  political in nature.

27.  Britain fought for control of India with
    a.  France.
    b.  Portugal.
    c.  Spain.
    d.  Holland.

28.  The British governor general of India who defeated the Mysore was
    a.  Charles Cornwallis.
    b.  Richard Wellesley.
    c.  Warren Hastings.
    d.  Robert Clive.

## GEOGRAPHY

1.  On the accompanying outline map and using Maps 16.1 and 23.1 on pages 455 and 711 in the text as a reference, locate the following:

    a.  The kingdoms of Kanem-Bornu and Hausaland

    b.  The Hausa city-states of Katsina and Kano

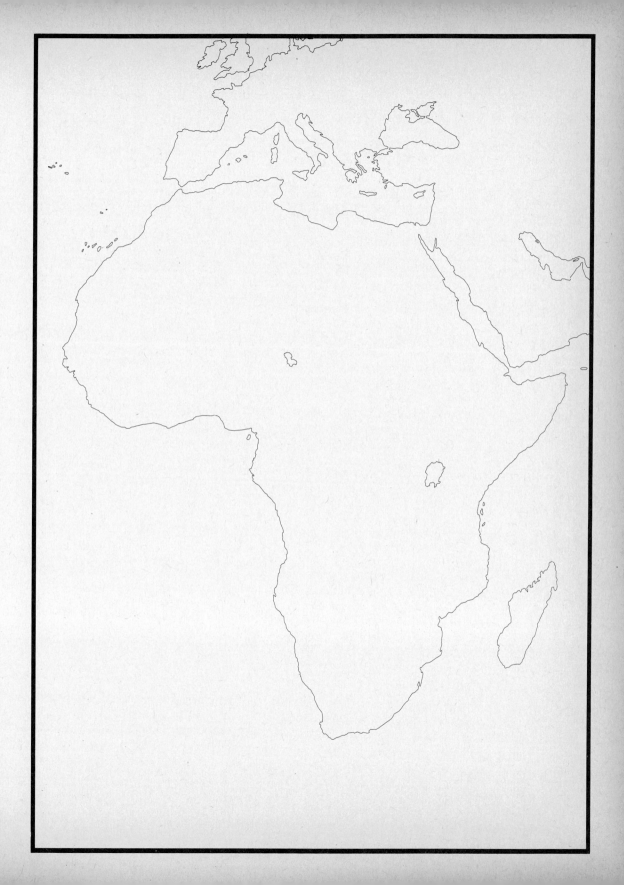

c.   The kingdom of Ethiopia

d.   The Swahili city-states of Mogadishu, Mombasa, Kilwa, and Sofala

2.   In the spaces above, describe briefly the kinds of products each of these areas traded and the directions in which its trade flowed.

## PROBLEMS FOR FURTHER INVESTIGATION

With ships and seamen no better than those of any other country in Europe, why did the Portuguese succeed where their Mediterranean predecessors failed? How did the unique combination of crusading zeal, desire for Guinea gold, the quest of Prester John, and the search for spices combine to spell success? Begin your investigation with C. R. Boxer, *Four Centuries of Portuguese Expansion* (1969).

Reading biographies is an excellent way of furthering your understanding of a particular period. The period covered in this chapter abounds with interesting personalities. Several good biographies are M. Edward, *Clive, The Heaven-Born General* (1977), L. Binyon, *Akbar* (1932), and H. Lamb, *Suleiman the Magnificent — Sultan of the East* (1951).

# CHAPTER 24

# CHINA AND JAPAN TO 1800

## CHAPTER OBJECTIVES

After reading and studying this chapter you should be able to answer the following questions:

Q-1.  What features characterized the governments of the Ming and Ch'ing in China and the Tokugawa shogunate in Japan?
Q-2.  How were Chinese and Japanese societies affected by agricultural and commercial developments?
Q-3.  How did Chinese thinkers interpret and explain the shift from the Ming to the Ch'ing?
Q-4.  What were the Chinese and Japanese attitudes toward western Christian missionary efforts?

## CHAPTER SYNOPSIS

In China the Ming dynasty replaced Mongol rule. Under the Ming, China experienced a remarkable upsurge in agricultural and commercial development. A remarkable and important agricultural revolution took place between 1370 and 1398, which included not only agricultural innovations and new crops but land reclamation (see Table 24.1), reforestation, and repopulation of devastated regions. This revolution encouraged advancements in culture and economics as well, and the state became highly centralized and rested on rule by bureaucracy (often to the dismay of the emperors), which, in the end, fell to corruption and greed. The founder of the Ming dynasty in 1368 was Hung Wu, who centralized government, instituted land reform, strengthened the civil service, and extended the Great Wall. The extravagances of Yung Lo and his court, his neglect of the merchant classes, high taxes, and a weakened military provoked riots and foreign intervention. The invading Manchus became the new Ch'ing dynasty in 1644. In turn, the Ch'ing replaced the Ming, which brought a long period of peace, prosperity, and population expansion. The Ch'ing Empire supported a population of 380 million in 1812, compared to only 193 million in all of Europe in 1800. China was also geographically larger than present-day China, and by the eighteenth century it enjoyed a favorable balance of trade, which brought to it a large portion of the bullion from Latin American mines. However, by the early nineteenth century China was stagnating under an excessive bureaucracy, graft, an extravagant court, and the opium trade.

At about the same time Japan was reaping the rewards of two centuries of peace and social order. Steady economic growth and improved agricultural technology had swelled the population. This chapter outlines the important aspects of Japanese feudalism and shows how the great samurai Nobunaga won control of most of Japan by the sword and went on to unite Japan with a central government and a policy of conciliation. Nobunaga was followed by the Tokugawa regime, which inaugurated a long era of peace while it sealed Japan's borders from the outside world. Prosperity led to urbanization and population increase, while the samurai class was transformed into urban consumers and bureaucrats.

Much of this chapter is devoted to Chinese and Japanese life. More than anywhere else, the family in China exercised great social control. Marriages were arranged, and education and employment were determined by the family. Life was very much influenced by agriculture, although important new jobs were created in the textile and porcelain-making industries. Women held an inferior position within China, but China did not have the hard-and-fast social lines found in Europe. Christianity's influence was limited, although the Jesuits were important agents in a scientific-mathematical exchange between Europe and China. Ordinary life in Japan is best seen in that of the oppressed peasant, although by 1800 a class of rich peasants existed and many peasants had turned to manufacture and urban life. The nobility were stripped of much of their power, the samurai lifestyle emerged, as did an important urban-merchant class.

## STUDY OUTLINE

I.   China: from the Ming dynasty to the mid-Manchu, ca 1368–1795
    A.   Hung Wu, founder of the Ming dynasty, pushed the Mongols out of China
    B.   The Ming agricultural and commercial revolutions
        1.   The Ming agricultural revolution was in part a recovery from the economic chaos of the Mongol rule
            a.   Improvements in rice production, such as Champa rice, led to two yearly harvests
            b.   Irrigation pumping, fish stocking, and new crops also resulted in increased food supply

    c.  Land reclamation, repopulation, and reforestation led to agricultural growth as well

  2.  The social consequences were threefold

    a.  A population boom began in about 1550

    b.  An intensification of labor and lower income per capita

    c.  Towns and small cities multiplied; here the marketplaces dominated commercial life

C.  The government of Hung Wu

  1.  Hung Wu founded the Ming dynasty in 1368 and instituted reform

    a.  He centralized his rule by confiscating noble and religious land and giving it to the peasants

    b.  He relied on land taxes and carried out a land survey and population census

    c.  All members of the three hereditary classes — peasants, artisans, and soldiers — had to provide service to the state

    d.  The emperor was absolute and all power was dispersed from his court

    e.  Later, Hung Wu divided China into principalities run by his sons

    f.  The civil service was reformed by the creation of an exclusive and arduous examination system based on the classics, literary abilities, and lack of originality

    g.  After 1426 the emperor's eunuchs came to hold much state power

  2.  In foreign affairs Hung Wu sought to strengthen China

    a.  He strengthened and extended the Great Wall

    b.  He demanded that foreign traders pay him tribute

    c.  However, Mongols and Japanese violated Chinese traditions

D.  Maritime expansion

  1.  The Ming era is also marked by important naval accomplishments under Yung Lo between 1405 and 1433.

  2.  They resulted in new trade, new tribute, navigational publications, and Chinese emigration into Asia and India

E.  Decline of the Ming dynasty

  1.  After Hung Wu died his son Yung Lo won a struggle for the throne, but the extravagances of his court hurt China's economy

    a.  Yung Lo moved the capital north to Peking and continued his father's policies

    b.  This, along with Yung Lo's extravagance, displeased the new gentry and mercantile groups

    c.  The emperor and his court lived in splendor in the Forbidden City, surrounded by the Imperial City

  2.  Yung Lo's successors had difficulties in foreign affairs

    a.  They could not hold back the Mongol invaders, and in 1449 the emperor was captured

       b.  Chinese invasion of Vietnam led to a Vietnamese liberation movement

       c.  Japan accelerated her raids on the China coast

       d.  The army was weak because taxes were not paid by the people

  3.  Nevertheless, Chinese trade with the West resulted in prosperity, as China exchanged her goods for the Europeans' silver

       a.  Silver became the medium of exchange

       b.  Foreign trade flourished

       c.  Large silk- and cotton-weaving and paper-making industries grew up

  4.  By 1600 China faced grave political and economic problems

       a.  The treasury was drained by war, royal extravagance, and enormous allowances for the extended imperial family

       b.  The military was weak and corrupt

       c.  New taxes provoked riots, and the eunuchs brought on terrorism and factionalism

       d.  The civil bureaucracy was faction-ridden and greedy and blocked imperial reform

  5.  Confucian theory has it that the Mings had forfeited the Mandate of Heaven because their own greed and self-interest had passed on to their officials — all of which invited unrest and eventual downfall

  6.  Under Nurhachi, the Manchus conquered Ming China

F.  Manchu rule

  1.  The Manchus established the Ch'ing dynasty in 1644

       a.  By 1681 their military control of China was complete

       b.  They purged the civil service of factions and eunuchs

       c.  Eighteenth-century China covered much of Asia, including Manchuria, Mongolia, Tibet, and Sinkiang, and received tribute from other states such as Burma, Laos, and Korea

  2.  Manchu rule rested on traditional Chinese methods

       a.  The emperor was supreme and ruled by the Mandate of Heaven

       b.  The central bureaucracy (civil service) continued to manage the state, but the Manchus kept themselves separate and above the Chinese

       c.  Ming and Manchu agricultural improvements continued to encourage population explosion (see Table 24.2), but by 1800 population was outpacing agriculture

       d.  Under Emperor K'ang-hsi, the emperorship was revitalized, domestic revolt crushed, and the Mongolian threat eliminated

       e.  K'ang-hsi's literary encyclopedia was a collection of all Chinese literature

       f.  K'ang-hsi encouraged literary and artistic work as China became a center for fine goods — including *china*

G.   The life of the people
1.   The family exercised greater social influence than elsewhere
a.   The family directed education of children, marriage, religious life, and welfare services
b.   Whereas poor families were "nuclear," middle- and upper-class families were "extended"; power in both rested with the father
c.   Marriages were arranged between parents; the bride became a part of the husband's family and was expected to bear sons
d.   Divorce was open only to men, and men held a higher position in society than women; girl babies were unwanted
e.   Young brides came under the control of their mothers-in-law, who were often cruel and severe
f.   Age was respected; wealthy women had little to do, whereas poor women worked in the fields
2.   The educational system during the Ming and Ch'ing periods had both virtues and weaknesses
a.   The village schools for boys stressed preparation for civil service examinations, but the curriculum was limited
b.   Still, they produced a highly literate society
c.   Girls received training that prepared them to be wives and mothers
3.   Unlike Europe, China did not have hard-and-fast social lines based on hereditary rights
a.   Upward mobility was possible for intelligent children
b.   Scholars held the highest rank in the social order
4.   The Chinese had a variety of forms of relaxation and recreation
a.   Gambling at cards, frequenting the tea houses, using alcoholic drink, and patronizing theaters were common entertainments
b.   Athletics and racing were looked down on
5.   Christian missionaries had little effect on the masses but were influential among the intellectual elite
a.   The Jesuit missionary Matteo Ricci found favor at the imperial court in the seventeenth and eighteenth centuries
b.   Christianity was rejected for a variety of reasons, including its stress on absolutes and its corrupting of Chinese morals
c.   A dispute between the Jesuits and other Catholic orders weakened the influence of the missionaries
6.   Christian missionaries (Jesuits) brought on the rebirth of mathematics and encouraged science, while Europeans took home ideas on bridge building, electrostatics, and magnetism

II.   Japan, ca 1400–1800
A.   During the Ashikaga shogunate (fourteenth to sixteenth centuries) Japan was thrust into civil war among the *daimyos*, or lords; historians call this an era of feudalism

B.  Feudalism in Japan
1.  Feudalism in Japan, unlike that in Europe, evolved in complete isolation from outside forces
2.  Two elements of Japanese feudalism appeared between the eighth and twelfth centuries
    a.  The shoen, or land, with its *shiki*, or rights
    b.  The military warrior clique — with its samurai warriors
3.  By 1550 the number of shoen decreased, while the *daimyos* consolidated their territories
4.  The nature of warfare changed as the cannon and musket made the mounted *samurai* obsolete
C.  Nobunaga and national unification
1.  The *samurai* Nobunaga slowly extended his power and emerged ruler of central Japan by 1568
    a.  1568–1600 is the "period of national unification" during which Nobunaga subdued most of Japan by force
    b.  To do so, he had to destroy Japan's most powerful Buddhist monastery
    c.  He augmented his conquests by force with able rule and a policy of reconciliation
    d.  Trusted *damyos* were favored, castles were built, and his reforms encouraged economic growth
2.  Nobunaga was succeeded by his general, Hideyoshi
    a.  Hideyoshi brought the province of Mori and the island of Kyushu under his domination
    b.  He reduced the threat of the *daimyos*
    c.  He extended his control over agriculture and peasants through a great land survey and through taxes
D.  The Tokugawa regime
1.  This regime was fashioned by Ieyasu
    a.  He left the emperor rich and sovereign in theory, but real power resided in his Tokugawa shogunate
    b.  The *daimyos* became his hostages at his capital at Edo
    c.  He used many devices similar to those used by Louis XIV and William the Conqueror in limiting the power of the nobility
    d.  Taxes were imposed on villages, not individuals
    e.  Class mobility ended, and class stratification was encouraged
2.  *Sakoku*, or the closed country policy, was instituted by Ieyasu's descendants
    a.  To maintain stability and peace, the Japanese were not allowed to leave; foreigners were excluded
    b.  Because of Catholic peasant revolts Christianity was associated with domestic disorder and was accordingly repressed

E.   The life of the people
    1.   Japanese life changed profoundly in the seventeenth and eighteenth centuries
        a.   Stripped of power, the nobility passed their lives in the pursuit of pleasure
        b.   This warrior class was gradually ruined by overindulgence in drink, sex, and costly living
        c.   The *kabuki* theater, with its crude and bawdy skits, was a favorite pastime of the nobility
        d.   Homosexuality, long accepted in Japan, was practiced by the samurai warrior class
    2.   Peasants were sometimes severely oppressed and led miserable lives
        a.   Peasant village life was highly regulated by the state
        b.   In the eighteenth century, 50 percent of the peasant rice crop was paid in taxes
        c.   Low rice prices and overpopulation led to frequent peasant revolts, such as in Iwaki in 1739
        d.   Famines in the 1780s and 1830s made the peasants' lot worse
    3.   The peasant society was not homogeneous
        a.   By the early 1800s, a large class of wealthy and educated peasants existed
        b.   A shortage of farm labor reflected the fact that many peasants worked in manufacturing
    4.   In theory the urban merchant class occupied the bottom rung of the social ladder
        a.   Merchants had no political power but accumulated great wealth
        b.   The growing cities offered social mobility to the poor peasants
        c.   Population growth, the *samurai* lifestyle, and urbanization encouraged the production of consumer goods and the formation of guilds and banks

## REVIEW QUESTIONS

Q-1.   Describe the various factors that gave rise to the so-called Ming Agricultural Revolution. What were the social consequences of this revolution?

Q-2.   How did Hung Wu strengthen and reform China? Compare and contrast the new and old Chinese methods of governing.

Q-3.   Why did the Ming Dynasty decline after Hung Wu's death? In what ways did the nation's economy reflect both decay and prosperity?

Q-4.   Describe the Forbidden City. In what ways does it symbolize China after Hung Wu's death?

Q-5.   What changes did the Manchus bring to China, and how successful were they in making China powerful?

Q-6.   Describe Chinese life during the Ming and Ch'ing periods by discussing Chinese marriage customs and family life, education, social status and entertainment.

Q-7.   What caused the civil war in Japan during the Ashikaga shogunate and by what term is this period known?

Q-8.   Briefly describe the evolution of feudalism in Japan, particularly the two distinctive elements that appeared between the eighth and twelfth centuries.

Q-9.   Who unified Japan and how did he encourage economic growth? Why did he have to destroy Japan's most powerful Buddhist monastery?

Q-10.   Compare the regime of Ieyasu and his Tokugawa shogunate with his European counterparts Louis XIV and William the Conqueror. What was the fate of Christianity during this period and why?

Q-11.   Why did Japanese life change profoundly during the seventeenth and eighteenth centuries? Describe the somewhat contradictory position of the urban merchant class.


## STUDY-REVIEW EXERCISES

*Define the following key concepts and terms.*

Ming Agricultural Revolution

Mandate of Heaven

china manufacture

Chinese civil service examinations

chinese family

Japanese *samurai*

*harakiri*

*kabuki*

*sakoku* policy

Japan's "period of national unification"

*Identify each of the following and give its significance.*

Forbidden City

Ming Dynasty

Ch'ing Dynasty

Emperor Hung Wu

Emperor K'ang-hsi

Matteo Ricci

Nobunaga

Japanese *daimyos*

Japanese *shoen*

Hideyoshi

Tokugawa shogunate

*Describe each of the following and note how each illustrates how Japanese nationalism was both alike and different from that of other Asian countries — such as China.*

Japan's "semi-divine mission"

*Zaibatsu*

Japanese "ultranationalism"

Japanese economy

*Test your understanding of the chapter by answering the following questions.*

1. The peasant founder of China's Ming Dynasty was _____.
2. Under the later Ming rulers, such as Yung Lo, the costs of the imperial court *increased/decreased*, while the balance of trade between China and Europe grew *more/less* favorable.

3. Compared to Europe at the time, China during the Ming and Ch'ing periods *was/was not* a society of hard-and-fast social lines.
4. Homosexuality *was/was not* accepted in Japan.
5. The eighteenth century was a period of economic and demographic *growth/decay* in both Japan and China.

## MULTIPLE-CHOICE QUESTIONS

1. During the Ming era in China, there was a proliferation of
   a. towns.
   b. small cities.
   c. large cities.
   d. both a and b

2. In Ming times the entire Chinese population was divided into three categories according to
   a. place of residence.
   b. occupation.
   c. religion.
   d. wealth.

3. Ming China regarded foreigners as
   a. pirates.
   b. curiosities.
   c. barbarians.
   d. enemies.

4. The flow of silver into China caused a(n)
   a. abandonment of the gold standard.
   b. prospering of the wealthy merchant class.
   c. decline in the value of paper money.
   d. sharp drop in the price of silver.

5. Emperor Wan-Li was unable to accomplish his ends because
   a. bureaucracy and precedent stood in his way.
   b. war interrupted his reforms.
   c. he died very young.
   d. the nobility opposed him.

6. Under the Tokugawa government, Japan was ruled by the
   a. emperor.

    b.  shogun.

    c.  Tokugawa regent.

    d.  council of *samurai.*

7.  *Kabuki* theater usually depicted
    a.  crude love and romance.
    b.  historical events.
    c.  scenes from court life.
    d.  folk tales.

8.  In more recent times, female roles in the *kabuki* theater were played by
    a.  boys.
    b.  prostitutes.
    c.  eunuchs.
    d.  divorcees.

9.  It may be generally said that during the Tokugawa era in Japan that
    a.  the country enjoyed peace and development.
    b.  the country suffered continuous civil strife.
    c.  people lost their faith in the monarchy.
    d.  the standard of living declined.

10.  The shogun Ieyasu kept effective control over the feudal lords by
    a.  executing their prominent leaders.
    b.  forcing them to spend alternate years in the capital.
    c.  imposing heavy taxes.
    d.  requiring their personal oath of loyalty.

11.  Japan expelled Christian missionaries because they
    a.  were spies for European nations.
    b.  encouraged Japanese Christians to participate in feudal revolts.
    c.  preached the overthrow of the shogun.
    d.  interfered with Japan's traditional culture.

12.  The founder of the Ming Dynasty and leader of the Red Turbans was
    a.  Hung Wu.
    b.  Wan-Li.
    c.  Wu Ti.
    d.  Wang Chih.

13.  The Ming agricultural and commercial revolutions were closely linked with
    a.  an expansion of foreign trade.
    b.  dramatic improvements in rice production.

    c.   deurbanization.

    d.   new methods of government spending.

14.  "Fish farming" refers to

    a.   big net fishing off the Chinese coast.

    b.   fish hatching in government aquariums.

    c.   farming for half the year and fishing the other half.

    d.   planting fish in the rice paddies.

15.  Hung Wu moved the Chinese capital to

    a.   Peking.

    b.   Nanking.

    c.   Chungking.

    d.   Shanghai.

16.  Hung Wu's most enduring reform was his

    a.   reorganization of the state ministry.

    b.   implementation of a yearly census.

    c.   reinstatement of civil service examinations.

    d.   hereditary categories.

17.  The naval expeditions of Yung Lo during the Ming period reached as far as

    a.   the east coast of India.

    b.   the east coast of Africa.

    c.   the west coast of India.

    d.   southeast Asia.

18.  Yung Lo moved the capital to

    a.   Peking.

    b.   Nanking.

    c.   Hong Kong.

    d.   Shanghai.

19.  The Forbidden city was built by

    a.   Hung Wu.

    b.   Yung Lo.

    c.   Wan-Li.

    d.   Liu Chin.

20.  During the later Ming Dynasty

    a.   China avoided all foreign trade.

    b.   China achieved peace with her northern invaders.

    c.  costs of the imperial court decreased.

    d.  China became involved in the world economy.

21.  The Ch'ing Dynasty was established by the
    a.  Manchus.
    b.  Mongols.
    c.  Japanese.
    d.  Vietnamese.

22.  Early on, the Ch'ing gained the support of
    a.  peasants.
    b.  intellectuals.
    c.  eunuchs.
    d.  landowners.

23.  The zenith of the Ch'ing Dynasty was achieved during the reign of
    a.  K'ang-hsi.
    b.  Wan-Li.
    c.  Wang Chih.
    d.  Liu Chin.

24.  The greatest controversy between papal authority and the Christian converts in China, which resulted in the missionaries' being expelled from China, surrounded
    a.  the use of Chinese in liturgical services.
    b.  the Chinese practice of ancestor worship.
    c.  the act of footbinding.
    d.  imperial religious authority.

25.  The code by which the samurai lived was called
    a.  harakiri.
    b.  seppuku.
    c.  Bushido.
    d.  shoen.

26.  The leader who began the Japanese period of national unification was
    a.  Ieyasu.
    b.  Tokugawa.
    c.  Nobunaga.
    d.  Ashikaga.

27.  In Tokugawa Japan the commercial class
     a.  were outlawed.
     b.  were considered lowly.
     c.  were highly esteemed.
     d.  rose to great power.

28.  To maintain dynastic stability and internal peace, the Japanese imposed measures called *Sakoku*, which
     a.  introduced the concept of primogeniture.
     b.  limited the power of the samurai.
     c.  was a closed-country policy.
     d.  outlawed Buddhism.

## UNDERSTANDING HISTORY THROUGH READING AND THE ARTS

Trade between China and the West is currently attracting much interest. But the movement of Chinese goods — including paintings, china ware, and the decorative arts — has been considerable and goes back many centuries. C. L. Crossman's *The China Trade\** (1972) looks at the export of furniture and other objects from China, and M. Tregear's *Chinese Art\** (1985) examines Chinese art since 5000 B.C., and Japan's art history is told in Stanley Baker, *Japanese Art\** (1984).

## PROBLEMS FOR FURTHER INVESTIGATION

Both the Meiji Restoration and the fall of the Manchus are now a part of global history. They should be read in the context of both Western imperialism and Japan and China's domestic problems of the nineteenth century. To begin this cross-cultural investigation, read G. B. Sansom, *The Western World and Japan* (1958), and F. Wakeman, *The Fall of Imperial China* (1975).

Japanese feudalism shared some similarities with its Western counterparts, and Japan's feudal values, such as loyalty and discipline, were to play a crucial role in the nation's modernization in the nineteenth century. For further investigation see G. B. Sansom, *Japan: A Short Cultural History* (1962), and E. Reischauer, *Japan: The Story of a Nation* (1981).

The rapid advancement of the Chinese economy around the tenth century led to important developments in Chinese art. For further investigation see M. Sullivan, *The Arts of China* (1979).

\*Available in paperback.

# CHAPTER 25

## THE REVOLUTION IN POLITICS,
## 1775–1815

## CHAPTER OBJECTIVES

After reading and studying this chapter you should be able to answer the following questions:

Q-1.  What were the causes of the political revolutions between 1775 and 1815 in America and France?

Q-2.  What were the ideas and objectives of the revolutionaries in America and France?

Q-3.  Who won and who lost in these revolutions?

## CHAPTER SYNOPSIS

The French and American revolutions were the most important political events of the eighteenth century. They were also a dramatic conclusion to the Enlightenment, and both revolutions, taken together, formed a major turning point in human history. This chapter explains what these great revolutions were all about.

The chapter begins with liberalism — the idea of popular sovereignty, individual rights, and self-determination. Liberalism was the fundamental ideology of the revolution in politics. It called for freedom and equality at a time when monarchs and aristocrats took their great privileges for granted. The author sees the immediate origins of the American Revolution in the British effort to solve the problem of war debts, which was turned into a political struggle by the American colonists, who already had achieved considerable economic and personal freedom. The American Revolution stimulated reform efforts throughout Europe.

It was in France that the ideas of the Enlightenment and liberalism were put to their fullest test. The bankruptcy of the state gave the French aristocracy the chance

169

to grab power from a weak king. This move backfired, however, because the middle class grabbed even harder. It is significant that the revolutionary desires of the middle class depended on the firm support and violent action of aroused peasants and poor urban workers. It was this action of the common people that gave the revolution its driving force.

In the first two years of the French Revolution, the middle class, with its allies from the peasantry and urban poor, achieved unprecedented reforms. The outbreak of an all-European war against France in 1792 then resulted in a reign of terror and a dictatorship by radical moralists, of whom Robespierre was the greatest. By 1795, this radical patriotism wore itself out. The revolutionary momentum slowed and the revolution deteriorated into a military dictatorship under the opportunist Napoleon. Yet until 1815 the history of France was that of war, and that war spread liberalism to the rest of Europe. French conquests also stimulated nationalism. The world of politics was turned upside down.

# STUDY OUTLINE

I. The new ideas of liberty and equality
   A. In the eighteenth century in the West, *liberty* meant human rights and freedoms and the sovereignty of the people
   B. *Equality* meant equal rights and equality of opportunity
   C. The roots of liberalism
      1. The Judeo-Christian tradition of individualism, reinforced by the Reformation, supported liberalism
      2. Liberalism's modern roots are found in the Enlightenment's concern for freedom and legal equality
      3. Liberalism was attractive to both the aristocracy and the middle class, but it lacked the support of the masses
II. The American Revolution (1775–1789)
   A. Some argue that the American Revolution was not a revolution at all but merely a war for independence
   B. The origins of the revolution are difficult to ascertain
      1. The British wanted the Americans to pay their share of imperial expenses
         a. Parliament passed the Stamp Act (1765) to raise revenue
         b. Vigorous protest from the colonies forced the act's repeal (1766)
      2. Many Americans believed they had the right to make their own laws
      3. The issue of taxation and representation ultimately led to the outbreak of fighting
   C. The independence movement was encouraged by several factors
      1. The British refused to compromise, thus losing the support of many colonists

2. The radical ideas of Thomas Paine, expressed in the best-selling *Common Sense*, greatly influenced public opinion in favor of independence
3. The Declaration of Independence, written by Thomas Jefferson and passed by the Second Continental Congress (1776), further increased the desire of the colonists for independence
4. Although many Americans remained loyal to Britain, the independence movement had wide-based support from all sections of society
5. European aid, especially from the French government and from French volunteers, contributed greatly to the American victory in 1783

D. The Constitution and Bill of Rights consolidated the revolutionary program of liberty and equality
   1. The federal, or central, government was given important powers — the right to tax, the means to enforce its laws, the regulation of trade — but the states had important powers too
   2. The executive, legislative, and judicial branches of the government were designed to balance one another
   3. Some people (the Anti-Federalists) feared that the central government had too much power; to placate them, the Federalists wrote the Bill of Rights, which spells out the rights of the individual

E. The American Revolution encouraged European revolution

III. The French Revolution: the revolution that began the modern era in politics
A. The influence of the American Revolution
   1. Many French soldiers, such as Lafayette, served in America and were impressed by the ideals of the revolution
   2. The American Revolution influenced the French Revolution, but the latter was more violent and more influential

B. The breakdown of the old order
   1. By the 1780s, the government was nearly bankrupt
   2. The French banking system could not cope with the fiscal problems, leaving the monarchy with no choice but to increase taxes

C. Legal orders and social realities: the three estates
   1. The first estate, the clergy, had many privileges and much wealth, and it levied an oppressive tax on the peasantry
   2. The second estate, the nobility, also had great privileges, wealth, and power, and it too taxed the peasantry
   3. The third estate, the commoners, was a mixture of a few rich members of the middle class, urban workers, and the mass of peasants

D. The formation of the National Assembly of 1789
   1. Louis XVI's economic reform plan to tax landed property was opposed by the nobles
   2. Louis called for a meeting of the Estates General, the representative body of the three estates

      a.   Traditionally, historians have viewed the bourgeoisie's class and economic interests as pushing it into a revolutionary role

      b.   Revisionist historians, however, claim that the bourgeoisie's interests did not differ from the interests of the upper class

      c.   The nobility represented both conservative and liberal viewpoints

      d.   The third estate representatives were largely lawyers and government officials

      e.   The third estate wanted the three estates to meet together so the third estate would have the most power

   3.   The dispute over voting in the Estates General led the third estate to break away and form the National Assembly

   4.   Louis tried to reassert his monarchial authority and assembled an army

  E.   The revolt of the poor and the oppressed

   1.   Rising bread prices in 1788–1789 stirred the people to action

   2.   Fearing attack by the king's army, angry Parisians stormed the Bastille (July 14, 1789)

      a.   The people took the Bastille, and the king was forced to recall his troops

      b.   The uprising of the masses saved the National Assembly

   3.   The peasants revolted, forcing the National Assembly to abolish feudal dues, and won a great victory

  F.   A limited monarchy established by the bourgeoisie

   1.   The National Assembly's Declaration of the Rights of Man (1789) proclaimed the rights of all citizens and guaranteed equality before the law and a representative government

   2.   Meanwhile, the poor women of Paris forced the king and government to move to Paris

   3.   The National Assembly established a constitutional monarchy and passed major reforms of France's laws and institutions

   4.   The National Assembly attacked the power of the church by seizing its land and subjugating the church to the state

   5.   This attack on the church turned many people against the revolution

IV.  World war and republican France (1791–1799)

  A.  War began in April 1792

   1.   The European attitude toward the French Revolution was mixed

      a.   Liberals and radicals such as Priestley and Paine praised it as the triumph of liberty

      b.   Conservatives like Burke and Gentz predicted it would lead to tyranny

   2.   Fear among European kings and nobility that the revolution would spread resulted in the Declaration of Pillnitz (1791), which threatened the invasion of France by Austria and Prussia

3. In retaliation, the patriotic French deputies declared war on Austria in 1792, but France was soon retreating before the armies of the First Coalition

4. In 1792 a new assembly (the National Convention) proclaimed France a republic

B. The "second revolution" and rapid radicalization in France

1. Louis XVI was tried and convicted of treason by the National Convention and guillotined in early 1793

2. French armies continued the "war against tyranny" by declaring war on nearly all of Europe

3. In Paris, the republicans — divided between the Girondists and the Mountain — struggled for political power

4. The *sans-culottes* — the laboring poor — allied with the Mountain and helped Robespierre and the Committee of Public Safety gain power

C. Total war and the Reign of Terror (1793-1794)

1. Robespierre established a planned economy to wage total war and aid the poor

2. The Reign of Terror was instituted to eliminate opposition to the revolution, and many people were jailed or executed

3. The war became a national mission against evil within and outside of France

D. The "Thermidorian reaction" and the Directory (1795-1799)

1. Fear of the Reign of Terror led to the execution of its leader, Robespierre

2. The period of the "Thermidorian reaction" following Robespierre's death was marked by a return to bourgeois liberalism

   a. Economic controls were established

   b. The Directory, a five-man executive body, was established

   c. Riots by the poor were put down

3. The poor lost their fervor for revolution

4. A military dictatorship was established in order to prevent a return to peace and monarchy

V. The Napoleonic era (1799-1815)

A. Napoleon's rule

1. Napoleon appealed to many, like Abbé Sieyès, who looked for authority from above

2. Napoleon became the center of a plot to overturn the weak Directory and was named first consul of the republic in 1799

3. He maintained order and worked out important compromises

   a. His civil code of 1804 granted the middle class equality under the law and safeguarded their right to own property

   b. He confirmed the gains of the peasants

        c.  He centralized the government, strengthened the bureaucracy, and granted amnesty to nobles

        d.  He signed the Concordat of 1801, which guaranteed freedom of worship for Catholics

    4.  He betrayed the ideals of the revolution by violating the rights of free speech and press, and free elections

B.  Napoleon's wars and foreign policy

    1.  He defeated Austria (1801) and made peace with Britain (1802)

    2.  Another war (against the Third Coalition — Austria, Russia, Sweden, and Britain) resulted in British naval dominance at the battle of Trafalgar (1805)

    3.  Napoleon used the fear of a conspiracy to return the Bourbons to power to get himself elected emperor

    4.  The Third Coalition collapsed at Austerlitz (1805), and Napoleon gained much German territory

    5.  In 1806, Napoleon defeated Prussia and gained even more territory

    6.  Napoleon's Grand Empire meant French control of continental Europe

    7.  The beginning of the end for Napoleon came with the Spanish revolt and the British blockade

    8.  The French invasion of Russia in 1812 was a disaster for Napoleon

    9.  He was defeated by the Fourth Coalition and abdicated his throne in 1814 — only to be defeated again at Waterloo in 1815

VI.  Was the French Revolution a success?

  A.  Yes, the liberal revolution in France succeeded in giving great benefits to the people

  B.  Although the revolution brought the Reign of Terror and a dictatorship, the old order was never reestablished, and thus a substantial part of the liberal philosophy survived

## REVIEW QUESTIONS

Q-1.  Define *liberalism*. What did it mean to be a liberal in Europe in the eighteenth and nineteenth centuries? How does this compare to twentieth-century liberalism?

Q-2.  Were great differences in wealth contradictory to the revolutionaries' idea of equality? Explain.

Q-3.  How did the writers of the Enlightenment differ on the method of establishing liberty?

Q-4.  According to Locke, what is the function of government?

Q-5.  Think back to the English Revolution of 1688 (Chapter 19). How does Locke's theory justify the English action of getting rid of one king and contracting for a new one?

Q-6.   Which side, American or British, had the better argument with regard to the taxation problem? How do the Seven Years' War, the Stamp Act, and the Boston Tea Party fit into your explanation?

Q-7.   Why is the Declaration of Independence sometimes called the world's greatest political editorial?

Q-8.   What role did the European powers play in the American victory? Did they gain anything?

Q-9.   What was the major issue in the debate between the Federalists and the Anti-Federalists?

Q-10.   How did Americans interpret *equality* in 1789? Has it changed since then? Are the definitions of *liberalism* and *equality* unchangeable, or do they undergo periodic redefinition?

Q-11.   Did the American Revolution have any effect on France?

Q-12.   Why was there fear in France that the tax-reform issue would have "opened a Pandora's box of social and political demands"?

Q-13.   Describe the three estates of France. Who paid the taxes? Who held the wealth and power in France?

Q-14.   With the calling of the Estates General, "the nobility of France expected that history would repeat itself." Did it? What actually did happen?

Q-15.   Discuss the reforms of the National Assembly. Did they display the application of liberalism to society?

Q-16.   What were the cause and the outcome of the peasants' uprising of 1789?

Q-17.   What role did the poor women of Paris play in the revolution?

Q-18.   Why were France and Europe overcome with feelings of fear and mistrust?

Q-19.   Why did the revolution turn into war in 1792?

Q-20.   What effect did the war have on the position of the French king and aristocracy?

Q-21.   Were the French armies conquerors or liberators?

Q-22.   Who were the sans-culottes? Why were they important to radical leaders such as Robespierre? What role did the common people play in the revolution?

Q-23.   Why did the Committee of Public Safety need to institute a Reign of Terror?

Q-24.   What event led to the takeover by Napoleon?

Q-25.   Was Napoleon a son of the revolution or just another tyrant? Explain.

Q-26.   Describe the Grand Empire of Napoleon. Was he a liberator or a tyrant?

Q-27.   What caused Napoleon's downfall?

## STUDY-REVIEW EXERCISES

*Define* the following key concepts and terms.

liberalism

Montesquieu's "checks and balances"

natural or universal rights

republican

popular sovereignty

tithe

Estates General

*Identify* each of the following and give its significance.

Stamp Act

battle of Trafalgar

American Bill of Rights

American Loyalists

American Constitutional Convention of 1787

Jacobins

Reign of Terror

National Assembly

Declaration of the Rights of Man

Bastille

Declaration of Pillnitz

*sans-culottes*

*assignats*

First Coalition

September Massacres

National Convention

Girondists

the Mountain

Thermidorian reaction

<u>Explain</u> *who the following people were and give their significance.*

"the baker, the baker's wife, and the baker's boy"

Lord Nelson

Thomas Paine

Edmund Burke

Marie Antoinette

Marquis de Lafayette

Thomas Jefferson

Maximilien Robespierre

John Locke

Abbé Sieyès

*Test your understanding of the chapter by answering the following questions.*

1. Napoleon's plan to invade England was made impossible by the defeat of the French and Spanish navies in the battle of

   _____ in 1805.
2. Overall, the common people of Paris played *a minor/an important* role in the French Revolution.
3. The author of the best-selling radical book *Common Sense* was

   _____ .
4. The French philosophe who argued for dividing government into legislative,

   judicial, and executive branches was _____ .
5. The sans-culottes *were/were not* the aristocratic supporters of the king in France.

6. The king who was executed in 1793 in France was _____ .
7. Most liberal thinkers of the eighteenth century *favored/opposed* the idea of democracy.
8. The radical and democratic faction of the Jacobins in revolutionary France was

   known as the _____ .
9. Napoleon's influence on European society resulted in the *decrease/increase* of serfdom.
10. The peasant uprising of 1789 in France ended in *victory/defeat* for the peasant class.
11. By the mid 1790s, people like Sieyès were increasingly looking to *the people/ a military ruler* to bring order to France.


## MULTIPLE-CHOICE QUESTIONS

1. Eighteenth-century liberals laid major stress on
   a. economic equality.
   b. equality in property holding.
   c. equality of opportunity.
   d. racial and sexual equality.

2. Which came first?
   a. Formation of the French National Assembly
   b. Execution of King Louis XVI

c.  American Bill of Rights
d.  Seven Years' War

3.  The French Jacobins were
    a.  aristocrats who fled France.
    b.  monarchists.
    c.  priests who supported the Revolution.
    d.  revolutionary radicals.

4.  The French National Assembly was established by
    a.  the middle class of the Third Estate.
    b.  King Louis XVI.
    c.  the aristocracy.
    d.  the sans-culottes.

5.  The National Assembly did all but which one of the following?
    a.  Nationalized church land
    b.  Issued the Declaration of the Rights of Man
    c.  Established the metric system of weights and measures
    d.  Brought about the Reign of Terror

6.  In 1789 the influential Abbé Sieyès wrote a pamphlet in which he argued that France should be ruled by the
    a.  nobility.
    b.  clergy.
    c.  people.
    d.  king.

7.  In the first stage of the Revolution the French established a (an)
    a.  constitutional monarchy.
    b.  absolutist monarchy.
    c.  republic.
    d.  military dictatorship.

8.  Edmund Burke's *Reflections on the Revolution in France* is a defense of
    a.  the Catholic church.
    b.  Robespierre and the Terror.
    c.  the working classes of France.
    d.  the English monarchy and aristocracy.

9.  Most eighteenth-century demands for liberty centered on
    a.  the equalization of wealth.

    b.  a classless society.
    c.  better welfare systems.
    d.  equality of opportunity.

10.  Americans objected to the Stamp Act because the tax it proposed
    a.  was exorbitant.
    b.  was required of people in Britain.
    c.  would have required great expense to collect.
    d.  was imposed without their consent.

11.  The American Revolution
    a.  had very little impact on Europe.
    b.  was supported by the French monarchy.
    c.  was not influenced by Locke or Montesquieu.
    d.  was supported by almost everyone living in the United States.

12.  The first successful revolt against Napoleon began in 1808 in
    a.  Spain.
    b.  Russia.
    c.  Germany.
    d.  Italy.

13.  The major share of the tax burden in France was carried by the
    a.  peasants.
    b.  bourgeoisie.
    c.  clergy.
    d.  nobility.

14.  The participation of the common people of Paris in the revolution was initially attributable to
    a.  their desire to be represented in the Estates General.
    b.  the soaring price of food.
    c.  the murder of Marat.
    d.  the large number of people imprisoned by the king.

15.  For the French peasants, the revolution of 1789 meant
    a.  a general movement from the countryside to urban areas.
    b.  greater land ownership.
    c.  significant political power.
    d.  few, if any, gains.

16.  The group that announced that it was going to cut off Marie Antoinette's head, "tear out her heart, [and] fry her liver" was the

    a. National Guard.
    b. Robespierre radicals.
    c. revolutionary committee.
    d. women of Paris.

17. The group that had the task of ridding France of any internal opposition to the revolutionary cause was the
    a. Revolutionary Army.
    b. secret police.
    c. republican mob of Paris.
    d. Committee of Public Safety.

18. Between 1789 and 1792, the revolutionary assemblies in France
    a. abolished free trade within France.
    b. worked harmoniously with the Catholic church.
    c. declared war on Austria.
    d. none of the above

19. During the Reign of Terror, Robespierre and his followers
    a. allowed Louis XVI to emigrate to Britain.
    b. controlled the price of bread.
    c. weakened French armies.
    d. failed to use French nationalism.

20. In 1765 the British government attempted to defray the costs of war by imposing on its colonies the
    a. income tax.
    b. Poll Tax.
    c. Intolerable Tax.
    d. Stamp Tax.

21. The Americans who remained loyal to the British crown at the time of the British-American colonial conflict tended to be
    a. urban workers.
    b. poor farmers.
    c. upper-class colonists.
    d. political radicals.

22. Most of the members elected to represent the third estate in the Estates General of 1789 were
    a. peasants.
    b. artisans and day laborers.

    c.  clergy.
    d.  lawyers and government officials.

23.  One reason that the French middle class was opposed to the Roman Catholic church was that
    a.  they advocated a national Protestant church.
    b.  the pope outlawed the charging of interest by the middle class.
    c.  the pope wanted to reorganize the church.
    d.  they had accepted the idea of the philosophes that the established religion was a "superstitious religion."

24.  After 1795 women and the laboring poor demanded
    a.  peace and a return to religion.
    b.  cheaper food.
    c.  land reform.
    d.  all of the above

25.  Napoleon's strongest support came from the
    a.  upper class.
    b.  middle class.
    c.  urban working class.
    d.  peasants.

26.  The class that benefited most from the French Revolution was the
    a.  nobility.
    b.  peasants.
    c.  middle class.
    d.  urban workers.

27.  Liberalism
    a.  tried to break the shackles of Judeo-Christian tradition.
    b.  opposed religious toleration.
    c.  supported individual human rights.
    d.  demanded democracy in government.

28.  In 1794, in reaction to the Reign of Terror, a new French government with a five-man executive was established. This government lasted until 1799, and is known as the
    a.  Committee for Public Safety.
    b.  Directory.
    c.  Second Coalition.
    d.  Mountain.

## GEOGRAPHY

1. Show on the outline map the boundaries of France before the outbreak of war in 1792. Now shade in the areas acquired by France by 1810. Was Napoleon successful in 1810 in expanding the boundaries of France? Who inhabited the territories newly acquired by France?

2. Shade in the dependent states in 1810. What nationalities inhabited these states? Were these large, powerful states?

3. Look closely at Map 25.1. Can you find the four small British fortified outposts scattered throughout Europe? How were these outposts necessary to and a reflection of Britain's military power? What did these outposts mean for smugglers and Napoleon's efforts to stop British trade with continental countries?

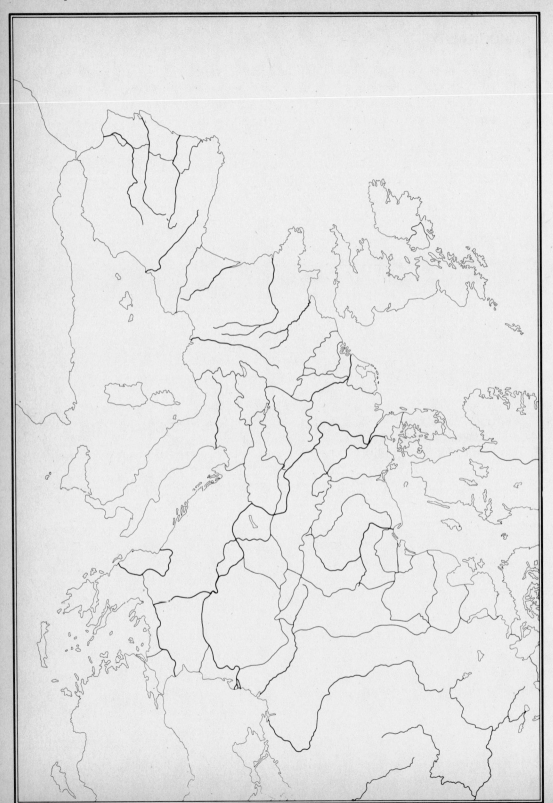

## PROBLEMS FOR FURTHER INVESTIGATION

This era of revolution is ideal for the study of both individual and group actions. The various arguments of scholars over the motives and contributions of Napoleon are brought together in D. H. Pinkney, ed., *Napoleon: Historical Enigma** (1969), and the story of Admiral Lord Nelson, Britain's hero and victor of great sea battles is interestingly told in R. Hough, *Nelson, A Biography* (1980). King George III of England has often been viewed, in American history, as the arch-enemy of liberty and constitutionalism. Is this a fair assessment? The debate over his role has gone on for a number of years and is the subject of a book of collected opinions, *George III: Tyrant or Constitutional Monarch?** (1964), edited by E. A. Reitan.

Group action in a revolution makes for an equally interesting study. The role of women in the revolution in France (and in other times) is well handled in E. Boulding, *The Underside of History: A View of Women Through Time* (1976). The "people" (which includes the Paris mob) who participated in the revolution in France are the subject of the interesting study by G. Rudé, *The Crowd in the French Revolution** (1959).

Students interested in the origins of the French revolution will want to check R. W. Greenlaw, ed., *The Economic Origins of the French Revolution** (1958), and those interested in political theory may want to consider a study of liberalism beginning with H. Schultz, ed., *English Liberalism and the State — Individualism or Collectivism?** (1972).

*Available in paperback.

## READING WITH UNDERSTANDING
### EXERCISE 3

## LEARNING HOW TO IDENTIFY MAIN POINTS THAT ARE EFFECTS, RESULTS, CONSEQUENCES

In the introduction to this *Study Guide* and in Reading with Understanding Exercises 1 and 2 we noted that learning to underline properly plays an important part in college work. Underlining (or highlighting with a felt-tipped pen) provides a permanent record of what you study and learn. It helps you review, synthesize, and do your best on exams.

We suggested three simple guidelines for effective underlining or highlighting:*

1. Be selective; do not underline or highlight too much.
2. Underline or highlight the main points.
3. Consider numbering the main points.

These guidelines will help you in courses in many different subjects.

### Cause and Effect in History

The study of history also requires learning to recognize special kinds of main points. These points are *explanatory* in nature. *They answer why and how questions*, thereby helping you to interpret and make sense of the historical record.

Two particularly important types of why and how questions focus on *cause* and *effect* in history. You are already familiar with questions of this nature, questions that provide much of history's fascination and excitement. "Why did the Roman Empire

---

*The guidelines for underlining are from *RSVP: The Houghton Mifflin Reading, Study, & Vocabulary Program*, second edition, by James F. Shepherd (Houghton Mifflin, 1984). We urge students to consult this very valuable book for additional help in improving their reading and study skills.

decline and fall?'' That is, what *causes* explain the decline and fall of the Roman Empire? ''What were the *effects* of the Black Death?'' You should pay particular attention to questions of cause and effect. They give history meaning. They help you increase your ability to think and reason in historical terms.

Two other insights will help you greatly in identifying main points involving cause and effect. First, historians use a number of different words and verbal constructions to express these concepts. Thus ''causes'' often become ''reasons'' or ''factors,'' or things that ''account for,'' ''contribute to,'' or ''play a role in'' a given development. ''Effects'' often become ''results'' or ''consequences,'' or are ''the product of an impact.'' In most cases students can consider such expressions as substitutes for cause and effect, although they should be aware that historians are not of one mind on these matters.

Second, cause and effect are constantly interrelated in the historical process. Yesterday's results become today's causes, which will in turn help bring tomorrow's results. To take examples you have studied, the *causes* of the fall of the Roman Empire (such as increasing economic difficulties) brought *results* (such as the self-sufficient agrarian economy) which contributed to—helped *cause*—the rise of Benedictine monasticism. In short, *a historical development can usually be viewed as a cause or an effect, depending on what question is being answered.*

## Exercise A

Read the following passage once as a whole. Read it a second time to underline or highlight it in terms of main points identified as effects or results. Consider numbering the effects in the margin. Then do Exercise B at the end of the passage.

The effects of the invention of movable-type printing were not felt overnight. Nevertheless, within a half-century of the publication of Gutenberg's Bible of 1456, movable type brought about radical changes. The costs of reproducing books were drastically reduced. It took less time and money to print a book by machine than to make copies by hand. The press also reduced the chances of error. If the type had been accurately set, all the copies would be correct no matter how many were reproduced. The greater the number of pages a scribe copied, the greater the chances for human error.

Between the sixteenth and eighteenth centuries, printing brought about profound changes in European society and culture. Printing transformed both the private and the public lives of Europeans. Governments that ''had employed the cumbersome methods of manuscripts to communicate with their subjects switched quickly to print to announce declarations of war, publish battle accounts, promulgate treaties or argue disputed points in pamphlet form. Theirs was an effort 'to win the psychological war.' '' Printing made propaganda possible, emphasizing differences between various groups, such as crown and nobility, church and state. These differences laid the basis for the formation of distinct political parties.

Printed materials reached an invisible public, allowing silent individuals to join causes and groups of individuals widely separated by geography to form a common identity; this new group consciousness could compete with older, localized loyalties. Book shops, coffee shops, and public reading rooms gradually appeared and, together with print shops, provided sanctuaries and meeting places for intellectuals and wandering scholars. Historians have yet to assess the degree to which such places contributed to the rise of intellectuals as a distinct social class.

Printing also stimulated the literacy of lay people and eventually came to have a deep effect on their private lives. Although most of the earliest books and pamphlets dealt with religious subjects, students, housewives, businessmen, and upper- and middle-class people sought books on all subjects. Printers responded with moralizing, medical, practical, and travel manuals. Pornography as well as piety assumed new forms. Broadsides and flysheets allowed great public festivals, religious ceremonies, and political events to be experienced vicariously by the stay-at-home. Since books and printed materials were read aloud to the illiterate, print bridged the gap between written and oral cultures.

## Exercise B

Study the last paragraph again. Can you see how it is a good example of the historical interaction of cause and effect? Do you see how a given development is an effect or a cause *depending on what historical question is being asked?* Be prepared for such "reversals" in the text, in lecture and class discussion, and on exams.

*Hint:* In the last paragraph, what is an *effect* of the invention of the printing press? (Ideas could be spread more rapidly.) What "stimulated"—helped *cause*—the spread of literacy? (The invention of the printing press. The author develops this point further in Chapter 14.)

# CHAPTER 26

# THE INDUSTRIAL REVOLUTION IN EUROPE

## CHAPTER OBJECTIVES

After reading and studying this chapter you should be able to answer the following questions:

Q-1.   What was the Industrial Revolution and what caused it?
Q-2.   How did the Industrial Revolution affect people and society in Europe? Was it a blessing or a disaster?

## CHAPTER SYNOPSIS

The world we live in today is largely a product of a revolution in industry and energy that began in England in the 1780s and lasted until about 1850. It changed the way people lived and worked, and it gave support to the Western expansion into non-Western lands. A number of important problems of interpretation relating to the revolution — the Industrial Revolution — are discussed in this chapter.

The chapter first considers why the Industrial Revolution occurred when it did and why it began in England. Important causes of English industrialization, some of which were discussed in detail in Chapter 22, were foreign and home demand for manufactured goods, agricultural improvements, a large free-trade area, good transportation, and a fairly advanced banking system. The pressure of a growing demand for textiles led to better spinning and weaving machinery, which, in turn, led to the creation of the world's first modern factories. In addition, a severe energy crisis presented the challenge that resulted in new production methods: abundant coal replaced scarce wood in the all-important iron industry and fueled Watt's magnificent new steam engine. For the first time, the English people had almost unlimited energy for useful work.

The chapter next considers the gradual spread of the new industrial methods from England to continental Europe. It was not easy for continental countries to copy the English achievement, but with the coming of the railroad rapid progress was made by the 1840s. The difficult problem of assessing the impact of the Industrial Revolution in the lives of the men and women of the working class is then examined. Was industrialization mainly a blessing or a disaster for the workers? After evaluating working conditions, family ties, wages, food, clothing, and health, the author concludes, with qualifications, that the lot of ordinary men and women improved as a result of industrialization. To carry this question of the standard of living one step further, the author takes a comparative look at what happened in Ireland, a poor agricultural country that did not industrialize. There, overpopulation and the potato famine combined to produce mass starvation and disease in the 1840s. One terrible alternative to industrial development was poverty and disaster.

## STUDY OUTLINE

I.  Initial breakthrough
    A.  The eighteenth-century origins of the Industrial Revolution
        1.  Stable government, economic freedom, available capital, and mobile labor in England encouraged growth
        2.  A large domestic market in England encouraged demand
    B.  An agricultural revolution, first in England and the Low Countries, promoted economic growth
        1.  Dutch leadership was due to population pressure, urban growth, and the quality of the people
        2.  Dutch land drainage techniques were skillfully adopted in England
        3.  Tull, Townsend, and others in England advocated new crops and new methods
        4.  Many historians and social observers have argued that enclosure left the small farmer without "common rights" and, generally, worse off
        5.  The fencing of open fields probably did not harm the poor people who lived off the land, as some historians have claimed
        6.  Enclosure resulted in more, not less, agricultural employment for wage workers
    C.  The first factories in the cotton textile industry
        1.  Growing demand for textiles led to new textile inventions and created a need for larger workshops — that is, factories
        2.  The factory system meant cheaper clothing and more jobs
        3.  But factories were often oppressive, and they utilized child labor
    D.  The growth of foreign trade
        1.  Mercantilism is an economic system whereby the state uses a variety of means to regulate the economy

2. The mercantilists claimed that a favorable balance of trade was necessary for the nation's survival
3. The Navigation Acts were a form of economic warfare against the Dutch and gave Britain a virtual trade monopoly with its colonies
4. The French quest for power in Europe and North America led to international wars
   a. The loss of the War of the Spanish Succession and the Seven Years' War forced France to cede all its North American possessions to Britain
5. Colonies helped relieve European poverty and surplus population as settlers eagerly took up farming
6. The English colonists made up for a decline in English trade on the Continent
7. Colonial and home demand encouraged industrial growth in England

II. Energy and transportation
   A. The problem of energy
     1. The search for a solution to the energy crisis was a cause of industrialization
     2. From prehistoric to medieval times the major energy sources were plants and animals, and human beings and animals did most of the work
     3. Energy from the land was limited
       a. By the eighteenth century, England's major source of fuel, wood, was nearly gone
       b. A new source of power and energy was needed, so people turned to coal
   B. "Steam is an Englishman"
     1. Before about 1700, coal was used to heat homes but not to produce mechanical energy or to run machinery
     2. Early steam engines, such as those of Savery (1698) and Newcomen (1705), were inefficient but revolutionary converters of coal into energy
     3. In the 1760s, James Watt increased the efficiency of steam engines, and with Matthew Boulton began to produce them
     4. Steam power was used in many industries, and it encouraged other breakthroughs
       a. It enabled the cotton industry to expand
       b. The iron industry was transformed as steam power made coke available
   C. The coming of the railroads
     1. Stephenson's *Rocket* (1825) was Europe's first locomotive; it was powered by a steam engine
     2. The railroad boom (1830–1850) meant lower transportation costs, larger markets, and cheaper goods

3.  Railroad building took workers from their rural life and transported them to an urban setting
4.  The railroad changed the outlook and values of the entire society
5.  Even painters such as Turner and Monet were inspired by railroads

D.  Prosperous Britain at mid-century
1.  The 1851 Crystal Palace fair reflected the growth of industry and population in Britain and confirmed that Britain was the workshop of the world
2.  Real income per person nearly doubled between 1801 and 1851

III.  The spread of the Industrial Revolution
A.  The challenge of industrialization
1.  Revolutions and wars on the Continent retarded economic growth
2.  Continental countries found it difficult to compete with Britain after 1815 because it was so economically and technologically advanced
3.  But continental countries had two advantages
   a.  Britain had done the developmental pathbreaking, so other countries could simply copy the British way of doing things
   b.  The power of strong central governments could be used to promote industry

B.  Agents of industrialization in continental Europe
1.  Cockerill, in Belgium, was one of many Englishmen who brought British industrial secrets to other parts of Europe
2.  In Germany, Harkort's business failure showed the problems of early industrialization and the need for government support
3.  Governments aided industrialists by erecting tariffs, building roads and canals, and financing railroads
4.  Many thinkers and writers, such as List in Germany, believed that industrialization would advance the welfare of the nation
5.  A tariff policy was established in Germany in 1834 with the Zollverein
   a.  Goods could move among the German member states without tariffs
   b.  Goods from other nations were subject to a tariff
6.  Banks played a more important role in industrialization on the Continent than in Britain

IV.  Capital and labor in the age of the Industrial Revolution
A.  The new class of factory owners
1.  Capitalist owners were locked into a highly competitive system
2.  The early industrial period offered opportunities for upward economic mobility, so owners came from a variety of backgrounds
3.  But by the later nineteenth century there was less mobility

B.  The new factory workers
1.  Overall, industrialization meant improvement of life

2. Many observers claimed that the Industrial Revolution brought misery to the workers
    a. The romantic poets Blake and Wordsworth protested the life of the workers and the pollution of the land and water
    b. Engels believed that the owners exploited the workers
3. Others, such as Ure and Chadwick, claimed that life was improving
4. The statistics with regard to wages, diet, and clothing paint a picture of overall improvement for the workers, with some qualifications
5. On the negative side, unemployment may have risen, hours of labor increased, and there was no improvement in housing

C. Conditions of work
1. Hours were long and monotonous
2. Working in the factory meant more discipline and less personal freedom
3. The refusal of men to work in factories led to child labor
4. As factories moved to urban areas, they attracted whole families and tended to preserve kinship ties
5. Factory acts limited child labor and ended the practice of families working as a unit in the factory

D. A mature working class
1. By 1850, workers were accustomed to factory discipline
2. Workers created a labor union movement despite antiunion laws — such as the Combination Acts
    a. Robert Owen formed a national union in 1834 in Britain, but it was short-lived
    b. The "new model," or craft union movement began about 1851 in Britain
3. Chartism was a political movement among British workers that sought universal male suffrage, shorter hours, and cheap bread

V. The alternative to industrialization
A. The growth of population
1. European population increased by nearly 40 percent between 1800 and 1850
2. Overpopulation led to underemployment, poverty, and migration in search of work

B. The potato famine in Ireland (1845–1851)
1. Irish peasants lived under the rule of English Protestant landlords who did little to improve conditions
2. Poverty among the Irish peasants was widespread
3. Because of the introduction of potato farming the Irish population grew from 3 to 8 million between 1725 and 1845
4. The potato crop failures in 1845, 1846, and 1851 resulted in widespread famine and migration

5.  The famine affected Ireland's growth and development
    a.  People were forced to migrate or marry late, and the country's population declined
    b.  Ireland's economy remained agricultural and impoverished; this, then, was the probable alternative to industrialization

## REVIEW QUESTIONS

Q-1.   Why did the Industrial Revolution begin in England? Was this a planned revolution? Explain.

Q-2.   What changes brought the open-field system to an end?

Q-3.   Where did the modern agricultural revolution originate? Why?

Q-4.   What is meant by *enclosure*? Was this movement a great swindle of the poor by the rich, as some have claimed?

Q-5.   Describe the energy crisis in England. How was it solved?

Q-6.   What was the relationship between the steam engine and the coal mine? The railroad and the coal mine?

Q-7.   How did the railroad affect (a) the factory system, (b) the rural workers, and (c) the outlook and values of society?

Q-8.   What did James Watt and Matthew Boulton do to multiply the uses of steam power?

Q-9.   How did the change in textile production affect employment in spinning and weaving for adults and children?

Q-10.   How did the French Revolution and the wars of 1792–1815 affect the economics of the continental states?

Q-11.   What disadvantages and advantages were felt by countries that industrialized *after* Great Britain?

Q-12.   What do the careers of Cockerill, Harkort, and List tell us about the problems and methods of industrialization on the Continent?

Q-13.   What was the purpose of the Zollverein? Of the Crédit Mobilier?

Q-14.   Did Britain's new industrial middle class ruthlessly exploit the workers?

Q-15.   Did real wages increase or decrease between 1790 and 1850? What about other factors such as diet and working conditions?

Q-16.   It has often been argued that the factory system in Britain caused a breakup of the family, especially as an economic unit. Explain why you agree or disagree.

Q-17.   What was the subcontract system and how did it work?

Q-18.   What were the goals and accomplishments of the Chartists?

Q-19.   How did the Irish land system work? How did the potato affect Irish economic and family life?

Q-20.   What was the result of the 1845–1851 potato blight in Ireland?

Q-21.   "The Industrial Revolution was the salvation rather than the curse of England and Europe." Defend or refute this statement.

*Test your understanding of the chapter by answering the following questions.*

1. The Industrial Revolution began in England about _____

   in the _____ industry.
2. A decrease in food prices led to a(n) *increased/decreased* demand for manufactured goods.
3. The Scots instrument maker who improved the steam engine was

   _____.

4. In Ireland, a single acre of _____ could support a family of six for a year.

5. The first railroad line was the _____ line, and the

   first effective locomotive was Stephenson's _____.
6. The railroads tended to *increase/decrease* the number of cottage workers.
7. The architectural wonder of the 1851 industrial fair in London was the build-

   ing called the _____.
8. Between 1801 and 1851, real income in Britain *increased/decreased*.
9. The role of the government in bringing about industrialization was *greater/less* in continental countries than in Britain.
10. The economic and trade agreement that allowed goods to move among German member states without tariffs was formed in 1834 and was called the

    _____.

11. The possibility of a European worker's becoming a big industrialist *increased/decreased* as the nineteenth century wore on.

12. With the _____ Act of 1833, the employment of children in British factories tended to *increase/decrease*.


## MULTIPLE-CHOICE QUESTIONS

1. In the 1830s, the most technologically advanced country in the world was
   a. Belgium
   b. the United States.
   c. France.
   d. Britain.

2. Which of the following was a period of falling real wages for English workers?
   a. 1750–1790
   b. 1792–1815
   c. 1815–1850
   d. 1850–1890

3. Which of the following was *least* likely to be a characteristic of a prefactory (cottage or agricultural) laboring person?
   a. Observed Holy Monday
   b. Worked beside other members of his or her family
   c. Worked hard but in spurts
   d. Would probably prefer factory work to railroad construction

4. The energy crisis of the eighteenth and nineteenth centuries was solved by reliance on
   a. wood.
   b. coal and steam.
   c. electricity.
   d. water power.

5. According to Friedrich List, the promotion of industry
   a. was dangerous for the well-being of the peasants.
   b. was vital for the defense of the nation.
   c. increased the poverty of the population.
   d. required free trade between nations.

6. The first steam railways were built in the
   a. 1790s.
   b. 1830s.
   c. 1850s.
   d. none of the above

7. Legislation passed by the British Parliament outlawing unions and strikes was
   a. the Labor Law of 1834.
   b. the Combination Acts.
   c. the Artisans Bill.
   d. none of the above

8. The first continental country to industrialize was
   a. Belgium.
   b. France.
   c. Italy.
   d. Germany.

9.  The industrial development of continental Europe was delayed by
    a. a lack of resources.
    b. the French Revolution and Napoleonic wars.
    c. the plague.
    d. a labor shortage.

10. To understand more fully the impact of the Industrial Revolution, historians think it best to concentrate their studies on
    a. England.
    b. France.
    c. Ireland.
    d. Belgium.

11. Before the 1830s, the
    a. family continued to work as a unit in the factories.
    b. factory employed only the females.
    c. mother and father worked together while their children went to factory schools.
    d. factory employed only the males.

12. The British workers' campaign to gain the franchise between 1838 and 1848 was called the
    a. Ten-Hours' movement.
    b. Luddite movement.
    c. Chartist movement.
    d. democratic movement.

13. Because of their economic problems, the Irish resorted to mass migration, primarily settling in
    a. Great Britain and Belgium.
    b. America and Canada.
    c. America and Great Britain.
    d. Wales and Scotland.

14. Those workers who smashed the machines that put them out of work were known as
    a. Luddites.
    b. anti-Modernists.
    c. Chartists.
    d. apprentices.

15. The battle in England against the enclosure movement has often been exaggerated. Proof of this is the fact that

    a.  no English land at all had been enclosed by 1750.
    b.  parliamentary actions after 1760 initiated the enclosure movement.
    c.  the proportion of landless laborers was very large after 1830.
    d.  enclosure actually created jobs.

16.  The mercantilist attitude toward the state was that
    a.  the government should regulate the economy.
    b.  governmental power should be increased at the expense of private profit.
    c.  using governmental economic power to help private interests is unethical.
    d.  the economy should be left to operate according to its natural laws.

17.  The new farming system consisting of crop rotation and the use of nitrogen-sorting crops caught on quickly in
    a.  the Low Countries and England.
    b.  Russia.
    c.  eastern Europe as a whole.
    d.  Scandinavia.

18.  In the mid-seventeenth century, England's major maritime competitor was
    a.  France.
    b.  the Netherlands.
    c.  Spain.
    d.  Denmark.

19.  The Seven Years' War (1756–1763) between France and Britain resulted in
    a.  British dominance in North America and India.
    b.  French dominance in North America and India.
    c.  a stalemate.
    d.  British dominance only in North America.

20.  The black-to-white ratio in America by 1774 was
    a.  one to four.
    b.  one to eight.
    c.  one to ten.
    d.  one to two.

21.  The group that used the new farming methods to the fullest in England was
    a.  independent farmers.
    b.  well-financed, profit-minded tenant farmers.
    c.  large landowners.
    d.  small landowning wage laborers.

22. The enclosure process
    a. caused large-scale unemployment compared with areas in which enclosure was not very far advanced.
    b. ruined the soil.
    c. helped to advance farming methods through the financing of tenant farmers by wealthy, large landowners.
    d. attracted people from the urban centers to the rural areas, where there was a scarcity of labor in the fields.

23. The impact of the Industrial Revolution could best be compared with
    a. the French Revolution.
    b. the American Revolution.
    c. the agricultural revolution of Neolithic times.
    d. Luther's Reformation.

24. The agricultural advancements made in England in the mid-eighteenth century
    a. stifled England's industrial development for a time.
    b. created a demand among the people for manufactured goods.
    c. precipitated a flow of people from the city to the country.
    d. raised food prices.

25. How was English technology transmitted directly to the Continent?
    a. Through political channels
    b. By spies of continental governments
    c. By Englishmen who migrated to the Continent to establish their own industrial enterprises
    d. Through English sponsorship of technical schools for both domestic and continental students

26. In the final analysis, the Industrial Revolution created circumstances whereby
    a. the rich got richer and the poor got poorer.
    b. the nation's wealth was close to evenly distributed by 1850.
    c. all industrial classes gained to some degree.
    d. the rich got richer and the poor agricultural workers made great gains.

27. The Factory Act of 1833
    a. raised wages significantly.
    b. forbade the employment of children under sixteen.
    c. forbade the employment of children under nine and limited the working hours of other youths under eighteen.
    d. made the family working unit even stronger.

28. Which of the following was a result of the early factory system?
    a. More expensive underclothing
    b. Unemployment for women
    c. The use of child labor
    d. A rising agricultural population

# GEOGRAPHY

1. In the space below, compare Maps 26.1 and 26.3 in the text in terms of their major industrial areas and their transportation networks. How do these maps explain why an ever-greater portion of the English population lived in the north as time passed? What different stages in the development of English transportation are illustrated by these maps?

2. Referring to Maps 26.3 and 26.4 in the text, use the space below to compare British and continental industrialization by 1850 in terms of (a) railroads, (b) coal deposits, and (c) industrial centers. What role did geography play in Britain's early industrial lead?

3. Four of Europe's most important centers of modern industry are (a) the large Manchester-Sheffield area, (b) the Ruhr valley, (c) the Liège region, and (d) the Roubaix region. Locate these regions on Maps 26.3 and 26.4. What countries are they in? What do they have in common?

## UNDERSTANDING HISTORY THROUGH READING AND THE ARTS

Few nineteenth-century inventions had as great an impact on society as did the invention of the camera in 1839. Photography allowed society to examine itself with a fullness never before experienced. In the late 1860s, for example, Thomas Annan took a series of photographs of the slums of Glasgow and thus encouraged interest in sanitary reform and urban improvement. Annan's photographs have been reproduced by Dover Press as T. Annan, *Photographs of the Old Closes and Streets of Glasgow, 1868-1877\** (1977), and M. Hiley, *Victorian Working Women* (1980) is a view of the habits and life of Victorian women through photography.

Emile Zola's *Germinal\** is a powerful novel about life and conditions in Belgian and French coal mines. Popular novels by Charles Dickens and Elizabeth Gaskell are among the suggested readings in the text.

The machine breakers in England (1811-1817) are the subject of M. I. Thomis's *The Luddites\** (1970-1972). Those interested in reading about the new industrial working class may want to begin with J. Kuczynski, *The Rise of the Working Class* (1967), or two collections of essays on the subject — M. L. McDougal, ed., *The Working Class in Modern Europe* (1975), and E. J. Hobsbawm, ed., *Labouring Men: Studies in the History of Labour\** (1964).

An unrivaled source of visual material associated with Britain's early industrial history is A. Briggs, *Iron Bridge to Crystal Palace, Impact and Images of the Industrial Revolution* (1979).

## PROBLEMS FOR FURTHER INVESTIGATION

Some historians do not agree with the traditional interpretation that the Industrial Revolution began in the late eighteenth century. One such historian is John Nef, who argues that it actually began in the sixteenth century. He places considerable emphasis on the importance of the coal industry and the early energy crisis. Some of his ideas are found in J. Nef, "The Early Energy Crisis and Its Consequences," *Scientific American* (November 1977), and "The Progress of Technology and the Growth of Large-scale Industry in Great Britain, 1540-1640," *Economic History Review* 5 (October 1934).

Students interested in the causes of the Industrial Revolution will want to see a series of debates by six historians in R. M. Hartwell, ed., *The Causes of the Industrial Revolution in England\** (1967).

No facet of the Industrial Revolution has been as controversial and long-lasting as the debate over whether it was a blessing or a curse for the working class. Many of the arguments of the optimists and the pessimists are collected together in two

*Available in paperback.

small books: P. A. M. Taylor, ed., *The Industrial Revolution in Britain* \* (rev. ed., 1970), and C. S. Doty, ed., *The Industrial Revolution* \* (1969). The impact of industrialization on women is one of the themes of Louise Tilly and Joan Scott in *Women, Work and Family* \* (1978). The most important (and controversial) book on the impact of industrialization on the working class is E. P. Thompson, *The Making of the English Working Class* \* (1966).

\*Available in paperback.

# CHAPTER 27

## IDEOLOGIES AND UPHEAVALS IN EUROPE,
## 1815-1850

## CHAPTER OBJECTIVES

After reading and studying this chapter you should be able to answer the following questions:

Q-1.  How and why did Western conservatives and radicals view liberalism and nationalism differently?
Q-2.  How and why did political revolution break out once again in Europe?
Q-3.  What ideas did thinkers develop to describe and shape the great political and economic transformation that was taking place in the West?

## CHAPTER SYNOPSIS

This chapter examines a number of extremely important ideas: liberalism, nationalism, socialism, and romanticism. Studying these ideas helps us understand the historical process in the nineteenth and twentieth centuries. A key aspect of that process was the bitter and intense struggle between the conservative aristocrats, who wanted to maintain the status quo, and the middle- and working-class liberals and nationalists, who wanted to carry on the destruction of the old regime of Europe that had begun in France in 1789. The symbol of conservatism was Prince Metternich of Austria, Europe's leading diplomat. Metternich was convinced that liberalism and nationalism had to be repressed, or else Europe (including his own Austria — see Map 27.2) would break up into warring states. In opposition to Metternich, liberals and nationalists saw their creeds as the way to free humanity from the burden of supporting the aristocracy and from foreign oppression. Metternich's convictions were shared by the other peacemakers at Vienna in 1814, while those of the liberals fanned the fires of revolution, first in 1830 and, more

201

spectacularly, in 1848. Political liberalism, combined with the principles of economic liberalism with its stress on unrestricted economic self-interest as the avenue
to human happiness, was extremely attractive to Europe's middle class. Of the
major powers, only Britain was transformed by reform and untouched by revolution.

The chapter shows that although many Westerners believed that nationalism
led toward human happiness, it contained the dangerous ideas of national and
racial superiority. To make the turbulent intellectual world of Europe even more
complex, socialism emerged as another, equally powerful set of ideas regarding
the creation of a just and happy society. Early socialists were idealistic and utopian,
but the socialism of Karl Marx, which later became dominant, claimed to be realistic
and scientific and argued that just as the rise of the bourgeoisie was the natural outcome of historical change, so was the rise of socialism. Socialism contributed to the
split between the middle and lower classes. This split explains the failure of these
classes in the face of the common enemies in the revolutions of 1848. The chapter
also discusses romanticism, which was a reaction to the rationalism of the previous
century. Romanticism was the central mood of the nineteenth century West and the
emotional background to its aesthetic landscape.


## STUDY OUTLINE

I.  The Vienna peace settlement
    A.  The Congress of Vienna
        1.  By 1814 the conservative monarchs of Europe had defeated French
            armies and checked the spread of the French Revolution
        2.  The victors restored the French boundaries of 1792 and the Bourbon
            dynasty
        3.  They made other changes in the boundaries of Europe and created a
            new kingdom out of Belgium and Holland
        4.  It was believed that the concept of the balance of power would pre-
            serve peace in Europe
        5.  But the demands of the victors, especially the Prussians and the
            Russians, for compensation threatened the balance
II. Radical ideas and early socialism
    A.  Liberalism — political and economic
        1.  Liberalism demanded representative government, equality before the
            law, and the freedom of speech and assembly
        2.  Economic liberalism was known as *laissez-faire* — the principle that
            the economy should be left unregulated
            a.  Adam Smith argued that a free economy would bring wealth for
                all — including workers
            b.  British businessmen often used the principle of laissez-faire in
                self-serving ways, backed up by the theories of Malthus, who be-

lieved that marrying late in life was the best means of population control, and Ricardo, who claimed that because of the pressure of population, wages would always be low

    3. After 1815, political liberalism became increasingly a middle-class doctrine in Europe, used to exclude the lower classes from government and business

B. Nationalism

    1. Most liberals believed that the nation was the source of freedom for the people

    2. Nationalists believed that common language and traditions would bring about unity and common loyalties and, therefore, self-government

    3. On the negative side, nationalism generated ideas of racial and cultural superiority

C. French utopian socialism

    1. Early French socialists proposed a system of greater economic equality organized by the government

    2. Saint-Simon and Fourier proposed a planned economy and socialist communities

    3. Blanc believed that the state should promote socialist programs and guarantee employment

    4. Proudhon claimed that the worker was the source of all wealth

D. Marxian socialism

    1. Marx saw history in terms of economic class struggle: the bourgeoisie exploited the working class

    2. He predicted that the future would bring a revolution by workers to overthrow the capitalists

    3. He claimed that labor was the source of all value

    4. His theory of historical evolution came from Hegel — stressing that each idea produces its opposite (antithesis)

III. Romantic movement

A. Romanticism was partly a European revolt against classicism and the Enlightenment

    1. Romantics rejected the classical emphasis on order and rationality

    2. Many romantics believed in the supremacy of emotion and the rejection of materialism and modern industry

    3. Romantics stressed a return to nature and the study of history

    4. Reading and writing history was viewed as the way to understand national destiny

    5. Rousseau was the most important forerunner of romanticism, as were "Storm and Stress" romantics of Germany

B. Romanticism in literature

    1. Romantic literature first developed fully in Britain, as exemplified by Wordsworth, Coleridge, Scott, Byron, Shelley, and Keats

    2. Romantics such as the Frenchwoman George Sand rebelled against social conventions

    3. In central Europe romanticism reinforced nationalism

  C. Romanticism in art and music

    1. Delacroix and Turner were two of the greatest romantic painters

    2. Romantic composers rejected well-defined structure in their efforts to find maximum range and intensity

    3. Beethoven was the first master of romantic music

IV. Reforms and revolutions

  A. National liberation in Greece (1821–1832)

    1. Greek nationalists led by Ypsilanti in 1821 fought for freedom from Turkey

    2. Britain, France, and Russia supported Greek nationalism, and Greece became independent in 1830

  B. Liberal reform in Great Britain

    1. The British aristocracy feared liberalism and worked to repress it

    2. The Corn Law, which protected the English landowners, is an example of aristocratic class power and selfishness

    3. Lower-class protest in Britain led to repressive laws (the Six Acts) and violence against the lower class

    4. The growth of the middle class and its desire for reform led to the Reform Bill of 1832, which increased the number of voters significantly

    5. The Chartist demand for universal male suffrage failed, but the Anti-Corn Law League succeeded in getting the Corn Law repealed and free trade established

    6. By 1846, both the Tory and Whig parties were interested in reform

  C. The revolution of 1830 in France

    1. Louis XVIII's Constitutional Charter of 1814 protected the people against a return to royal absolutism and aristocratic privilege

    2. Charles X, Louis's successor, tried to reestablish the old order and repudiated the Constitutional Charter

    3. The reaction was an immediate revolution that brought the expulsion of Charles X

    4. The new king, Louis Philippe, accepted the Constitutional Charter but did little more than protect the rich upper middle class

V. The revolutions of 1848

  A. A democratic republic was established in France in 1848

    1. King Louis Philippe's regime (since 1830) refused to bring about electoral reform

    2. A revolt in Paris in 1848 led to the establishment of a provisional republic that granted universal male suffrage and other reforms

    3. The revolutionary coalition couldn't agree on a common program, as the "liberal" republicans split with the "socialist" republicans

    4. National workshops were a compromise between the socialists' demands for work for all and the moderates' determination to provide only temporary relief for the massive unemployment
    5. The fear of socialism led to a clash of classes
    6. The closing down of the workshops led to a violent uprising (the June Days)
    7. Class war led to the election of a strongman, Louis Napoleon, as president in 1848

B. The Austrian Empire in 1848
    1. The revolution in France resulted in popular upheaval throughout central Europe, but in the end conservative reaction won
    2. Hungarian nationalism resulted in revolution against the Austrian overlords
    3. Conflict among the different nationalities (Hungarians against Croats, Serbs, and Rumanians; Czechs against Germans) weakened the revolution
    4. The alliance of the working and middle classes soon collapsed
    5. The conservative aristocrats crushed the revolution
    6. The Russian army helped defeat the Hungarians

C. Prussia and the Frankfurt Assembly in 1848
    1. Middle-class Prussians wanted to create a unified liberal Germany
    2. Inspired by events in France, the working-class people of Prussia demanded and received a liberal constitution
    3. Further worker demands for suffrage and socialist reforms caused fear among the aristocracy
    4. The Frankfurt National Assembly of 1848 was a middle-class liberal body that began writing a constitution for a unified Germany
    5. War with Denmark ended with a rejection of the Frankfurt Assembly and the failure of German liberalism

## REVIEW QUESTIONS

Q-1. Discuss how political and economic change in nineteenth-century Europe might fuse to form the "dual revolution."
Q-2. Describe the treatment of defeated France by the victors in 1814. Why wasn't the treatment harsher?
Q-3. What is meant by *balance of power*? What methods were used by the Great Powers to preserve the balance of power?
Q-4. What were the Hundred Days?
Q-5. Who were the participants and what was the purpose of the Holy Alliance and the congress system?

Q-6.    Describe the make-up of the Austrian Empire. How and why were nationalism and liberalism regarded as dangerous to those in power?

Q-7.    Describe laissez-faire economic philosophy. Why did the laissez-faire liberals see mercantilism as undesirable?

Q-8.    "The ideas of economic liberals like Smith, Malthus, and Ricardo were used by the industrialist middle class for their own interests." Explain.

Q-9.    Define *nationalism*. What were its links to liberalism?

Q-10.    What are the goals of socialism? How do the ideas of Saint-Simon, Fourier, Blanc, and Proudhon illustrate socialist thought? Do you agree with them?

Q-11.    What was Marx's view of history? What was the role of the proletariat in history?

Q-12.    What were the romantics rebelling against?

Q-13.    The Enlightenment writers believed that life could be understood through reason, but the romantics of the next century believed that life could be understood only through experience, emotion, and feeling. Explain this by making reference to the romantic writers and artists.

Q-14.    In what ways was romantic music a radical departure from the past? What was the purpose of romantic music? Why is Beethoven considered a genius?

Q-15.    Compare and contrast the political developments in Britain and France between 1814–15 and 1832. Who were the winners and the losers?

Q-16.    What were the causes and the outcome of the Greek revolution of 1821–1832?

Q-17.    Is there any evidence that between 1815 and 1830 Britain was in a period of the repression of liberalism?

Q-18.    What were the goals of the Chartists? The Anti-Corn Law League?

Q-19.    "The Reform Bill of 1832 was a middle-class triumph." Explain.

Q-20.    Why did Charles X lose his throne?

Q-21.    Describe what happened in France in 1848. Why did the French voters turn their backs on the revolution and elect a strongman as president?

Q-22.    Was the national workshop plan a wise compromise for the French socialists?

Q-23.    Why did the revolutionary coalition in Hungary in 1848 break down?

Q-24.    Why couldn't the middle-class liberals and the urban poor in Austria cooperate in destroying their common enemies?

Q-25.    Describe the role of the Archduchess Sophia in the preservation of the Austrian Empire.

Q-26.    What were the goals of the Frankfurt Assembly? Why did it fail?

## STUDY-REVIEW EXERCISES

*Define the following key concepts and terms.*

romanticism

conservatism

dual revolution

liberalism

nationalism

radicalism

laissez-faire

iron law of wages

socialism

Marx's theory of historical evolution

classicism

republicanism

*Identify each of the following and give its significance.*

Quadruple Alliance

Constitutional Charter of 1814 (France)

Napoleon's Hundred Days

Congress of Troppau

congress system

Corn Law

Ten Hours Acts of 1847 (Britain)

national workshops

*The Wealth of Nations*

Frankfurt Assembly

Schleswig-Holstein question

Louis Kossuth

Jules Michelet

Johann Herder

Frederick William IV

Alexander Ypsilanti

Chartists

Thomas Malthus

Karl Marx

Louis Philippe

*The Communist Manifesto*

Robert Peel

<u>Explain</u> *what ideas the following romantic figures attempted to convey to their audiences.*

William Wordsworth

Walter Scott

George Sand

Eugène Delacroix

Ludwig van Beethoven

John Martin

*Explain the objectives of the following participants at the peace conference of* <u>*1814–1815.*</u>

| Name of diplomat | Country | Objective |
| --- | --- | --- |
| Metternich | Austria | |
| Castlereagh | Great Britain | |
| Alexander I | Russia | |
| Talleyrand | France | |
| Hardenburg | Prussia | |

<u>*Explain*</u> *the objectives of the revolutionaries in the following countries and how* <u>*successful they were.*</u> *In each case explain why the revolution failed or succeeded.*

| Country | Year | Revolutionary Goals and Outcome |
| --- | --- | --- |
| Spain | 1820–1823 | |
| Two Sicilies | 1820–1821 | |
| Greece | 1821–1832 | |
| France | 1830 | |
| France | 1848 | |
| Hungary | 1848 | |
| Prussia | 1848 | |

*Test your understanding of the chapter by answering the following questions.*

1.  In the long run, the revolutions in Germany in 1848 resulted in the *victory/defeat* of German liberalism.

2.  The new president of France in 1848 was _____.

3.  The great and moving romantic painter whose masterpiece was *Liberty Leading the People* was _____.

4.  The laissez-faire economists believed that the state *should/should not* regulate the economy.

5.  Hungary was a part of the _____ Empire.

6.  This German pastor and philosopher argued that every national group has its own particular spirit and genius. _____

7.  This mid–nineteenth-century Frenchman, author of *Organization of Work*, believed that the right to work was sacred and should be guaranteed by the state.

    _____

8.  The revolutions of 1848 in Austria saw *cooperation/competition* between national groups and the eventual *victory/defeat* of the old aristocracy and conservatism.

## MULTIPLE-CHOICE QUESTIONS

1.  The British Corn Laws were passed to give economic advantage to the
    a.  landed aristocracy.
    b.  middle class.
    c.  urban working class.
    d.  agricultural workers.

2.  The so-called dual revolution that began in the late eighteenth century refers to
    a.  political revolution in France and Russia.
    b.  an economic and political revolution.
    c.  a joint revolution in improved health care and population increase.
    d.  a religious and cultural revolution.

3.  The problem that almost led to war among the major powers in 1815 was
    a.  the refusal of France to participate in the Vienna conference.
    b.  the British takeover of the South American trade routes.
    c.  Russian and Prussian territorial demands.
    d.  the refusal of Italy to participate in the Frankfurt Assembly.

4.  The major demand of the English Chartists was for
    a.  universal male suffrage.
    b.  improved prison conditions.
    c.  tariff protection for poor farmers.
    d.  government-sponsored cooperative workshops.

5.  All of the following were members of the Quadruple Alliance *except*
    a.  Russia.
    b.  Great Britain.
    c.  Prussia.
    d.  France.

6.  Metternich's conservative policies prevailed in
    a.  South America.
    b.  western Europe.
    c.  central Europe.
    d.  Great Britain and its colonies.

7.  Adam Smith would have been likely to agree that
    a.  monopolies are good for a state.
    b.  increased competition benefits all classes of society.
    c.  increasing workers' wages is harmful in the long run.
    d.  population will always grow too fast.

8.  One of the most influential French utopian socialists was
    a.  the count de Saint-Simon.
    b.  Talleyrand.
    c.  Louis Philippe.
    d.  Eugène Delacroix.

9.  In 1848, great revolutions occurred in all of the following countries *except*
    a.  Prussia.
    b.  Hungary.
    c.  Italy.
    d.  Great Britain.

10. Classical liberalism called for the unrestricted activity of
    a.  labor unions.
    b.  the European aristocracy.
    c.  business interests.
    d.  the clergy.

11.  All but one of the following were major ideas of liberalism.
    a.  Representative government
    b.  Equality before the law
    c.  Individual freedoms, such as freedom of the press and freedom of speech
    d.  Legally separated classes

12.  The first great nationalist rebellion of the 1820s involved the
    a.  Germans against the Austrians.
    b.  Greeks against the Turks.
    c.  Irish against the English.
    d.  Greeks against the Russians.

13.  The English Corn Law prohibited
    a.  the exporting of British grain.
    b.  raising the price of British grain above that of continental prices.
    c.  the importing of foreign grain unless the price of British grain reached harvest disaster prices.
    d.  the domination of the British grain market by the aristocracy.

14.  The English Reform Bill of 1832 did not
    a.  give the new industrial areas proper representation in Parliament.
    b.  relieve the pressure for reform.
    c.  gain the House of Commons supremacy over the House of Lords.
    d.  establish universal manhood suffrage.

15.  Generally the revolutions of 1848 provided
    a.  some immediate gains for the liberal forces, only to be crushed later by the combined forces of monarchy, aristocracy, and army.
    b.  slow gains at first for the liberals, followed by complete realization of their goals.
    c.  immediate and complete success by the liberals.
    d.  none of the above.

16.  Nationalists of the early nineteenth century believed that
    a.  people are basically ignoble and corrupt.
    b.  elections are a waste of money.
    c.  the existence of many independent nations would promote world harmony.
    d.  common language is unimportant in forming a nation.

17.  The order in which the following three movements appeared in the eighteenth and nineteenth centuries was
    a.  romanticism, classicism, realism.

   b.  realism, classicism, romanticism.
   c.  romanticism, realism, classicism.
   d.  classicism, romanticism, realism.

18.  Louis XVIII's successor, Charles X,
   a.  supported the constitutional charter of Louis XVIII.
   b.  wanted to restore the prerevolutionary order in France.
   c.  extended suffrage to the majority of Frenchmen.
   d.  upheld the freedom of the press.

19.  The artists and writers of the romantic movement were
   a.  uninterested in nature.
   b.  in revolt against classicism.
   c.  not to be found in Germany.
   d.  opposed to innovation and emotion in art and music.

20.  The Austrian foreign minister was
   a.  Castlereagh.
   b.  Talleyrand.
   c.  Metternich.
   d.  Alexander I.

21.  In 1815, after Napoleon's hopes were crushed at Waterloo, he was
   a.  exiled to Elba.
   b.  executed.
   c.  exiled to St. Helena.
   d.  imprisoned in England.

22.  After the peace settlement of Vienna there were
   a.  still over three hundred independent German political entities.
   b.  thirty-eight independent German states, including Austria and Prussia.
   c.  only two German states: Austria and Prussia.
   d.  approximately one hundred independent German states dominated by Austria.

23.  Metternich's conservative and repressive political and social policies were primarily a response to
   a.  growing nationalism and liberalism in Europe.
   b.  Russia's growing political power.
   c.  Napoleon's Hundred Days.
   d.  Prussia's threat to Austria's power.

24. Adam Smith advocated
    a. a free market economy, free of government controls.
    b. mercantilism.
    c. government control of the national economy.
    d. socialism.

25. The country that led the way in utopian socialist thought was
    a. England.
    b. Germany.
    c. France.
    d. Austria.

26. Marx believed that the proletariat would come to power
    a. through peaceful, gradual change.
    b. through revolution.
    c. by uniting with the middle class against the aristocracy.
    d. by uniting with the aristocracy against the middle class.

27. The art form that best expressed romanticism was
    a. literature.
    b. painting.
    c. architecture.
    d. music.

28. Two major powers that did not suffer mid–nineteenth-century revolutions were
    a. Portugal and Spain.
    b. England and Russia.
    c. England and Belgium.
    d. Russian and Austria.

# GEOGRAPHY

1. Study carefully Map 27.1, Europe in 1815, which is important for understanding the Vienna peace settlement and the entire nineteenth century. Identify the five Great Powers and fix their boundaries in your mind. Also study the boundaries of the reorganized German confederation. What are the two main states in the confederation, and what are some of the smaller ones? Now refer to Map 25.1 and see how (a) France had lost and (b) Prussia had gained in the Rhineland area. Finally, what two Central European nationalties were politically most fragmented in 1815?

Now close the text and test your understanding with the outline map on the following page. Shade in the five Great Powers and their boundaries, trace the boundary of the German confederation, and name and position (approximately) the capital cities of the five Great Powers.

2. Study Map 27.2 and then list below the national groups that made up the Habsburg (Austrian) Monarchy in 1815. Can you predict a logical reorganization of this along nationalist lines? (See Map 32.4.)

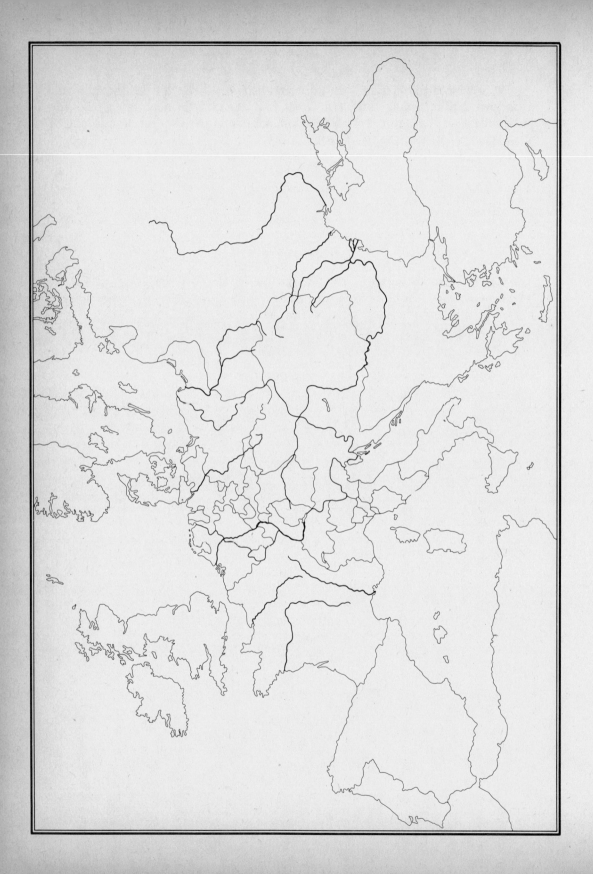

## UNDERSTANDING HISTORY THROUGH READING AND THE ARTS

Great novels that accurately portray aspects of the times are Victor Hugo, *Les Misérables,** an exciting story of crime and passion among France's poor; Honoré de Balzac, *Cousin Bette** and *Père Goriot**; Thomas Mann, *Buddenbrooks** (1902), a wonderful historical novel that traces the rise and fall of a prosperous German family over three generations during the nineteenth century; and Charles Dickens, *A Tale of Two Cities,** a portrait of London and Paris during the "dual revolution." One of the best recent historical novels about nineteenth-century life is J. Fowles, *The French Lieutenant's Woman** (1969).

Ludwig van Beethoven was the first great master of romantic music, even though in his early period he was influenced by the classical works of Haydn and Mozart. Beethoven's Symphony No. 9, the Choral Symphony, was greatly influenced by the ideas of the French Revolution — liberty, equality, and fraternity — and the symphony's "Ode to Joy" is based on Schiller's "Ode to Freedom." The score was dedicated to Frederick William III, the king of Prussia.

## PROBLEMS FOR FURTHER INVESTIGATION

Was the 1848 revolution in France a modern class struggle in the Marxist sense? Much of the answer depends on whether or not one can show that the working class was of the new proletarian type — that is, modern factory workers rather than traditional artisan craftsmen. Begin your investigation with G. Rudé, *The Crowd in History: A Study of Popular Disturbances in France and England, 1730–1848** (1964), Chapters 9 and 11, and then for the other side of the argument see C. Tilly, "The People of June, 1848," in R. Price, ed., *Revolution and Reaction* (1977).

Did the British aristocrats give power to the middle class (in the Reform Bill of 1832) because they were afraid that it was the only alternative to violent revolution? This and other questions of interpretation of the famous bill are considered by seventeen different historians in W. H. Maehl, Jr., ed., *The Reform Bill of 1832** (1967).

Those interested in the subject of romanticism should see J. B. Halsted, ed., *Romanticism: Definition, Explanation, and Evaluation** (1965), and a good starting point for an investigation of nationalism in H. Kohn, *Nationalism: Its Meaning and History** (1955).

*Available in paperback.

# CHAPTER 28

# LIFE IN EUROPEAN URBAN SOCIETY

## CHAPTER OBJECTIVES

After reading and studying this chapter you should be able to answer the following questions:

Q-1.   What did the emerging urban-industrial society in Europe mean for its members? Did the quality of life improve?

Q-2.   What impact did the city have on European family life, sexuality, marriage, and childrearing in the nineteenth century?

Q-3.   What changes in thought and culture inspired and reflected the new urban civilization in Europe?

## CHAPTER SYNOPSIS

This chapter looks at the exciting and complex world of European towns and cities, which expanded greatly because of the Industrial Revolution and which came to dominate life in the later nineteenth century. The chapter shows that although the urban environment had long been crowded and unhealthy, the rapid growth of urban population made such problems worse. However, by the 1840s, urban problems were attacked and partly solved both in Great Britain and in the continental countries. For example, throughout Europe a movement for better public health brought about sewer and water systems and gradually cleaned up the worst filth. Likewise, there were revolutionary breakthroughs in preventive medicine in the 1860s and after as Pasteur and his followers discovered how germs spread disease and how disease could be controlled. Urban planning and public transportation helped people move to better, less crowded housing. Thus, by the

late nineteenth century the quality of life in Western cities had improved dramatically for ordinary people and the working classes.

However, enormous social and economic differences between upper and lower
classes continued to exist in Europe as urban and industrial growth created new
classes, class conflict, and a more complex social hierarchy. The chapter illustrates
these differences by describing the different classes and some of the fascinating
details of their distinctive lifestyles. During this period Western family life, sexual
practices, and the role of women changed dramatically. In general, family life
became more stable and affectionate in the later nineteenth century, but economic
activities became rigidly separated according to sex. The results of these developments were both good and bad for Western women and young people.

Major intellectual developments in urban European society included a major
expansion of scientific knowledge and the rise of realism as the dominant artistic
mood. Scientific thought scored theoretical triumphs, which resulted in practical
improvements, a growing faith in progress, and great prestige for scientists and
their methods. Influential thinkers such as Comte and Marx sought to determine
society's unalterable scientific laws, while Social Darwinists applied Darwin's
theory of natural selection to human affairs. The trend toward secular thinking
strengthened. Literary realism, fascinated by scientific laws, ordinary people, and
urban problems, fully reflected the spirit of the age in the West.

## STUDY OUTLINE

I.   Taming the European city
    A.  Industry and the growth of cities
        1.  Deplorable urban conditions of congestion, filth, and disease existed
            before the Industrial Revolution
        2.  The Industrial Revolution and population growth made urban reform
            necessary
        3.  Housing was crowded and poor and living conditions unhealthy
            a.  A lack of transportation, which necessitated the crowding, and
                the slowness of government enforcement of sanitary codes con-
                tributed to the problem
            b.  The legacy of rural housing also contributed to the problem
    B.  The public health movement
        1.  The reformer Chadwick was influenced by Bentham's ideas of the
            greatest good for the greatest number
            a.  He believed that cleaning the city would curtail disease
            b.  He proposed the installation of running water and sewers
        2.  New sanitation methods and public health laws were adopted all over
            Europe

C. The bacterial revolution
   1. The prevailing theory of disease in the West was that it was caused by bad odors
   2. Pasteur's theory that germs caused disease was a major breakthrough, and its application meant disease could be controlled through vaccines
   3. Lister developed the concept of sterilization of wounds
D. Urban planning and public transportation
   1. Better urban planning contributed to improved living conditions
   2. After 1850, Paris was transformed by the urban planning of Haussmann; it became a model city
   3. Electric streetcars revolutionized urban life and enabled the cities to expand
II. Social groups in Europe
A. Social structure
   1. The standard of living for the average European improved substantially
   2. But differences in wealth continued to be enormous; society remained stratified in a number of classes
B. The middle classes were diverse
   1. The upper middle class was composed of successful business families who were attracted to the aristocratic lifestyle
   2. The middle middle-class group contained merchants, lawyers, and doctors — people who were well off but not wealthy
   3. Next came the lower middle class: shopkeepers, small businessmen, white-collar workers
   4. Experts, such as engineers, chemists, accountants, and managers, were also considered members of the middle class
   5. The middle-class lifestyle included large meals, dinner parties, servants, an interest in fashionable dressing, and a good education for the family's children
   6. The code of expected behavior stressed hard work, self-discipline, religion, and restraint from vice
C. The working class
   1. The vast majority of people belonged to the working class, yet the class had varying lifestyles and little unity
   2. The most highly skilled workers constituted a "labor aristocracy"
      a. They developed a lifestyle of stern morality
      b. They considered themselves the leaders of the working class
   3. Next came the semi-skilled and unskilled urban workers
      a. Domestic servants constituted one of the largest subgroups of the unskilled workers
      b. Women employed in the "sweated industries" were another large group

        c.   Drinking was a favorite leisure activity of the working class; other pastimes included sports and the music halls

    4.  In Europe, church attendance by the working class declined, while in the United States working-class churches thrived

III.  Changes in family life in Europe

    A.  Premarital sex and marriage

        1.  "Romantic love" had triumphed by 1850 — and premarital sex and illegitimacy had increased compared to the eighteenth century

        2.  After 1850, illegitimacy decreased, indicating the growing morality and stability of the working class

        3.  Economic factors remained more important in middle-class marriages than in working-class marriages

    B.  Prostitution

        1.  Men commonly turned to prostitutes because marriages were often made later in life, especially in the middle and upper classes

        2.  Brutal sexist behavior was a part of life

    C.  Kinship ties

        1.  Marriage and family ties were often strong

        2.  Kinship networks were an important source of mutual support and welfare

    D.  Women and family life

        1.  The preindustrial pattern of women working disappeared except for working-class women

        2.  Women became full-time mothers and homemakers, not wage earners

        3.  Women were excluded from good jobs but wielded power in the family

        4.  The home increased in emotional importance in all social classes; it symbolized shelter from the harsh working world

        5.  Strong emotional bonds between mothers and children and between wives and husbands developed

    E.  Childrearing

        1.  There was more breast-feeding and less abandonment of babies

        2.  The birthrate declined, so each child became more important and could receive more advantages

        3.  Many children were too controlled by parents, however, and suffered the effects of excessive parental concern

        4.  Relations between fathers and children were often tense; fathers tended to be very demanding

        5.  In studying family dynamics, Freud developed his theory of the Oedipal complex: that sons compete with their fathers for their mothers' love

        6.  Working-class youths probably had more avenues of escape from family tensions than middle-class youths

IV.  Scientific and intellectual developments in Europe

A. The triumph of science
   1. Theoretical discoveries resulted increasingly in practical benefits, as in chemistry and electricity
   2. Scientific achievements strengthened faith in progress and gave science unrivaled prestige
B. Social science and evolution
   1. Many thinkers, such as Auguste Comte, tried to study society "scientifically" and find general social laws
   2. Theories of dynamic development and evolution fascinated nineteenth-century Westerners
      a. Charles Darwin theorized that all life had evolved gradually through an unending "struggle for survival"
      b. Social Darwinists, such as Herbert Spencer, applied Darwin's ideas to human affairs
C. Realism in literature
   1. Realism replaced romanticism as the dominant artistic trend after 1850
   2. Realists gloried in everyday life, taboo subjects, and urban problems
   3. French novelists, notably Balzac, Flaubert, and Zola, led the way
      a. As a typical realist, Zola saw himself as an objective scientist depicting life exactly as it was
      b. They focused on the working classes and on taboo subjects such as strikes, sex, violence, and alcoholism
      c. They believed that heredity and environment determined human behavior
   4. Mary Ann Evans (George Eliot), Hardy, and Tolstoy were also great realists
      a. Evans and Hardy sought to explain what determines human action
      b. Tolstoy set forth a fatalistic theory of history
   5. Exposure of inequality and faith in science were favorite themes of realist novelists

## REVIEW QUESTIONS

Q-1.  To what extent was industrialization responsible for the deplorable conditions of European cities in the early nineteenth century?

Q-2.  Who was Edwin Chadwick? What role did he play in the health movement?

Q-3.  What was the miasmatic theory of disease? How did it retard progress?

Q-4.  What contributions did Pasteur, Koch, and Lister make to life in urban Europe? Give examples.

Q-5.  What were the reasons for the rebuilding of Paris? Who was responsible for this change?

Q-6.   Why was the electric streetcar so important in improving urban life?

Q-7.   Marx claimed that as a result of industrialization there was an increasing polarization of society into rich and poor. Do the facts warrant such a conclusion?

Q-8.   Describe the differences and similarities between groups within the middle class in nineteenth-century Europe. What separated and what united them?

Q-9.   What were the goals of the middle class in the West?

Q-10.   Describe the labor aristocracy. What were the interests of its members? How did they differ from the rest of the working class?

Q-11.   What were the interests, motives, and lifestyle of the European working class? How were they changing by the late nineteenth century?

Q-12.   Why was there a decline in illegitimacy in Europe after 1850?

Q-13.   Why did middle-class European men marry late? What effect did this have on their sexual behavior?

Q-14.   How common was prostitution in Europe in the nineteenth century? What sort of evidence on the subject exists?

Q-15.   Did kinship ties disappear in the new urban environment? Explain.

Q-16.   What was the social and economic position of women in Europe in the nineteenth century? Were they better off than in preindustrial society?

Q-17.   What kind of changes occurred in child care and the attitudes toward children in Europe in the nineteenth century?

Q-18.   What was the nineteenth-century European view of masturbation?

Q-19.   Overall, did European family life improve in the nineteenth century? Explain.

Q-20.   In what practical ways did breakthroughs in scientific inquiry transform life for the general population of nineteenth-century Europe?

Q-21.   How did science affect the study of society — that is, "social science"?

Q-22.   Explain the new evolutionary views of biological development and how these views influenced religious and social thought.

Q-23.   What was the realist movement in Western literature? Who were the major writers of this movement, and how did they differ from previous writers?

## STUDY-REVIEW EXERCISES

*Define the following key concepts and terms.*

antiseptic principle

Darwin's theory of biological evolution

sweated industries

labor aristocracy

literary realist movement

miasmatic theory

middle-class morality

Comte's positivism

*Study Figures 28.2 and 28.4 in the text. What important characteristics of nineteenth-century society do they reveal?*

*Explain how each of the following people contributed to the improvement of nineteenth-century life.*

Edwin Chadwick

Louis Pasteur

Robert Koch

Jean Baptiste Lamarck

Charles Darwin

Sigmund Freud

Gustave Flaubert

Emile Zola

Auguste Comte

Joseph Lister

Baron Haussmann

Gustave Droz

*Test your understanding of the chapter by answering the following questions.*

1. The European birthrate *increased/decreased* in the last half of the nineteenth century.
2. He advocated the principle of "the greatest good for the greatest number."

   _____

3. Lister believed that infection could be controlled by the application of his

   "_____ principle."

4. Electric streetcars first came to the city in about the year _____.
5. Overall, treatment of children and infants *improved/deteriorated* in the nineteenth century.
6. Generally speaking, the European aristocracy experienced *no change/a decrease* in relative income in the nineteenth century.
7. The highly skilled upper 15 percent of the working class was known as the

   _____.

8. The status and income of schoolteachers and nurses *rose/fell* during the nineteenth century.
9. "It is to the _____ that the vast body of the working people look for recreation and entertainment."
10. By 1850, working-class European young people tended to marry for *love/ economic reasons.*
11. Kinship ties tended to grow *stronger/weaker* as a result of urban society.
12. Sex roles for men and women in the nineteenth century tended to become *more/less* rigid.
13. Women's economic power in Europe in the nineteenth century *increased/ decreased* as compared to that of the eighteenth century.

## MULTIPLE-CHOICE QUESTIONS

1. As compared to preindustrial society, the relative distribution of wealth among the three classes in industrial society in Europe
   a. probably did not change.
   b. shifted in favor of the working class.
   c. shifted significantly in favor of the middle class.
   d. shifted in favor of the aristocracy.

2. Which level of European society was most opposed to drinking?
   a. Aristocracy
   b. Middle class
   c. Working class
   d. Monarchy

3. Comte's "stages of knowledge" theory held that the third and final stage of all intellectual activity was the
   a. scientific.
   b. theological, or fictitious.
   c. metaphysical, or abstract.
   d. psychological, or analytic.

4. The new movement in writing, as found in the works of Zola, Flaubert, and Hardy, which pursued the typical and commonplace and claimed that human action was a result of heredity and environment, was called
   a. romanticism.
   b. secularism.
   c. realism.
   d. fauvism.

5. The development of urban Western society between 1850 and 1900 brought
   a. a decrease in wages.
   b. a drop in the average standard of living.
   c. less of a gap between the income of rich and poor.
   d. more diversity of occupation in the middle and lower classes.

6. By 1900, people of the lower class
   a. were subdivided into well-defined subclasses.
   b. had generally similar lifestyles.
   c. were united against the rich.
   d. hated to go to music halls.

7. One change that the nineteenth century brought to Western women was
   a. less distinction between the duties of husband and wife.
   b. a rise in factory employment after marriage.
   c. more equal employment opportunities.
   d. increased control over money and family decisions.

8. After 1850, ordinary European women
   a. were more likely to marry for money.
   b. were more likely to breast-feed their babies.

    c.  hardly ever got pregnant before marriage.

    d.  generally cut themselves off from parents and relatives after they got married.

9.  White-collar workers generally
    a.  grew in importance in the nineteenth century.
    b.  were uninterested in moving up in society.
    c.  kept many servants.
    d.  felt a common tie with manual workers.

10.  The Western country in which the problems of urban congestion and deplorable conditions were felt first and most acutely was
    a.  France.
    b.  Germany.
    c.  Great Britain.
    d.  Ireland.

11.  Sigmund Freud's most revolutionary idea was that
    a.  unconscious psychological energy was sexual energy.
    b.  masturbation was a source of psychological disturbance.
    c.  spontaneous affection was damaging.
    d.  family life had little to do with mental illness.

12.  Comte's social philosophy of positivism was based on the idea that the laws of human relations were discoverable through
    a.  God.
    b.  political action.
    c.  social science.
    d.  Marxism.

13.  After the Industrial Revolution, the gap between the rich and poor
    a.  decreased.
    b.  increased.
    c.  stayed about the same as previously.
    d.  none of the above.

14.  The typical Western nineteenth-century *middle-class* social occasion was
    a.  a trip to the music hall.
    b.  gambling.
    c.  a dinner party.
    d.  a relaxing evening at the local pub.

15. By the late nineteenth century, indulging in heavy drinking and practicing cruel sports, such as cockfighting,
    a. were on the increase because of more leisure time.
    b. were both in decline.
    c. fluctuated from year to year.
    d. resulted in the prohibition of such activities.

16. After 1850, the illegitimacy rate in Europe
    a. increased.
    b. decreased.
    c. remained about the same.
    d. fluctuated depending on economic conditions.

17. It is possible that kinship ties within nineteenth-century working-class homes in the West
    a. hardly existed.
    b. were greater than often believed.
    c. did not exist after marriage.
    d. existed *only* in crisis situations.

18. The division of labor by sex in the last half of the nineteenth century tended to
    a. increase.
    b. decrease.
    c. not change from the earlier period.
    d. decrease only for middle-class women.

19. Late-nineteenth-century roles of father and mother tended to become
    a. more alike.
    b. more rigid.
    c. more democratic, with the father showing more affection.
    d. more flexible.

20. The so-called labor aristocracy in Great Britain in the late nineteenth century comprised
    a. more than 30 percent of the working class.
    b. about 50 percent of the working class.
    c. about 15 percent of the working class.
    d. less than 2 percent of the working class.

21. Which of the following groups within the working classes was closest to the middle class in terms of values and behavior?
    a. Domestic servants

    b.   The labor aristocracy
    c.   Self-employed street vendors
    d.   Music-hall patrons

22.  "Sweated" workers were most frequently found in
    a.   the clothing trades.
    b.   large textile factories.
    c.   domestic service.
    d.   the shipbuilding industry.

23.  The eleven-volume *My Secret Life* deals with
    a.   sexual adventure.
    b.   the war against immorality.
    c.   investigations into working-class health.
    d.   insanity in the nineteenth century.

24.  By 1900 the birthrate in Europe was
    a.   increasing dramatically.
    b.   on a slight rise.
    c.   declining generally.
    d.   declining only in rural areas.

25.  Sigmund Freud believed that mental illness often originated in
    a.   environmental forces acting on the individual.
    b.   alienation resulting from industrialization.
    c.   emotional stress.
    d.   childhood experiences.

26.  The realist writers held to which of the following principles in their writing?
    a.   The romantic search for the sublime
    b.   An emphasis on subjective nonscientific observations
    c.   A general criticism of middle-class values and life
    d.   A focus on the special days of special people

27.  The birthrate declined in the later nineteenth century for which of the following reasons?
    a.   The desire to give less individual care and attention to children
    b.   The desire to give fewer opportunities to children in education
    c.   The acceptance of birth-control practices by the Catholic church
    d.   The declining value of children as an economic asset

28. In the nineteenth century, prostitution
    a. increased.
    b. decreased.
    c. stayed about the same.
    d. disappeared for a short time.

## GEOGRAPHY

Study Map 28.1, European Cities of 100,000 or More, 1800 and 1900. (a) In what regions or countries of Europe did urban growth largely occur? (b) Why did this urban growth take place?

## UNDERSTANDING HISTORY THROUGH READING AND THE ARTS

The best way to learn about life for the common folk is to read historical novels. The life of a family in early twentieth-century Scotland (Ayrshire) is told in W. McIlvanney's *Docherty* (1975); the London underworld of crime is mixed with upper-class life in M. Crichton's exciting *The Great Train Robbery*\* (1975); and life in a slum is the subject of Robert Robert's autobiography, *The Classic Slum*\* (1973). Charles Dickens' *Hard Times*\* has become a classic statement about life in the new industrial society, as has E. Gaskell's *Mary Barton.*\* Another interesting fictional account of hardship and survival in the nineteenth century is C. Kingsley, *Alton Locke.*\* The text section "Realism in Literature" lists a number of the realist classics, and these are a way to understand urban life and how writers viewed the world in which they lived.

Victorian social and moral codes were expressed in painting. These highly popular works of the time are known as modern-life or "narrative" paintings and are interestingly described (and shown) in C. Wood, *Victorian Panorama: Paintings of Victorian Life* (1977), and J. Hadfield, *Every Picture Tells a Story: Images of Victorian Life* (1985). Impressionist painting is very popular today, but a new light on how it related to social change of the time is sketched out in

\*Available in paperback.

T. Clark, *The Painting of Modern Life: Paris in the Art of Manet and His Followers* (1985). The student interested in architecture and the city should begin with the general work taken up by M. Girouard, *Cities and People* (1985), and socialism and art was a subject taken up by the influential Englishman William Morris — who is the subject of A. Briggs, *William Morris, Selected Writings and Designs* (1957).

The tragedy of industrial-urban life for the lower classes is woven into Puccini's highly popular and romantic opera *La Bohème*, which takes place in Paris. Many recordings of his opera are available.

## PROBLEMS FOR FURTHER INVESTIGATION

What was life like for members of the nineteenth-century working class in Europe? Historians are just now beginning to understand how they lived. One of the problems, however, is that the working people wrote little about themselves. Some autobiographical and biographical material that exists for the British working classes is H. Mayhew, *London Labour and London Poor** (reprint, 3 vols., 1969); E. Yeo, *The Unknown Mayhew** (1972); J. Burnett, ed., *Annals of Labour* (1974); P. Thompson, *The Edwardians* (1975); and J. Saville and J. Bellamy, eds., *Dictionary of Labour Biography* (4 vols., 1973). The problems faced by working-class women in the "sweated trades" are set forth in J. Schmiechen, *Sweated Industries and Sweated Labor, the London Clothing Trades, 1860–1914* (1984).

*Available in paperback.

# CHAPTER 29

# THE AGE OF NATIONALISM IN EUROPE,
1850-1914

## CHAPTER OBJECTIVES

After reading and studying this chapter you should be able to answer the following questions:

**Q-1.** How did "nation building" transform the major states of nineteenth-century Europe?

**Q-2.** Why did nationalism become a universal faith in Europe between 1850 and 1914?

**Q-3.** How did it evolve so that it gained the support of the broad masses of society?

## CHAPTER SYNOPSIS

The theme of this chapter is the triumph of European nationalism after the unsuccessful nationalist revolutions of 1848. Between 1850 and 1914, strong nation-states developed, which won the enthusiastic support of all the social classes, caused a shift in the balance of international political power, and pulled the masses away from the socialist doctrine of class war.

Napoleon III of France played a pioneering role in this triumph of nationalism. His mild dictatorship, which came into being illegally and which lasted from 1852 to 1870, showed how the national state and its programs could appeal to rich and poor, conservative and radical. In this way, the national state became a way of coping with the challenge of revolutionary political and economic change. In Italy, Count Cavour, the moderate nationalist leader of the kingdom of Sardinia, managed to unify most of Italy in 1860 into a single political state that was far from radical in social and economic matters. Shortly thereafter, in 1862, Otto von Bismarck became chief minister of Prussia. A master of power politics, Bismarck skillfully

233

fought three wars to unify the states of Germany into a single nation under Prussian leadership. In doing so, Bismarck strengthened German nationalism and gave it a conservative and antiliberal thrust. Nationalism was also important in Russia. There it led to major reforms after the Crimean War: in 1861 the serfs were freed, and the government encouraged the development of railroads and modern industry. Frustrated nationalism was an important factor in the Russian revolution of 1905, after defeat in a war with Japan.

Nationalism continued to grow in strength in the emerging European urban society of the late nineteenth century. This was because national governments and politicians responded effectively to many of the political demands and social needs of the people. Throughout most of Europe, socialists and socialist political parties looked increasingly toward unions and parliaments for continued gradual improvement. They paid only lip service to the idea of radical, violent revolution and class war. The growing moderation of European socialists reflected the great appeal of nationalism for the masses. Only in multinational states, most notably the Austro-Hungarian Empire, did the growth of competing nationalisms promote fragmentation as opposed to unity.

## STUDY OUTLINE

   I.   Napoleon III and the French tradition of authoritarian rule
        A.  The Second Republic and Louis Napoleon
            1.  The reasons for Napoleon's election include middle-class and peasant fears of socialism and a disgust with class politics
            2.  Many people wanted a strong national leader who would serve all the people and help them economically
            3.  Napoleon cooperated with the conservative National Assembly, but it refused to change the constitution so he could run for another term
            4.  Therefore, he seized power in a coup d'état in 1851 and dismissed the assembly; these actions were approved by the voters
        B.  Napoleon III's Second Empire
            1.  Napoleon III's greatest success was improving the economy of France
            2.  His political system allowed only limited opposition
            3.  His dilemma was to reconcile a strong state with democracy
  II.   National building in Italy and Germany
        A.  Italy to 1850: a battleground for great powers
            1.  "Italy" was divided; much of it was under the control of Austria and the pope
            2.  Between 1815 and 1848, the goal of national unity began to appeal to Italians

      3. Sardinia was the logical leader in the nationalist movement

      4. Pope Pius IX opposed nationalism and other modern ideas

  B. Cavour and Garibaldi

      1. Count Cavour, the liberal minister of Sardinia, built Sardinia into a liberal and economically sound state

         a. He was a moderate nationalist who sought unity only for the northern and perhaps central areas of Italy

         b. He worked to consolidate Sardinia as a liberal state capable of leading northern Italy

      2. Cavour used France to engineer a war with Austria to further his plans for unification

      3. Central Italy was united with Sardinia in 1860

      4. Garibaldi "liberated" southern Italy and Sicily, and Italy was further unified

      5. Except for Rome and Venice, Italy was politically united by 1860

         a. But there were strong class divisions

         b. There were also strong cultural divisions between the northern and southern areas

  C. Bismarck takes command

      1. Bismarck's "blood and iron" policy was centered on nationalism and war as a means of increasing Prussia's power

      2. Competition between Prussia and Austria caused a stalemate in Germany

      3. The Zollverein encouraged the move toward a non-Austrian Germany

      4. The Prussians, William I and Bismarck, supported militarism rather than liberalism to strengthen Germany and defeat Austria

  D. The Austro-Prussian War of 1866 — the first step toward unification

      1. Denmark's attempted annexation of Schleswig-Holstein led to the war with Austria

      2. Bismarck isolated Austria from France and Russia

      3. Prussian victory meant Austria had to give up its role in Germany

  E. The taming of Parliament

      1. The middle class preferred national unity to liberal institutions

      2. Bismarck outmaneuvered the liberals in the parliament, and the middle class ended up supporting monarchial authority

  F. The Franco-Prussian War (1870–1871)

      1. Bismarck used war with France to bring southern Germany into the union

      2. As a result of military success, semi-authoritarian nationalism in Germany won out over liberalism

III. The modernization of Russia

  A. The "Great Reforms"

1. Serfdom was still the basic social institution of agrarian nineteenth-century Russia
2. The Crimean War (1853–1856) speeded up the modernization of Russia
   a. Russia's defeat showed how badly the country had fallen behind the industrializing West
   b. The war also created the need for reforms because its hardships led to the threat of peasant uprisings
3. Serfdom was abolished in 1861, and other reforms were undertaken
   a. Local assemblies (zemstvos) were established
   b. The legal system was reformed

B. The industrialization of Russia (1860–1900)
1. Railroad construction stimulated the economy and inspired nationalism and imperialism
2. The assassination of Alexander III (1881) brought political reform to an end
3. Economic reform was carried out by Sergei Witte, the minister of finance from 1892 to 1903
   a. More railroads were built
   b. Protective tariffs were raised
   c. Foreign ideas and money were used to build factories

C. The revolution of 1905
1. Defeat at the hands of Japan brought political upheaval at home
2. Popular revolution forced Nicholas II to issue the October Manifesto, which granted full civil liberties and promised some form of representative government
3. Partially modernized Russia became a conservative constitutional monarchy, dominated by the bureaucracy and the propertied classes.

IV. The responsive national state (1871–1914)
A. Characteristics of the new national state
1. Ordinary people felt increasing loyalty to their governments
2. By 1914, universal male suffrage was the rule, and women were beginning to demand the right to vote too

B. The German Empire
1. The German Empire was a union of twenty-five German states in 1871 governed by a chancellor (Bismarck) and a parliament (the Reichstag)
2. Bismarck and the liberals attacked the Catholic church (the *Kulturkampf*) in an effort to maintain the superiority of state over church, but abandoned the attack in 1878
3. Worldwide agricultural depression after 1873 resulted in the policy of economic protectionism in Germany
4. Bismarck outlawed socialist parties
5. Bismarck gave Germany an impressive system of social-welfare legislation, partly to weaken socialism's appeal to the workers

6. King William II dismissed Bismarck to try to win the support of the workers, but he couldn't stem the rising tide of socialism
7. The Social Democratic Party became the largest party in the parliament, but it was strongly nationalistic, not revolutionary

C. Republican France (the Third Republic)
1. The defeat of France in 1871 led to revolution in Paris (the Commune)
2. The Paris Commune of 1871 was brutally defeated
3. A new Third Republic was established and led by skilled men such as Gambetta and Ferry
4. The Third Republic passed considerable reforms, including legalizing trade unions and creating state schools, and it built a colonial empire
5. The Dreyfus affair (1898–1899) weakened France and caused anti-Semitic reaction

D. Great Britain and Ireland
1. The reform bills of 1867 and 1884 further extended the franchise in Britain
2. Others, like Mill, looked to safeguarding the individual
3. Led by David Lloyd George, the Liberal party ushered in social-welfare legislation between 1906 and 1914
4. The issue of home rule divided Ireland into the northern Protestant Ulsterites, who opposed it, and the southern Catholic nationalists, who favored it

E. The Austro-Hungarian Empire
1. After 1866, the empire was divided in two, and the nationalistic Magyars ruled Hungary
2. Austria-Hungary suffered from competing nationalisms, which pitted ethnic groups against one another and weakened the state
3. Anti-Semitism grew rapidly, especially in Vienna

V. Marxism and the socialist movement
A. The Socialist International
1. A rapid growth of socialist parties occurred throughout Europe after 1871
2. Socialists united to form an international socialist movement

B. Unions and revisionism
1. There was a general rise in the standard of living for workers in the late nineteenth century, so they became less revolutionary
2. Unions were gradually legalized in Europe, and they were another factor in the trend toward moderation
3. Revisionist socialists believed in working within capitalism (through labor unions, for example) and no longer saw the future in terms of capitalist-worker warfare

4.  In the late nineteenth century, the socialist movements within each nation became different from one another and thereby more and more nationalistic

## REVIEW QUESTIONS

Q-1.   How did "nation building" transform the major states of nineteenth-century Europe?

Q-2.   Why did nationalism become a universal faith in Europe between 1850 and 1914?

Q-3.   How did it evolve so that it gained the support of the broad masses of society?

Q-4.   Why did the voters of France elect Louis Napoleon president in 1848? Why did they elect him emperor a few years later?

Q-5.   What were some of the benefits Napoleon bestowed on his subjects?

Q-6.   Did Napoleon allow any political opposition to exist? Explain his political system and why it eventually broke down.

Q-7.   Italy before 1860 was merely a "geographical expression." Explain.

Q-8.   What were the three basic approaches to Italian unification? Which one prevailed?

Q-9.   What was the nature and significance of Garibaldi's liberation of Sicily and Naples in 1860? Why was Cavour so nervous about Garibaldi?

Q-10.   What were the causes and results of the Austro-Prussian War?

Q-11.   What was the significance of the Zollverein in German history?

Q-12.   Why did the Prussian liberals make an about-face and support their old enemy Bismarck after 1866?

Q-13.   Describe the status of the Russian serf in the early nineteenth century. How beneficial was the reform of 1861 to the serf?

Q-14.   Why was the Crimean War a turning point in Russian history?

Q-15.   Describe the economic nationalism of the Russian minister of finance, Sergei Witte.

Q-16.   Russia used the West to catch up with the West. Explain by citing examples.

Q-17.   Compare and contrast the consequences of the Crimean and Russo-Japanese wars.

Q-18.   What does it mean to say that "Russia was partially modernized on the eve of World War One"?

Q-19.   Was the new Germany a democracy? Where did power reside in the Germany of 1871?

Q-20.   What was Bismarck's relationship (after 1871) with (a) the Catholic church, (b) the liberals, and (c) the socialists?

Q-21.   What were the German social-welfare laws? What were their origin?

Q-22.   Describe the fortunes and misfortunes of the German socialists (Social Democratic Party) from about 1878 to 1912.

Q-23.   Discuss the causes and the outcome of the Dreyfus affair in France in 1898–1899.

Q-24.   What were the major political developments and issues in Britain and Ireland? Was the Irish problem solvable?

Q-25.   In what ways were ethnic rivalries and growing anti-Semitism related in Austro-Hungary?

Q-26.   How does one account for the rapid growth of socialist parties in Europe in the last quarter of the nineteenth century?

Q-27.   What was the purpose of the socialist Internationals? To what degree did they represent working-class unity?

Q-28.   What were the general arguments of the revisionist and gradualist socialists? Were they true Marxists?

## STUDY-REVIEW EXERCISES

*Identify each of the following people and give his or her significance.*

David Lloyd George

Benjamin Disraeli

Emmeline Pankhurst

Jules Ferry

Sergei Witte

Alexander II

Camillo Benso di Cavour

Eduard Bernstein

Pius IX

William Gladstone

Giuseppe Garibaldi

William II

John Stuart Mill

*Explain the following events, who participated in them, and why they were important.*

"People's Budget" (Britain)

Napoleon III's coup d'état

May Day

assassination of Tsar Alexander II

establishment of the Zollverein (1834)

establishment of the Austro-Hungary monarchy

Treaty of Villafranca

Paris Commune of 1871

Ulster revolt of December 1913

*Explain the outcome and significance of each of the following wars.*

|  | Year | Outcome and Significance |
|---|---|---|
| Danish War |  |  |
| Austro-Prussian War |  |  |
| Franco-Prussian War |  |  |
| Crimean War |  |  |
| Russo-Japanese War |  |  |

<u>*Test*</u> *your understanding of the chapter by answering the following questions.*

1. In 1851, the French voters *approved/disapproved* of Louis Napoleon's seizure of power.
2. Increasingly, the main opposition to Napoleon III came from the *middle class/working class/upper class.*
3. The Russian *victory/defeat* in the Crimean War of 1853–1856 contributed to *freedom/serfdom* for the Russian peasants after 1861.
4. After 1848, the pope *supported/opposed* Italian unification.
5. After 1873, the price of wheat on the world market *rose/fell* rather dramatically.
6. The minority Irish Ulsterites were *Catholic/Protestant* and *for/against* home rule.
7. Bismarck used war with *Austria/France/Russia* in order to bring the south Germans into a united Germany.

## MULTIPLE-CHOICE QUESTIONS

1. The most industrialized, socialized, and unionized continental country by 1914 was
   a. France.
   b. Germany.
   c. Italy.
   d. Belgium.

2. The Russian zemstvo was a(n)
   a. industrial workers' council.
   b. local government assembly.
   c. terrorist group.
   d. village priest.

3. The *Kulturkampf* in Germany was an attack on
   a. liberals.
   b. socialists.
   c. the Catholic church.
   d. Prussian culture.

4. The first modern social security laws were passed in the 1880s in
   a. Britain.
   b. France.
   c. Russia.
   d. Germany.

5. The general tendency of unions toward the end of the century was
   a.   to move closer to Marxism.
   b.   to move toward evolutionary socialism.
   c.   to reject socialism altogether.
   d.   increasingly to favor revolution.

6. After 1850, the disciples of nationalism in Italy looked for leadership from
   a.   Prussia.
   b.   the papacy.
   c.   Sardinia-Piedmont.
   d.   the Kingdom of the Two Sicilies.

7. Russian social and political reforms in the 1860s could best be described as
   a.   revolutionary.
   b.   totally ineffective.
   c.   halfway measures.
   d.   extremely effective.

8. Witte's plans for the economic development of Russia included
   a.   lowering protective tariffs.
   b.   taking Russia off the gold standard.
   c.   encouraging foreign investment.
   d.   bringing Russian Marxists into the government.

9. Among those opposing home rule in Ireland were
   a.   Catholics.
   b.   Ulsterites.
   c.   Irish peasants.
   d.   William Gladstone.

10. After 1870, Marxian socialists
   a.   accepted the revisionist theories of Eduard Bernstein.
   b.   failed to grow in number.
   c.   formed a second international organization.
   d.   refused to participate in national elections.

11. After 1871, the European balance of power
   a.   shifted in favor of Russia.
   b.   broke down because of British naval supremacy.
   c.   shifted in favor of Germany.
   d.   shifted in favor of France.

12. The German Zollverein was
    a. a trade union.
    b. a customs union.
    c. an "all-German" parliament.
    d. a system of roads.

13. Bismarck's policy toward the Social Democrats was one of
    a. limited support.
    b. political alliance to defeat the military party.
    c. total repression.
    d. indifference.

14. Louis Napoleon believed that
    a. universal manhood suffrage was bad.
    b. all elections should be abolished.
    c. Austria should be supported by Italy.
    d. poverty could be reduced by government action.

15. In the 1850s, Prussia's economic growth was encouraged largely because of its
    a. rapid development within the Zollverein.
    b. seizure of Alsace and Lorraine from France.
    c. lack of a parliament.
    d. defeat of Cavour in Italy.

16. Bismarck wanted
    a. to form a state that would include every person who spoke German.
    b. to increase the power of Prussia.
    c. the business classes to rule Germany.
    d. to avoid war at all costs.

17. In the 1880s, Bismarck pushed laws through the parliament that
    a. nationalized the steel and coal industry.
    b. provided workers with social security benefits.
    c. eliminated socialism.
    d. lowered tariffs on imported wheat.

18. The individual least responsible for playing a role in Italian unification was
    a. Mazzini.
    b. Garibaldi.
    c. Pope Pius IX.
    d. Count Cavour.

19. In 1870, Pope Pius IX alarmed many Europeans when he
    a. denounced German unification.
    b. called for a "holy war" against communism.
    c. refused to support Greek refugees.
    d. made a declaration of papal infallibility.

20. The German social welfare legislation of 1883–1884, which included old-age pensions and national health and accident insurance, was pushed through parliament by
    a. the Social Democrats.
    b. the Catholic Center party.
    c. Bismarck.
    d. Emperor William I and his wife.

21. The main opposition to Napoleon III came from
    a. the working class.
    b. the middle class.
    c. the upper class.
    d. all of the above.

22. Germany in 1871 took Alsace-Lorraine from
    a. Austria.
    b. Turkey.
    c. France.
    d. Denmark.

23. The new national states of Europe after 1871 were
    a. police states.
    b. opposed to universal male suffrage.
    c. increasingly responsive to the needs of the people.
    d. governed by an aristocratic oligarchy.

24. The south Germans were reluctant to go beyond economic unification with the rest of Germany because of different religious and political traditions. In the end, then, why did the south Germans agree to join the German Empire?
    a. Bismarck threatened to overrun them.
    b. The Franco-Prussian War settled the issue for them.
    c. They sought protection from the threat of Austrian invasion.
    d. They feared expulsion from the customs union.

25. The country *least* able to use nationalism to strengthen the state in the nineteenth century was

    a.  Great Britain.
    b.  France.
    c.  Germany.
    d.  Austria-Hungary.

26.  Which of the following is true in regard to German unification?
    a.  It was completed in 1871 through a war with France.
    b.  The chief architect of the movement was William I.
    c.  The unification process was directed by the German state of Austria.
    d.  Unification included liberal and democratic ideas and methods.

27.  Cavour's program for the unification of northern Italy included which of the following?
    a.  Improved transportation
    b.  Increased power for the Catholic church
    c.  Elimination of civil liberties
    d.  Peace and open diplomacy

28.  The Jewish captain in the French army who was falsely accused of treason was
    a.  Léon Gambetta.
    b.  Jules Ferry.
    c.  Adolphe Thiers.
    d.  Alfred Dreyfus.

## GEOGRAPHY

1.  Using Map 29.1 as your guide, list when and how the major regions of Italy were brought into a "united" Italy. What territory went to France in the process? Why?

2.  Using Map 29.2 describe why and how the major German states or regions became a part of Prussian-dominated Germany. Why did this unification process result in war between France and Prussia?

## UNDERSTANDING HISTORY THROUGH READING AND THE ARTS

The nineteenth century saw the publication of a good number of books based on the idea that humanity could transform itself and build a new world ruled by justice and equality. One of the most popular of these utopian works in Europe was the American author Edward Bellamy's *Looking Backward*,* which was first published in 1888. Life and revolutionary activity among rural workers is told in the fascinating *Autobiography of Joseph Arch*, J. O'Leary, ed. (1966). One of the most interesting women of the nineteenth century was Queen Victoria, whose life is dealt with in the lively biography *Queen Victoria** (1964), by E. Longford.

In music the mood of the last half of the nineteenth century was romantically nationalistic. Brahms wrote the *Song of Triumph* to celebrate the German victory over France in 1870, while Smetana, the first great Czech nationalist composer, glorified the folk history of the Czech people in his *My Country*. In opera Moussorgsky wrote *Boris Godunov* (1874), a historical drama about Russia during the time of Ivan the Terrible. The popularity of German heroic music-drama continued to grow, and it drew added inspiration from Wagner's *The Ring of the Nibelungs* (four parts, 1869–1876), a monumental national epic of Germany based on Nordic mythology. All of these works are available on a number of recordings.

## PROBLEMS FOR FURTHER INVESTIGATION

Who was Napoleon III and what were his motives — a police state or a unified and prosperous France? Begin your investigation with the problem series book *Napoleon III — Man of Destiny*,* B. D. Gooch, ed. (1963).

The problems of interpreting the Italian unification movement are discussed by a number of historians in C. F. Delzell, *The Unification of Italy** (1963).

*Available in paperback.

Those interested in the political activities of British workers will want to start with H. Pelling, *The Origins of the Labour Party* (1954), and for the interesting story of the politicization of the German working class, from Marx to the present, begin with H. Grebing, *The History of the German Labour Movement* (1969).

How did the Franco-German War change the course of history? French-German relations and French history took a tragic turn in 1870 with the siege of Paris and the grim civil war that followed. This is the subject of A. Horne, *The Fall of Paris: The Siege and the Commune of 1870-1** (1965, 1981).

What were the goals and interests of women in the nineteenth-century women's rights movement? Begin with T. Lloyd, *Suffragettes International: The World Wide Campaign for Women's Rights** (1971), M. Thomis and J. Grimmett, *Women in Protest, 1800-1850** (1983), and O. Banks, *Faces of Feminism* (1981). Further, in an era in which most women were confined to either the kitchen or drawing room, three Victorian women (Josephine Butler, Octavia Hill, and Florence Nightingale) became important makers of social policy. This is the subject of N. Boyd, *Three Victorian Women Who Changed Their World* (1982). The problems faced by working-class women in the "sweated trades" are set for in J. Schmiechen, *Sweated Industries and Sweated Labor: The London Clothing Trades, 1860-1914* (1984).

*Available in paperback.

## READING WITH UNDERSTANDING
## EXERCISE 4

## LEARNING TO CLASSIFY INFORMATION ACCORDING TO SEQUENCE

As you know, a great deal of historical information is classified by sequence, in which things follow each other in time. This kind of *sequential order* is also known as *time order* or *chronological order*.

Attention to time sequence is important in the study of history for at least two reasons.

1.  It helps us organize historical information effectively.

2.  It promotes historical understanding. If the student knows the order in which events happened, he or she can think intelligently about questions of cause and effect. The student can begin to evaluate conflicting interpretations.

Since time sequences are essential in historical study, the authors have placed a number of timelines in the text to help you organize the historical information.

### Two Fallacies Regarding Time Sequences

One common fallacy is often known by the famous Latin phrase *post hoc, ergo propter hoc:* "after this, therefore because of this." This fallacy assumes that one happening that follows another *must* be caused by the first happening. Obviously, some great development (such as the Protestant Reformation) could come after another (the Italian Renaissance) without being caused by it. *Causal relationships must be demonstrated, not simply assumed on the basis of the "after this, therefore because of this" fallacy.*

A second common, if old-fashioned, fallacy assumes that time sequences are composed only of political facts with precise data. But in considering social, intellectual, and economic developments, historians must often speak with less chronological exactitude—in terms of decades or even centuries, for example. Yet they still use time sequences, and students of history must recognize them. For example, did you realize that the sections on "The Scientific Revolution" and "The Enlightenment" in Chapter 18 are very conscientious about time sequence, even though they do not deal with political facts?

### Exercise

Reread the large section in Chapter 18 on "The Scientific Revolution" with an eye for dates and sequential order. Then take a sheet of notebook paper and with the book open make a "Timeline for the Scientific Revolution." Pick out at least a dozen important events and put them in the time sequence, with a word or two to explain the significance when possible.

*Suggestion:* Do not confine yourself solely to specific events with specific dates. Also, integrate some items from the subsection on the causes of the Scientific Revolution into the sequence. You may find that constructing timelines helps you organize your study.

After you have completed your timeline, compare it with the one on the following page, which shows how one of the authors of the text did this assignment.

**Timeline on the Scientific Revolution**

| | |
|---|---|
| (1300-1500) | Renaissance stimulates development of mathematics |
| early 1500s | Aristotle's ideas on movement and universe still dominant |
| 1543 | Copernicus publishes *On the Revolution of the Heavenly Spheres* |
| 1572, 1577 | New star and comet create more doubts about traditional astronomy |
| 1546-1601 | Tycho Brache—famous astronomer, creates mass of observations |
| 1571-1630 | Johannes Kepler—his three laws prove Copernican theory and demolish Aristotle's beliefs |
| 1589 | Galileo Galilei (1564-1642) named professor of mathematics |
| 1610 | Galileo Galilei studies moon with telescope and writes of experience |
| 1561-1626 | Francis Bacon—English scientific enthusiast, advocates experimental (inductive) method |
| 1596-1650 | René Descartes—French philosopher, discovers analytical geometry in 1619 and advocates theoretical (deductive) method |
| to about 1630 | All religious authorities oppose Copernican theory |
| about 1632 | Galileo tried by papal inquisition |
| 1622 | Royal Society of London founded—brings scientists and practical men together |
| 1687 | Isaac Newton publishes his *Principia*, synthesizing existing knowledge around idea of universal gravitation |
| to late 1700s | Consequences of Scientific Revolution primarily intellectual, not economic |

# CHAPTER 30

## THE WEST AND THE WORLD

### CHAPTER OBJECTIVES

After reading and studying this chapter you should be able to answer the following questions:

Q-1.  What is "global inequality" and "new imperialism," and how and why did they occur?

Q-2.  What were the consequences for Europe and the new colonial peoples?

### CHAPTER SYNOPSIS

This chapter explains how and why we live in a lopsided world of rich nations and poor nations. We live in a world today in which the consequences of nineteenth-century Western imperialism are still being felt. In the nineteenth century, Western civilization reached the high point of its longstanding global expansion. Western expansion in this period took many forms. There was, first of all, economic expansion. Europeans invested large sums of money abroad, building railroads and ports, mines and plantations, factories and public utilities. Trade between nations grew greatly, a world economy developed, and a huge gap between rich and poor nations also developed. European economic penetration was very often peaceful, but Europeans (and Americans) were also quite willing to use violence to force isolationist nations such as China and Japan to throw open their doors to Westerners. Second, millions of Europeans migrated abroad. The pressure of poverty, over-population in rural areas, and oppression encouraged this migration, but once in the United States and Australia, European settlers passed laws to prevent similar mass migration from Asia.

A third aspect of Western expansion was that European states established vast political empires, mainly in Africa but also in Asia. This was called the "new imperialism," and it occurred primarily between 1880 and 1900, when European governments scrambled frantically for territory. White people came, therefore, to rule millions of black and brown people in Africa and Asia. The causes of the new imperialism are still hotly debated. Competition for trade, superior military force, European power politics, and a racist belief in European superiority were among the most important. Some Europeans bitterly criticized imperialism as a betrayal of Western ideals of freedom and equality.

Western imperialism produced various reactions in Africa and Asia. The first response was simply to try to drive the foreigners away. The general failure of this violent response then led large masses to accept European rule, which did bring some improvements. A third response was that of Western-educated natives, who were repelled by Western racism and attracted by Western ideals of national independence and economic progress. Thus, imperialism and reactions to it spread Western civilization to non-Western lands.

## STUDY OUTLINE

I.   Industrialization and the world economy
   A.   The global economic system was built so that wealth flowed from non-Western nations to the West
   B.   The rise of global inequality
      1.   The Industrial Revolutions of Europe and North America caused a lopsided world of rich and poor nations
      2.   Not until the nineteenth century did the Third World's (meaning Africa, Asia, and Latin America) standard of living begin to fall behind that of Europe — but by 1970 the gap was very wide (see Figure 30.1)
      3.   The reason for the gap was industrialization, but historians debate whether or not the gap was due to exploitation of the non-West by the West
   C.   Trade and foreign investment
      1.   The nineteenth century saw an enormous growth in world trade, with Britain playing a key role
      2.   Britain, for example, used non-Western markets to buy its cotton textiles, while it absorbed vast quantities of raw materials from the non-West
      3.   The railroad, the steamship, refrigeration, and other technological innovations revolutionized trade patterns
      4.   The Suez and Panama canals fostered intercontinental trade
      5.   Beginning about 1840, Europeans continuously invested large amounts of capital abroad and in other European countries

6. Investment resulted in cheap raw materials, an increased demand for European manufactured goods, and more white settlement, while it victimized the natives

D. The opening of China and Japan
1. European trade with China increased, but not without a struggle
   a. China had never been interested in European goods
   b. British merchants and the Chinese clashed over the sale of opium and the opening of Chinese ports to Europeans
   c. The Opium War of 1839–1842 led to the British acquisition of Hong Kong and the opening of Chinese ports to Europeans
   d. A second war in 1856–1860 resulted in more gains for Europeans on terms unfavorable to China
2. Japan also was unwilling to trade with the West or to have diplomatic relations with it
   a. Japan wanted to maintain its long-standing isolation
   b. An American fleet under Perry "opened" Japan in 1853 with threats of naval bombardment

E. The Western penetration of Egypt
1. Mohammed Ali built a modern state in Turkish-held Egypt that attracted European traders
2. Egyptian landlords profited from the new European economic control, but the once self-sufficient peasants were hurt
3. Khedive Ismail continued the modernization of Egypt but also drew the country deeply into debt
4. To prevent Egypt from going bankrupt, Britain intervened politically — thus a new phase of direct control was underway
5. Foreign financial control provoked a violent nationalistic reaction in Egypt that led to British occupation of the country
6. British rule of Egypt (under Baring) — based on military force, reform, and economic control — became a new model for European expansion

II. The great migration from Europe and Asia
A. The pressure of population
1. The population of Europe more than doubled between 1800 and 1900
2. This population growth was the impetus behind emigration
3. Migration patterns varied from country to country, depending largely on economic opportunities at home and abroad
4. Only about half the migrants came to the United States

B. European migration
1. Most European migrants were peasants who lacked adequate land holdings or craftsmen who were threatened by industrialization
2. After 1881 many Jews left Russia; likewise many Germans came to the Midwest in America

3.  Most were young and unmarried
4.  Many returned home after some time abroad
5.  Many were spurred on by the desire for freedom and change

C.  Asian migration
   1.  Many Asians became plantation laborers — under near-slavery conditions
   2.  Asian migration led to racist reactions in the West

III.  Western imperialism

A.  The new imperialism of 1880–1914
   1.  Europeans scrambled for political and economic control of Asia and Africa
   2.  This led to new tensions between European states and wars with non-European powers

B.  The scramble for Africa
   1.  Prior to 1880, European control of Africa was limited — British and Dutch defeat of the Zulus and Xhosas of South Africa is a major exception
   2.  British occupation of Egypt and Belgian penetration into the Congo started the race for colonial possessions
   3.  The Berlin Conference (1884–1885) laid ground rules for this new imperialism
      a.  European claims to African territory had to be based on military occupation
      b.  No single European power could claim the whole continent
   4.  Germany entered the race for colonies and cooperated with France against Britain
   5.  The British massacred Muslim tribesmen at Omdurman (1898) in their drive to conquer the Sudan and nearly went to war with the French at Fashoda

C.  Imperialism in Asia
   1.  The Dutch extended their control in the East Indies while the French took Indochina
   2.  Russia and the United States penetrated Asia

D.  The causes of the new imperialism
   1.  Economic motives — especially trade opportunities — were important, but in the end general economic benefits were limited
   2.  Political and diplomatic factors encouraged imperialism
      a.  Colonies were believed to be crucial for national security, military power, and international prestige
      b.  Colonies were also needed to provide naval bases
   3.  Nationalism and racism contributed to imperialism
   4.  Humanitarians, including missionaries, as well as military men often encouraged imperial growth

      5.  Europeans saw themselves as giving a superior civilization to the world

  E.  Critics of imperialism

      1.  The British journalist Hobson argued that imperialism was the result of capitalism and benefited only special-interest groups

      2.  Others — such as Conrad — were critical for humanitarian or liberal reasons

IV.  Responses to Western imperialism

  A.  Imperialism disrupted traditional society in many ways

      1.  Traditionalists wanted to drive Western culture out and preserve the old culture and society

      2.  Modernizers believed it was necessary to adopt Western practices

      3.  Anti-imperialist leaders found inspiration in Western liberalism and nationalism

  B.  Empire in India

      1.  The last traditionalist response in India was the Great Rebellion of 1857–1858

      2.  After 1858, India was ruled by a white British elite that considered itself superior to the Indians

      3.  An Indian elite was educated to aid the British in administration

      4.  Imperialism brought many benefits, including unity and peace

      5.  But nationalistic sentiments grew among the Western-educated Indian elite

  C.  The example of Japan

      1.  The Meiji Restoration (1867) was a reaction to American intrusion, the unequal treaties, and humiliation of the shogun

      2.  The Meiji leaders were modernizers, and they brought liberal and economic reforms

      3.  Japan looked increasingly toward the German empire and rejected democracy in favor of authoritarianism in the 1890s

      4.  Japan became an imperial power in the Far East

  D.  Toward revolution in China

      1.  The traditionalist Manchu rulers staged a comeback after the opium wars

      2.  The Chinese defeat by Japan in 1894–1895 led to imperialist penetration and unrest

      3.  Modernizers hoped to take over and strengthen China

      4.  Boxer traditionalists caused violence and a harsh European reaction

      5.  Revolutionary modernizers overthrew the Manchu dynasty in 1912

# REVIEW QUESTIONS

Q-1.   Describe the enormous increase in world trade after 1800. What were the reasons for this growth? Why did the "Third World" fall behind in its standard of living?

Q-2.   Discuss the Opium wars (1839–1842, 1856–1860) by describing the motives of both the British merchants and the Chinese government.

Q-3.   Trace the flow of European capital in the nineteenth century, and note its effects.

Q-4.   Khedive Ismail once said, "My country is no longer in Africa; we now form part of Europe." What did he mean?

Q-5.   Explain the British-Egyptian conflict of 1882. What were the causes and the results?

Q-6.   What were some of the differences in migration patterns among the various European states?

Q-7.   Where did the European migrants go?

Q-8.   Why did the migrants leave? Why did so many return?

Q-9.   Why was migration from Italy so heavy? Who were the migrants and where did they go?

Q-10.   What distinguished the "new imperialism" from earlier forms of European expansion in the nineteenth century?

Q-11.   Why was Leopold II of Belgium interested in Africa?

Q-12.   What was meant by "effective occupation"? Did it cause or curtail further imperialism?

Q-13.   In 1898, a British army faced a French army at Fashoda in north-central Africa. How did each power get to such a location, and how was the confrontation resolved?

Q-14.   What do you believe was the chief cause of European imperialist expansion? Was it an inevitable result of capitalism, as some have argued?

Q-15.   What impact did Christianity have on both imperialism and the contrast between imperialists and natives?

Q-16.   What was the purpose of the Great Rebellion in India in 1857–1858?

Q-17.   What were the advantages and disadvantages of British rule for the Indians?

Q-18.   What was the Meiji Restoration in Japan? Why was it a turning point in Japanese history?

Q-19.   How well did the Japanese copy the Europeans? What European ideas were most attractive to them?

Q-20.   Does the Manchu dynasty in the period 1860–1912 represent a traditionalist or modernist response to Europe and imperialism?

Q-21.   In the light of Chinese history and Chinese-European relations in the nineteenth century, what do you consider to be the causes of the Chinese Revolution of 1911–1912?

## STUDY-REVIEW EXERCISES

*Define* the following key concepts and terms.

Third World

new imperialism

European foreign investment

traditionalist response to imperialism

modernist response to imperialism

Social Darwinism

racism

nationalism

*Identify* each of the following and give its significance.

Manchu dynasty

Pale of [Jewish] Settlement

Evelyn Baring

International Association for the Exploration and Civilization of Central Africa

Egyptian Nationalist Party

Suez Canal

Omdurman

British opium trade

Pierre de Brazza

Mohammed Ali

Leopold II

Matthew Perry

Boers

Emile Aguinaldo

Empress Dowager Tzu Hsi

John Hobson


*Explain* what the following events were, who participated in them, and why they were important.

Japanese "opening" of Korea in 1876

Berlin Conference of 1884–1885

Fashoda crisis of 1898

Great Trek of the Boers

Alexandria riots of 1882

Treaty of Nanking, 1842

*Clermont* experiment of 1807

Meiji Restoration of 1867

Sino-Japanese War (1894–1895)

the Opium wars


*Test* your understanding of this chapter by filling in the blank line with the letter of the correct answer.

_____ 1. He took the Sudan for the British with     a. Sun Yat-sen
his victory at Omdurman.     b. Evelyn Baring

_____ 2. His attempt to modernize Egypt resulted in bankruptcy and foreign intervention
_____ 3. He was a journalist, explorer, and employee of Leopold II.
_____ 4. He was a British paternalistic reformer in Egypt.
_____ 5. He argued that the strongest nations tend to be the best.
_____ 6. He "opened" Japan to the West in 1853.
_____ 7. He was a Chinese revolutionary and republican.
_____ 8. Under her leadership China was able to strengthen itself and maintain its traditional culture.

c. Lord Kitchener
d. Walter Bagehot
e. Khedive Ismail
f. Commodore Perry
g. Empress Dowager Tzu Hsi
h. H. M. Stanley
i. Rudyard Kipling

## MULTIPLE-CHOICE QUESTIONS

1. The Treaty of Nanking of 1842 ended a war between Great Britain and China that had started over
   a. Chinese expulsion of British diplomats from Canton.
   b. disagreement over shipping rights in Chinese ports.
   c. opium smuggled into China from British India.
   d. the British annexation of Manchuria.

2. The most persuasive Western argument against European imperialism was that
   a. it was not economically profitable.
   b. European control of nonwhites was immoral and hypocritical.
   c. not enough investment was made in colonies.
   d. it was unworthy of great nations.

3. Western influence on Japan resulted in
   a. a Westernized country that began to practice its own form of imperialism.
   b. a country subject to Britain in the same way that India was.
   c. a country subject to the United States in the same way that India was subject to Britain.
   d. no effect at all.

4. After the Opium wars China
   a. began to industrialize rapidly.
   b. recovered for a number of years under the Empress Dowager.

    c.   defeated Japan in the Sino-Japanese War of 1894–1895.

    d.   established a communist dictatorship to crush the Boxer Rebellion.

5.  After 1840, world trade
    a.   grew slowly as prices increased.
    b.   grew rapidly as prices decreased.
    c.   remained about the same as during the early decades of the century.
    d.   declined because of the rise of protective barriers.

6.  Which of the following characterizes the traditional attitude of Chinese society toward European society?
    a.   Great interest in European products
    b.   A desire to open trade ports to European capitalists
    c.   A need for Europe as a source of capital and market for Chinese tea
    d.   Considerable disinterest in Europe

7.  The war between Britain and China, which ended in 1842, was caused by
    a.   Chinese penetration into southeast Asia.
    b.   British merchants' demand to sell opium to the Chinese.
    c.   the Chinese naval blockade of the Japanese coast.
    d.   Chinese piracy.

8.  Japan was "opened" by the United States as a result of
    a.   a military display of force.
    b.   long and arduous negotiations.
    c.   a willingness on the part of Japan.
    d.   the Opium wars.

9.  Throughout the nineteenth century, European population and emigration tended to
    a.   increase.
    b.   decrease slightly.
    c.   remain about the same.
    d.   decrease significantly.

10.  As a percentage of the total population, the area that was most affected by the entrance of Europeans into its land was
    a.   the United States.
    b.   Argentina.
    c.   Russia.
    d.   Peru.

11. For the most part, the people who left Europe to settle elsewhere were
    a. the poorest and least skilled of society.
    b. middle-class adventurers in search of new fortunes.
    c. small landowners and village craftsmen.
    d. aristocratic profit-seekers.

12. The return of the migrant to his or her native land was
    a. rare.
    b. not uncommon.
    c. common only among the Irish.
    d. common only among those migrating to Argentina.

13. In the nineteenth century, two out of three migrants to Argentina and Brazil came from
    a. Italy.
    b. Africa.
    c. Ireland.
    d. northern Europe.

14. The east European migrants *least* likely to return to Europe were
    a. Poles.
    b. Jews.
    c. Germans.
    d. migrants from the Balkan lands.

15. The great European scramble for possession of Africa occurred
    a. prior to 1850.
    b. after 1900.
    c. between 1880 and 1900.
    d. around 1850.

16. The victor of the Fashoda incident in Africa was
    a. Britain.
    b. France.
    c. Germany.
    d. Belgium.

17. The radical English economist J. S. Hobson argued in his book *Imperialism* that the motive for colonial imperialism was
    a. economic.
    b. political.
    c. military.
    d. overpopulation.

18. During the nineteenth century international trade
    a. hardly increased at all.
    b. was facilitated by Britain's commitment to free trade.
    c. was helped by the building of the Suez and Panama canals.
    d. between Germany and Britain was very small because of nationalism.

19. European foreign investment
    a. came mainly from Britain, France, and Germany.
    b. avoided Canada and the United States.
    c. was concentrated in European colonies and protectorates in Asia and Africa.
    d. did not increase between 1890 and 1914.

20. Italians migrated to North and South America because of
    a. political repression in Italy.
    b. agricultural depression and industrial stagnation.
    c. the expulsion of landless workers from large estates.
    d. war in Europe.

21. Although the migration of Asians to the West was considerable, this flow was eventually stopped because of
    a. world war.
    b. growth and modernization in the Asian nations.
    c. white racism in the new lands.
    d. all of the above

22. Imperialism in Africa was characterized by
    a. a scramble for control of various African territories by European nations early in the nineteenth century.
    b. the establishment of "ground rules" at the Berlin Conference.
    c. European indifference in the late nineteenth century.
    d. a war between France and Britain over control of Egypt and the Sudan.

23. The United States' imperialistic conquest in Asia was
    a. Indochina.
    b. New Zealand.
    c. the Philippines.
    d. Burma.

24. One reason for European expansion was
    a. a desire to copy the technology of other cultures.
    b. to ensure access to foreign markets.

   c.  altruism.
   d.  a keen interest in primitive art and religion.

25.  British colonies in Africa included
   a.  Libya.
   b.  Ethiopia.
   c.  the Congo.
   d.  South Africa.

26.  A major reason that Third World nations lag behind European nations economically is that they
   a.  are primitive.
   b.  do not need to earn as much income.
   c.  are, for the most part, non-Christian.
   d.  are not as industrialized.

27.  In 1850, the average income per person in Europe was
   a.  five times greater than that of the Third World.
   b.  three times greater than that of the Third World.
   c.  twice as great as that of the Third World.
   d.  roughly the same as that of the Third World.

28.  Which of the following characterizes the economic relationship between an industrialized nation and a nonindustrialized nation?
   a.  The industrialized nation tends to gain more benefit.
   b.  Both nations benefit equally.
   c.  The nonindustrialized nation tends to gain more benefit.
   d.  Neither benefits.

## GEOGRAPHY

1.  On the map of Africa, locate and label each of the following colonies and indicate to which European nation it belonged. Indicate which ones were controlled by Europeans prior to 1878 (see Map 30.2 in text).

| | | |
|---|---|---|
| Union of South Africa | Madagascar | French Equatorial Africa |
| Algeria | Belgian Congo | Orange Free State |
| Transvaal | Libya | German East Africa |

Nigeria                    Gold Coast                    Egypt

Morocco                    British East Africa

2. Explain why and how Britain and France acquired so much African territory.

3. Locate Fashoda. What happened here, and where else did the British and the French come into conflict?

4. Use earlier history to help explain why little Portugal got so much African territory.

5. On the map of Asia, locate and label the following places and indicate which western nation exercises control or domination.

French Indochina          Port Arthur                   Philippine Islands

India                     Canton                        Korea

Macao                     Manchuria                     Suez Canal

Hong Kong                 Formosa                       Dutch East Indies

Vladivostok

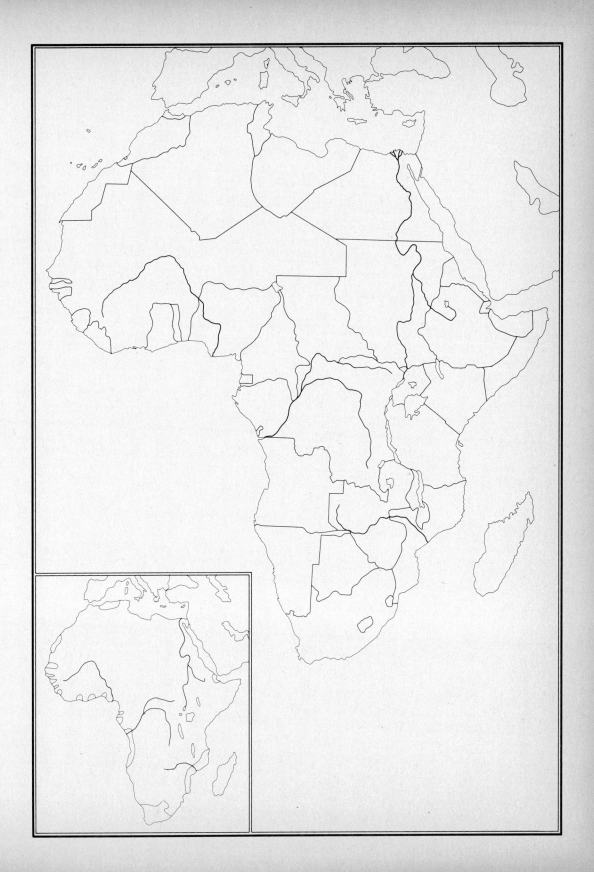

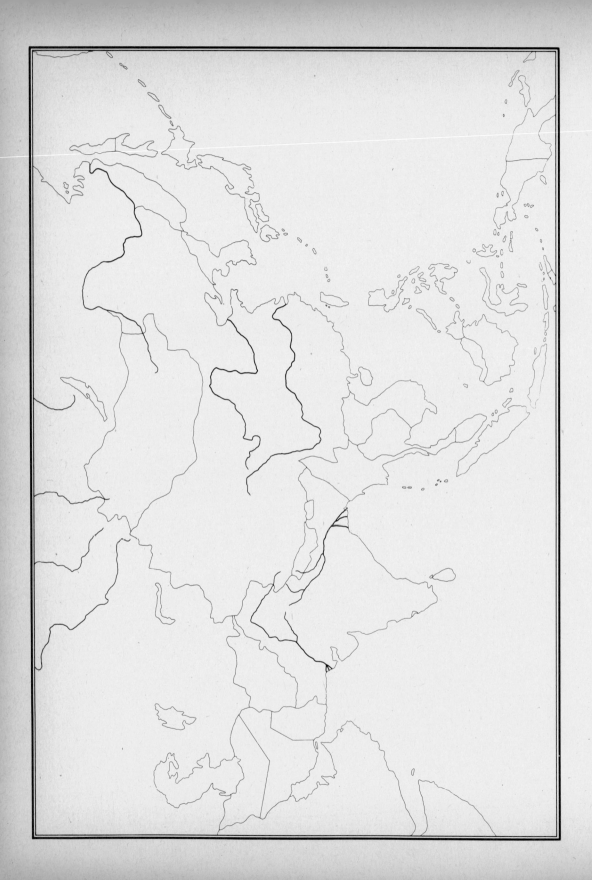

6.  Why were Russian and Japanese imperialists likely to collide in Korea?

7.  What were the economic and political motives of the British concerning Asia? What was the importance of the Suez Canal to the British military and to British merchants?

## UNDERSTANDING HISTORY THROUGH READING AND THE ARTS

A striking and fascinating study of one of the greatest of the imperialist-militarists is P. Magnus, *Kitchener: Portrait of an Imperialist** (1959, 1968). Imperialist adventure, as found in works such as R. Kipling, *Kim* and *In Black and White*, and J. Conrad, *Lord Jim*, has become part of the classical literature of our time.

One woman's life in Africa is the subject of the award-winning film *Out of Africa* (1984) and can be found in I. Dinesen, *Letters from Africa, 1914–1931** (1981, trans. by A. Born).

Few operas have enjoyed the popularity of Giacomo Puccini's *Madame Butterfly* (1904). This Italian tragic grand opera is set in Japan and centers on the marriage of an American naval lieutenant and a Japanese woman.

## PROBLEMS FOR FURTHER INVESTIGATION

How did the non-Westerners view the Western imperialists? One place to begin is with China; see A. Waley, *The Opium War Through Chinese Eyes* (1958). What were the causes of imperialism and what made the system of "empire" work? Was empire a system that developed its own internal logic and reason for being? The various causes for the changed nature of imperialism in the 1880s are discussed in H. M. Wright, ed., *The "New Imperialism"** (1961). Imperialism in Africa is ana-

*Available in paperback.

lyzed by a number of historians in R. F. Betts, ed., *The "Scramble" for Africa\** (1966), and a good general description of the greatest imperialist nation, Great Britain, is to be had in B. Porter, *The Lion's Share, A Short History of British Imperialism, 1850–1970\** (1976), as well as D. Judd's *The Victorian Empire* (1970), which is a pictorial history.

\*Available in paperback.

# CHAPTER 31

## THE WESTERN HEMISPHERE
## IN THE NINETEENTH CENTURY

## CHAPTER OBJECTIVES

After reading and studying this chapter you should be able to answer the following questions:

Q-1.  How did the transformation of the United States into a great world power come about?

Q-2.  Why and how did the Spanish colonies of Latin America shake off European domination and become nation-states?

Q-3.  What role did "manifest destiny" play in United States history?

Q-4.  How did the Americas absorb new peoples, and what was their social impact?

Q-5.  How did the issue of race create serious tensions throughout the hemisphere?

## CHAPTER SYNOPSIS

It was during the nineteenth century that millions of immigrants populated and built ethnically diverse nations. This chapter examines that process.

Between 1806 and 1825, the Latin American colonies acquired independence from Spain and Portugal and established a unique racial-social structure consisting essentially of four racial groups: *Creoles*, *peninsulares*, *mestizos*, and *mulattos*. Much of the political and social history of Latin America evolves from this arrangement. Although the independence struggles grew out of a common reaction to the colonial policies of Spain — particularly the economic policies of Charles III — the struggles took different forms in different places. The *Creole* rulers, like the white landowners of the United States, interpreted the Enlightenment ideals in a manner that applied only to them and left the Indian and black majorities without human rights. The racism of Latin America was less rigid than that of the United States, however, because Indian and black individuals of mixed blood were more easily assimilated and enjoyed a degree of social and economic mobility. As the Comunero Revolution of 1781 illustrates, non-white revolt proved partially successful.

With independence in Latin America came instability, which led to military dictatorships, such as Rosas' in Argentina. The price of economic development was another kind of dictatorship — neocolonialism — as Britain and the United States came to dominate the railroads, mineral resources, banking, and much else. Economic development also meant a deterioration of conditions for the Latin American Indians, who were deprived of their land and fell into a cycle of debt peonage and plantation labor.

Meanwhile, massive immigration from Europe led to rapid urbanization, tenement living, and (for some) assimilation into the elite and wealthy upper class. Furthermore, because a vast majority of the immigrants were single males, immigration resulted in a mixture of Europeans, Asians, and Indians. For blacks in Latin America, however, immigration proved a calamity. They were reduced to the fringes of the labor market and became the victims of racial prejudice.

The concept of manifest destiny played an important role in U.S. history. Overall, it gave the young nation justification for its relentless push across the continent and its inhuman treatment of native Americans. Another issue, that of slavery, preoccupied Americans and eventually caused a civil war. Although a powerful array of arguments — including the human rights arguments of the Enlightenment — characterized slavery as a great evil, many Americans of the liberal-democratic tradition were nonetheless committed to slavery. The reason for this dilemma was profits: Cotton was king in the South, and slavery was necessary for the survival and expansion of the cotton economy. It was President Lincoln's Emancipation Proclamation that transformed the war from a political struggle to a moral crusade for the liberty of all Americans. The author discusses the impact of slavery on the black family. He shows how black women fought sexual abuse and how the black family held itself together in spite of slavery.

After the Civil War the United States experienced a gigantic industrial boom and a surge of immigration and urbanization, all of which brought a high degree of cultural-ethnic pluralism to the new industrial cities. But industrialization and urbanization brought serious problems: poverty and slum life, anti-immigration prejudice, and industrial unrest.

From its origin in 1608 as a French trading post located in present-day Quebec, Canada also developed into an independent nation during the nineteenth century. Control passed to the British following the prolonged "French and Indian Wars," an event central to the history of French Canadians. Widespread discontent over the lack of popular representation led to parliamentary reforms, most notably those outlined in the British North America Act of 1867, which established the Dominion of Canada and brought the Canadian constitution to its modern form. Under the Dominion's first prime minister, John A. Macdonald, Canada underwent significant expansion (incorporating all of northern North America by 1873) and development; by the century's end Canada was enjoying an impressive industrial boom.


## STUDY OUTLINE

I.  Latin America, ca 1800–1929
    A.  The Spanish Empire in the West underwent a series of upheavals that can be called revolutions, wars of independence, or civil wars
        1.  *Creoles* (American Spanish), *peninsulares* (Spanish or Portuguese natives), *mestizos* (mixed Spanish and Indian) and *mulattos* (mixed Spanish and black) fought the Spanish and one another
        2.  After 1850 millions of new immigrants flooded Latin America
    B.  The origins of the revolutions
        1.  By the late seventeenth century, the Spanish colonies had achieved much economic diversity and independence
            a.  Mercantilist imperialism of Spain had faded away
            b.  Intercolonial trade had grown, and dependence on Spain had lessened
        2.  Spain's new economic policies reversed this trend after the War of the Spanish Succession
            a.  Colonial manufacture and agriculture were taxed highly, and economic development was frustrated
            b.  Under Charles III, preference was shown to Spaniards in political offices — at the expense of the Creoles
            c.  Tax reforms aggravated colonial discontent
    C.  Race relations in the colonial period
        1.  Creoles did not extend the idea of "rights of man" to nonwhites
            a.  The lack of women led to mixed marriages of Indian, Spanish, and African blood
            b.  *Peninsulares* and *Creoles* held privileged status
            c.  Dark skin was a sign of servile manual labor
            d.  Indian majorities existed in Peru and Bolivia, whereas European majorities existed in Argentina and Chile
        2.  The Spanish controlled the economy
            a.  Indian land was taken by the Spanish as the Indians became slave laborers
            b.  Nevertheless, manumission was more frequent than in North America, and social mobility was not uncommon
            c.  Many black slaves fled to the jungles or mountains
            d.  Indians were subject to the *mita*, the *repartimiento*, and the new taxes of the 1770s and 1780s

D.  The Comunero Revolution
  1.  First, Amaru led an Indian uprising in Peru
    a.  The rebels demanded abolition of the *alcabala*, the *mita*, and Indian governors
    b.  The revolt was crushed by the Spanish but some reforms were granted
  2.  Revolution then occurred in Socorro in New Granada
    a.  Socorro had prospered as an agricultural and manufacturing center of Colombia
    b.  A large *mestizo* population existed
    c.  Tax increases and a new *alcabala* led to the Comunero Revolution
    d.  Creole captains led an Indian army on Bogotá
    e.  The government agreed to the rebels' demands but later pardoned the Creoles and turned against the rebels
E.  Independence
  1.  The removal of the Spanish king by Napoleon led to revolt in Latin America
    a.  The wealthy Creoles seized power for themselves
    b.  Otherwise, there was a variety of doctrines, leaders, and organization throughout Spanish America
    c.  Each separate area went its own way
    d.  Bolívar's dream of a continental union broke down
  2.  Only Brazil won its independence without violent upheaval
    a.  The Portuguese kings had fled to Brazil
    b.  King Pedro I proclaimed Brazil's independence in 1822
    c.  Factional disputes and separatist movements were not settled until Pedro II's reign
F.  The consequences of independence
  1.  The expulsion of the Spanish left a power vacuum filled by civic disorder
    a.  Creole inexperience in politics led to rule by military dictators
    b.  The dictator Rosas ruled in Argentina and Santa Anna, while other dictators ruled in Venezuela
    c.  Continual revolutions occurred in Bolivia and Venezuela
    d.  Economic prosperity was lost as warfare disrupted the economy
  2.  Slavery was abolished (except in Brazil and Cuba)
    a.  Most slaves were freed and were given legal equality but there was no redistribution of property
    b.  Blacks enjoyed greater economic and social mobility than in the United States
    c.  Some blacks, such as Guerrero, Flores, Santa Cruz, Guzman, and Castilla, led their countries

        d.  A three-tiered socioracial structure existed: white, colored, and black
        e.  Colored people gradually assimilated upward — partly due to the small number of poor whites
        f.  The mass of blacks continued to experience racism
  G.  Neocolonialism
     1.  The advent of stable dictatorship led to economic growth
        a.  Political stability encouraged foreign investment
        b.  British and American investment in Mexico and British investment in Brazil and Chile encouraged economic development — but at a high price
        c.  By 1900 foreigners — especially the British and Americans — controlled Latin American economies
        d.  Each economy revolved around one or two export products, making them overly vulnerable to world market changes
     2.  Demand for *hacienda* land, because of internal and export demand, led to further loss of land by the Indians
        a.  In Mexico the Diaz government encouraged appropriation of Indian land
        b.  The Indians were then exploited as laborers
        c.  Some argue that the hacienda owners, such as the Sanchez Navarros family in Mexico, were efficient capitalist enterprises
  H.  The impact of immigration
     1.  Argentina and other Latin American countries adopted Alberdi's idea that immigration was crucial, and many European countries, in turn, were overpopulated and promoted emigration
     2.  Italian, Spanish, and Portuguese people poured into Latin America
        a.  Cities like Buenos Aires grew rapidly and were cosmopolitan in nature
        b.  Immigrants worked hard and often lived in poverty in tenement dwellings known as *conventillos*
        c.  Many immigrants enjoyed upward mobility and imitated the lifestyle of the rich Europeans
     3.  This vast immigration changed the economy and society
        a.  Agriculture and industry grew
        b.  Immigrant men often married Indian women, thus advancing ethnic integration
        c.  Because nonblack immigrants controlled factory jobs, urban blacks were forced into unemployment or marginal employment and experienced racism
II.  The United States, ca 1789–1929
  A.  Manifest destiny

1. Many agreed with O'Sullivan that God had foreordained the United States to cover the entire continent
2. The United States pushed its borders across the continent
   a. During the colonial period, the Indians and the British blocked expansion westward to the Pacific
   b. The purchase of Louisiana from France, that of Florida from Spain, and the settlement of 1814 with Britain pushed the United States south, southwest, northwest, and to the Gulf Plains
   c. The absorption of Texas, an independent republic since 1836, led to a push further west and to war with Mexico
   d. President Polk's war with Mexico led to U.S. acquisition of California and New Mexico

B. The fate of the Indians
   1. Government treatment of the Indian population was wanton and cruel
      a. Trickery was used to obtain Indian land
      b. Indians were moved to reservations, where many of them died
      c. President Jackson refused to enforce the Supreme Court decision recognizing Cherokee Indian land rights

C. Black slavery in the South
   1. The liberal and democratic beliefs of the Americans conflicted with their devotion to black slavery
      a. Some argue that social prestige and political power were the reasons for slavery
      b. Economic historians show that economic gain was the main motive for slavery
   2. Slavery produced a considerable sense of guilt and psychological conflict among the planter class — particularly among women
      a. The conflict between religious beliefs and slaveholding produced deep psychological stresses
      b. Many white women of the South were abolitionists

D. Westward expansion and the Civil War
   1. The growth of the cotton industry raised the question of the further expansion of slavery
   2. Lincoln's election caused South Carolina (and then other states) to secede from the Union in 1860
   3. Lincoln became a spokesman for the antislavery and free-labor movements
      a. However, he wanted to conduct the Civil War for the preservation of the status quo
      b. Pressures to win the war brought Lincoln to declare the Emancipation Proclamation

       c.   The Proclamation freed slaves only in the rebel states

       d.   It transformed the war into a moral crusade for all Americans

   4.   The shortage of American cotton led English textile manufacturers to secure cotton outside of the southern United States

   5.   The war had important political consequences in Europe

       a.   The English masses used the North's victory as a signal for democracy over the aristocracy

       b.   The Civil War was the first modern war

   6.   "Reconstruction" (1865–1877) of the South saw slavery disappear, but there was no practical application of social-legal equality or suffrage

       a.   Lacking cash, blacks became poor sharecroppers

       b.   Despite the Fifteenth Amendment, whites used violence and Jim Crow laws to keep blacks from their rights

E.  The black family

   1.   In spite of slavery, blacks established strong family units

       a.   Most slave couples had long marriages

       b.   Slave owners encouraged slave marriage and large families

       c.   Separated couples tried to maintain the family unit

       d.   Slave women fought to retain their marriage choice of sexual partners, and they frequently used abortion to limit family size

       e.   Sexual activity outside of marriage was rare among slave women

       f.   Until the 1920s, most black households were headed by two parents

F.  Industrialization and immigration

   1.   Following the Civil War, the United States underwent an industrial boom

       a.   Government land turned over to the railroads encouraged industrial expansion

       b.   The entry of millions of new immigrants met the labor needs of growing industry

       c.   Cheap farm land in the West encouraged cultivation by pioneers

       d.   Immigration led to rapid urbanization — nearly 40 percent of the population was urban by 1900

       e.   New inventions, large factories, and manufacturing techniques (such as Ford's assembly line) led to increased production and new ways of living

       f.   Depressions led to huge trusts and monopolies

       g.   Employers constantly tried to cut labor costs and they often neglected worker safety

   2.   Urbanization brought serious problems

       1.   Riis's investigation pointed to the sordidness of slum life for many new immigrants

   b. Anti-immigrant prejudices — largely against non-Anglo-Saxons, Catholics, and Orientals — arose among Americans born here

   c. Economic depression in the 1890s meant unemployment, exploitation of workers, and industrial unrest

   d. Racist immigration laws established quotas on some groups and completely restricted others

  3. The notion of "manifest destiny" and the process of urbanization and industrialization led to U.S. intervention in the Philippines, Cuba, and elsewhere in Latin America

   a. The United States acquired Cuba and the Philippines as a result of the Spanish-American War of 1898

   b. The United States practiced intervention in Latin America on numerous occasions — including in Nicaragua in 1926 to bolster conservative governments

III. Canada: from colony to nation

 A. Colonization and conflict

  1. Frenchman Samuel de Champlain established a trading post in 1608 on site of present-day Quebec; the colony of New France was founded

  2. British challenged French for control of lucrative fur trade, initiating the "French and Indian Wars"

  3. British defeated French in 1759 on the Plains of Abraham, ending the French Empire in North America; by the Treaty of Paris of 1763, France ceded Canada to Great Britain

 B. Colonial government

  1. British Parliament passed the Quebec Act of 1774, placing power in hands of appointed governor and council and denying Canadians a legislature

  2. Civil discontent led to the Constitution Act of 1791, which divided Canada into Lower and Upper Canada; though the Act provided for elective assemblies in both provinces, it gave the governor and his council the right to veto assembly decisions

  3. British Parliament appointed Lord Durham to recommend reforms when open rebellion broke out in Upper and Lower Canada in 1837

 C. Age of confederation, 1841–1867

  1. Lord Durham's *Report on the Affairs of British North America* led to the Union Act of 1840, which united Lower and Upper Canada under one government composed of a governor, an appointed legislative council (cabinet), and an elective assembly

  2. The British North America Act of 1867 brought the Canadian constitution to its modern form; the Dominion of Canada was established

   a. Dominion cabinet received complete jurisdiction over internal affairs; Britain retained control over foreign policy

   b. John A. Macdonald became Dominion's first prime minister

D.  Expansion and Development
    1.  Under Macdonald, Canada expanded to include all of northern North America (1868–1873)
    2.  Canadian Pacific Railroad opened November 7, 1885
    3.  Between 1897 and 1912, a wave of immigrants arrived in Canada, French Canadians resisted assimilation
    4.  Supported by population growth, Canada experienced an agricultural and industrial boom between 1891 and 1914
E.  Participation in World War I
    1.  Canadians powerfully supported Allied cause
    2.  The Imperial War Cabinet, composed of chief British ministers and prime ministers of the Dominion, was established
    3.  Canada received in 1918 the right to participate in the Versailles Peace Conference and in the League of Nations

## REVIEW QUESTIONS

Q-1.  Describe how the Spanish economic policies of Charles III affected Spanish America.

Q-2.  What were the Spanish attitudes toward nonwhites, and how were their attitudes incorporated into colonial society?

Q-3.  The upheavals in the Spanish colonies have been described as revolutions, wars of independence, and civil wars. Why? What are the differences among the three?

Q-4.  How and why did racial mixing and freedom for slaves come about?

Q-5.  Why did the revolutions in Peru and Colombia (Socorro) take place? What were the outcomes?

Q-6.  How and why did the independence movement occur in Latin America? What roles did Bolívar and King Pedro I play?

Q-7.  Why did military dictatorships evolve, and what were their effects on the economy?

Q-8.  Describe how the abolition of slavery affected the blacks of Latin America.

Q-9.  Discuss how foreign immigration affected the new independent states of Latin America in terms of the economy and the racial structure of society.

Q-10.  Define and describe the notion of "manifest destiny." What were its origins, and what results did it produce?

Q-11.  By citing examples, explain, in general, the U.S. government attitude and policy toward native Americans.

Q-12.  What were the motives for slavery in the United States?

Q-13.  Explain why a U.S. liberal democrat in the early nineteenth century could also be a slave owner. What was the impact of this dilemma on society?

Q-14.  Describe how slavery affected the black family. How accurately do the facts fit heretofore-accepted notions of slaves' family life and sexuality?

Q-15.  What was the effect of "Reconstruction" on blacks in the United States? Had racial discrimination disappeared?

Q-16.  The urbanization and industrialization that followed the Civil War brought growth as well as serious problems. Explain.

Q-17.  What were the causes of U.S. intervention in Latin America? Give some examples and discuss the effects that intervention had on Latin American politics.

Q-18.  Why did the Quebec Act prove unpopular in Canada? What reforms in colonial government did the British proceed to make?

## STUDY-REVIEW EXERCISES

*Define the following key concepts and terms.*

alcabala

mita

repartimiento

peninsulares

Creoles

mestizo

conventillos

hacienda

manifest destiny

*Identify each of the following and give its significance.*

Charles III of Spain

Comunero Revolution

Tupac Amaru

Simon Bolívar

Pedro I of Portugal

Juan Bautista Alberdi

Emancipation Proclamation

frontier women in the American West

Chinese Exclusion Act of 1882

Jacob Riis, *How the Other Half Lives* (1890)

Treaty of Guadalupe Hidalgo (1848)

Spanish-American War of 1898

Louisiana Purchase

Toussaint L'Ouverture

Jim Crow laws

Lord Durham

John A. Macdonald


*Test your understanding of the chapter by answering the following questions.*

1.  The people of Spanish descent born in America were known as

    _____,

    whereas the natives of Spain and Portugal were called the

    _____.

2.  In his effort to make himself emperor of Europe, Napoleon indirectly *encouraged/discouraged* independence movements in Latin America.
3.  During the colonial period, nonwhites in Latin America experienced *more/less* social mobility than those in North America.

4. The Comunero Revolution was led by (a) Creoles, (b) Indians, (c) peninsulares,

   (d) King Pedro I. _____

5. Generally, the vast immigration from Europe had a(n) *favorable/unfavorable*
   impact on the blacks of Latin America.

6. The countries that led the way in foreign investment in Latin America were

   _____ and _____ .

7. Most slave couples in the United States had *long/short* marriages, and sexual
   activity outside of marriage among slave women was *common/rare*.

8. The Emancipation Proclamation of President Lincoln (a) freed all slaves,

   (b) freed the slaves only in rebel states. _____

9. From slaveholding times until the 1920s, a large majority of black families were
   headed by *one/two* parent(s).

10. The man whose book *How the Other Half Lives* brought many people to
    recognize the wretchedness of life for immigrants in New York was

    _____ .

11. French Canadians *did/did not* resist assimilation with the immigrants who
    arrived in Canada in the late nineteenth century.

## MULTIPLE-CHOICE QUESTIONS

1. The *Creoles* were
   a. persons of mixed Spanish-Indian blood.
   b. Americans of Spanish ancestry.
   c. Indians who absorbed European culture.
   d. the ruling class in Spanish America.

2. In the late eighteenth century, most government posts in Latin America were
   held by
   a. *peninsulares.*
   b. mestizos.
   c. mulattos.
   d. Creoles.

3. Spanish colonies resented the imposition of taxes without
   a. arbitration.
   b. consultation.
   c. representation.
   d. legislation.

4. Social status in Spanish America depended on
   a. wealth.
   b. titles of nobility.
   c. religion.
   d. racial background.

5. The majority of the population in Latin America was
   a. Indian.
   b. mestizo.
   c. European.
   d. Creole.

6. The independence movement in Latin America
   a. intended a radical redistribution of property.
   b. sought to give rights to the Indians.
   c. fought to eliminate Spanish rule.
   d. desired to place a Creole king on the throne.

7. The Latin American wars of independence ended with
   a. the election of the South American constitutional convention.
   b. a chaotic political situation.
   c. Spanish recognition of the new nations.
   d. Bolívar's election to the presidency.

8. The typical Latin American nation of the nineteenth century was a
   a. monarchy.
   b. democratic republic.
   c. republic ruled by a dictator.
   d. totalitarian state.

9. Nonwhites in Latin America
   a. had ample opportunity to rise socially.
   b. could rise economically but seldom socially.
   c. could not get ahead unless they "passed" for white.
   d. might rise socially if they were light-skinned.

10. Large-scale development of Latin American economies began when
    a. oil was discovered.
    b. foreign investment started.
    c. slavery was abolished.
    d. dictators introduced economic planning.

11. A serious economic weakness in South America was
    a. dependence on imported food.
    b. the possibility of U.S. intervention.
    c. dependence on one or two products.
    d. the use of domestic capital.

12. The term *manifest destiny* refers to the
    a. belief that the United States was destined to cover the continent.
    b. Confederacy's justification for southern independence.
    c. reason that the United States purchased Louisiana.
    d. belief that blacks were destined to be slaves.

13. The author of this text argues that
    a. slavery was not profitable.
    b. slaves were kept for reasons of prestige.
    c. slaveholders were aristocrats, not businessmen.
    d. slavery was profitable business.

14. The experience of slavery led to
    a. a weak family structure among blacks.
    b. a strong family tradition among blacks.
    c. a pattern of fatherless families among blacks.
    d. marriages of short duration among blacks.

15. Immigrants to the United States most often
    a. settled on western farms.
    b. found employment in urban industries.
    c. had difficulty finding work.
    d. worked in the mines.

16. Experiences on the U.S. frontier led to
    a. increased differentiation of sex roles.
    b. the belief that women were morally superior.
    c. a contempt for the arts as effeminate.
    d. a blurring of the sex roles.

17. The assembly line became popular because
    a. quality was more important than quantity.
    b. quantity was more important than quality.
    c. industrialists wanted interchangeable workers.
    d. industrialists like to use interchangeable parts.

18. One explanation suggested for the recurring economic depressions of the nineteenth century is
    a. strikes.
    b. overproduction.
    c. unsound monetary policy.
    d. legalization of trusts.

19. The immigrants most disliked by nativist Americans were the
    a. Roman Catholics.
    b. Slavics.
    c. Chinese.
    d. Jews.

20. The insurrections in nineteenth-century Latin America were
    a. wars of independence.
    b. civil wars.
    c. wars of revolution.
    d. all of the above

21. *Peninsulares* were
    a. natives.
    b. whites born in the Americas.
    c. mulattos.
    d. native-born Spanish or Portuguese.

22. The Comunero and Tupac Amaru rebellions
    a. were total successes.
    b. were put down, yet led to some reforms.
    c. failed utterly.
    d. ended in even more severe treatement of the Indians.

23. Brazil's independence was
    a. secured peacefully by royal proclamation.
    b. obtained by treaty with Portugal.
    c. won in a bloody civil war.
    d. won by Bolívar.

24. In the late nineteenth century,
    a. land reform gave farms to millions of Indians.
    b. many Indians lost their land to corrupt businessmen.
    c. foreign capitalists bought up huge tracts of land.
    d. the Mexican government nationalized vacant lands.

25. Methods of operation on the *haciendas*
    a. were inefficient and old-fashioned.
    b. were businesslike and efficient.
    c. were the reason for high corn prices.
    d. are disputed by scholars.

26. Juan Bautista Alberdi advocated immigration for Argentina because
    a. the nation's labor supply was totally inadequate.
    b. Indians and blacks lacked basic skills.
    c. the constitution required it.
    d. he wished that the nation would become predominantly white.

27. The vast majority of immigrants to Argentina were
    a. family groups.
    b. unmarried males.
    c. skilled workers.
    d. northern Europeans.

28. Which of the following is *not* a reason that blacks could seldom obtain urban industrial jobs in Latin America?
    a. The lacked basic skills.
    b. Immigrants would work for lower wages.
    c. Whites were racially prejudiced.
    d. Their backgrounds were usually rural.

29. California became part of the United States as a result of the
    a. Louisiana Purchase.
    b. Treaty of Ghent.
    c. Mexican War.
    d. War of 1812.

30. It may be generally said of the American Indians that they
    a. were bloodthirsty savages.
    b. were fairly compensated for their lands.
    c. endured terrible treatment at the hands of whites.
    d. went to war out of a desire for revenge.

31. South Carolina seceded from the Union because
    a. Lincoln wanted to free the slaves.
    b. Fort Sumter had been fired on.
    c. Lincoln had been elected president.
    d. it wished to form a Southern Confederacy.

33.  John A. Macdonald's crowning achievement was
     a.  his *Report on the Affairs of British North America.*
     b.  the opening of the Canadian Pacific Railroad.
     c.  the defeat of the French on the Plains of Abraham in 1759.
     d.  his championship of the Constitution Act of 1796.


## GEOGRAPHY

1.  Study Map 31.2. Referring to the text when necessary, answer the following
    questions:
    a.  Name the present-day countries that made up the Spanish viceroyalties
        of Peru, New Granada, and La Plata. Draw all of these areas on the accom-
        panying outline map.




    b.  In the space below, describe the products that were exported by these areas
        to Spain. What affect did the French revolutionary and Napoleonic wars have on
        on Spain's administration of its colonies?







    c.  Indicate the location of the Suarez River and Bogotà in New Granada. In
        the space below, describe the sequence of events that made up the Com-
        unero Revolution.

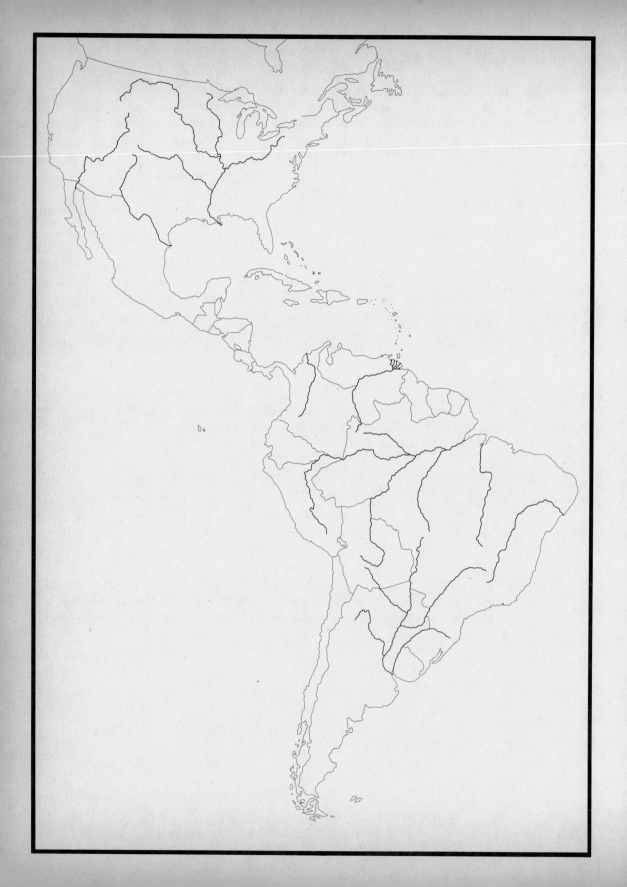

2.  Using Map 31.1 in the text as your guide, answer the following questions
    as you locate the appropriate areas:
    a.  What was the economic, political, and social importance of Buenos Aires
        in the era after independence was gained?

    b.  What were the countries which received their independence through the
        leadership of Simon Bolívar? Why did Bolívar say that "America is
        ungovernable"?

## UNDERSTANDING HISTORY THROUGH READING AND THE ARTS

Photography has greatly aided the historian in the documentation of work and
life in the new industrial societies that emerged out of the nineteenth century.
When Jacob Riis began his investigation of the underprivileged living in the crime-
ridden slums of New York's Lower East Side, he turned to the camera to supplement the printed word. Riis was one of the first Americans to use flashlight power.
Seventeen of his startling photographs were printed in his book *How the Other
Half Lives* (1890) and have been reprinted in *U.S. Camera 1948* (1948). Other
glimpses of urban life by Riis came in his second book, *Children of the Poor* (1895).
The best history of photography is Beaumont Newhall, *The History of Photography*
(fifth edition, 1982).

## PROBLEMS FOR FURTHER INVESTIGATION

Students interested in the age of nation-state in Latin America may want to begin
with an examination of the life and work of Simon Bolívar — the man responsible

for the creation of the five modern states of Venezuela, Colombia, Ecuador, Bolivia, and Peru. A good short biography that includes relevant primary source reading is J. Johnson's *Simon Bolivar and Spanish American Independence, 1783-1830* (1968). One of the first comprehensive accounts of the evolution of racial mixture and racial acculturation in Latin America is M. Morner's *Race Mixture in the History of Latin America* (1967). For further study of nation-building in Canada, see the highly readable account by R. Cook, *Canada: A Modern Study* (1971). Another sound survey of Canadian history, which emphasizes cultural developments, is K. McNaught, *The Pelican History of Canada** (1976).

*Available in paperback.

# CHAPTER 32

## THE GREAT BREAK: WAR AND REVOLUTION

## CHAPTER OBJECTIVES

After reading and studying this chapter you should be able to answer the following questions:

Q-1.   What were the causes of the First World War?
Q-2.   How and why did the war have such enormous and destructive consequences?
Q-3.   How did the war affect the ways in which people lived and thought?

## CHAPTER SYNOPSIS

The First World War had enormous and destructive consequences. Western civilization would never be the same again — as the war caused not only death and destruction, but a variety of revolutions as well. The First World War was long and destructive, opening a new era in European history. This chapter shows how and why this was so. Beginning with the system of alliances that had formed two hostile military blocs by 1914, the author shows how nationalism and fears of nationalism touched off a world war in 1914. Contrary to expectations, the First World War became a ghastly military stalemate. The stalemate forced each government to make a total war effort, which demanded great sacrifices and major social changes. Economic life was strictly controlled, women entered defense plants, and nationalistic propaganda strengthened genuine popular support for the war. By 1916, however, there was growing discontent and war weariness in all countries.

Russia broke first under the enormous strains of total war. In March 1917, a moderate patriotic revolution established a Russian republic. In November 1917, Lenin and the Bolsheviks took power in a socialist revolution. Lenin was a dedicated revolutionary who had reinterpreted Marxism in a radical way before 1914, and he took Russia out of the war and established a harsh dictatorship. This dictatorship allowed the Bolshevik government to survive and to defeat many different foes in a bloody civil war. Revolution also occurred in Germany and Austria. Germany established a republic, and Austria-Hungary broke into pieces. In 1919, the world of 1914 lay in ruins, due to the impact of total war and radical revolution. Nor did the peace settlement of Versailles bring stability, since the defeated Germans hated the peace treaty and the victorious Americans rejected it.

## STUDY OUTLINE

I. The First World War (1914–1918)
   A. The Bismarckian system of alliances
      1. Germany was the powerful European country after 1871
      2. Bismarck sought to guarantee European peace through alliances
      3. The Three Emperors' League (Austria, Russia, and Germany) was created (1873) to maintain the status quo
      4. Because of tensions with France, Italy joined Germany and Austria to form the Triple Alliance (1882)
      5. In 1887, the Russian-German Reinsurance Treaty promised neutrality by each state if the other was attacked
   B. The rival blocs
      1. William II's termination of the German-Russian Reinsurance Treaty led to a new Russian-French alliance
      2. Under William II, the British-German "natural alliance" deteriorated into a rivalry
         a. The Boer War, German envy of British imperialism, and economic and military rivalry drove the British and the Germans apart
         b. Then Britain turned to France and formed the Anglo-French Entente of 1904, which further alienated Germany
      3. As a result, Germany became increasingly distrustful, and other European countries began to see Germany as a threat
   C. The outbreak of war (August 1914)
      1. Nationalism in the Balkans threatened the Ottoman Empire and European peace
      2. Independence was acquired by Serbia, Rumania, and part of Bulgaria in 1878
      3. Austria's annexation of Bosnia in 1908 greatly angered Serbia, which was forced to turn southward in its nationalistic desire to expand, and so began the first Balkan War (1912)
      4. The Balkan wars of 1912–1913 were a victory for Balkan nationalism
      5. The assassination of the Austrian archduke Francis Ferdinand (1914) resulted in a Balkan war between Serbia and Austria

    6. Germany gave Austria full support in her foreign policy

    7. Military considerations dictated policy, and an all-European war resulted

  D. Reflections on the origins of the war

    1. With German support, Austria was the immediate cause

    2. Germany's failure to keep Bismarck's system of alliances was fateful

    3. Nationalism contributed to war fever

    4. All the European leaders underestimated the consequences of war

  E. The first battle of the Marne (September 1914)

    1. The original plan — a German invasion of France through Belgium — had to be altered when British troops landed to help the Belgians

    2. The battle of the Marne turned the war into a long stalemate

  F. Stalemate and slaughter

    1. A line of trenches stretched from the Belgian coast to Switzerland

    2. Trench warfare meant much horrible death but no end to the war

    3. The war's horrors caused a profound disillusionment with society and mankind

  G. The widening war

    1. Despite huge Austrian losses, Austria and Germany defeated Russia and Serbia on the eastern front (1914–1915)

    2. Italy and Bulgaria entered the war (1915)

    3. With Arab help Britain defeated the Ottoman Empire (1918)

    4. The United States entered the war in 1917 because of German submarine warfare

II. The home front

  A. Mobilizing for total war

    1. Most people saw the war in nationalistic terms

    2. Total war meant that economic planning was necessary

    3. This control of economic and social life ultimately strengthened socialist ideas

    4. In Germany, food and raw materials were rationed and universal draft was initiated, but war profits were not taxed

  B. The social impact

    1. Labor shortages brought about benefits for organized labor

    2. The role of women changed dramatically as many women entered the labor force

     a. Some women gained equal pay for equal work, and the right to vote was applied to women in Britain, Germany, and Austria

     b. Women displayed a growing spirit of independence

    3. War brought about greater social equality

  C. Growing political tensions

    1. Wartime propaganda was widespread

      2.  By 1916, people were growing weary of war; morale had declined

      3.  Demands for social reform and national self-determination re-emerged

III.  The Russian Revolution (1917)

    A.  The fall of imperial Russia

      1.  War losses and mistakes pointed to the incompetence of the tsar and the Russian government

      2.  Tsar Nicholas II's poor leadership contributed to military defeat

      3.  The Duma sought a more responsive and democratic government

      4.  The influence of Rasputin on the royal family further weakened the government and created a national scandal

      5.  Food shortages led to revolution in March 1917

          a.  A provisional government was proclaimed by the parliament (Duma)

          b.  The tsar abdicated

    B.  The provisional government (March 1917)

      1.  After the March Revolution, Russia became the freest country in the world

      2.  Yet the new revolutionary government, led by Kerensky, wanted to postpone land reform, fearing it would further weaken the peasant army; the continuation of the war was Kerensky's primary concern

      3.  The provisional government had to share power with the Petrograd Soviet (council) of Workers' and Soldiers' Deputies

          a.  The Petrograd Soviet's Army Order No. 1 placed military authority into the hands of the ordinary soldiers

          b.  Army discipline broke down completely, and massive desertions began

      4.  Liberty was rapidly turning into anarchy

    C.  Lenin and the Bolshevik Revolution

      1.  Lenin believed that revolution was necessary to destroy capitalism

      2.  He also believed that Marxist revolution could occur in Russia if led by an intellectual elite

      3.  Russian Marxists became divided over Lenin's theories

          a.  Lenin's Bolsheviks demanded a small, disciplined, elitist party

          b.  The Mensheviks wanted a democratic party with mass membership

      4.  Lenin led an attack against the provisional government in July 1917, but it failed and he went into hiding

      5.  Kerensky's power was weakened by an attack on the provisional government by his commander in chief, Kornilov, and he lost favor with the army

    D.  Trotsky and the seizure of power

      1.  A radical Marxist and supporter of Lenin, Trotsky centered his power in the Petrograd Soviet

      2.  Trotsky engineered a Soviet overthrow of the provisional government (November 1917)

E. Dictatorship and civil war
1. Lenin gave approval to the peasants' seizure of land and the urban workers' takeover of the factories
2. Lenin arranged for an end of the war with Germany, but at a high price: the sacrifice of all of Russia's western territories (the Treaty of Brest-Litovsk, 1918)
3. Opposition to the Bolsheviks led to civil war (1918–1921)
   a. The officers of the old army (the Whites) organized the opposition to the Bolsheviks (the Reds)
   b. The Whites came from many social groups and wanted self-rule, not Bolshevik dictatorship
4. The Bolshevik victory in the civil war was due to a number of factors: unity, a better army, a well-defined political program, mobilization of the home front, an effective secret police force, and an appeal to nationalism in the face of foreign aid to the Whites
5. World War I brought on the Russian Revolution, which signaled the rise of world communism
IV. The peace settlement (1918–1919)
A. The end of the war
1. By early 1917, the German populace was weary of war, and the German army was decisively defeated in the second battle of the Marne
2. The Allies were strengthened by U.S. intervention
3. The German military arranged for a new liberal German government to accept defeat, but it tried to bargain for an advantageous settlement
4. German soldiers and workers began to demonstrate for peace, and Germany surrendered (1918)
B. Revolution in Germany
1. Revolution in Austria-Hungary led to the breakup of the Austro-Hungarian Empire into new national states
2. Revolution in Germany led to a socialist government
3. Moderate German socialists attacked the radical socialists, who then founded the German Communist party
C. The Treaty of Versailles
1. President Wilson advocated national self-determination and the creation of a League of Nations to avert future wars
2. Clemenceau of France and Lloyd George of England were more interested in permanently weakening Germany and making it pay for the war; Clemenceau wanted a buffer state between France and Germany
3. The conflicting desires of the Allies led to a deadlock and finally a compromise
   a. France gave up its demand for a protective buffer state in return for a defensive alliance with Britain and the United States

      b.  The League of Nations was created

    4.  Germany lost her colonies and territory in Europe — largely Alsace-Lorraine to France and Danzig and eastern land to Poland

    5.  Germany had to admit responsibility for the war and thus pay enormous damages

    6.  Austria-Hungary and Turkey were the big losers in the separate peace treaties; the principle of self-determination still applied only to Europeans, and thus Western imperialism lived on

D.  U.S. rejection of the Versailles Treaty

    1.  World peace rested on

        a.  The success of upholding the principle of national self-determination

        b.  The success of the new democratic German government

        c.  U.S. support of the Western alliance — including the League of Nations, which the United States refused to join

    2.  President Wilson refused to accept any Senate modifications to the treaty, so it was never ratified, and the Senate also refused to ratify the defensive alliance with France

    3.  France felt bitterly betrayed by its allies, the United States and Britain

E.  World War I had revolutionary consequences

    1.  The war was a result of nationalism

    2.  The war swept away monarchs and multinational empires, and national self-determination triumphed

    3.  The war brought on the Russian Revolution

    4.  It ushered in a new age that saw the increased presence of government in everyday life, more economic planning, and greater social equality

## REVIEW QUESTIONS

**Q-1.**  Discuss the motives and interests of each of the Great Powers between 1871 and 1914.

**Q-2.**  What was the purpose of the German-Russian Reinsurance Treaty? Why did it end in 1890 and with what results?

**Q-3.**  What were the reasons for Britain and Germany's so-called love-hate relationship?

**Q-4.**  Why was the Moroccan crisis of 1905 a turning point in European diplomacy?

**Q-5.**  What impact did the Congress of Berlin (1878) have on the Balkan area? Who was bound to be the loser in the Balkans?

**Q-6.**  Describe the origins and causes of the "third Balkan war" in 1914.

**Q-7.**  Which of the major powers do you believe most responsible and least responsible for the war? Explain.

**Q-8.**  How did the war affect the economy and the people at home? How cooperative was the population?

Q-9.   How did the war affect the power of organized labor? Women in society?

Q-10.   "The war tended to have an equalizing effect on society." Explain.

Q-11.   What evidence is there that the strain of war was beginning to take its toll on the home front in Russia, Austria, France, and Germany by 1916?

Q-12.   What were the reasons for the Russian Revolution in March 1917? Was revolution inevitable?

Q-13.   What were the soviets? What role did they play in the Bolshevik Revolution?

Q-14.   What was it about Lenin's character that made him a successful revolutionary? Why were his ideas popular with peasants and urban workers?

Q-15.   Why did Kerensky and the provisional government fail?

Q-16.   What were the reasons for the Bolshevik victory in the civil war?

Q-17.   Were there one, two, or many Russian revolutions in 1917? Explain.

Q-18.   What happened to the Austro-Hungarian and Turkish empires after 1918?

Q-19.   What were the goals of Wilson, Lloyd George, and Clemenceau at the Versailles peace conference?

Q-20.   The Treaty of Versailles is often seen as a major reason for the Second World War. Do you agree? Why?

Q-21.   Compare and contrast the Versailles settlement of 1919 with the Vienna settlement of 1815. What similarities do you see? What were the most striking differences?

Q-22.   What were the revolutionary consequences of the First World War?


## STUDY-REVIEW EXERCISES

*Explain* who or what each of the following was and what role each played in the Russian Revolution.

Petrograd Soviet

Leon Trotsky

Petrograd bread riots (1917)

Congress of the Soviets

Kiev mutiny (1918)

Alexander Kerensky

Vladimir Lenin

Army Order No. 1

Constituent Assembly

White opposition

Treaty of Brest-Litovsk (1918)

*Number the following events in Russian history in chronological order.*

1. _____    Marx writes the *Communist Manifesto*

2. _____    Lenin's return from Switzerland

3. _____    The establishment of the provisional government

4. _____    The outbreak of war between Russia and Germany

5. _____    The Kornilov plot

6. _____    The abolishment of the Constituent Assembly

7. _____    The overthrow of Kerensky and the provisional government

8. _____    American, British, and Russian invasion of Archangel and Vladivostok

*Define the following key concepts and terms.*

German War Plan of 1914

"total war"

totalitarian

first battle of the Marne

"blank check" policy

western front

Bolsheviks

"war communism"

principle of national self-determination

war reparations

Treaty of Versailles

League of Nations

*Identify* each of the following and give its significance.

Lawrence of Arabia

Reinsurance Treaty

Algeciras Conference of 1906

Anglo-French Entente of 1904

Third Balkan War (1914)

*Lusitania*

Admiral Tirpitz

(German) Auxiliary Service Law of 1916

David Lloyd George

Rasputin

Francis Ferdinand

Georges Clemenceau

Duma

British Ministry of Munitions

*Test your understanding of the chapter by answering the following questions.*

1.  Germany violated the neutrality of _____
    in 1914.

2.  _____ was exiled to Siberia for
    socialist agitation.

3.  The date of the assassination of Archduke Francis Ferdinand was

    _____.

4.  The president of the Russian revolutionary provisional government was

    _____.

5.  Russian workers' councils were called _____.

6.  The Arab princes were roused to revolt in 1917 by

    _____.

7.  The treaty between the Germans and the Russian Bolshevik government in 1918

    was called _____.

8.  The German chancellor fired by William II was

    _____.

9.  A Serbian revolutionary group was named

    _____.

## MULTIPLE-CHOICE QUESTIONS

1.  The Bismarckian system of alliances was meant to
    a.  expand Germany's borders.
    b.  help German allies expand their borders.
    c.  restrain Russia and Austria-Hungary and isolate France.
    d.  encourage relations with France.

2.  Which group of events is in chronological order?
    a.  The Three Emperors' League, the Alliance of the Three Emperors, the
        Russian-German Reinsurance Treaty
    b.  The Russian-German Reinsurance Treaty, the Alliance of the Three
        Emperors, the Three Emperors' League

c.  The Alliance of the Three Emperors, the Russian-German Reinsurance Treaty, the Three Emperors' League
d.  The Russian-German Reinsurance Treaty, the Three Emperors' League, the Alliance of the Three Emperors

3.  The German war plan was to knock out
    a.  England by marching through France.
    b.  Russia by marching through Poland.
    c.  France by marching through Belgium.
    d.  Belgium by marching through France.

4.  The end of the war in 1918 brought revolution to which of the following countries?
    a.  France and Britain
    b.  Germany and Italy
    c.  Germany and Austria-Hungary
    d.  France and Italy

5.  The phrase that best describes Bismarck's attitude toward German expansion after 1871 is
    a.  German control of all Europe.
    b.  the annexation of Austria-Hungary to Germany.
    c.  no territorial ambitions.
    d.  a great German navy and German colonies.

6.  The young Emperor William II of Germany made the fateful decision to reverse Bismarck's foreign policy by refusing to renew the treaty between Germany and
    a.  Austria.
    b.  Britain.
    c.  France.
    d.  Russia.

7.  As a result of the Moroccan crisis, European powers viewed which of the following countries as a threat to peace and stability?
    a.  France
    b.  Germany
    c.  Britain
    d.  Japan

8.  The countries with the most at stake in the Balkans and most fearful of nationalism were
    a.  Germany and Austria.

b.  France and Turkey.

c.  Turkey and Austria.

d.  Russia and Germany.

9.  The first country to mobilize in 1914 for general warfare was
    a.  France.
    b.  Germany.
    c.  Russia.
    d.  Britain.

10. The chief feature of the war on the western front was
    a.  inconclusive battles fought in ceaseless trench warfare.
    b.  the invasion of Germany by French and British troops.
    c.  a series of German victories at the German-French border.
    d.  a propaganda war with little actual fighting.

11. The major impact of World War I on economic thought was the
    a.  promotion of government planning and involvement in the economy.
    b.  strengthening of capitalism based on laissez-faire principles.
    c.  reaffirmation of imperialism.
    d.  proof that civilizn populations were unimportant to the war economy.

12. For women in European society, the First World War brought about
    a.  overall economic and political improvement.
    b.  some economic gains but no political gains.
    c.  a setback in the struggle for women's rights.
    d.  a deterioration of their economic position.

13. The Petrograd Soviet's "Army Order No. 1" resulted in
    a.  a renewed and effective war effort.
    b.  a complete breakdown of army discipline.
    c.  increased authority of the Russian military elite.
    d.  large numbers of new recruits.

14. As a result of the Treaty of Brest-Litovsk, Russia
    a.  acquired considerable territory.
    b.  re-entered the war on the German side.
    c.  agreed to spread the revolution to western Europe.
    d.  lost one-third of its population.

15. The most anti-German of the major power representatives at the Versailles treaty conference in 1919 was

    a.  Clemenceau of France.
    b.  Lloyd George of Britain.
    c.  Wilson of the United States.
    d.  Orlando of Italy.

16.  The Austrian annexation of Bosnia and Herzegovina resulted in a direct threat to the national aspirations of
    a.  Italy.
    b.  Serbia.
    c.  Germany.
    d.  Turkey.

17.  Austria-Hungary's decision to go to war against Serbia was in large part due to
    a.  German encouragement of Austria and their pledge of unlimited support.
    b.  the Russian pledge of neutrality.
    c.  the French pledge of neutrality.
    d.  British support.

18.  Before World War I started, the German chancellor believed that Britain would
    a.  remain neutral.
    b.  join the Germans against Russia.
    c.  prevent France from invading Germany.
    d.  side against Germany.

19.  The Russian parliament that Nicholas adjourned in 1914 was
    a.  Soviet.
    b.  a provisional government.
    c.  the Duma.
    d.  Petrograd.

20.  The Bolshevik war commisar was
    a.  Lenin.
    b.  Trotsky.
    c.  Kornilov.
    d.  Kerensky.

21.  The Russian who was called "our Friend Grigori" by Tsarina Alexandra was
    a.  Rasputin.
    b.  Kerensky.
    c.  Lenin.
    d.  Kornilov.

22. The heir to the Russian throne suffered from
    a. polio.
    b. multiple sclerosis.
    c. leukemia.
    d. hemophilia.

23. Control over Iraq and Palestine was gained in 1919 by
    a. Britain.
    b. France.
    c. the United States.
    d. the Soviet Union.

24. As a result of the First World War
    a. the world economy became more integrated.
    b. the power of government decreased.
    c. greater social equality arose.
    d. national self-determination was defeated.

25. In regard to the Treaty of Versailles and the League of Nations the United States
    a. ratified the treaty and went on to play a more important role in Europe through the League.
    b. ratified the treaty but failed to participate fully in the League.
    c. did not ratify the treaty but entered the League anyway.
    d. did not ratify the treaty and failed to join the League.

26. Around the turn of the century, the policy of "splendid isolation" was abandoned by
    a. the United States.
    b. Germany.
    c. Italy.
    d. Great Britain.

27. During the First World War, the Ottoman Turks
    a. remained neutral.
    b. remained neutral until the United States entered the war.
    c. were allied with Germany.
    d. were allied with the Greeks and Serbians against Austria-Hungary.

28. The United States entered the First World War
    a. at its beginning.
    b. within a few months after it began.

c.  almost one and one-half years after it began.
d.  almost three years after it began.

## GEOGRAPHY

1.  Study Maps 32.1 and 32.2. Referring to the text when necessary, answer the following questions.
    a.  Using Map 32.2, describe the ethnic make-up of the Balkans.

    b.  Locate the extent of Ottoman (Turkish) control in the Balkans in 1878 and in 1914. Describe how and why it lost territory.

    c.  What were the territorial ambitions of Serbia and Austria-Hungary in the Balkans?

2.  Study Map 32.2. Referring to the text when necessary, answer the following questions.
    a.  What was the western front and where did it exist? Compare it with the eastern front.

b.  Locate the following important battles of the First World War: Gallipoli, Passchendaele, Tannenberg, and Verdun. In each case, who fought, what was the outcome, and was the significance?

3.  Study Map 32.4 to understand some of the changes brought by the First World War. Answer the following questions.
   a.  Locate the Polish corridor, Alsace and Lorraine, the three new Baltic states, and Galicia. What happened to each of these areas because of the First World War, and what was the significance?

   b.  Locate the demilitarized zone along the Rhine. How did this strengthen the French military position?

   c.  Locate the territorial losses experienced by the three great empires — Germany, Austria, and Russia. How did the losses reflect the principle of self-determination?

## UNDERSTANDING HISTORY THROUGH READING AND THE ARTS

Few books have captured the tragedy of World War I as well as Erich Remarque's novel *All Quiet on the Western Front** (1929), while A. Horne's *The Price of Glory: Verdun 1916* (1979) recounts the horror of the western-front battle that cost 700,000 lives.

The war, the hemopiliac child, Rasputin, and the murder of the royal family by the Bolsheviks are all brought together in an interesting book about Russia in the era of the revolution, *Nicholas and Alexandra** (1971) by R. Massie. Lenin's impact on history is best covered in L. Fischer, *The Life of Lenin** (1964, 1965), and in C. Hill, *Lenin and the Russian Revolution** (1947, 1971), while the standard life of Leon Trotsky is a three-volume work (1954–1963) by I. Deutscher. Bismarck's important foreign policy is covered in W. Medlicott and D. Coveney, eds., *Bismarck and Europe* (1972).

## PROBLEMS FOR FURTHER INVESTIGATION

Was Germany responsible for the Great War? This has been one of the most-debated subjects in political-diplomatic history in recent years. One of the chief revisionists is A. J. P. Taylor, *The Struggle for Mastery in Europe, 1848–1919* (1954), while a recent anti-German argument has come from E. Fischer, *The German War Aims in World War I* (1967). The debate is discussed in D. E. Lee, *The Outbreak of the First World War** (1970).

The problems of interpreting the revolution in Russia, current interpretations, and key themes are examined in a short but valuable book, *The Russian Revolution and Bolshevik Victory: Why and How?** by A. E. Adams (1960).

*Available in paperback.

# CHAPTER 33

## NATIONALISM IN ASIA, 1914-1939

## CHAPTER OBJECTIVES

After reading and studying this chapter you should be able to answer the following questions:

Q-1.   How did modern nationalism develop in Asia between World War One and World War Two?

Q-2.   How did national movements arise in different countries, and how did some of these parallel movements come into brutal conflict?

## CHAPTER SYNOPSIS

What is nationalism, and why did many Asians view it as the solution to all of their problems? This chapter begins by answering this question in general terms, noting three reasons that nationalism was so popular an ideology, and then goes on to give a history of nationalism in Asia at its height — the 1914-1939 era.

The promises of independence that the imperialist Europeans made to their subject peoples during the First World War were not kept. By the end of the war neither Britain nor France was in a mood to give up its old holdings; in fact, they used the League of Nations mandate system (giving them much control over the old Turkish empire and the Middle East) to increase the size of their empires. At the same time, the war enhanced the national consciousness of peoples heretofore dominated by the West as it convinced them that the Europeans were beatable. Nationalism was also encouraged by the ideas of equality and national freedom that flowed out of wartime Europe and revolutionary Russia.

During the war the British had encouraged Arab revolt against Turkey and had promised the Zionist Jews a homeland in Palestine, Then, after the war and at

305

the point of a gun, a British and French takeover of the Middle East brought on violent reaction from the Arab, Turkish, Iranian, and Jewish nationalists and, in some instances, brought them into conflict with each other. Rejection of self-determination for the non-Western world and the smashing of the new Syrian and Iraqi states by the Allies convinced the Arabs of the European betrayal. Meanwhile, under the great Mustafa Kemal, Turkey — dismembered and reduced to a puppet state of Britain and France — rose up against the foreigners and laid the foundations for a modern, highly nationalistic, and secularized state. Equally important, nationalism transformed Iran and Afghanistan — both of which had to first cast off the British and in both of which the Islamic religion remained a counter against secularism and modernization.

In the 1920s and 1930s the Arabs won a considerable number of victories as independence came at a gradual pace. Iraq, Egypt, and Syria freed themselves, and a new, communally directed Jewish state was created in Palestine. From the beginning, however, the Arabs and the Jews were engaged in an undeclared civil war. A similar nationalist movement unified and divided India. Here the British policy of gradualism was deemed too gradual by Indian nationalists, who, under the great Hindu social activist Gandhi, successfully used the tactics of militant nonviolence to reform India and gain self-rule — although India was now divided between Hindu and Muslim.

Also in the 1920s the revolutionary Chinese nationalist movement, which had strengthened China and had redefined Chinese family life, was tragically undermined by a communist vs. non-communist civil war and by war with Japan. Sun Yat-sen's Nationalist program to institute land reform and to crush the warlords was eventually abandoned, only to become the key to Mao's communist victory in 1949. Meanwhile in Japan, rapid industrial development had created an imbalanced economy under *zaibatsu* control, while in the political sphere Japan moved from liberalism to ultranationalism. Japanese expansion into Manchuria led to war with China — an event that changed the course of Chinese and world history.

Elsewhere in Asia, nationalism transformed French Indochina, the Dutch East Indies, and the Philippines. While the Americans' encouragement of independence in the Philippines laid the foundations for popular government, Dutch and French reluctance to set their holdings free led to nationalist reaction and, as we will see later in Vietnam, a complex and bloody war.

## STUDY OUTLINE

I.  The First World War and Western imperialism
   A.  The First World War greatly altered relations between Asia and Europe
       1.  The Asians saw the war as a family quarrel that divided Europe and made it vulnerable

2. The British and the French needed the aid and the resources of their colonial peoples
   a. Many Asians and Africans served in the French and British armies
   b. The war experience gave Asians an exposure to Western democratic and republican ideas
   c. The British and French, in turn, made promises of postwar reform and self-rule
   d. Wilson's idea of self-determination raised hopes for the end of foreign domination

B. However, after the war, the Western imperialists worked to retain and expand their possessions
   1. The idea of self-determination was subordinated to the British and French plan for continued Western rule
   2. The League of Nations mandate system increased the size of the empires of France and Britain
   3. This caused Asians to react by turning to nationalist movements

C. Soviet communism denounced imperialism and encouraged national independence movements
   1. Lenin and the communists announced that the end of foreign exploitation was the immediate goal
   2. Nationalists, like the Vietnamese Ho Chi Minh, were inspired by Lenin's plea for national self-determination

D. National self-determination also appealed to countries that were subject to indirect Western control and exploitation
   1. The Western-dominated world economy created hostility toward Europe and the United States
   2. Nationalism went hand in hand with the promises of modernization

II. The Middle East
A. The Arab revolt
   1. Beginning with the Revolution of 1908, the Young Turks strengthened the Ottoman state at the expense of the Arabs, largely Syria and Iraq
      a. They were determined to hold the vast and diverse empire together
      b. After defeat in Europe (Balkan War, 1912), they concentrated on control over their Asian possessions
      c. Instead of liberal reform, they implemented a narrow Turkish nationalism
      d. Turkish nationalism was narrow and unwilling to recognize other ethnic and religious groups — e.g., the Turks killed over a million Armenians
   2. In 1914 the Arabs sided with Britain and successfully revolted
      a. The *sharif* Hussein Ibn Ali led the Arabs in revolt against Turkey
      b. He was joined by the British leader of the Arabs, T. E. Lawrence

     c.  The Arabs expected the British to support Arab national independence

3.  Meanwhile, Britain and France secretly agreed (Sykes-Picot Agreement) to divide and rule the Ottoman Empire themselves

     a.  France received modern-day Lebanon, Syria, and much of southern Turkey

     b.  Britain received Palestine, Jordan, and Iraq

4.  The British Balfour Declaration of 1917 promised the Jews a national home in Palestine — a promise that dismayed the Arabs, who thought it wrong for a small minority to be able to found an exclusive religious and ethnic state

5.  Faisal and the Arabs felt betrayed

     a.  The idea of self-determination was not carried out by the Allies

     b.  The mandate system and the Balfour Declaration were forced on the Arabs

6.  A Syrian revolt in 1920 led to French repression

B.  The Turkish Revolution

1.  The war left Turkey dismembered and reduced to a puppet state of France and Britain, while the Greeks conquered part of western Turkey

2.  Mustafa Kemal led the Turkish national liberation movement

     a.  Kemal's forces won a great victory over the foreigners

     b.  The Treaty of Lausanne abolished hated foreign controls, but Turkey lost its Arab provinces

3.  Kemal was a secularist and a modernizer

     a.  He deposed the sultan and established a republic with himself as president

     b.  He crushed the Armenians and the Kurds and built a one-party system in Turkey

     c.  He ended religious influence in government and education and modernized the law and schools

     d.  Women were enfranchised, divorce was open to women, Western dress codes were enforced, and a new non-Arabic script was introduced

4.  Kemal's nationalist revolution made Turkey into a modern secular state

C.  Iran and Afghanistan

1.  Iran was not as successful as Turkey in building a modern state

     a.  By the late nineteenth century, Iran was weak and subject to outside demands

     b.  The Iranian revolution of 1906 ended with Russian and British occupation of Iran

     c.  By 1919, all of Iran was under British control

     d.  The new shah, Reza Shah, limited foreign influence, modernized Iran, and ruled harshly

      e.  Reza Shah's secularization and tyrannical ways weakened Iran as a modern state

  2.  Afghanistan won independence but found modernization difficult

      a.  British influence was thrown off by a holy war (1919) led by Amir Ammanullah

      b.  Ammanullah's attempt to modernize and secularize Afghanistan was opposed by tribal and religious traditionalists

D.  The Arab states, Palestine, and the breakdown of the mandate system

  1.  The British appointed King Faisal in Iraq, who in turn secured independence and moderate reforms for Iraq

  2.  Egypt was given independence, but British troops remained

  3.  The French mandates of Syria and Lebanon were given indpendence but remained under French influence

  4.  The situation in the British mandate of Palestine grew worse in the interwar years

      a.  Arab nationalists were united against the Jewish settlers

      b.  Zionism, the movement to re-create a Jewish state in Palestine, was founded by Theodor Herzl

      c.  Conditions in Europe and America in the 1920s and 1930s encouraged large-scale Jewish immigration to Palestine

      d.  The Jewish National Fund bought land from rich Arabs and gave it to settlers; many Jewish immigrants, however, preferred urban settlement

      e.  Civil war between Arab and Jew resulted in British pressure to slow down and limit Jewish immigration

      f.  Jewish settlers responded by forging Jewish cultural unity and a new form of economic community — the *kibbutz*

      g.  The *kibbutz* was a cooperative farm in which each member shared equally in work, rewards, and defense

III.  Toward self-rule in India

A.  Promises and repression, 1914–1919

  1.  India gave loyal and significant support to the British cause during World War One

      a.  Over one million Indians volunteered for duty in Europe

      b.  Economic and health problems grew and revived the prewar Nationalist movement

      c.  The Lucknow Pact brought the Muslim minority and the Hindu majority together under the banner of self-government

  2.  The British response was contradictory

      a.  The Government of India Act (1919) gave Indians participation in government

      b.  Meanwhile, the repressive Rowlatt Acts were designed to root out opposition

      c.  The British massacre of Indian civilians at Amritsar brought India to the verge of violent civil war

B.  Hindu society and Mahatma Gandhi

   1.  Mahatma Gandhi's background was in Hindu society

     a.  Gandhi grew up in one of the "protected" states, the part of India least affected by British rule

     b.  Gandhi grew up in a wealthy Indian family of the merchant class — the *gandhi*

     c.  This typical extended-family structure stressed group harmony, kindness, and patience

     d.  Gandhi studied law in England and eventually became a lawyer in British South Africa

C.  The roots of Gandhi's militant nonviolence

   1.  Gandhi's encounters with racial discrimination caused him to examine the "new system" of slavery in British South Africa

   2.  Gandhi undertook the legal defense of Indians who had finished their terms as indentured laborers

   3.  Gandhi's spiritual theory of social action was *Satyagraha* — meaning "soul force" to gain truth and social justice

   4.  Its tactic of nonviolent resistance owed a good deal to the teachings of Christ

   5.  Gandhi's movement brought tax and immigration reforms and recognition of non-Christian marriages for the nonwhites of South Africa

D.  Gandhi leads the way toward national independence

   1.  On his return to India in 1915, Gandhi traveled among the common people and led agricultural and industrial strikes

   2.  The Amritsar Massacre pushed him to boycott British goods and jobs and not to pay taxes

   3.  The call to militant nonviolence appealed to the heretofore passive masses of Hindus and pushed them and the Muslims into the Congress

   4.  Gandhi ended this campaign in 1922 when violence broke out, and he turned to helping the poor help themselves

   5.  By 1929 Indian desire for a speedier path to self-rule led to Gandhi's famous march to the sea

   6.  In 1931 the British and Gandhi negotiated a new constitution (1935) that strengthened India's parliament

   7.  Gandhi's tactics and philosophy brought the masses into politics and nurtured national identity and self-respect — although he failed to heal the split between Hindu and Muslim

IV.  Turmoil in East Asia

A.  Chinese movement toward independence from the West and toward modernism was undermined by internal conflict and war with Japan

B. The rise of Nationalist China
   1. The fall of the Manchu dynasty in the Revolution of 1911–1912 ended the hope of preserving traditional China
   2. Yüan, the leader of the revolution against the Manchus, dissolved the parliament and ruled as a dictator
   3. This led to warlordism
      a. Yüan's death led to a shift of power to the local warlords
      b. Their taxes, wars, and corruption created terrible suffering
   4. Foreign imperialism made matters worse
      a. Japan's seizure of Shantung and southern Manchuria led to the patriotic protest called the "May Fourth Movement"
   5. This led to an alliance between Sun Yat-sen's Nationalists and the Chinese Communists
      a. Sun placed nationalism above all else — including communism
      b. To him, democracy meant order and land reform for the peasants
      c. Sun's goal was that the Nationalist Party crush the warlords to unite China under a strong government
   6. In 1926–1928 the Nationalists under Chiang Kai-shek unified China under a new government at Nanking
      a. However, the Japanese threat remained
      b. Chiang's Nationalists purged the Chinese Communists, who vowed revenge
C. China's intellectual revolution
   1. Nationalism was only one part of the New Culture Movement
      a. It was also a Western-oriented movement that attacked traditional culture, particularly Confucian ethics
      b. Through its widely read magazines, *New Youth* and *New Tide*, the movement advocated Western ideas such as individualism, democracy, science, and a new language
      c. Its greatest thinker was Hu Shih, who advocated a gradual adoption of Western ideas
   2. Another aspect of the New Culture Movement was Marxian Socialism
      a. Marxism was attractive because it was a single, all-encompassing creed
      b. It provided a means for criticizing Western dominance and explaining Chinese weakness
      c. It was appealing as a way to free the poor peasants from their parasitic landlords
   3. Mao Tse-tung believed that peasant revolution would free China
      a. He advocated equal distribution of land
      b. He built up a self-governing communist soviet at Juichin in southeastern China

D. The changing Chinese family
  1. The Confucian principle of subordination placed the group over the individual and tied women to husband and family
    a. Women were given in marriage by parents at an early age
    b. The wife owed unquestioning obedience to her husband, could be bought and sold, and had no property rights
  2. Lao T'ai T'ai's autobiography illustrates both old and new Chinese attitudes toward the family
    a. Footbinding died out
    b. Marriages for love became common, and polygamy declined
    c. Economic and educational opportunities opened for women
E. From liberalism to ultranationalism in Japan
  1. World War One accelerated economic expansion and imperial growth in Japan
  2. The early 1920s saw a period of peaceful and democratic pursuit of its goals, although most nationalists held that Japan's mission was to protect all of Asia
  3. Serious problems accompanied Japan's rise
    a. Japan's population grew while natural resources and food remained scarce
    b. Her "dualistic economy" consisted of a few giant conglomerate firms and a mass of peasants and craftsmen — and a weak middle class
    c. Struggle between old and new political elites resulted in a lack of cohesive leadership
  4. The most serious problem was that of ultranationalism
    a. The ultranationalists were violently anti-Western and rejected Western ideas and institutions
    b. They wanted to restore traditional Japanese practices — such as the samurai code
    c. They preached foreign expansion and "Asia for Asians"
    d. The Great Depression caused many Japanese to turn to the ultra-nationalists
F. Japan against China
  1. Japanese army officers in Manchuria turned to ultranationalism as a solution to Japan's problems
  2. All of Manchuria was taken from China in 1931–1932 by the Japanese army, and Japan's politics became increasingly chaotic
  3. Japanese aggression caused the Chinese Nationalist government to abandon modernization and social and land reform
    a. Half of China's land was owned by the rich landlords, while the peasants owned little land and lived in poverty

   b.  Now opposed to land reform, the Nationalist goal was the elimina-
       tion of Mao's Communist movement
   c.  Mao's Long March in 1934 saved communism, which then under-
       took land reform — thus winning peasant support
4.  Communist-Nationalist cooperation in the late 1930s could not halt
    further Japanese aggression
   a.  By late 1938 sizable portions of coastal China were under Japanese
       control (see Map 33.2)
   b.  Both the Communists and the Nationalists retreated to the interior
G.  Southeast Asia and the Philippines
   1.  Events elsewhere in Asia inspired nationalism in French Indochina and
       the Dutch East Indies
   2.  French imperialism in Vietnam stimulated the growth of a Communist-
       led nationalist opposition movement
   3.  In Indonesia, Dutch determination to keep its colonies led to the rule
       of a successful nationalist movement
   4.  The Philippine nationalist movement succeeded
      a.  Highly educated, the Philippine people sought independence from
          the United States
      b.  The United States encouraged economic growth, education, and
          popular government
      c.  But U.S. racism encouraged radical nationalism in the Philippines
      d.  The Great Depression encouraged the United States (in 1934) to
          schedule self-government for the Philippines in 1944
H.  Conclusion
   1.  The Asian revolt against the West became a mass movement only
       after 1914
   2.  The nationalists usually adopted Western techniques and favored
       modernization
   3.  The diversity of their history explains why Asian people also became
       defensive in their relations with each other

## REVIEW QUESTIONS

Q-1.  What role did the colonial peoples play in the First World War? How did
most Asians view that war?

Q-2.  Compare and contrast the British and French attitude toward their colonial
peoples during and after the war.

Q-3.  Who benefited from the League of Nations mandate system? Who lost?

Q-4.  What happened to President Wilson's idea of national self-determination?
Why was it not applied to colonial peoples?

Q-5.   In what way did the Russian Revolution encourage Asian nationalism?

Q-6.   Why did the Arabs hope that the French and British would champion the cause of Arab nationalism? Why did this hope turn into a feeling of betrayal?

Q-7.   Describe Faisal's efforts to bring about Syrian independence. What was the outcome?

Q-8.   What factors were responsible for the Young Turk nationalist movement in Ottoman Turkey, and what changes did the movement bring to that society?

Q-9.   In what sense was the Turkey of Kemal a true student of the enlightenment and Western liberalism? In what sense was it not?

Q-10.   Why was the Iranian Revolution of 1906 "doomed to failure"?

Q-11.   Describe the position of the Jews, that of the Arabs, and that of the British on the issue of a Jewish homeland in Palestine. In what way was the British position contradictory?

Q-12.   Describe the League of Nations "mandate system." How did it work, whom did it affect, and why was it established?

Q-13.   Describe the Zionist movement by commenting on its origins, its goals, and its implementation.

Q-14.   How did World War One affect the Indian people, the Indian nationalist movement, and the British government in India?

Q-15.   Describe Gandhi's idea of militant nonviolence based on *Satyagraha.* Why were his cultural background and his experience in South Africa important?

Q-16.   Give examples of Gandhi's militant nonviolent tactics. What impact did this movement have on the poor masses of India?

Q-17.   Describe the British government's position in India. What was the Hindu-Muslim problem, and how did it make British rule easier?

Q-18.   Describe events in China in the fifteen or so years after 1912. What problems did China face, and how successful was it in establishing unity and order?

Q-19.   Discuss and explain the three major currents in China's New Culture Movement: nationalism, modernism, and Marxian socialism. Why was each appealing to many Chinese?

Q-20.   Describe Mao Tse-tung's philosophy and his program of revolutionary reform for China. Why were the warlords opposed?

Q-21.   What were the pros and cons of traditional Confucian ethics as it related to the family and womanhood? What changes in marriage and womanhood occurred after about 1911?

Q-22.   How did World War One affect Japan? What events can you cite to show the trend toward liberalism and democracy?

Q-23.   Describe Japanese-Chinese relations in the twentieth century up to about 1938.

Q-24.   What problems did Japan face in the 1920s and 1930s? How did the ultra-nationalists propose to solve these problems?

**Q-25.** How did Japanese conquest affect the Chinese Nationalist Party? Explain the reasons for the Nationalist versus Communist struggle.

**Q-26.** What were the reasons for a Nationalist movement in the Philippines? What were the attitudes of the Americans toward the Filipino people?

## STUDY-REVIEW EXERCISES

*Test your understanding of the chapter by answering the following questions.*

1. Territories of the defeated German and Ottoman empires that were turned over by the League of Nations to the victorious powers are known as

   _____.

2. With the end of the First World War, Turkey faced all but which one of the following? (a) British and French occupation, (b) Greek invasion, (c) strong support from its Arab subjects, (d) practically no territory in Europe. _____

3. In general, most Asian and Arab nationalists *accepted/rejected* the ideas of the Western Enlightenment and Western modernization.

4. Both the nationalist movement in Turkey under Kemal and that in Iran under Reza Shah were *opposed to/in favor of* weakening traditional religion.

5. The country of Lebanon was a mandate of *Britain/France* and was dominated by its *Christian/Muslim* majority.

6. The key unit of Jewish agricultural organization in Palestine was the

   _____.

7. After the First World War was over, the British government was *more/less* sympathetic to the Indian demands for national independence.

8. In India, Hindu family tradition and the subordination of women were *included in/excluded from* the development of Gandhi's nationalist movement, while in China, traditional Confucian ethics was *included in/excluded from* the New Culture nationalists.

## MULTIPLE-CHOICE QUESTIONS

1. President Wilson and the Russian leader Lenin had a common
   a. dislike of communism.
   b. desire to continue colonial rule by Europeans.
   c. disinterest in the ideas of nationalism.
   d. belief in self-determination.

2.  The position of the Paris Peace Conference (1919) and the League of Nations on the subject of Syria was
    a.   acceptance of the idea of self-determination.
    b.   establishment of a French mandate.
    c.   acceptance of a merger of Syria with Iraq.
    d.   establishment of a Zionist state in Syria.

3.  The great revolutionary and nationalist leader of Turkey and "father of the Turks" was
    a.   Mustafa Kemal.
    b.   Hussein Ibn Ali.
    c.   T. E. Lawrence.
    d.   Jamal al-Din al Afghani.

4.  The cultured Austrian journalist and founder of Zionism was
    a.   Mustafa Kemal.
    b.   Theodor Herzl.
    c.   Karl Lueger.
    d.   Ferdinand Lassalle.

5.  In order to forge a cohesive community that could face the dangers of Arab opposition, the Jewish settlers of Palestine
    a.   turned to rural development through cooperative farming.
    b.   adopted a program of rapid industrialization and urbanization.
    c.   adopted a philosophy of monopoly capitalism.
    d.   all of the above.

6.  The Arab nationalist who was deposed in Syria and then made King of Iraq by the British was
    a.   Faisal.
    b.   Ammanullah.
    c.   Henri II.
    d.   Lenin.

7.  In 1907, and until 1919, Iran was divided into spheres of influence by
    a.   Turkey and Russia.
    b.   Turkey and Iraq.
    c.   Russia and Britain.
    d.   Britain and France.

8.  As the examples of Egypt, Syria, and Lebanon indicate, by the 1930s the Arab states

a.   freed themselves from Western mandates.
b.   freed themselves from Western influence.
c.   acquired genuine independence.
d.   all of the above.

9.   The foremost Arab leader, a direct descendant of Muhammad, who proclaimed
     himself king of the Arabs, was
     a.   T. E. Lawrence.
     b.   Hussein Ibn Ali.
     c.   Reza Shah.
     d.   Prince Henri.

10.  During the First World War, Arab nationalists and the British found they had
     a common enemy in
     a.   France.
     b.   Soviet Russia.
     c.   India.
     d.   Turkey.

11.  The "Great Idea" of the Greek nationalists in the post–World War I years was
     a.   a return to classical learning.
     b.   a modern Greek empire.
     c.   the building of a Bolshevik state in Greece.
     d.   liberation from Turkey.

12.  After about 1921 the majority of Jewish emigrants to Palestine came from
     a.   the United States.
     b.   Europe (largely Poland and Germany).
     c.   the Arab states.
     d.   France and Italy.

13.  The two Western imperialist countries that had traditionally extended influ-
     ence and control over Iran were
     a.   Russia and Britain.
     b.   France and Britain.
     c.   the United States and France.
     d.   the United States and Russia.

14.  The Balfour Declaration of 1917 expressed British commitment to
     a.   self-rule in India.
     b.   the spirit of the Versailles Treaty.
     c.   unobstructed sea lanes.
     d.   a Jewish homeland in Palestine.

15. In the secret Sykes-Picot Agreement, France and Britain agreed on
    a. how to defeat Germany.
    b. unconditional German surrender.
    c. how to divide the Ottoman Empire after the war.
    d. spheres of influence in Southeast Asia.

16. Shortly after World War I, Greece invaded
    a. Italy.
    b. Albania.
    c. Egypt.
    d. Turkey.

17. Mustafa Kemal in Turkey
    a. granted autonomy to ethnic minorities.
    b. created a two-party system, on the British model.
    c. moved the capital to Ankara.
    d. revived the sultanate.

18. Mustafa Kemal strove to
    a. revive the Islamic religion.
    b. recover the lost Arab lands.
    c. reacquaint his people with their historic tradition.
    d. modernize on the Western model.

19. The Muslim League called for the creation of a Muslim nation in British India.
    They wished to call it "land of the pure," or
    a. Pakistan.
    b. Afghanistan.
    c. Ceylon.
    d. Punjab.

20. Compared to Kemal in Turkey, Reza Shah's drive to modernize Iran was
    a. less successful.
    b. equally successful.
    c. slightly more successful.
    d. much more successful.

21. The main reason Ammanullah failed to reform and modernize Afghanistan was
    a. British overlordship.
    b. Islam.
    c. Indian invasions.
    d. a lack of natural resources.

22. Zionism is
    a. the Jewish political system.
    b. a highly advanced system of agriculture.
    c. Jewish nationalism.
    d. a sect of Judaism.

23. It is true of the Jewish settlement in Palestine that
    a. much of the land was purchased by the U.S. government.
    b. most of the early immigrants preferred to live in urban areas.
    c. the British gave no support to the idea of a Jewish homeland.
    d. the Zionists encouraged only wealthy Jews to settle in Palestine.

24. Mohandas Gandhi was
    a. Hindu.
    b. Buddhist.
    c. Moslem.
    d. Christian.

25. Hindu women
    a. were considered equal to men.
    b. were subordinate to men.
    c. could remarry if widowed.
    d. were targets of disrespect.

26. Gandhi was
    a. from the Indian peasant class.
    b. a grocer.
    c. a trained lawyer.
    d. a bachelor.

27. Mohandas Gandhi advocated
    a. war between Hindus and Muslims.
    b. British rule.
    c. violent overthrow of British rule.
    d. nonviolent action protesting British rule.

28. The founder of the Kuomintang, or Nationalist Party, in China was
    a. Mao Tse-tung.
    b. Chiang Kai-shek.
    c. Yuan Shih-k'ai.
    d. Sun Yat-sen.

## GEOGRAPHY

1.  Show on the outline map the changes in the size of the Turkish state following the First World War. How does this size compare to that of pre-war Turkey?

2.  Note the location of Ankara, Istanbul, and the Smyrna Coast.

3.  Describe the causes of these changes. What role did Greece and Britain play in this process?

4.  On the same map show the states that were mandated to Britain and France after the First World War.

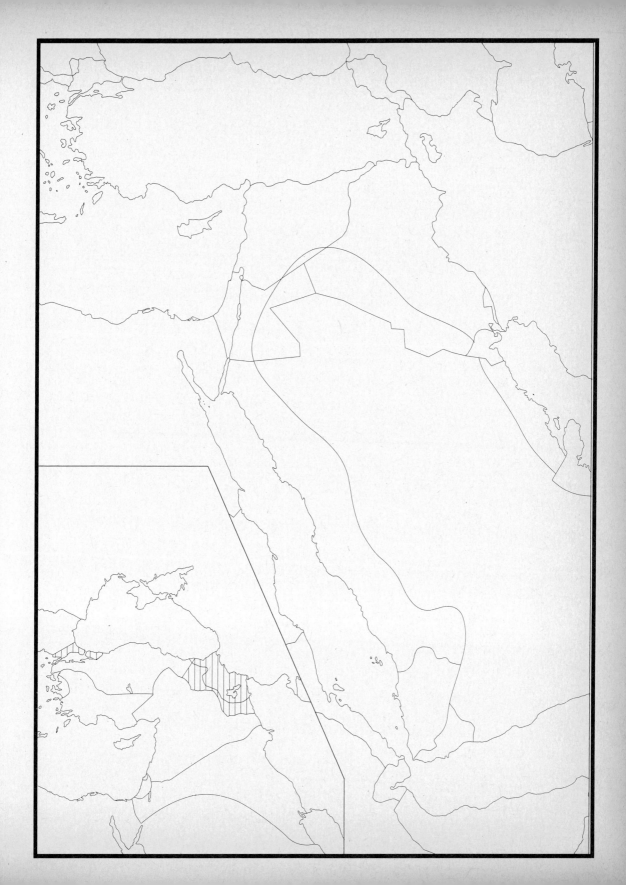

## UNDERSTANDING HISTORY THROUGH READING AND THE ARTS

Few men of the twentieth century have had as important an impact on world
political thought and action as the nationalist leaders Mohandas Gandhi in India,
Sun Yat-sen and Mao Tse-tung in China, and Ho Chi Minh in Vietnam. A good
place for the reader to begin with Gandhi is his autobiography, *The Story of My
Experiments with Truth* (first published in 1927). Other helpful and interesting
works on Gandhi are *The Life of Gandhi* (1950) by L. Fischer, and *The Conquest
of Violence* (1959), by M. Bondurant. For Sun Yat-sen, see H. Shriffrin, *Sun Yat-sen
and the Origins of the Chinese Revolution* (1970); and for Mao, S. Schram, *Mao
Tse-tung* (1966).

## PROBLEMS FOR FURTHER INVESTIGATION

There is no parallel in history to the control that the small and distant Britain held
over vast India for so long a time. A good starting point in an analysis of the impact
of imperial rule in India is a book of debates: *The British in India: Imperialism or
Trusteeship?* (1962), edited by M. D. Lewis. The massacre of Indian civilians at
Amritsar is pointed to as one of the low points in British imperial history. If you
are interested in trying your hand at working with primary source documents and
have access (as most large libraries do) to the British Parliamentary Papers, you may
want to look at two government reports that tell of the massacre: the *Rowlatt
Report* (1918, Cmd. 9190) and the *Hunter Committee Report* (1920, Cmd. 681).
For an account of the work of the last viceroy, Lord Mountbatten, see *Mission with
Mountbatten* (1951) by A. Campbell-Johnson.

## READING WITH UNDERSTANDING
### EXERCISE 5

## LEARNING HOW TO IDENTIFY MAIN POINTS
## THAT ARE CAUSES OR REASONS

In Exercise 3 we considered cause and effect and underlined a passage dealing with effects or results. This exercise continues in this direction by focusing on causes or reasons.

### Exercise

Read the following passage as a whole. Reread it and underline or highlight each cause (or factor) contributing to the Industrial Revolution in England.

Note that there are several causes and that they are rather compressed. (This is because the author is summarizing material presented in previous chapters before going on to discuss other causes or factors—notably technology and the energy problem—in greater detail.) Since several causal points are presented in a short space, this is a very good place to number the points (and key subpoints) in the margin. After you have finished, compare your underlining or highlighting with that in the suggested model on pages E-4 to E-5.

## Eighteenth-Century Origins

The Industrial Revolution grew out of the expanding Atlantic economy of the eighteenth century, which served mercantilist England remarkably well. England's colonial empire, augmented by a strong position in Latin America and in the African slave trade, provided a growing market for English manufactured goods. So did England itself. In an age when it was much cheaper to ship goods by water than by land, no part of England was more than twenty miles from navigable water. Beginning in the 1770s, a canal building boom greatly enhanced this natural advantage (see Map 22.1). Nor were there any tariffs within the country to hinder trade, as there were in France before 1789 and in politically fragmented Germany.

Agriculture played a central role in bringing about the Industrial Revolution in England. English farmers were second only to the Dutch in productivity in 1700, and they were continuously adopting new methods of farming as the century went on. The result, especially before 1760, was a period of bountiful crops and low food prices. The ordinary English family did not have to spend almost everything it earned just to buy bread. It could spend more on other items, on manufactured goods—leather shoes or a razor for the man, a bonnet or a shawl for the woman, toy soldiers for the son, and a doll for the daughter. Thus, demand for goods within the country complemented the demand from the colonies.

England had other assets that helped give rise to the Industrial Revolution. Unlike eighteenth-century France, England had an effective central bank and well-developed credit markets. The monarchy and the aristocratic oligarchy, which had jointly ruled the country since 1688, provided stable and predictable government. At the same time the government let the domestic economy operate fairly freely and with few controls, encouraging personal initiative, technical change, and a free market. Finally, England had long had a large class of hired agricultural laborers, whose numbers were further increased by the enclosure movement of the late eighteenth century. These rural wage earners were relatively mobile—compared to village-bound peasants in France and western Germany, for example—and along with cottage workers they formed a potential industrial labor force for capitalist entrepreneurs.

All these factors combined to initiate the Industrial Revolution, which began in the 1780s—after the American war for independence and just before the French Revolution. Thus the great economic and political revolutions that have shaped the modern world occurred almost simultaneously, though they began in different countries. The Industrial Revolution was, however, a longer process. It was not complete in England until 1830 at the earliest, and it had no real impact on continental countries until after the Congress of Vienna ended the era of revolutionary wars in 1815.

### Eighteenth-Century Origins

causes

1

a

b

c

2

a

b

c

3

4

5

6

The Industrial Revolution grew out of the expanding Atlantic economy of the eighteenth century, which served mercantilist England remarkably well. England's colonial empire, augmented by a strong position in Latin America and in the African slave trade, provided a growing market for English manufactured goods. So did England itself. In an age when it was much cheaper to ship goods by water than by land, no part of England was more than twenty miles from navigable water. Beginning in the 1770s, a canal building boom greatly enhanced this natural advantage (see Map 22.1). Nor were there any tariffs within the country to hinder trade, as there were in France before 1789 and in politically fragmented Germany.

Agriculture played a central role in bringing about the Industrial Revolution in England. English farmers were second only to the Dutch in productivity in 1700, and they were continuously adopting new methods of farming as the century went on. The result, especially before 1760, was a period of bountiful crops and low food prices. The ordinary English family did not have to spend almost everything it earned just to buy bread. It could spend more on other items, on manufactured goods—leather shoes or a razor for the man, a bonnet or a shawl for the woman, toy soldiers for the son, and a doll for the daughter. Thus, demand for goods within the country complemented the demand from the colonies.

England had other assets that helped give rise to the Industrial Revolution. Unlike eighteenth-century France, England had an effective central bank and well-developed credit markets. The monarchy and the aristocratic oligarchy, which had jointly ruled the country since 1688, provided stable and predictable government. At the same time the government let the domestic economy operate fairly freely and with few controls, encouraging personal initiative, technical change, and a free market. Finally, England had long had a large class of hired agricultural laborers, whose numbers were further increased by the enclosure movement of the late eighteenth century. These rural wage earners were relatively mobile—compared to village-bound peasants in France and western Germany, for example—and

a

along with cottage workers they formed a potential industrial labor force for capitalist entrepreneurs.

All these factors combined to initiate the Industrial Revolution, which began in the 1780s—after the American war for independence and just before the French Revolution. Thus the great economic and political revolutions that have shaped the modern world occurred almost simultaneously, though they began in different countries. The Industrial Revolution was, however, a longer process. It was not complete in England until 1830 at the earliest, and it had no real impact on continental countries until after the Congress of Vienna ended the era of revolutionary wars in 1815.

# CHAPTER 34

## THE AGE OF ANXIETY

## CHAPTER OBJECTIVES

After reading and studying this chapter you should be able to answer the following questions:

Q-1. How were the postwar feelings of crisis and anxiety reflected in Western thought, art, and culture?

Q-2. How did political leaders try to maintain peace and prosperity between 1919 and 1939? Why did they fail?

## CHAPTER SYNOPSIS

Because war and revolution had shattered many traditional ideas, beliefs, and institutions, many people of the postwar era found themselves living in an age of anxiety and continuous crisis. The first half of this chapter deals with major changes in ideas and culture that were connected to this age of anxiety. Some of these changes began before 1900, but they became widespread only after the great upheaval of World War I affected millions of ordinary people and opened an era of uncertainty and searching. People generally became less optimistic and had less faith in rational thinking. Radically new theories in physics associated with Albert Einstein took form, while Sigmund Freud's psychology gave a new and disturbing interpretation of human behavior. Philosophy and literature developed in new ways, and Christianity took on renewed meaning for thinking people. There was also great searching and experimentation in architecture, painting, and music, all of which went in new directions. Much painting became abstract, as did some music. Movies and radio programs, which offered entertainment and escape, gained enormous popularity among the general public. In short, there were revolutionary changes in thought, art, and popular culture.

The second half of this chapter discusses efforts to re-establish real peace and political stability in the troubled era after 1918. The author believes Germany was the key area. In 1923, hostility between France and Germany led to an undeclared war when French armies occupied Germany's industrial heartland. This crisis was resolved, though, and followed by a period of cautious hope in international politics between 1924 and 1929. The stock market crash in the United States in 1929, however, brought renewed economic and political crisis to the Western world. Attempts to meet this crisis in the United States, Sweden, Britain, and France were only partly successful. Thus, economic and political difficulties accompanied and reinforced the revolution in thought and culture. It was a hard time in Western society.

## STUDY OUTLINE

I.  Uncertainty in modern thought
    A.  The effects of World War I
        1.  Many people rejected the long-accepted Western beliefs in progress and the power of the rational mind to understand a logical universe and an orderly society
            a.  Even before the war, Nietzsche believed that civilization had lost its creativity by neglecting emotion and overstressing reason and traditional values
            b.  Bergson and Sorel pointed out the limits of rational and scientific thinking
            c.  Valéry wrote about the crisis of the cruelly injured mind
        2.  Throughout the 1920s and 1930s there arose a growing pessimism
    B.  Physics and psychology
        1.  The challenge to Newtonian physics by scientists such as Einstein undermined belief in constant natural laws
        2.  The 1920s was the "heroic age of physics"
            a.  Rutherford split the atom
            b.  Subatomic particles were identified, notably the neutron, which led to atomic power
        3.  The new physics described a universe that lacked absolute objective reality and direct relevance to human experience
        4.  According to Freud, human behavior is basically irrational
            a.  The key to understanding the mind is the irrational unconscious (the id)
            b.  Behavior is a compromise between the needs of the id (which is driven by sexual and instinctual desires) and the controls of the

ego (which tries to determine what a person can do) and the super-ego (moral values that tell what a person should do)

5. Instinctual drives can easily overwhelm the control mechanisms; yet rigid repression can cripple people with guilt and neuroses

C. Philosophy: logical empiricism and existentialism
1. In English-speaking countries, the main development in philosophy was logical empiricism, while on the Continent the primary development was existentialism
    a. Logical empiricism, as defined by Wittgenstein, claimed that philosophy was nothing more than the logical clarification of thought; it could not answer the great issues of the ages
    b. Modern existentialism was the search for human and moral values in an uncertain world
    c. Despair and meaninglessness can be overcome by individual action and choice
2. Unlike logical empiricism, existentialism offered a positive answer to profound moral issues and contemporary crises

D. The revival of Christianity
1. A revitalization of fundamental Christianity took place after the First World War
2. Christian Protestant theologians, who had previously sought to harmonize religious belief with scientific findings, stressed a return to faith and traditional doctrines, as in the writings of Kierkegaard and Barth
3. Christian Catholic theologians, such as Marcel, found new hope in religion

E. Twentieth-century literature
1. The postward moods of pessimism, relativism, and alienation influenced novelists
2. Literature focused on the irrationality of the human mind
3. Writers embraced psychological relativity — the attempt to understand oneself by looking at one's past — and the stream-of-consciousness technique (Woolf, Joyce)
4. Much literature, such as that of Spengler, Kafka, and Orwell, was anti-utopian; that is, it predicted a future of doom

II. Modern art and music rejected old forms and values
A. Architecture and design
1. The new idea of functionalism, or usefulness, revolutionized architecture with its emphasis on efficiency and clean lines instead of ornamentation
2. The Chicago school of architects, led initially by Sullivan, pioneered in the building of skyscrapers

3. Frank Lloyd Wright then used the same ideas to design truly modern houses
4. The German Bauhaus school under Gropius became the major proponent of functional and industrial forms
5. Mies van der Rohe took European functionalism to Chicago

B. Modern painting
1. French impressionism yielded to nonrepresentational expressionism, which sought to portray the worlds of emotion and imagination, as in the works of van Gogh, Cézanne, and Matisse
2. Cubism (founded by Picasso) and abstract painting emerged from expressionism
3. Surrealism became prominent in the 1920s and 1930s

C. Modern music
1. The concept of expressionism also affected music, as in the work of Stravinsky
2. Some composers, led by Schönberg, abandoned traditional harmony and tonality

D. Movies and radio
1. The general public embraced movies and radio enthusiastically
2. The movie factories and Charlie Chaplin created a new medium and a new culture
3. Moviegoing became a form of escapism
4. Radios and film were used for propaganda as well as entertainment

III. The search for peace and political stability
A. Germany and the Western powers
1. Germany was the key to lasting peace, and the Germans hated the Treaty of Versailles
2. France, fearful and isolated, believed that an economically weak Germany was necessary for peace in Europe
3. Britain needed a prosperous Germany in order to maintain the British economy
   a. J. M. Keynes, an economist, argued that the Versailles treaty crippled the European economy and needed revision
   b. His attack on the treaty contributed to guilt feelings about Germany in Britain
   c. As a result, France and Britain drifted apart
4. When Germany refused to continue its heavy reparation payments, French and Belgian armies occupied the Ruhr (1923)

B. The occupation of the Ruhr
1. Because Germany would not pay gold, France wanted to collect reparations in coal, steel, and machinery

2. The Germans stopped work in the factories and France could not collect reparations, but the French occupation affected the German economy drastically
    a. Inflation skyrocketed
    b. Resentment and political unrest among the Germans grew
3. Germany agreed to revised reparations payments and France withdrew its troops, but many Germans were left financially ruined and humiliated

C. Hope in foreign affairs (1924–1929)
1. The Dawes and Young plans provided a solution to the reparations problem: the United States loaned money to Germany so it could pay France and Britain so they could pay the United States
2. The treaties of Locarno eased European disputes
    a. Germany and France accepted their common border
    b. Britain agreed to fight if either country invaded the other
3. The Kellogg-Briand Pact (1928) condemned war

D. Hope in democratic government
1. Although republican democracy appeared to have the support of most Germans, Germany split into extreme right and left groups
    a. The extreme nationalists, such as Hitler's followers, were insignificant until 1929
    b. The Communists on the far left attacked the moderate leftist Social Democrats
2. In France, the democratically elected government rested in the hands of the middle-class-oriented moderates, while the Communists battled for the support of the workers
3. Northern France was rebuilt, and Paris became the world's cultural center
4. Britain's major problem was unemployment, and the government's efforts to ease it led the country gradually toward socialism

IV. The Great Depression (1929–1939)
A. The economic crisis
1. The depression began with the U.S. stock market crash (October 1929)
2. Financial crisis led to a decline in production in Europe and the United States and an unwise turn to protective tariffs
3. The absence of international leadership and poor national policies added to the depression

B. Mass unemployment
1. As production decreased, workers lost their jobs and had no money to buy goods, which cut production even more

2.  Mass unemployment also caused great social and psychological problems
C.  The New Deal in the United States
1.  Roosevelt's goal was to preserve capitalism through reform
2.  Government intervention in and regulation of the economy first took place through the National Recovery Administration (NRA), whose task it was to fix prices and wages for everyone's benefit
3.  The NRA was declared unconstitutional (1935), and Roosevelt decided to attack the problem of unemployment directly by using the federal government to employ as many people as possible
    a.  The Work Projects Administration was set up (1935) and employed millions of people
    b.  It was very popular and helped check the threat of social revolution
4.  Other social measures, such as Social Security and government support for labor unions, also eased the hardships of the depression
5.  Although the New Deal helped, it failed to pull the United States out of the depression
    a.  Some believe that Roosevelt should have nationalized industry so that national economic planning could have worked
    b.  Many economists argued that the public works projects were not extensive enough
D.  The Scandinavian response to economic depression
1.  Backed by a strong tradition of community cooperation, socialist parties were firmly established in Sweden and Norway by the 1920s
2.  Deficit spending to finance public works and create jobs was used to check unemployment and revive the economy after 1929
3.  Scandinavia's welfare socialism offered an appealing middle way between capitalism and communism or fascism in the 1930s
E.  Recovery and reform in Britain and France
1.  Britain's concentration on its national market aided its economic recovery
2.  Government instability in France prevented recovery and needed reform
    a.  The Socialists, led by Blum, became the strongest party in France and attempted New Deal-type reforms
    b.  France was drawn to the brink of civil war, and Blum was forced to resign (1937), leaving the country to drift aimlessly

## REVIEW QUESTIONS

Q-1.  Define *quanta* and its implications for the definition of matter and energy.
Q-2.  Define and discuss the relationships among the id, ego, and superego.

Q-3.　Freud's view that human beings are basically irrational coincides with the picture of the universe drawn by modern physics. Discuss this relationship between psychology and science.

Q-4.　Discuss the meaning of Sartre's statement that "man is condemned to be free." How is this thought connected to the existential belief that man must seek to define himself?

Q-5.　How did the loss of faith in reason and progress affect twentieth-century Christian thought?

Q-6.　French impressionism has been defined as "superrealism." Explain.

Q-7.　Compare and contrast Gauguin's and Le Corbusier's concepts of art.

Q-8.　How do impressionism and expressionism reflect the rationality and irrationality of the nineteenth and twentieth centuries, respectively?

Q-9.　What influence did Freud have on twentieth-century painting?

Q-10.　Discuss the attitudes of Britain, France, and Germany with regard to the Treaty of Versailles.

Q-11.　The most serious international crisis of the 1920s occurred in the German Ruhr in January 1923. What was the crisis, and what were its consequences?

Q-12.　Describe the part played by the United States in the economic and political settlements of the mid-1920s in Europe.

Q-13.　What problems faced the British governments of the 1920s, and with what ideas did the Labour Party approach these problems?

Q-14.　Discuss the origins, interests, and goals of the Labour and Liberal parties in Britain.

Q-15.　What were the causes of the Great Depression?

Q-16.　Trace the cause and effect of the recall of public and private loans to European countries.

Q-17.　Roosevelt's goal was to preserve capitalism through reform. Explain.

Q-18.　What was the NRA, and why did it not work well?

Q-19.　The New Deal ultimately failed to halt mass unemployment. Why? Why is it said that the WPA helped prevent social revolution in the United States?

Q-20.　Why was the Scandinavian response to the economic crisis the most successful one in the Western democracies?

## STUDY-REVIEW EXERCISES

*Explain who the following people were and note how their work contributed to and reflected the uncertainty and anxiety in modern thought.*

Friedrich Nietzsche

Georges Sorel

Henri Bergson

Sigmund Freud

Ludwig Wittgenstein

Jean-Paul Sartre

James Joyce

Oswald Spengler

Franz Kafka

*Define the following philosophic and artistic schools and movements by describing their basic aims and characteristics and naming some participants and works.*

modern existentialism

functionalism in architecture

Bauhaus school

Chicago school of architecture

expressionism in painting

cubism

dadaism

surrealism

expressionism in music

atonality

logical empiricism

*Identify* each of the following and give its significance.

Ramsay MacDonald

Treaty of Versailles

"Little Entente" of 1921

Ruhr crisis of 1923

Locarno meetings of 1925

Munich beer hall "revolution" of 1923

principle of uncertainty

French Popular Front

National Recovery Administration

BBC

Léon Blum

Raymond Poincaré

John Maynard Keynes

Walter Gropius

Leni Riefenstahl

*Test* your understanding of the chapter by answering the following questions.

1.  Most modern (postimpressionist) artistic movements *were/were not* concerned with the visible world of fact.

2.  The Dawes Plan provided that _____ would get

    loans from the United States to pay reparations to _____

and _____ so that they could

repay their loans to _____.

3. After 1914, people tended to *strengthen/discard* their belief in progress.
4. The works of modern physics tended to *confirm/challenge* the dependable laws of Newton.
5. The British economist who criticized the Versailles treaty and advocated a "counter-cyclical policy" to deal with depressed economies was

_____.

## MULTIPLE-CHOICE QUESTIONS

1. The country most interested in strict implementation of the Treaty of Versailles was
   a. France.
   b. Britain.
   c. the United States.
   d. Italy.

2. Existentialists believed that
   a. the world was perfectible.
   b. only God was certain in this lost world.
   c. human beings can conquer life's absurdity.
   d. no human action can bring meaning to life.

3. The trend in literature in the postwar period was
   a. toward a new faith in God and mankind.
   b. the glorification of the state.
   c. the new belief in a world of growing desolation.
   d. utopian dreams of the future.

4. The German philosopher Friedrich Nietzsche believed that Western civilization
   a. had lost its creativity by neglecting emotion.
   b. should be rebuilt around Christian morality.
   c. needed to increase political democracy.
   d. should place more stress on social equality.

5. According to the British economist J. M. Keynes, the key to lasting peace and prosperity in Europe after World War I was

    a.  a powerful France and Russia.
    b.  the growth of the British empire.
    c.  the enforcement of the Treaty of Versailles.
    d.  a prosperous and strong Germany.

6. The British Labour Party leader and prime minister in 1924 and 1929 was
    a.  MacDonald.
    b.  Blum.
    c.  Sartre.
    d.  Keynes.

7. The "spirit of Locarno" after 1924 was a general European feeling that
    a.  the communist overthrow of European governments was inevitable.
    b.  Germany must be forced to pay her original reparation debts.
    c.  European peace and security were possible.
    d.  Hitler would bring about the recovery of Germany.

8. The decade following World War I was generally a period of
    a.  uncertainty and dissatisfaction with established ideas.
    b.  increasing belief in the goodness and perfectibility of humanity.
    c.  emphasis on the idea that a new science and technology would build a more democratic and liberal world.
    d.  religious revival based on the human nature of Christ, and the basic goodness of human beings.

9. The philosophy of logical empiricism held that
    a.  great philosophical issues can never be decided.
    b.  humanity must accept all truths as being absolute.
    c.  humanity is basically sinful.
    d.  there is no God.

10. The writings of Virginia Woolf and James Joyce reflect the postwar concern with the
    a.  reconstruction of society.
    b.  attempt to discover the reasons for the loss of faith in God.
    c.  conflict between materialism and spiritualism.
    d.  complexity and irrationality of the human mind.

11. Modern painting grew out of a revolt against
    a.  classicism.
    b.  capitalism.
    c.  French impressionism.
    d.  German romanticism.

12. The movement in painting that attacked all accepted standards of art and behavior and delighted in outrageous conduct was
    a.  the Bauhaus movement.
    b.  brutalism.
    c.  dada.
    d.  cubism.

13. For the people of Britain, the greatest problem of the 1920s was
    a.  increased class tension.
    b.  the Irish problem.
    c.  the rise of socialist dictatorship.
    d.  unemployment.

14. The antifascist movement in France in 1936–1937, led by Léon Blum, was known as the
    a.  Radical Alliance.
    b.  Communist Coalition.
    c.  Popular Front.
    d.  New Deal Republic.

15. In January 1923 the German Ruhr was occupied by
    a.  Russia.
    b.  France.
    c.  Britain.
    d.  Austria.

16. In both France and Germany in the 1920s the socialist and communist parties
    a.  declined in strength.
    b.  opposed democratic methods.
    c.  gained increased support from the working classes.
    d.  became overwhelmingly revolutionary.

17. Nietzsche believed that Western civilization had
    a.  found the eternal secret for a dynamic and vital civilization.
    b.  fallen away from liberalism and rationalism and thus was in danger of being conquered by the East.
    c.  lost its creativity and decayed into mediocrity.
    d.  had been strengthened by nationalism and socialism.

18. Albert Einstein theorized that
    a.  atoms were stable, basic building blocks of nature.
    b.  matter and energy are not interchangeable.

c. time and space are not absolute.
d. all of the above

19. To Freud, the key to understanding the mind, and thus human behavior, is the primitive irrational unconscious, which he called the
   a. ego.
   b. id.
   c. superego.
   d. supernatural.

20. The general trend in architecture and design in the postwar era, as seen in the Bauhaus movement, was toward
   a. monumental building to glorify the state.
   b. renewed emphasis on ornamentation.
   c. good, simple, functional design for everyday living.
   d. all of the above

21. One of the foremost figures in the functionalist movement in architecture and a founder of the Bauhaus school was
   a. Le Corbusier.
   b. William Morris.
   c. Louis H. Sullivan.
   d. Walter Gropius.

22. In the so-called atonal music of Schönberg, musical notes were
   a. independent and unrelated.
   b. based on the works of classical composers.
   c. brought together in recognizable harmonies.
   d. none of the above

23. Of all the Western democracies, the countries that responded most successfully to the challenge of the Great Depression were
   a. France and Britain.
   b. the United States and Britain.
   c. Sweden and Norway.
   d. Britain and Italy.

24. In responding to the Great Depression, the New Deal in America
   a. was not very successful in solving the problems of unemployment and low production levels.
   b. achieved considerably reduced unemployment.

    c.   was very successful because it turned to Keynesian views.

    d.   was successful in its program of wide-scale nationalization of the banks and railroads.

25.  War was condemned and renounced as an instrument of foreign policy in 1928 by the

    a.   Dawes Plan.

    b.   Kellogg-Briand Pact.

    c.   Treaty of Versailles.

    d.   New Deal.

26.  As the main opposition to the Conservatives in Britain, the Liberal Party was slowly being replaced after 1918 with a new party called the

    a.   Tory Party.

    b.   Socialist Party.

    c.   Labour Party.

    d.   Social Democratic Party.

27.  The U.S. film industry in the 1920s included screen stars such as

    a.   Lillian Gish.

    b.   Linda Parolini.

    c.   Mary Pickford.

    d.   both *a* and *c*

28.  The great filmmaker who made "The Triumph of the Will," a masterpiece of Nazi documentary propaganda, was

    a.   Sergei Eisenstein.

    b.   Mack Sennett.

    c.   Alban Berg.

    d.   Leni Riefenstahl.

## GEOGRAPHY

Using Map 34.1 in the text and using employment as a measure of the impact of the depression on society, what European countries were hurt most by the depression? How did this compare to the United States? What accounts for the regional differences within Britain (see Map 26.2)?

## UNDERSTANDING HISTORY THROUGH READING AND THE ARTS

The message of existentialist philosophy is movingly told in Albert Camus's *The Myth of Sisyphus** (1942), and the Paris that Gertrude Stein claimed was "where the twentieth century was" is the subject of Ernest Hemingway's *A Moveable Feast** (1964) and of Janet Flanner's *Paris Was Yesterday** (1972). The text bibliography lists a number of excellent books, including several on life during the depression. George Orwell's *Animal Farm** (1954) and *1984** (1949) are classics for good reason, and his book *The Road to Wigan Pier** (1937) is a view of British working class life in the era of the Great Depression.

Functionalism in architecture (including the Chicago school) is treated in N. Pevsner, *Pioneers of Modern Design** (1960). The international style and the man who made Chicago the most important architectural center in America are the subjects of P. Blacke, *Mies van der Rohe: Architecture and Structure** (1964), and more recently, *Mies van der Rohe: A Critical Biography* (1985) by F. Schulze. An excellent review of Le Corbusier's buildings and his writings is found in S. von Moos, *Le Corbusier** (1985), and the aims and achievements of the German Bauhaus movement are examined in two books by G. Naylor: *The Bauhaus** (1968) and *The Bauhaus Reassessed** (1985).

A good example of how art, including painting, became an expression of political-social attitudes is the work of George Grosz, a German painter. His work is shown and discussed in *George Grosz: The Berlin Years** (1985) by S. Sabarsky.

One of the most chilling examples of the use of film for the ideological transformation of a country is Leni Riefenstahl's documentary *The Triumph of the*

*Available in paperback.

*Will* (1934), showing the 1934 Nazi party rally at Nuremberg. It reveals a great deal about what Nazis wanted to believe about themselves and their leader, Adolf Hitler. It is available on video and film.

## PROBLEMS FOR FURTHER INVESTIGATION

Those interested in the complexities of interwar economic history will find B. W. E. Alford, *Depression and Recovery? British Economic Growth, 1918–1939** (1972), a short and readable discussion of a number of interpretations on the nature of the British economy. The Versailles treaty is dealt with in the Problems in European History book *The Versailles Settlement** (1960), edited by I. J. Lederer.

   The dramatic changes in domestic life, sport, amusement, politics, sex, and other aspects of life in the twenty-one-year period between the two great wars make a stimulating subject for student research. Begin your investigation with R. Graves and A. Hodge, *The Long Weekend, A Social History of Great Britain, 1918–1939** (1940, 1963).

*Available in paperback.

# CHAPTER 35

## DICTATORSHIPS AND THE
## SECOND WORLD WAR

## CHAPTER OBJECTIVES

After reading and studying this chapter you should be able to answer the following questions:

Q-1.   What are the characteristics of the twentieth-century totalitarian state?
Q-2.   How did the totalitarian state affect ordinary people?
Q-3.   How did it lead to war?

## CHAPTER SYNOPSIS

The anxiety and crisis that followed the First World War contributed to the rise of powerful dictatorships in parts of Europe. Some of these dictatorships were old-fashioned and conservative, but there were new totalitarian dictatorships as well, notably in Soviet Russia and Nazi Germany. This chapter examines the different kinds of dictatorship in a general way and then looks at Stalin's Russia and Hitler's Germany in detail.

In Soviet Russia, Lenin relaxed rigid state controls in 1921 after the civil war in order to revive the economy successfully. After defeating Trotsky in a struggle for power, Stalin established a harsh totalitarian dictatorship, which demanded great sacrifices from the people. But Soviet Russia built up its industry while peasants lost their land and a radically new socialist society came into being. Mussolini's government in Italy was much less radical and totalitarian.

This chapter concludes with Adolf Hitler and the totalitarian government of the Nazis in Germany. The roots of Nazism are found in racism, extreme nationalism, and violent irrationality, all of which drove Hitler relentlessly. Hitler was also a master politician, and this helped him gain power legally. His government was popular, especially because it appeared to solve the economic problems of the Great Depression. Hitler also had the support of the German masses because of his success in foreign affairs. He used bullying and fears of communism in Britain and France to rearm and expand, until finally war broke out over Poland in 1939. By 1942, Hitler and the Nazis had temporarily conquered a great empire and were putting their anti-Jewish racism into operation.

## STUDY OUTLINE

I.  Authoritarianism and totalitarianism in Europe after the First World War
    A.  Conservative authoritarianism
        1.  Conservative authoritarianism had deep roots in European history and led to an antidemocratic form of government that believed in avoiding change but was limited in its power and objectives
        2.  Conservative authoritarianism revived after the First World War in eastern Europe, Spain, and Portugal
        3.  The new authoritarian governments were more concerned with maintaining the status quo than with forcing society into rapid change
    B.  Modern totalitarianism
        1.  Modern totalitarianism emerged from World War I and the Russian civil war when individual liberties were subordinated to military efforts
        2.  Nothing was outside of the control of the all-important state: it was a dictatorship that sought to control the political, economic, social, intellectual, and cultural components of its subjects' lives
        3.  Unlike old-fashioned authoritarianism, which was based on elites, modern totalitarianism was based on the masses
        4.  Totalitarian regimes believed in mobilizing society toward some great goal
    C.  Totalitarianism of the left and the right
        1.  In Stalinist Russia, the leftists prevailed, and private property was taken over by the state
        2.  In Nazi Germany, private property was maintained
II. Stalin's Russia
    A.  From Lenin to Stalin
        1.  By 1921, the economy of Russia had been destroyed
        2.  Lenin's New Economic Policy (NEP) restored some capitalistic incentive
            a.  Peasants bought and sold goods on the free market
            b.  Agricultural production grew and industrial production surpassed the prewar level
        3.  Economic recovery and Lenin's death brought a struggle for power between Stalin and Trotsky, which Stalin won

      a. Stalin met the ethnic demands for independence within the multi-national Soviet state by granting minority groups limited freedoms

      b. Stalin's theory of "socialism in one country," or Russia's building its own socialist society, was more attractive to many Communists than Trotsky's theory of "permanent revolution," or the overthrow of other European states

    4. By 1927, Stalin had crushed all opposition and was ready to launch an economic-social revolution

  B. The five-year plans

    1. The first five-year plan to increase industrial and agricultural production was extremely ambitious, but Stalin wanted to erase the NEP, spur the economy, and catch up with the West

    2. Stalin waged a preventive war against the better-off peasants, the *kulaks*, to bring them and their land under state control

      a. Collectivization of the kulaks' land resulted in disaster for agriculture

      b. But it was a political victory for Stalin and the Communist party, as the peasants were eliminated as a potential threat

    3. The five-year plans brought about a spectacular growth of heavy industry, especially with the aid of government control of the workers and foreign technological experts

    4. Massive investment in heavy industry, however, meant low standards of living for workers

  C. Life in Stalinist society

    1. The Communists wanted to create a new kind of society and human personality

    2. Stalin's reign of terror and mass purges eliminated any opposition

    3. Propaganda and indoctrination were common features of life, and even art and literature became highly political

    4. Life was hard, but people were often inspired by socialist ideals and did gain some social benefits and the possibility of personal advancement through education

  D. Women in Soviet Russia

    1. Women were given much greater opportunities in industry and education

    2. Medicine and other professions were opened to them

    3. Most women had to work to help support their families in addition to caring for the home and the children

III. Mussolini's Italy

  A. The seizure of power

    1. The First World War and postwar problems ended the move toward democracy in Italy

    2. By 1922, most Italians were opposed to liberal parliamentary government

      3. Mussolini's Fascists (the Black Shirts) opposed the "socialist threat" with physical force

      4. Mussolini marched on Rome in 1922 and forced the king to name him head of the government

  B. The regime in action

      1. Mussolini's Fascists manipulated elections and killed the Socialist leader Matteotti

      2. Between 1924 and 1926 Mussolini built a one-party Fascist dictatorship — but never really totalitarian

        a. Much of the old power structure remained — particularly the capitalists

        b. The Catholic Church supported the Fascists

        c. Women were repressed, but Jews were not persecuted until late in the Second World War

IV. Hitler's Germany

  A. The roots of Nazism

      1. Hitler became a fanatical nationalist while in Vienna, where he absorbed anti-Semitic and racist ideas

      2. He believed that Jews and Marxists lost the First World War for Germany

      3. By 1921, he had converted the tiny extremist German Workers' group into the Nazi party

        a. The party grew rapidly

        b. Hitler and the party attempted to overthrow the Weimar government, but he was defeated and sent to jail (1923)

  B. Hitler's road to power (1923–1933)

      1. The trial after Hitler's attempted coup brought him much publicity, but the Nazi party remained small until 1929

      2. Written in jail, his autobiography, *Mein Kampf*, was an outline of his desire to achieve German racial supremacy and domination of Europe, under the leadership of a dictator (*führer*)

      3. The depression made the Nazi party a major party that was especially attractive to the lower middle class and to young people

      4. By 1932, the Nazi party was the largest in the Reichstag

      5. The Weimar government's orthodox politics intensified the economic collapse and convinced the middle class that its leaders were incompetent; hence, they welcomed Hitler's attacks on the republican system

      6. The Communists refused to ally with the socialists to block Hitler

      7. Hitler was a skilled politician, a master of propaganda and mass psychology, who generated enormous emotional support with his speeches

      8. Hitler was appointed chancellor in 1933

  C. The Nazi state and society

      1. The Enabling Act of March 1933 gave Hitler absolute dictatorial power

      2.  Nazis took over every aspect of German life — political, social, economic, cultural, and intellectual

      3.  Hitler took over total control of the military

      4.  The Gestapo, or secret police, used terror and purges to strengthen Hitler's hold on power

      5.  Hitler set out to eliminate the Jews

         a.  The Nuremberg Laws deprived Jews of their citizenship

         b.  Jews were constant victims of violence and outrages

  D.  Hitler's popularity

      1.  Hitler promised and delivered economic recovery through public works projects and military spending

      2.  Hitler reduced Germany's traditional class distinctions

      3.  He appealed to Germans for nationalistic reasons

      4.  Communists, trade unionists, and some Christians opposed Hitler; many who opposed him were executed

V.  Nazi expansion and the Second World War

  A.  Aggression and appeasement (1933–1939)

      1.  Hitler's main goal was territorial expansion for the superior German race

      2.  In violation of the Treaty of Versailles, he occupied the demilitarized Rhineland

      3.  The British policy of appeasement led to their approval of Hitler's aggression

      4.  Mussolini attacked Ethiopia and joined Germany in supporting the Fascists in Spain

      5.  Germany, Italy, and Japan formed an alliance

      6.  Hitler annexed Austria and demanded part of Czechoslovakia in 1938

      7.  Chamberlain flew to Munich to appease Hitler and agree to his territorial demands

      8.  Hitler accelerated his aggression and occupied all of Czechoslovakia

      9.  Hitler and Stalin signed a secret pact that divided eastern Europe into German and Russian zones

    10.  Germany attacked Poland, and Britain and France declared war on Germany (1939)

  B.  Hitler's empire (1939–1942)

      1.  The key to Hitler's military success was speed and force

      2.  He crushed Poland quickly and then France; by July 1940 the Nazis ruled nearly all of Europe except Britain

      3.  He bombed British cities in an attempt to break British morale but did not succeed

      4.  In 1941 Hitler's forces invaded Russia and conquered the Ukraine and got as far as Leningrad and Moscow

5. After Japan attacked Pearl Harbor (1941), Hitler also declared war on the United States
6. Hitler was determined to rid Europe of Slavs and Jews, and millions died in forced-labor or concentration camps

## REVIEW QUESTIONS

Q-1.   Evaluate the rise of conservative authoritarianism in Poland, Hungary, Yugoslavia, and Portugal. How do you explain this development?

Q-2.   What are the characteristics of modern totalitarianism? How does it differ from conservative authoritarianism?

Q-3.   What was the purpose of Lenin's New Economic Policy?

Q-4.   How successful was Stalin's program of five-year plans for the industrialization of Soviet Russia? What were its strengths and weaknesses?

Q-5.   How does one explain that despite a falling standard of living, many Russians in the 1920s and 1930s willingly worked harder and were happy?

Q-6.   Generally, did women gain or lose status and power in the new Stalinist Russian state?

Q-7.   What were the circumstances under which Mussolini rose to power in Italy? What were his goals and tactics?

Q-8.   Many Germans in the 1920s and 1930s viewed Hitler as a reformer. What were his ideas about the problems and the future of Germany?

Q-9.   Evaluate the impact of the Great Depression on German political life.

Q-10.   Discuss the role of mass propaganda and psychology in Hitler's rise to power.

Q-11.   Why did Hitler acquire such a mass appeal? Did he improve German life?

Q-12.   Describe the Munich Conference of 1938 and Chamberlain's policy of appeasement. Why were so many British willing to appease Hitler? What was the result of the Munich Conference?

Q-13.   Describe Hitler's foreign and military policy up to 1938. Was there enough evidence of aggression to convince the world that Hitler was dangerous?

Q-14.   What was the "final solution of the Jewish question"?

Q-15.   Describe German-Soviet relations between 1939 and 1941. Was war between the two inevitable?

## STUDY-REVIEW EXERCISES

*Define the following key concepts and terms.*

Hitler's final solution policy

modern totalitarianism

"socialism in one country"

appeasement

fascism

anti-Semitism

*Blitzkrieg*

*Identify* the following people and give their significance.

Béla Kun

Weimar Republic

National Socialist German Workers' Party

Benito Mussolini

Oliviera Salazar

Leon Trotsky

Chancellor Heinrich Brüning

General Paul Hindenburg

King Alexander of Yugoslavia

Neville Chamberlain

Russian kulaks

Nazi Storm Troopers (the SA)

Joseph Goebbels

German Social Democrats

*Explain* *what the following events were, who participated in them, and why they were important.*

Stalin's collectivization program

Lenin's New Economic Policy (1921)

Mussolini's march on Rome (1922)

Hitler's Munich plot (1923)

Great Depression in Germany (1929–1933)

Nuremberg Laws (1935)

Munich Conference (1938)

Russo-German ("Nazi-Soviet") nonaggression pact (1939)

Stalin's five-year plans

Battle of Britain


*Test* *your understanding of the chapter by answering the following questions.*

1. Unlike his rival Trotsky, Stalin *favored/opposed* the policy of "socialism in one country."
2. In Germany, the Communists *agreed/refused* to cooperate with the Social Democrats in opposition to Hitler.
3. Stalin's forced collectivization of peasant farms was a political *victory/failure* while it was an economic *success/disaster*.
4. Hitler's Nazi party ruled a modern totalitarian state of the *right/left*.
5. Totalitarian states of the right usually *do/do not* advocate state takeover of private property.
6. The antisocialist leader of the Italian Black Shirts was

_____.

7. Lenin's New Economic Policy *was/was not* a return to capitalism.
8. He was legally appointed chancellor of Germany in 1933.

_____

9.  The standard of living of the average Russian worker in the 1930s *improved/ declined* as a result of Stalin's five-year plans.
10. The foreign policy of Prime Minister Chamberlain tended to be *pro-German/ anti-German*.
11. Mussolini's Italy *did/did not* have all the characteristics of a modern totalitarian state.


## MULTIPLE-CHOICE QUESTIONS

1.  The German Nuremberg laws related to
    a.  antidepression programs.
    b.  the Versailles Treaty.
    c.  the elimination of the Fascists.
    d.  Jewish citizenship.

2.  The Vichy government of 1940 was established in
    a.  Poland.
    b.  Germany.
    c.  Czechoslovakia.
    d.  France.

3.  The two countries in which modern totalitarianism reached its most complete form in the 1930s were
    a.  Russia and Germany.
    b.  Italy and France.
    c.  Germany and Italy.
    d.  Russia and Italy.

4.  Before the modern totalitarian state, the traditional form of antidemocratic government in Europe was
    a.  conservative authoritarianism.
    b.  absolutism.
    c.  republicanism.
    d.  oligarchy.

5.  The modern totalitarian state is
    a.  lethargic in its approach.
    b.  built on elite groups.
    c.  concerned only with survival.
    d.  characterized by rapid and profound changes.

6. Lenin's New Economic Policy of 1921
   a. nationalized industries.
   b. called for the collectivization of agriculture.
   c. restored limited economic freedom.
   d. set five-year goals.

7. Before Lenin died, he named what man as his successor?
   a. Stalin
   b. Trotsky
   c. No one
   d. Dzhugashvili

8. Stalin became Lenin's successor because he
   a. was chosen by Lenin.
   b. was able to work outside the party.
   c. successfully related Russian realities to Marxist teachings.
   d. devised a system whereby minorities enjoyed total freedom.

9. Stalin's plans for rapid industrialization were based on
   a. importing coal from Japan.
   b. factories staffed exclusively by party members.
   c. depriving peasants in order to feed workers.
   d. a huge domestic market for consumer goods.

10. Under Stalin, women's greatest real benefits were
    a. sexual liberation and abortion.
    b. easy divorce and day-care centers.
    c. work freedom and accessible education.
    d. easier work than in the past and freedom from family worries.

11. Most Germans reacted to Hitler's purge of Jews with
    a. hostility and anger.
    b. protests and demonstrations.
    c. apathy and indifference.
    d. joy and celebration.

12. For Italian women, the fascist regime of Mussolini meant
    a. no improvement and a probable decline in status.
    b. considerable gains, especially in finding new careers in industry.
    c. more birth control and better-paying jobs.
    d. greater political participation and legal rights.

13. The people within German society whom Hitler appealed to most were
    a.  industrial workers.
    b.  the poor.
    c.  Social Democrats.
    d.  the middle class.

14. Conservative authoritarianism differed from modern totalitarianism in that it
    a.  did not result in dictatorships.
    b.  allowed popular participation in government.
    c.  was more concerned with maintaining the status quo than with rapid change or war.
    d.  did not persecute liberals or socialists.

15. One major reason for British appeasement of Hitler was that
    a.  he was seen as a way to block German capitalist expansion.
    b.  he was seen as the bulwark against communism.
    c.  the British government was prosocialist.
    d.  none of the above

16. After becoming dictator Hitler did which one of the following?
    a.  Strengthened labor unions
    b.  Limited the number of political parties to three
    c.  Gave awards for intellectual achievement
    d.  Eliminated the Nazi Storm Troopers

17. The Russian *kulaks* were
    a.  rich farmers who rejected Christianity.
    b.  bureaucrats who joined the Communist party.
    c.  peasants who opposed collectivization.
    d.  industrial workers.

18. For the Russian people, Stalin's Five-Year Plans meant
    a.  great gains in industrial growth plus an improved standard of living.
    b.  great gains in industrial growth but no improvement in the individual's standard of living.
    c.  improvement for the life of the industrial worker but not for the farm worker.
    d.  an increase in consumer goods available for all Russians.

19. By 1938 in Germany there were
    a.  greater equality and exceptional opportunities for the middle and lower classes.

b. exploitation and terrorism.

c. greater opportunities for the upper classes.

d. a severe economic recession.

20. The Second World War
    a. slowed down the totalitarian movement.
    b. eliminated most of the totalitarian states in eastern Europe.
    c. resulted in a totalitarian state in Germany.
    d. speeded up the movement toward modern totalitarianism.

21. Hitler's "final solution" policy was created to
    a. defeat France and Russia in a two-front war.
    b. kill all the Jews in Europe.
    c. end capitalism in Germany.
    d. create a new all-German Europe.

22. The British prime minister who gave in to Hitler's territorial demands was
    a. Winston Churchill.
    b. David Lloyd George.
    c. Neville Chamberlain.
    d. Bonar Law.

23. Mussolini
    a. drew support from the Catholic church.
    b. drew support from Jews.
    c. usurped Vatican lands and angered the Pope.
    d. kept religion out of politics.

24. The act that gave Hitler absolute dictatorial power in 1933 was the
    a. Munich Conference.
    b. Enabling Act.
    c. *Blitzkrieg.*
    d. resignation of Brüning.

25. *Mein Kampf*, written by Hitler, was
    a. a lurid, anti-Semitic novel.
    b. dictated while he was serving a prison sentence.
    c. autobiographical and apolitical.
    d. basically economic in nature.

26. Which of the following was found in Stalinist society?
    a. Police terrorism

b. Religious toleration
c. Freedom of expression
d. Large-scale discrimination against women in the job market

27. Lenin's New Economic Program
    a. did nothing to appease the peasant majority.
    b. created a massive recession.
    c. denationalized heavy industry and banks.
    d. brought rapid economic recovery.

28. Stalin's collectivization
    a. increased agricultural output markedly.
    b. caused agricultural output to plummet.
    c. was a total political disaster.
    d. did not cause any drastic change in agricultural output.

## UNDERSTANDING HISTORY THROUGH READING AND THE ARTS

There has been a burst of literature on Hitler and Nazi Germany in recent years. Two of the most readable books are A. Speer, *Inside the Third Reich\** (1971), and L. S. Davidowicz, *The War Against the Jews, 1933–1945\** (1975). Speer was an architect who became Hitler's chief war planner and one of the persons closest to Hitler. His picture of Hitler is revealing in many ways. Davidowicz writes about the German "final solution." It's a horrible story but one that needs to be told to every generation. The relationship between anti-Semitism and German Fascism is further examined in Y. Bauer, *A History of the Holocaust\** (1982), and the motives of a concentration camp commandant are evaluated in G. Sereny, *Into That Darkness\** (1974, 1982). The least known of the Nazi atrocities is dealt with in F. Rector, *The Nazi Extermination of Homosexuals* (1981).

A large number of first-rank films have been made about Europe in the 1930s. *The Shop on Main Street* (1966) is a drama of a man living under Nazi occupation in Czechoslovakia who is sent to take over a button shop from an old Jewish woman. Similarly moving is *The Diary of Anne Frank* (1959), which is about a Jewish family hiding in an attic in Amsterdam in World War II. John Gielgud and Irene Worth narrate a French documentary about the Spanish Civil War entitled *To Die in Madrid* (1965). The film *Night and Fog*, by Resnais, is a chilling documentary of the Nazi concentration camps.

*Available in paperback.

## PROBLEMS FOR FURTHER INVESTIGATION

The period considered in this chapter is constantly undergoing reinterpretation, and new material appears each year. Helpful is A. Funk et al., *A Select Bibliography on Books on the Second World War\** (1975). This is a bibliography of books published from 1966 to 1975.

Those interested in examining the tangle of views on the life and motives of Hitler should begin with R. G. L. Waite, ed., *Hitler and Nazi Germany* (1965), and A. Bullock, *Hitler: A Study in Tyranny* (revised, 1962), and for Hitler's impact on German society, D. G. Williamson, *The Third Reich* (1984). About the Italian dictator, the student should read D. M. Smith, *Mussolini* (1982). A highly scholarly account of Hitler's appeal to the German people is R. Hamilton, *Who Voted for Hitler?\** (1982). The problem of the origins of the Second World War is the subject of W. L. Kleine-Ahlbrandt, ed., *Appeasement of the Dictators* (1970).

Stalin's contribution to history has been the subject of much debate. The best overall summary of this debate is M. McCauley, *Stalin and Stalinism\** (1983), while the chilling horrors of one aspect of Stalin's regime are dealt with (including photographs) in I. Deutscher and D. King, *The Great Purges* (1985). And a good short discussion of the origins and motives of the political extremes of the decades between the two world wars is D. Smith, *Left and Right in Twentieth-Century Europe\** (1970).

# CHAPTER 36

## THE RECOVERY OF EUROPE AND
## THE AMERICAS

## CHAPTER OBJECTIVES

After reading and studying this chapter you should be able to answer the following questions:

Q-1.   What were the strengths and weaknesses of the Grand Alliance, and how did it defeat Germany?
Q-2.   How did Western society recover from the Second World War?
Q-3.   What were the causes of the cold war?
Q-4.   How did "economic nationalism" transform Latin America?
Q-5.   What were the major political developments in the United States after the Second World War, and why did the United States become involved in Vietnam?

## CHAPTER SYNOPSIS

This chapter shows how Europe, especially Western Europe, recovered from the destruction of 1945, how the cold war split the continent into communist and non-communist blocs, how the old European empires were replaced by neocolonialism, why the Soviets intervened in Czechoslovakia and the United States in Vietnam, and how North and South America also revived and evolved in the postwar era.

The author examines why the Grand Alliance of Britain, the Soviet Union, and the United States failed to hold together after it succeeded in defeating Nazi Germany. Military discussions, ideological differences, and disputes over eastern Europe were key factors in the origins of the cold war. By 1950 the Iron Curtain was in place, and western and eastern Europe were going their separate ways. Battered western Europe rebuilt quickly and successfully, helped by new leaders and attitudes, U.S. aid, and the creation of the Common Market. In the United States, prosperity contributed to the popular desire to hold on to the social policies of the liberal New Deal era of Roosevelt, and an important civil rights movement and a war on poverty resulted in significant changes. Developments in east European countries closely followed those in Soviet Russia. Stalin reimposed a harsh dictatorship after the war, which Khrushchev relaxed (de-Stalinization). The policy of détente was furthered with East-West agreements at Helsinki. Meanwhile, the Cold War was reheated as the United States, in an effort to "roll back communism" and after refusing to allow free elections in Vietnam, carried on a long and unsuccessful war in Vietnam — which, by the end, had brought down two U.S. presidents and left the United States divided and with diminished world prestige. The Soviet leaders engaged themselves in successfully putting down a revolution in 1968 in Czechoslovakia. which sought "socialism with a human face," and carried out at home a program of re-Stalinization that aimed at ending internal opposition and reasserting a unified national spirit. Since 1985 Gorbachev has worked to increase Soviet productivity. An anticommunist popular revolt in Hungary failed, while material conditions in communist countries gradually improved and communist governments remained firmly in control.

European empires in Asia went out of business after the Second World War. India led the way to national independence right after the war, and other British territories in Africa followed. Most important, a kind of neocolonization emerged whereby Europe and the United States used their economic power to make Africa, much of Asia, and Latin America subordinate to the West.

## STUDY OUTLINE

I.  Allied victory and the cold war (1942–1950)
    A.  The Grand Alliance
        1.  The twenty-six allied nations were led by Britain, the United States, and the Soviet Union
        2.  America's war policy was to defeat Germany before Japan
        3.  The Allies put military decisions, such as the Allied invasion of Germany, above political questions, such as the political makeup of postwar Europe
        4.  The Allies decided that the unconditional surrender of Japan and Germany would be necessary
        5.  Allied strength was enormous, and it was aided by the resistance groups, many of which were communist
            a.  America's strength lay in its industry and national unity
            b.  Britain drew on its empire and on the United States for resources and also effectively mobilized its own economy
            c.  Russia drew on its large industrial capacity and the heroic determination of its people

B. The tide of battle
1. The Germans were turned back at Stalingrad at the end of 1942
2. American victories in the Pacific in 1942 put Japan on the defensive
3. British-American victories in North Africa in 1942 gave the Allies a springboard for the Italian campaign
4. Italy surrendered in 1943, but fighting continued as the Germans seized Rome and northern Italy
5. The Allies pushed into Germany from the east and the west; Germany surrendered in May 1945, and Hitler committed suicide
6. The United States dropped two atomic bombs on Japan, and it too surrendered, in August 1945

C. The origins of the cold war
1. American-British invasion via France meant that Soviet Russia alone would occupy Eastern Europe
2. At the Yalta Conference the Allies decided to divide Germany into occupation zones and to demand that Germany pay reparations to the Soviet Union
3. The British and the Americans wanted free elections in eastern Europe
4. To prevent another German invasion the Russians wanted pro-Russian, pro-communist governments
5. In general, Soviet control over eastern Europe could not be prevented by the United States after 1945

D. West versus East
1. Truman cut off aid to Russia because of Stalin's insistence on having communist governments in eastern Europe
2. By 1947, many Americans believed that Stalin was trying to export communist revolution throughout Europe
3. The Marshall Plan was established to help European recovery; the Truman Doctrine was meant to prevent further spread of communism
4. The Soviet blockade of Berlin led to a successful allied airlift
5. In 1949, the United States formed an anti-Soviet military alliance of Western governments, the North Atlantic Treaty Organization (NATO); in return, Stalin united his satellites in the Warsaw Pact
6. In 1949, Communists won in China
7. In 1950, when communist North Korea invaded the south, American-led UN troops intervened
8. The Western attempt to check Stalin probably came too late and may have encouraged Russian aggression

II. The western European renaissance
A. The postwar challenge
1. The war left Europe physically devastated and in a state of economic and moral crisis

2. New leaders and new parties, especially the Catholic Christian Demo-crats, emerged in Italy, France, and Germany and provided effective leadership and needed reforms

3. In many countries, such as Britain, France, and Italy, socialists and communists emerged from the war with considerable power and a strong desire for social reform

4. Socialists and Communists emerged with strong popular support and pushed for welfare measures and nationalization of certain industries

5. The Marshall Plan aided in economic recovery and led to the Organiza-tion for European Economic Cooperation (OEEC), while NATO led to military protection

B. Economic "miracles"
1. Led by West Germany, a European economic miracle was underway by 1963
2. A free-market economy — with a social welfare net — brought rapid growth to West Germany
3. A mixed state and private economy brought rapid growth to France
4. Old skills, new markets, cheap labor, and the Common Market stimu-lated economic development in western Europe

C. Toward European unity
1. Democratic republics — with a stress on civil liberties — were reestab-lished in France, West Germany, and Italy
2. Christian Democrats and others opposed traditional nationalism and sought a unified Europe, but economic unity proved to be more realis-tic than political unity
3. The six-nation Coal and Steel Community marked the beginning of a movement toward European unity and led to further technical and economic cooperation
4. The Treaty of Rome (1957) created the European Economic Com-munity (EEC, or Common Market), whose immediate goal was to create a free-trade area and reduce tariffs
5. But regenerated hopes for political union in Europe were frustrated by a resurgence of nationalism in the 1960s
   a. De Gaulle, a romantic nationalist, wanted France to lead the Common Market
   b. He withdrew from NATO and blocked British attempts to join the Common Market

D. Decolonization of Asia and Africa
1. The causes of imperial decline between 1947 and 1962
   a. Internal demands for political self-determination and equality had spread in old colonial areas, especially after the First World War
   b. The Second World War reduced European power and destroyed the Western sense of moral and racial superiority

    2.  Britain under the Labour Party gave up India, but France tried to reestablish colonial rule in Indochina and Algeria

    3.  African states gained independence, but many increased economic and cultural ties with their former European rulers

    4.  As a result, a renewed economic subordination (or neocolonialism) was imposed on Africa by western Europe and the United States

  E.  Political trends since 1968

    1.  Student and worker unrest in France in 1968 signaled the end of the era of postwar recovery

    2.  Economic problems of the 1970s did not cause Europe to return to economic nationalism; instead, more nations joined the Common Market and the movement toward European unity

    3.  Democracy was strengthened as Spain, Portugal, and Greece turned toward democratic rule, and as the Italian and French Communist parties participated in democratic governments

III.  Soviet Eastern Europe

  A.  Stalin's last years

    1.  The national unity of the war period ended in rigid dictatorship again

    2.  Stalin began a new series of purges and enforced cultural conformity

      a.  Soviet citizens living outside Russia were forced to return, and nearly a million of them plus other Russians died in labor camps

      b.  Culture, art, and the Jewish religion were attacked

    3.  Five-year plans were reintroduced

    4.  Stalin's repressive system was exported to eastern Europe

      a.  Only Tito in Yugoslavia was able to build an east European communist state free from Stalinist control

      b.  Tito's success led Stalin to purge the Communist parties of eastern Europe in an attempt to increase their obedience to him

  B.  Reform and de-Stalinization

    1.  Khrushchev and fellow reformers won the leadership of Russia over the conservatives, who wanted to make as few changes as possible in the Stalinist system

    2.  Khrushchev denounced Stalin and began a policy of liberalization

      a.  The Soviet standard of living was improved, and greater intellectual freedom was allowed

      b.  Writers such as Pasternak and Solzhenitsyn criticized the Stalinist past

      c.  Khrushchev pushed for "peaceful coexistence" with the West and a relaxation of cold war tensions

    3.  This de-Stalinization caused revolution in eastern Europe

      a.  Poland won greater autonomy

      b.  Hungary expelled Soviet troops and declared its neutrality but was invaded by Russia and the reformers defeated

C.  From Brezhnev to Gorbachev
1.  Re-Stalinization began with Khrushchev's fall (1964)
    a.  Khrushchev was opposed by some party members and by conservatives in foreign policy
    b.  He was successful in Berlin but lost to the United States over Cuba
    c.  Brezhnev stressed the ties with the Stalinist era and launched an arms buildup
2.  Under the reformer Dubček, the Czech communist party instituted reforms that stressed socialism with freedom and democracy
    a.  The reforms were popular but frightened entrenched powers
    b.  The Soviet and other East bloc leaders feared Czech nationalism or even pro-Western policy
    c.  The Soviets responded in August of 1968 with brutal repression
    d.  The Czech leaders backed down; reforms were canceled
    e.  Later, the Brezhnev Doctrine was announced, declaring it rightful for the Soviets to intervene in any socialist country
    f.  Western Europe stood by without responding because it believed in the sphere-of-influence principle
3.  In the Soviet Union the Czech crisis caused a step backward toward Stalinization
    a.  However, the standard of living continued to improve
    b.  Russian national pride contributed to stability
    c.  The Great Russians feared demands for autonomy from East European and non-Russian nationalities
    d.  Massive party bureaucracy and centralization hindered economic growth
    e.  Gorbachev is interested in economic reform
IV.  The Western Hemisphere
A.  Postwar prosperity in the United States
1.  Conversion to a peacetime economy went smoothly, and a generation experienced ever-greater prosperity
2.  Until the 1960s, domestic politics consisted largely of consolidating the New Deal and maintaining the status quo
B.  The civil-rights revolution in the United States
1.  School segregation was declared unconstitutional by the Supreme Court in 1954
2.  Blacks used militant nonviolence and growing political power to gain reforms in the 1960s, while the United States became more of a welfare state
C.  The Vietnam trauma and beyond
1.  U.S. involvement in Vietnam grew out of its fear of communism
    a.  The United States refused to allow free elections in Vietnam, and it deposed uncooperative leaders

      b.  President Johnson vowed not to "lose" Vietnam and therefore carried out a massive military buildup and bombing, but without victory

  2.  Public criticism of the war brought the defeat of Johnson and in 1968 the election of President Nixon

      a.  Nixon cut war costs and brought many troops home, but the war continued for another four years

      b.  Nixon's illegal activities led to the Watergate crisis and his resignation

  3.  Vietnam became unified, and the United States was left divided and uncertain about its world policy

  4.  The policy of détente resulted in an East-West agreement at Helsinki guaranteeing frontiers and human rights

      a.  But Soviet involvement in Afghanistan and elsewhere convinced some Americans that the Soviets were violating the spirit of détente

      b.  President Reagan undertook a U.S. arms buildup and sought to overthrow pro-Marxist governments

D.  Economic nationalism in Latin America

  1.  Latin American countries had long been the victims of neocolonial practices on the part of Europe and the United States

  2.  Beginning with the Great Depression, more popularly based governments encouraged the development of local manufacturing to reduce their dependence on raw-materials production and foreign markets

  3.  In Mexico the revolution of 1910 opened a new era of economic nationalism, social reform, and industrialization

      a.  President Cardenas nationalized U.S. oil companies

      b.  The Mexican state successfully promoted industrialization from the early 1940s to the late 1960s

  4.  Under the strongman Vargas and then under Kubitschek Brazil also embraced economic nationalism and moderate social reform

E.  The Cuban Revolution

  1.  Cuba was relatively rich but suffered from dictatorship, corruption, and a tradition of U.S. intervention

  2.  The magnetic Fidel Castro led a successful revolution, which had major consequences

      a.  Castro repelled a U.S.-supported invasion by Cuban exiles, thereby winning great prestige

      b.  He established a communist and authoritarian society

      c.  Castro's success encouraged leftist hopes throughout Latin America

F.  Authoritarianism and democracy in Latin America

  1.  Democratic government has been in retreat in Latin America since the Cuban Revolution, and the gap between rich and poor has widened

2. In Brazil and Argentina the military has generally ruled since 1964, with the support of conservatives and most of the middle class

3. In Chile the army overturned a leftist government and imposed a harsh dictatorship

4. The new authoritarians oppose communism, but they are also determined modernizers, committed to national independence and industrialization

5. In the 1980s, Peru, Bolivia, and Ecuador reestablished elected governments, and in Argentina military defeat led to democratic and antimilitary action

6. Brazil's government was turned over to civilian rule

7. In Nicaragua in 1979 the Sandinista reform government overthrew the U.S.-supported Somoza dictatorship — to the dismay of the Reagan government in the United States

## REVIEW QUESTIONS

Q-1.   What were the strengths and weaknesses of the Grand Alliance? Can you identify any sources of future problems?

Q-2.   If the Americans and the British did not open the western front against Germany until June 1944, on what fronts was the war against Hitler carried on?

Q-3.   One of the controversies over World War II military strategy is whether the bombing of cities and civilians helped to defeat the enemy. What is the answer?

Q-4.   Why was the Teheran Conference important in shaping the map of postwar Europe? What were the alternatives?

Q-5.   Describe the dispute between the United States and Russia at the end of the war. How and why did it escalate into a cold war?

Q-6.   What are the sources of the Soviet Union's paranoia about Germany and vice versa? What do they tell us about the cold war?

Q-7.   How did Europe accomplish economic recovery after the war? What factors contributed to its growth?

Q-8.   Which approach toward European unity was more successful, the political or the economic? Why?

Q-9.   Describe the steps taken toward European economic unity. How does this unity affect the European and world economy?

Q-10.   Was nationalism completely dead in postwar Europe? Who was Charles de Gaulle, and what was his ambition?

Q-11.   What is neocolonialism? Give examples to support your definition.

Q-12.   "Postwar domestic politics in the United States consisted largely of making modest adjustments to the status quo." Why was this so?

Q-13.   What were the milestones in the civil-rights revolution?

Q-14.   What are some of the key components of economic nationalism? How and why did it arise in Latin America?

Q-15.   Compare and contrast Mexico under Cardenas with Brazil under Vargas.

Q-16.   What were the causes and the consequences of the Cuban Revolution?

Q-17.   What is meant by "the new authoritarianism in Latin America"? Are military governments in Latin America reacting to fears of social reform or communist revolution?

Q-18.   Evaluate Soviet foreign policy toward eastern Europe by discussing Poland and Hungary in 1956.

Q-19.   Evaluate Stalin's postwar policy and actions. Why were many Russian nationalists disappointed in them? How would you judge Stalin's place in Soviet history?

Q-20.   Describe the circumstances surrounding Khrushchev's famous Twentieth Party Congress speech in 1956. What were the results of his policy?

Q-21.   What were the reasons for Khrushchev's fall from power and the beginning of the re-Stalinization of Russia in 1964?

Q-22.   Why did the United States become involved in a war in Vietnam? Why did the Vietcong win?

Q-23.   What were the consequences of the Nixon-Watergate crisis?

Q-24.   What were the motives of the Czechoslovakian communist party reform movement of 1968 under Dubček? Why did the experiment fail? Why didn't western Europe give support to Czechoslovakia?

## STUDY-REVIEW EXERCISES

<u>Define</u> *the following key concepts and terms.*

neocolonialism

economic nationalism

"containment of communism" policy

cold war

"socialism with a human face" (Czechoslovakia)

mixed economy

détente

Truman Doctrine

de-Stalinization/re-Stalinization

decolonization

"European nation"


*Identify* each of the following and give its significance.

Sandinista government of Nicaragua

battle of Stalingrad

NATO

European Coal and Steel Community

British Labour party

Hiroshima and Nagasaki

National Association for the Advancement of Colored People

Vietcong

Tet offensive

Geneva accords (of 1954)

Brezhnev Doctrine

Civil Rights Act of 1964

Kuomintang

Atlantic Charter

Alliance for Progress

Marshall Plan

Warsaw Pact

Common Market

Taft-Hartley Act

*Identify the following people and explain their importance.*

Josip Tito

Ho Chi Minh

Nikita Khrushchev

Lázaro Cárdenas

Clement Attlee

Salvador Allende

Charles de Gaulle

Fidel Castro

Winston Churchill

Leonid Brezhnev

Juan Perón

João Goulart

Richard Nixon

Alexander Dubček

Getulio Vargas

Mikhail Gorbachev

*Explain* what the following events were, who participated in them, and why they were important.

Normandy invasion (June 6, 1944)

Schuman Plan (1950)

Twentieth Party Congress of the Soviets (1956)

Berlin Blockade of 1961

U.S. Civil Rights Act of 1964

election of the Allende government (1970)

Chinese civil war (1945–1949)

partition of Palestine (1948)

Bay of Pigs invasion (1961)

Falkland Islands War (1982)

*Explain* what happened at the following wartime conferences of the Big Three and what impact each one had on the postwar world.

*Conference and Date*

Casablanca (January 1943)

Teheran (November 1943)

Yalta (February 1945)

*Test your understanding of the chapter by answering the following questions.*

1.  The American aid program that led to the establishment of the Organization for European Economic Cooperation was known as the

_____.

2. The post–World War II Soviet bloc's military alliance is known as the

   _____.

3. The resurgence of traditional nationalism in France was led, from 1958 to 1969,

   by President _____.

## MULTIPLE-CHOICE QUESTIONS

1. French economic recovery following World War II centered on
   a. free-market capitalism alone.
   b. socialism.
   c. a mixed state and private economy.
   d. trade unionism.

2. Khrushchev
   a. denounced Stalinist policies and Stalin himself.
   b. carried on the Stalinist traditions.
   c. opposed reconciliation with the West.
   d. placed restrictions on cultural freedom.

3. The only eastern European communist leader to build an independent communist state free from Stalinist control was
   a. Nagy.
   b. Tito.
   c. Dubček.
   d. Schuman.

4. In Italy, the leading political party in the immediate postwar elections was the
   a. Communists.
   b. Catholic Center.
   c. Socialists.
   d. Christian Democrats.

5. American-Soviet conflict in the post–World War II era first centered on the problem of the future of
   a. France.
   b. East Germany.
   c. Yugoslavia.
   d. Poland.

6.  All but which one of the following had embraced military authoritarian government by the 1970s?
    a.  Chile
    b.  Mexico
    c.  Brazil
    d.  Argentina

7.  Prior to June 1944, most of the fighting on land against Hitler's Germany was carried out by
    a.  France.
    b.  Britain.
    c.  Russia.
    d.  the United States.

8.  During and after World War Two, U.S. leaders were most concerned that after the war the east European countries would
    a.  become U.S. allies.
    b.  be friendly toward Russia.
    c.  have freely elected governments.
    d.  reject German fascism.

9.  The Frenchman who came to symbolize the resurgence of European nationalism was
    a.  Jean Monnet.
    b.  Charles de Gaulle.
    c.  Robert Schuman.
    d.  André Malraux.

10. Since the Second World War, communist participation in west European governments has
    a.  decreased.
    b.  disappeared entirely.
    c.  been outlawed in most countries.
    d.  increased.

11. The only east European communist country able to remain free of Stalin's control was
    a.  Poland.
    b.  Yugoslavia.
    c.  East Germany.
    d.  the Ukraine.

12. The country that blocked British entry into the Common Market and that withdrew its forces from NATO was
    a. Belgium.
    b. West Germany.
    c. Italy.
    d. France.

13. Under Stalin, top priority in production in the Soviet Union was given to
    a. consumer goods.
    b. military goods.
    c. aid for rebuilding East Germany.
    d. building new housing.

14. The turning point of the Second World War on the eastern front was fought at
    a. Leningrad.
    b. Brest-Litovsk.
    c. Stalingrad.
    d. El Alemein.

15. The allied nations of the Second World War included each of the following except
    a. the Soviet Union.
    b. the United States.
    c. Austria.
    d. Britain.

16. In 1954 the French lost control of
    a. Indochina.
    b. Algeria.
    c. South Sudan.
    d. Teheran.

17. The de-Stalinization program in the Soviet Union led to revolts in
    a. Italy and Turkey.
    b. Poland and Hungary.
    c. Volgograd and Leningrad.
    d. Mongolia and Afghanistan.

18. The Treaty of Rome in 1957
    a. ended the Second World War.
    b. created the United Nations.
    c. declared war on world communism.
    d. created the European Common Market.

19. For the most part, it appears that Soviet control over Eastern Europe
    a. could not have been prevented by the United States.
    b. was a part of Stalin's plan to control all of Europe.
    c. was welcomed by the east European countries.
    d. all of the above.

20. West German economic recovery following World War II centered on
    a. free-market capitalism.
    b. socialism.
    c. a mixed state and private economy.
    d. welfare-statism.

21. All but which one of the following were goals of the de-Stalinization program in Russia?
    a. Relaxation of cold-war tensions
    b. Acceptance of different paths to socialism
    c. Cultural and literary freedom
    d. A shift in economy toward consumer goods and agriculture

22. United States involvement in Vietnam had its origins in
    a. fear of French imperialism.
    b. the U.S. attempt to impose free elections on the Vietnamese.
    c. an attempt to stop communism.
    d. U.S. economic interests in Asia.

23. The Czechoslovakian experiment of 1968 sought
    a. socialism with a human face.
    b. the end of communism.
    c. the expulsion of the Soviets.
    d. the adoption of a capitalist economy.

24. The U.S. President who vowed not to lose Vietnam was
    a. Lyndon Johnson.
    b. Richard Nixon.
    c. John Kennedy.
    d. Dwight Eisenhower.

25. The Brezhnev Doctrine declared that the
    a. Soviets will go ahead with arms buildup.
    b. Chinese were not true Socialists.
    c. party must reform itself.
    d. Soviets had the right to intervene in any socialist country.

26. The Czechoslovakian reform movement had the following impact on everyday life in the Soviet Union.
    a. Fall in the standard of living
    b. Decline in nationalistic spirit
    c. Decline in bureaucratic influence
    d. Re-Stalinization

27. The Helsinki agreements of 1975 centered on
    a. the guarantee of human rights and existing political frontiers.
    b. a reduction of military spending and arms production.
    c. an international ban on nuclear testing.
    d. the reunification of Europe.

28. At the Yalta Conference on 1945, the Allied leaders agreed to
    a. demand unconditional surrender of Germany.
    b. Russian hegemony in eastern Europe.
    c. divide Germany into zones of occupation.
    d. let East European governments be anti-Russian.

## GEOGRAPHY

1. Show on the outline map the location of the so-called Iron Curtain that has divided Europe since the Second World War.
2. Shade in the territory lost by Germany after the Second World War. Should East Germany be considered "lost" territory?
3. Shade in the territory gained by the Soviet Union after the Second World War. Did Poland gain anything in return for its losses to the Soviet Union?

4. Locate on the map and label the original members of the Common Market. Label the countries that have joined in later years. How does the subsequent expansion illustrate the success of the Common Market?

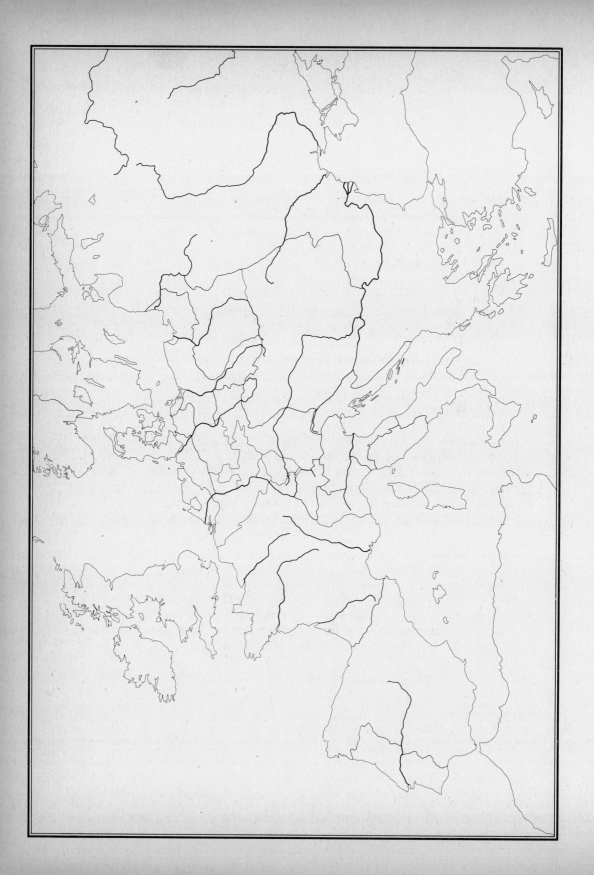

5.  Locate on the map and label the following places.

| | | | |
|---|---|---|---|
| Berlin | Brussels | Paris | London |
| Warsaw | Rome | Belgrade | Moscow |
| Bonn | Prague | | |

What do all of these cities have in common?

## UNDERSTANDING HISTORY THROUGH READING AND THE ARTS

Alexander Solzhenitsyn's *One Day in the Life of Ivan Denisovich*\* (1962) is a powerful and moving story of one human being in a postwar prison camp in Stalinist Russia. One of the best books on the origins of the cold war is L. Halle, *The Cold War as History* (1967).

The release from Nazi occupation gave an enormous boost to popular song throughout Europe. Nowhere were songwriters and young artists as inspired as in France, and no one was as loved by the French people as Edith Piaf. Piaf was a nightclub singer who sang *chanson réalistes* — songs about the joys, frustrations, and sorrows of the people of the streets. She made her first recording in 1936. Her first recording after the war, *Les Trois Cloches*, was described as "the folklore of the future." She died in 1963 after a full and sometimes tragic life. Many recordings of her performances are available.

## PROBLEMS FOR FURTHER INVESTIGATION

Why were the Vietnamese peasants able to withstand the onslaught of U.S. military technology? Did the war contribute to the Watergate scandal? Could the United States have won the war? These questions and many others are considered in H. Higgens, *Vietnam*\* (1982 edition), in G. McT. Kahin, *Intervention: How America Became Involved in Vietnam* (1986), and S. Karnow, *Vietnam, A History*\* (1983).

Who were the men who shaped the great postwar alliance among Europe, the United States, and Japan? What were the key events and ideas behind this alliance? Based on interviews, memoirs, and documents, the key figures of the postwar era — Eisenhower, De Gaulle, Kennedy, Schmidt, MacArthur, and others — come alive in R. Barnet, *The Alliance* (1983).

\*Available in paperback.

Those interested in the military history of the Second World War and the postwar era will want to begin with P. Paret, *Makers of Modern Strategy, from Machiavelli to the Nuclear Age** (1986). The origins of the cold war, according to its earliest interpreters, were rooted in the conflict between communist aggression and U.S. benevolence. Preoccupied with the task of defeating the Axis powers, the United States misjudged the intentions of the Soviet Union and, unknowingly, opened the door to communist expansion. U.S. policy makers then adopted policies designed to "contain" Russian aggression. For example, see G. F. Kennan, *American Diplomacy, 1900–1950* (1951).

Then the turbulent sixties, which were characterized by a reappraisal of American truths, led some historians to reexamine the origins of the cold war. Revisionists such as W. A. Williams, *The Tragedy of American Diplomacy** (1959), and W. Lafeber, *America, Russia, and the Cold War, 1945–1975** (1976), emphasized U.S. economic expansion as a major reason for the confrontation between East and West. Armed with a monopoly of atomic weapons, the United States threatened Soviet security and thereby forced communist leaders to forge eastern Europe into a protective buffer under Soviet hegemony. For a good brief survey of cold war literature see the pamphlet by B. Tierney, et al., *The Cold War — Who Is to Blame?** (1967).

*Available in paperback.

# CHAPTER 37

## ASIA AND AFRICA IN THE CONTEMPORARY WORLD

## CHAPTER OBJECTIVES

After reading and studying this chapter you should be able to answer the following questions:

Q-1.   Why and how have Asian and African countries risen so rapidly since World War Two?
Q-2.   How are the emerging nation-states facing the economic, social, and cultural challenges of today's world?

## CHAPTER SYNOPSIS

A turning point in modern world history has been the resurgence and political self-assertion of Asian and African peoples since 1945. Under Mao Tse-tung, China transformed itself from a weak nation to a major world power. The Communist victory of 1949 was due to its strong guerrilla army, its program of land redistribution, and the failure of the Nationalists to gain peasant support. At first Mao followed the Soviet model as it stressed the development of heavy industry and totalitarian social controls. Then, with Mao's Great Leap Forward, China turned its back on Russia by placing emphasis on peasant communal agriculture. This was followed by a cultural revolution, reconciliation with the United States, and, more recently, a Second Revolution that has resulted in a return to peasant family agriculture — as opposed to communal agriculture.

While China looked to communism, Japan turned to a mix of traditionalism, capitalism, and democratic liberalism to induce national recovery. Here a sweeping American revolution brought demilitarization and a liberal constitution, but it was largely the characteristic Japanese stress on social cooperation that brought on the economic miracle. In India independence was accompanied by a hate-filled and bloody struggle between Hindu and Muslim, and then a population explosion that threatened economic development and parliamentary democracy. The old British India was divided (in 1947) into two (and then three) different states and more recently another religious-cultural group, the Sikhs, have fought for an independent state. One outcome of this was a bloody struggle in which Indira Gandhi, the Prime Minister, was killed. Ethnic conflict followed independence in Malaya as well, while in the Philippines the democratic system of 20 years fell to a dictatorship, as did the experiment in democracy in Indonesia, but with more brutal consequences. One of the most violent struggles for independence was in Vietnam, where the French refusal to grant independence led to a bitter war in which the Communists emerged as the champions of the nationalistic cause.

In the Muslim world, anti-Western nationalism true to Islam has been the dominant political force. Here change and bewildering conflict have prevailed as we witness, for example, war over Palestine, revolution in Egypt and Iran, and war in Algeria. Arab opposition to Israel has been the most important factor in unifying the Arab states. Most recently, an Arab-Persian conflict (which is a Shi'ite-Sunni conflict as well) has taken place since 1979 in the form of the bloody Iran-Iraq war.

By 1900 black Africa was bound to a somewhat uniform imperialist system of bureaucratic rule, a world economy, and few social services. But within this pattern there were numerous varieties. In British Ghana and French Senegal, for example, a black elite benefited from imperialist rule, whereas in Kenya, South Africa, and the Congo, a system of indirect slave labor and rigorous segregation prevailed. When the Europeans carved out their African states, they did so without regard to ethnic and tribal boundaries — a fact that has both fostered and hindered African unity and national development.

African nationalism was encouraged by the idea of African unity and wartime promises of self-determination. The Great Depression and the Second World War, however, encouraged black nationalism the most. Following the example of radical mass politics in Ghana, most of Africa was free of foreign control by the mid-1960s, although Algeria (like the Belgian Congo) won its independence only after a bitter struggle. Unfortunately, by the late 1960s, the tendency toward democratic government slipped into reverse gear — and a trend toward one-party or military government emerged. Nigeria illustrates a number of these patterns of nationalist development: a lack of ethnic/tribal homogeneity, civil war, and military rule. South Africa remains the exception to African nationalism, because its white minority succeeded in implementing a sophisticated and harsh system of apartheid. In South Africa, where the white minority system reserves the best jobs and housing and most political power for itself, black opposition centers in the African National Congress. Over the years Afrikaner constitutional reform has given some power to nonwhites, but none to the black majority. The Afrikaners, in 1985 and 1986, increasingly turned to ruling through hard-line military power and press censorship.

**STUDY OUTLINE**

I.  The resurgence of East Asia
   A.  The Communist victory in China
      1.  The triumph of communism was the result of two forces
         a.  Mao's strong communist guerrilla movement based on peasant interests
         b.  War with Japan, which weakened the Nationalists and resulted in 3 million dead or wounded
      2.  After Japan surrendered, civil war between the Nationalists and the Communists resumed
         a.  The Communists were a smaller force but were better led
         b.  Chiang Kai-shek and 1 million Chinese fled to the island of Taiwan in 1949
      3.  The Communists transformed China
         a.  Land was redistributed to the poor peasants as collective farms
         b.  They liquidated many "class enemies"
         c.  They used reeducation, self-criticism sessions, and other means to eliminate their opposition
         d.  They created a strong unified and centralized state
      4.  The American threat to China during the Korean War caused the people of China to rally to the Communist government
   B.  Mao's China
      1.  At first China followed the Soviet model and allied itself with Stalin's Soviet Union
         a.  Soviet aid and Soviet-type five-year plans brought about industrialization and attention to the sciences
         b.  Soviet totalitarian techniques were used to control culture and thought
         c.  Prostitution and drug abuse were eliminated, and women were given equality and new opportunities
      2.  In 1958 Mao led China in an independent "Great Leap Forward"
         a.  Economic growth via small-scale peasant economy was planned
         b.  A new socialist personality was to be sought by all
         c.  The Great Leap ended in economic disaster and hostility between Russia and China
      3.  To save his position and his revolution, Mao launched the Great Proletarian Cultural Revolution
         a.  His goal was to eliminate the bureaucrats and recapture the fervor of the revolution
         b.  He also sought to eliminate revisionism and Russian influence

4. The Cultural Revolution was an important youth rebellion carried out by the Red Guards
   a. They were encouraged to practice rebellion
   b. They intended to purge China of feudal and bourgeois culture and thought
   c. The Revolution mobilized the masses, shook up the party, and created greater social equality, but, as well, it caused chaos and resentment among officials and others

C. Deng's "Second Revolution"
   1. After Mao's death in 1976 and the defeat of the "Gang of Four," a counterattack, led by Deng Xiao-ping, took place
   2. Called the "Second Revolution," this counterattack opened the door to reconciliation between China and the USA (1971)
      a. Major reforms were initiated (the "four modernizations") — the most important being a switch from communal to a free-market peasant family agriculture
      b. Communist party control over politics and family size led to university student protest demonstrations in 1986

D. Japan's American revolution
   1. After the war, power in Japan resided in the hands of the American occupiers
      a. General Douglas MacArthur and his advisers exercised almost absolute authority
      b. The Americans carried out a plan of demilitarization and radical reform
      c. MacArthur wisely allowed the Emperor to remain as figurehead
      d. A new constitution created a popular government with a bill of rights and also abolished the armed forces
   2. A powerful Japanese bureaucracy pushed reforms through the Diet
      a. A labor movement was promoted
      b. American-style antitrust laws broke the old *zaibatsu*
      c. Women were liberated and education was reformed and democratized
      d. Land reform made the peasants supporters of democracy
   3. The cold war and American fears of communism influenced the United States to push Japan in a more conservative direction
      a. Left-wingers were purged
      b. Labor and antitrust reforms were dropped
      c. Occupation ended in 1952; Japan became independent but a military protectorate of the United States

E. "Japan, Inc." — the rebuilding of the country

1. Slow economic recovery turned into a great economic burst between 1950 and 1970, so that by 1986 per capita income exceeded that in the United States
2. Japan's success brought both foreign imitation and foreign criticism
3. Japan's economic success is related to its history and national character
   a. Its geography contributed to political unity and cultural homogeneity
   b. Traditionally, Japanese society puts the needs of the group before those of the individual
4. Government and big business shared leading roles in bringing about economic growth
   a. As during the Meiji era, government supported and encouraged big business
   b. In return for lifetime job guarantees, workers and unions are loyal to their companies
   c. Distance between workers and managers is less than in the West
   d. Workers are quickly retained, and efficiency, quality, and quantity are stressed
5. Japan's emphasis on cooperation and compromise led to a decrease in crime and solutions to pollution and energy resources problems

II. New nations in South Asia and the Muslim world
  A. Independence on the Indian subcontinent
    1. The Second World War accelerated India's desire for independence and worsened Indian-British relations
    2. The Muslim League demanded the division of India to allow for a Muslim state
       a. The Muslim leader Jinnah feared Hindu political and cultural domination
       b. Gandhi opposed the division of India
    3. The British promise of independence led to clashes between Hindu and Muslim
       a. Jinnah and the Muslim League would not accept a proposed federal constitution
       b. The partition (India/Pakistan) of 1947 led to massacres; Gandhi was assassinated
       c. War between India and Pakistan took place in 1948-1949, 1965-1966, and 1971
  B. Pakistan
    1. Although an authoritarian state, Pakistan did not remain unified
    2. East Pakistan's Bengalis constituted the majority but were neglected by the ruling elite in West Pakistan
    3. In 1971 a Bengali revolt led to an independent Bangladesh

C.  India
   1.  After 1947 India was ruled by Jawaharlal Nehru
       a.  Nehru and the Congress Party initiated major social reforms
       b.  Women were granted new rights
       c.  The untouchable caste classification was abolished
   2.  India's population growth canceled out much of its economic growth
       as poverty increased
   3.  Indira Gandhi took on the task of population control
       a.  She subverted parliamentary democracy and carried out a campaign
           of mass sterilization
       b.  She won a great electoral victory, but conflict between Punjab
           Sikhs and the government led to her assassination in 1984
       c.  Her son, Rajiv Gandhi, was elected prime minister
D.  Southeast Asia
   1.  Sri Lanka (Ceylon) gained independence quickly and smoothly
   2.  Independence in Malaya led to warfare between the Islamic Malays and
       the Chinese minority
       a.  A federated Malaysia was formed
       b.  In 1965 the largely Chinese city of Singapore was pushed out of
           the federation
   3.  Philippine independence was granted in 1946
       a.  President Marcos subverted the constitution and ruled as a dictator
       b.  In 1986 Corazon Aquino led a successful campaign to oust Marcos,
           but the gap between the rich elite and the poor remains enormous
   4.  The Netherlands East Indies became the independent Indonesia
       a.  The anti-Western Sukarno attempted to forge a "guided democracy"
       b.  Supposed communist influence led to Sukarno's downfall and a
           military regime
   5.  France's attempt to re-impose its rule in Vietnam led to an independ-
       ence movement led by the nationalist Ho Chi Minh
       a.  Despite American help, the French were defeated in 1954
       b.  The agreed-on elections to unify Vietnam were never held
       c.  Civil war between Communists and anti-Communists led, eventually,
           to a Communist victory and a defeat for the United States
E.  The Muslim World
   1.  Arab nationalism has two faces
       a.  The practical side has concentrated on nation building
       b.  The idealistic side has concentrated on Arab unification
       c.  Arab nationalism is unified on anticolonial and anti-Jewish levels,
           but regional and ideological rivalry has hurt the pan-Arab dream
   2.  After the Second World War, conflict over Jewish immigration led to
       conflict between the Jews and the Palestinian Arabs and the Arab League
       states

3. In 1947, the United Nations proposed that Palestine be divided into Jewish and Arab states
   a. The Jews accepted, but the Arabs rejected the proposal
   b. War between the two sides led to an Israeli victory
   c. While the Israelis conquered more territory, 900,000 Arab refugees left old Palestine

4. The Arab humiliation triggered a nationalist revolution, led by Nasser, in Egypt
   a. Nasser drove out the pro-Western King Farouk in 1952
   b. Nasser instituted radical land reform

5. Nasser's Egypt sought neutrality and took aid from Russia
   a. The United States canceled its offer to build a great new dam on the Nile
   b. Nasser retaliated by nationalizing the Suez Canal Company
   c. In turn, the British, French, and Israelis invaded Egypt
   d. The United States and Russia forced the invaders to withdraw
   e. Although Arab victory encouraged anti-Western radicalism in the Arab world, the Arabs remained divided

6. War recurred in 1967 and in 1973

7. Sadat of Egypt, with U.S. President Carter's support, engineered a settlement between Israel and Egypt
   a. Other Arab leaders continued their opposition to Israel and their support of the PLO
   b. With Sadat's assassination, Egypt-Israeli relations deteriorated over the issue of the Israeli West Bank settlement
   c. Egypt stood by as Israel occupied southern Lebanon in 1982, in an effort to destroy the PLO

8. An independence movement in the French colony of Algeria resulted in the Algerian war
   a. Tunisia and Morocco had won independence from France in 1956
   b. The 1 million French-Europeans in Algeria were determined to prevent a Muslim nationalist state in Algeria
   c. A military coup in Algeria brought General De Gaulle to power in France
   d. However, De Gaulle accepted the idea of Algerian independence

9. Turkey followed Ataturk's vision of a modern, secularized and Europeanized state

10. Once again, Iran tried to follow Turkey's example
    a. Shah Muhammad Reza Pahlavi angered Iranian nationalists because he courted the West
    b. The shah nationalized Iranian oil, but the West retaliated with a boycott that hurt the economy

      c.   In 1953, Mosaddeq forced the shah to flee, but the Americans supported his return and his harsh dictatorship

      d.   With an Islamic revolution (led by Ayatollah Khomeini) in 1978, the shah fled and U.S. diplomats were imprisoned

      e.   Fearing the Iranian Shi'ites, Iraq began a long and bloody war against Iran

III.  Imperialism and nationalism in black Africa

    A.  All but two areas of black Africa — Portugal's territory and South Africa — won political independence after the Second World War

    B.  The imperial system, 1900–1930

      1.  By 1900 most of black Africa had been taken by the Europeans

        a.   Trade in raw materials had replaced trade in human beings

        b.   Imperialism shattered the existing black society

        c.   This society had consisted of thousands of political units and hundreds of languages

        d.   The imperialists themselves ruled differently, and the number of settlers varied

      2.  The British and French goal was that of "good government"

        a.   In reality this meant a military order to prevent rebellion

        b.   The imperialists spent little on social services and feared that education would encourage revolt

      3.  The economic goal was to draw raw materials out of the interior

        a.   Railroads and roads were built from coast to interior to move raw materials out and manufactured goods in

        b.   Railroads and roads enabled the imperialists to put down rebellions quickly, and they provided wage jobs for former peasants

        c.   Forced labor was widespread until about 1920

        d.   Agricultural self-sufficiency gave way to export production for the world market

    C.  Ghana and Kenya illustrate the variations of the impact of imperialism

      1.  Precolonial Ghana was the powerful and economically vigorous kingdom of Ashanti

      2.  The British made Ashanti into a crown colony (the Gold Coast), which set the pace for West Africa's westernization

        a.   They introduced large-scale cocoa bean production

        b.   Much of the economic success in cocoa was due to native, not British, entrepreneurship

        c.   A black elite participated in colonial government

      3.  British-controlled Kenya experienced a more harsh colonial rule

        a.   These East African peoples were less numerous and less interested in commerce

        b.   Indian and white settlers exploited the territory

      c.  The British imposed a rigorous system of segregation on the blacks and Indians

D.  The growth of African nationalism

   1.  Western imperialism caused the rise of African nationalism, but it was of a different nature than the nationalism of elsewhere

      a.  Imperialism and Western ideas came later than in other parts of the world

      b.  A multiplicity of ethnic groups and arbitrary boundaries complicated political nationalism

   2.  The impetus for black nationalism came from the United States and the British West Indies

      a.  W. E. B. DuBois was the most influential of the black nationalists

      b.  Based on Wilson's idea of self-determination, DuBois's Pan-African Congress called for the union of all African peoples

      c.  A minority of blacks in Senegal favored union with France

      d.  The Senegal poet and leader Senghor articulated the idea of joy and pride in "blackness" — or *négritude*

      e.  In British West Africa the Westernized blacks pushed for moderate steps toward greater self-government

   3.  With the Great Depression, African nationalism became more radical

      a.  The black elite became hostile to the system

      b.  Like Azikiwe in Nigeria, they became the leaders who spread nationalist ideas

      c.  The Depression resulted in cooperative "holdups" by farmers and a racial interpretation of economic conflict

E.  Achieving independence with new leaders

   1.  The Second World War speeded up the nationalist movement

      a.  The growth of towns and the shortage of goods increased discontent

      b.  The wartime experiences and antiracist ideals of blacks encouraged nationalism

      c.  The British and French began to push for economic and social improvement

      d.  Wartime ideals encouraged adoption of the principle of self-determination

   2.  New leaders like Nkrumah, Azikiwe, and Touré succeeded in bringing independence to Africa

      a.  The postwar leaders were of humble social origins and were influenced by Western thought

      b.  They accepted the prevailing colonial territorial boundaries

      c.  They channeled the hopes and discontent of the masses into organized politics

F.  Ghana shows the way to African independence
    1.  Under Nkrumah, Ghana became the first independent African state
        a.  Nkrumah was influenced by European socialists and the "Back to Africa" movement of Marcus Garvey
        b.  Garvey preached the idea of "Africa for the Africans"
    2.  Nkrumah's independence movement followed the Second World War
        a.  Economic discontent turned into anti-imperialist rioting
        b.  The British encouraged constitutional reform
        c.  Nkrumah built a radical mass party that demanded "self-government now"
        d.  In and out of prison, Nkrumah led his radical nationalist party to victory over all rivals
        e.  Ghana's independence encouraged speedy independence for other African states
    3.  In some areas, white settlers tried to retain their privileged position
        a.  Eventually the blacks of Southern Rhodesia won over the whites and renamed their country Zimbabwe
        b.  In Zambia and East Africa, the whites were too few to block black nationalism for long
G.  Nationalism in French-speaking regions of Africa
    1.  With some black support, France under De Gaulle developed an alternative to independence
        a.  French West Africa and French Equatorial Africa were formed into a federation and participated in French government
        b.  The black elite, led by Senghor, wanted to retain ties with France
        c.  Under Touré's leadership, Guinea rejected the French plan and won independence
        d.  All others followed — although many retained close ties with France
    2.  Belgium's harsh rule in its Congo colony ended with civil war and tribal conflict, an exception to the general African experience
IV.  Black Africa since 1960
  A.  In the 20 years since independence, democracy has given way to one-party rule or military dictatorship
    1.  Corruption is widespread and dictatorship common
    2.  White racist rule in South Africa represents a ticking time bomb for Africa
    3.  Some developments have proved beneficial
        a.  Imperialism has been thrown off
        b.  Some degree of unity and modernization has been created
  B.  Building national unity
    1.  Imperialism had affected Africa in several positive ways

      a. About 40 states were created

      b. Some modernization and urbanization took place

      c. A modern, diversified social structure was established

  2. Other features of imperialism were negative

      a. Disruption of traditional life caused suffering and unfulfilled expectations

      b. The economy was geared to export and was under foreign control

      c. Artificial boundaries did not consider ethnic-cultural groupings — and hence many states were faced with multiethnic problems

  3. Western-style democracy and political system have not worked well

      a. Parties based on ethnic/regional lines encouraged conflict

      b. Leaders turned to tough measures to hold countries together

  4. For example, Nkrumah built a "revolutionary" one-party state in Ghana

      a. He used communist and totalitarian models

      b. His grandiose projects failed, and he was deposed by the army in 1966

  5. Also, French-speaking Mali and Guinea adopted one-party governments, whereas Senegal and the Ivory Coast remained moderate

  6. Naturally, then, military takeovers have been common in Africa

      a. Some military governments, like that in Amin's Uganda, have terrorized the people

      b. Others, such as Ethiopia in the late 1970s, had redeeming qualities: They held the country together and were committed to modernization

      c. Military leaders often believe in the ultimate goal of free democratic government

C. Nigeria, Africa's giant, illustrates the difficulties of nation-building

  1. In Nigeria are many religious, regional, and tribal groups

  2. Modern Nigeria was a creation of the British consolidation of two administrative districts

      a. The key issue in preindependence years was the relationship between central government and the regions

      b. A federal system was worked out that shared power with the three state governments

  3. Ethnic rivalry in 1964 led to violence, a military coup, and civil war

      a. A military council killed many politicians and officers and abolished regional governments

      b. Ibo domination led to civil war and the creation of an independent Ibo state of Biafra

      c. After three years of bloodshed, Biafra was forced to remain in Nigeria

4. A new Nigerian federal government was formed, with nineteen states
   a. Iboland was rebuilt as oil revenues soared
   b. An elected civilian government took over in 1979
   c. However, military rule returned in 1983, followed by a more liberal military coup in 1985
D. The struggle in southern Africa
   1. Black nationalist guerrillas moved Portugal and the white population out of Angola and Mozambique
   2. The roots of racial conflict in the Republic of South Africa are complex
      a. After conquest, Britain allowed the Dutch settlers self-rule
      b. Britain also allowed the whites (Afrikaners) to limit black land-ownership
      c. The black land reserves were a pool for indirect forced labor
   3. The Afrikaner racist-totalitarian system is the efficient and well-organized system of *apartheid* (meaning separation or segregation)
      a. The population is divided into four legally unequal racial groups
      b. Whites control the economy and enjoy the wealth
      c. Despite poverty and exploitation, a distinct black urban culture has emerged
   4. Black nationalist protest has a long history
      a. Peaceful civil disobedience has existed since the 1950s but has not worked
      b. The moderate nationalists were destroyed and a more radical African National Congress movement took its place
      c. A new parliamentary reform made no provision for black representation
      d. Despite internal and foreign protest the white government moved closer toward dictatorship for all

## REVIEW QUESTIONS

Q-1.  Explain why Mao's Communists won in war against the Nationalists. Why did the Communists appeal to many peasants?

Q-2.  How did the Soviet Union affect China during the early years of Communist rule?

Q-3.  Describe the cultural and economic policies of Chairman Mao. How successful was he in transforming China into a country based on modernization and equality?

Q-4.  Compare the cultural and economic goals of China during Mao's Cultural Revolution to those of China following his death.

Q-5.  Describe Japan's "American revolution." In what ways did the United States influence postwar Japan?

Q-6.   What are the reasons for the Japanese economic miracle?

Q-7.   What role has big business played in the Japanese economy? How does this differ from the relationships among labor, big business, and government in the United States?

Q-8.   Explain Japan's group-centered and cooperative ideals. Give examples of how these have contributed to Japan's economic and social success.

Q-9.   What effect did the coming of national independence have on Hindu and Muslim relations in India? What was the outcome? Could it have been avoided?

Q-10.   Explain the reason for the Bangladesh revolt of 1971.

Q-11.   How successful was Indira Gandhi in solving India's problems and preserving democracy in India?

Q-12.   What were the results — in terms of political order and social reform — when Malaya and the Philippines gained their independence?

Q-13.   What were the goals of the Vietnamese nationalists? Describe the process and the outcome of the nationalist struggle.

Q-14.   What were the reasons for the Jewish-Arab conflict? What was its outcome?

Q-15.   Describe the goals and the achievements of both Nasser and Sadat of Egypt.

Q-16.   Why did the Iranian revolution of 1978 occur? Explain by making reference to the shah, U.S. interests, the Iranian nationalists, and how this revolution affected Iran-Iraq relations.

Q-17.   Discuss the various ideas that influenced and emerged out of the black nationalist movements. Pay particular attention to the ideas of DuBois, Senghor, Garvey, Nkrumah, and Touré.

Q-18.   Nkrumah's movement in Ghana was a mass movement based on radical nationalism. Explain.

Q-19.   Describe De Gaulle's plan to keep French Africans within the French empire. What were the results and what was Touré's role?

Q-20.   Why did Belgium's rule in the Congo come to such a violent end? How did Belgian colonial policy differ from that of France and Britain?

Q-21.   How did European imperialism affect black Africa in terms of human life and economic arrangements?

Q-22.   What were the objectives of the French and British rulers in black Africa, and how did they achieve these objectives?

Q-23.   Explain what social and economic rearrangements took place in Ghana and Kenya as a result of British colonial rule.

Q-24.   Discuss the positive and negative ways in which imperialism affected Africa.

Q-25.   Why hasn't the Western-style political system worked well in Africa? Use Ghana and Nigeria as examples.

Q-26.   In what ways does Nigeria illustrate the difficulties of nation building in Africa? Why did the Biafran war take place and what was its outcome?

Q-27.   How does the Afrikaner *apartheid* system work, and how has it affected the blacks of South Africa?

## STUDY-REVIEW EXERCISES

*Define the following key concepts and terms.*

pan-Africanists/"black Frenchmen"

French ideology of assimilation

*négritude*

*apartheid*

Shi'ite Muslims/Sunni Muslims

*Identify each of the following and give its significance.*

Mao's Great Proletarian Cultural Revolution

Mao's Great Leap Forward

Red Guards

Deng's Second Revolution

Japan's Democratic Liberal Party

Battle of Dien Bien Phu

General Douglas MacArthur

Jawaharlal Nehru

Ho Chi Minh

Punjab Sikhs

Indira Gandhi

Rajiv Gandhi

Achmed Sukarno

Ferdinand Marcos

Muhammad Ali Jinnah

Muslim League

Bengali Hindus

Bengali Revolt of 1971

Gamal Abdel Nasser

Arab League

Suez Crisis of 1956

Palestine Liberation Organization (PLO)

Ayatollah Khomeini

Anwar Sadat

W. E. B. DuBois

"Back to Africa" Movement

Lord Louis Mountbatten

Kwame Nkrumah

Marcus Garvey

Nnamdi Azikiwe

Léopold Senghor

Afrikaner

South African Native Land Act of 1913

*Explain when, how, and from whom each of the following colonial states received its independence.*

Palestine

India

Pakistan

Malaya

Philippine Islands

Vietnam

Nigeria

South Africa

Ghana


*Test your understanding of the chapter by answering the following questions.*

1. U.S. military movement across the thirty-eighth parallel eventually *weakened/ strengthened* the Chinese Communist position.
2. Mao's Great Leap Forward *did/did not* improve relations between China and Russia.
3. The U.S. general who exercised great power in postwar Japan was General

   _____.
4. Japan's economic success after the Second World War *is/is not* related to its history and national character.
5. Compared to the United States, the relationship between worker and employer

   in Japan is (a) more combative, (b) based more on cooperation. _____

6. Led by the Muslim leader _____ India's Muslims

   were given a separate homeland called _____.
   The eastern part of this new country was eventually given its own independence

   and named itself _____.

7. The Philippine experiment with the U.S. style of government *did/did not* bring true democracy and constitutionalism to that country.
8. The South African Native Land Act of 1913 was an important step in *limiting/expanding* the land-use rights of blacks.
9. The nationalist leader of Indonesia whose authoritarian and anti-Western regime

   was toppled by the army in 1965 was _____.


## MULTIPLE-CHOICE QUESTIONS

1. After their victory in 1949, the early Communist regime under Mao
   a. was unwilling to carry out land reform.
   b. was greatly influenced by the Soviet model of five-year plans.
   c. completely divorced itself from Soviet influence.
   d. turned to the capitalist West for its economic ideas.

2. Compared to the Russian land redistribution of the 1930s, Mao's land redistribution program and the creation of the collectives
   a. was rapid, brutal, and unsuccessful.
   b. was opposed by the masses.
   c. was gradual and less brutally carried out.
   d. did not affect the holdings of the old landlords and the rich peasants.

3. Mao's Great Leap Forward was intended to
   a. bypass the Russians to arrive at true communism.
   b. jump from communism to bureaucratic capitalism.
   c. prepare China for the Olympics.
   d. make the family the basis of communist society.

4. U.S. occupation of Japan
   a. left Japan's powerful bureaucracy intact.
   b. resulted in the elimination of the emperor.
   c. restored the military.
   d. all of the above

5. The "reverse course" that U.S. policy toward Japan took as a result of the cold war refers to a(n)
   a. U.S. decision to withdraw from Japanese affairs.
   b. economic war between Japan and the United States.
   c. purge of the left wing in Japanese politics.
   d. return of all land to the big landlords.

6. The Muslim leader Jinnah pushed the British for
    a. an independent Pakistan.
    b. continued British presence in India.
    c. a unified federal India for Muslim and Hindu.
    d. none of the above

7. According to Indira Gandhi's government, improvement of living standards could be obtained only after
    a. the British paid reparations to the Indians.
    b. India was reunited with Pakistan.
    c. heavy industry was developed.
    d. the rate of population growth was greatly reduced.

8. The U.S. black nationalist whose goals were solidarity among blacks everywhere and eventually a union of all African peoples was
    a. Léopold Senghor.
    b. W. E. B. DuBois.
    c. Kwame Nkrumah.
    d. Sekou Touré.

9. The Great Depression of the 1930s
    a. had little if any effect on black Africa.
    b. hurt only the elite Westernized blacks.
    c. did not affect agricultural production.
    d. produced extreme hardship and discontent among the African masses.

10. Nkrumah's independence movement was based on
    a. support of the demands of tribal leaders.
    b. moderate and gradual transition to independence.
    c. immediate self-government.
    d. independence through elite leadership rather than mass participation.

11. The Belgian policy toward its Congo colony was different than that of France to its colonies in that it
    a. discouraged the development of an educated population.
    b. supported a plan of imperial federation.
    c. welcomed the idea of self-determination for Africans.
    d. none of the above

12. The South African Native Land Act of 1913
    a. limited the land ownership of the white population.
    b. turned the land over to anyone who could prove ownership.

    c.  brought about wide-scale British ownership.
    d.  greatly limited black ownership of land.

13.  The largest barrier to Nigerian unity has been
    a.  British reluctance to grant independence.
    b.  regional and tribal rivalries.
    c.  lack of natural resources.
    d.  white supremacy.

14.  Indira Gandhi's defeat at the polls and much of her unpopularity was due to her
    a.  refusal to call for free elections.
    b.  failure to attack dishonest officials and black marketeers.
    c.  mass sterilization campaign.
    d.  foreign policy.

15.  In the end, the war with Japan
    a.  weakened the Chinese Communists.
    b.  weakened the Chinese Nationalists.
    c.  weakened Mao's appeal to the peasants.
    d.  allowed the Nationalists to eliminate the Communists in China.

16.  To save China from "revisionist" influence and to recover his lost influence after the failure of the Great Leap Forward, Mao
    a.  gave more power to the party bureaucrats.
    b.  reinstituted some capitalist practices in China.
    c.  strengthened China's relations with Russia.
    d.  launched a cultural revolution.

17.  Which of the following is true of postwar Japan?
    a.  It was allowed to remilitarize.
    b.  It rid itself of the emperor.
    c.  It rejected a constitution.
    d.  It became a military protectorate of the United States.

18.  Which of the following is true of the black nationalist movement?
    a.  The Great Depression and the Second World War made it less radical.
    b.  It was influenced by the ideas of Marcus Garvey.
    c.  It proceeded most rapidly and peacefully in the Belgian Congo.
    d.  It rejected the ideas of the American W. E. B. DuBois.

19. The city of Singapore was pushed out of the Malaysia Federation because it
    a.  refused to agree to federation.
    b.  was dominated by the communists.
    c.  was dominated by Chinese.
    d.  was too large.

20. Mao's radical cadres of young people who were encouraged to denounce their teachers and practice rebellion were known as the
    a.  Red Guards.
    b.  Student Youth Movement.
    c.  Revolutionary Youth Corps.
    d.  Red Terror.

21. The leader who fled to Taiwan with his Nationalist followers was
    a.  Emperor Hirohito.
    b.  Chiang Kai-shek.
    c.  Deng Xiao-ping.
    d.  Mao Tse-tung.

22. The first black African state to gain independence from its colonial overlord was
    a.  Kenya.
    b.  Ghana.
    c.  Guinea.
    d.  Congo.

23. The successor to Ferdinand Marcos as president of the Philippines was
    a.  Indira Gandhi.
    b.  Ho Chi Minh.
    c.  Achmed Sukarno.
    d.  Corazon Aquino.

24. The successful leader of the black nationalist movement in Ghana was
    a.  Sekou Touré.
    b.  Léopold Senghor.
    c.  Kwame Nkrumah.
    d.  Nnamdi Azikiwe.

25. The Egyptian president who signed a peace settlement with Israel was
    a.  Anwar Sadat.
    b.  Gamal Abdel Nasser.
    c.  Menachem Begin.
    d.  Muhammad Reza Pahlavi.

26. The European leader who accepted the principle of self-determination for Algeria in 1959 was
    a. Charles De Gaulle.
    b. Winston Churchill.
    c. Helmut Schmidt.
    d. Leonid Brezhnev.

27. The battle of Dien Bien Phu in 1954 marked the end of French control of
    a. Algeria.
    b. Indochina.
    c. South Sudan.
    d. Teheran.

28. The British, French, and Israelis were forced to withdraw from Egypt by
    a. Egypt and Syria.
    b. Russia and Egypt.
    c. the United States and Russia.
    d. the Palestinians and Libya.

## GEOGRAPHY

On the outline map of Africa, show the locations of the following new black African states: Ghana, Kenya, Senegal, Zambia, Zimbabwe, Guinea, Zaire, Mali, and the Ivory Coast.

Next, briefly describe to what European power each had been attached, and compare and contrast the process of achieving independence (such as peacefully, through war, or through revolution). Which of the imperialist countries — France, Britain, or Belgium — provided the smoothest and least violent transition to independence?

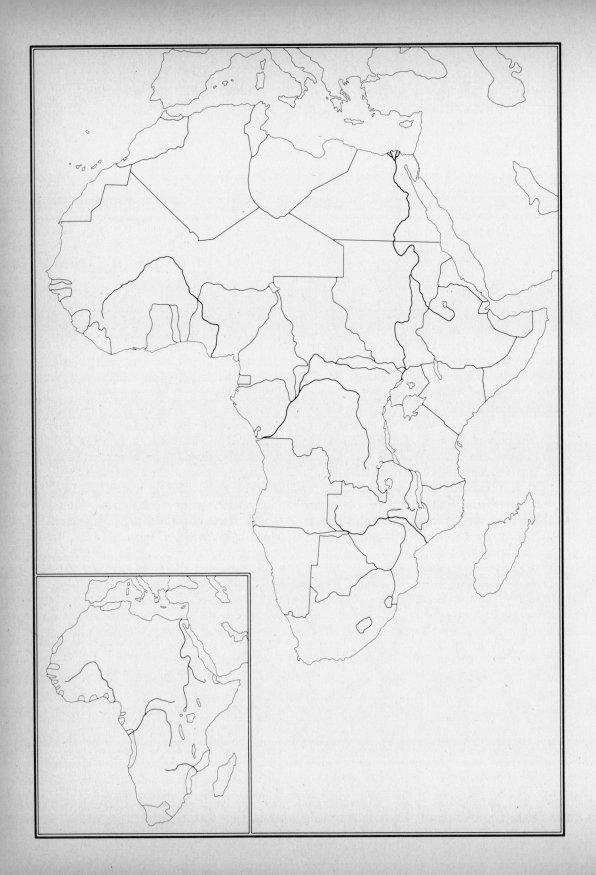

## UNDERSTANDING HISTORY THROUGH READING AND THE ARTS

The study of black Africa has been largely a one-way street, as Westerners try to uncover the impact that Western society has had on black society. In the work *The Image of Black in Western Art* (2 vols., 1979), however, attention is focused on the popularity of the black African image in Western art since the fifteenth century B. C.

The revival of the power of Islam is one of the most salient features of the contemporary world. In the book *Among the Believers: An Islamic Journey* (1980), the famous writer V. S. Naipaul takes the reader through four Islamic countries, observing, conversing, and reflecting: Iran, Pakistan, Malaysia, and Indonesia.

## PROBLEMS FOR FURTHER INVESTIGATION

How have Africans met and dealt with modernization and Westernization, colonialism and Christianity? An excellent way to pursue this subject is through the novels of Chinua Achebe. His novel *Things Fall Apart\** (1959), set in an Ibo village in what is now Biafra, vividly re-creates pre-Christian tribal life, and shows how the coming of the white man led to the breaking up of the old ways. In *No Longer at Ease\** (1960), Achebe describes the tragic predicament of a young African idealist whose foreign education has converted him to modern standards of moral judgment.

Two excellent books with which to start a research project on modern South Africa are *South Africa: Time Running Out\** (1981), a report by the Study Commission on United States Policy Toward Southern Africa, and L. Thompson and A. Prior, *South African Politics\** (1982). R. Omond's book, *The Apartheid Handbook: A Guide to South Africa's Everyday Racial Policies\** (1985) uses specific examples to show exactly how the apartheid system works today, and the book *Black Politics in South Africa Since 1945\** (1983) by T. Lodge is an excellent history of the development of mass protest movements in South Africa since 1945. Those interested in the use of biography as history will want to read the biography of the first secretary of the African National Congress, a man whose life included childhood on a German mission station, work in the diamond town of Kimberley, and experience in journalism and political activism. The book is *Sol Plaatje\** (1984) by B. William.

*Available in paperback.

# CHAPTER 38

# LIFE IN INDUSTRIALIZED NATIONS

## CHAPTER OBJECTIVES

After reading and studying this chapter you should be able to answer the following questions:

Q-1. How has everyday life changed in the postwar era and why?

Q-2. What have these changes meant to people?

Q-3. Why did economic problems return to plague the industrialized nations from the early 1970s, and what were the social consequences?

## CHAPTER SYNOPSIS

This chapter focuses on three of the most important areas of change in today's Western world: science, class structure, and the family.

Examining first science and technology, the author shows how the Second World War speeded up scientific achievement and gave rise to very large scientific projects involving great numbers of researchers and large government grants. This development has led to major changes in the lives of scientists and technicians, who have great influence in modern society. A second trend has been toward a more flexible and democratic class structure, where white-collar professionals and highly trained specialists provide the model for a new middle class. Reforms in education and expanded social security have strengthened the move toward social democracy. Although discontent like that which brought a student revolution in France in 1968 has not been eliminated, changes in education and new opportunities for men and women of talent resulted in a more fluid and less antagonistic class structure. The family and the role of women also underwent well-publicized changes. The divorce rate went up, while the marriage rate and birthrate fell.

397

Married women were having fewer children and were ever more likely to work outside the home for wages. This trend reflects and encourages a growing spirit of independence among women. Women and the family experienced a truly revolutionary transformation.

After about 1968 the self-confidence and the social and economic stability that came to mark the postwar era evaporated. What followed were two decades of upheaval. First, in the early 1970s a combination of factors, including the collapse of the U.S.-dominated world monetary order and a dramatic rise in energy prices, led to a worldwide recession that was to last well into the 1980s. Spurred on by war in the Middle East and revolution in Iran, oil prices skyrocketed, thereby setting into motion the worst world economic decline since the 1930s. Particularly hard hit, western European countries faced massive unemployment and economic stagflation, and the people faced a falling standard of living. All of this was accompanied by increased government spending on benefits for the unemployed and needy and, correspondingly, by a buildup of huge national debts and inflation. By the late 1970s some, like Thatcher and Reagan, perceived a need to eliminate huge deficits and cut spending, while a whole generation of young people became concerned about their job prospects. The student idealism of the 1960s was over.

## STUDY OUTLINE

I.  Science and technology
    A.  The union of science and technology
        1.  Generally, science and technology were joined together only occasionally before the 1930s
        2.  The Second World War focus on military problems brought them together
        3.  The results have been both good and bad
            a.  New industries were created, and rapid economic growth was achieved after 1945
            b.  Harmful environmental effects became increasingly possible
    B.  The stimulus of World War Two
        1.  With the Second World War pure science lost its independence as leading scientists worked for their governments to help fight the war
        2.  The war led to major technological breakthroughs, such as radar, improved jet engines, computers, and the atomic bomb
    C.  The rise of Big Science
        1.  Big Science could attack difficult problems by combining theoretical work with engineering techniques
        2.  It needed a great deal of money, which it received from government
        3.  Russia pioneered in the development of a manned space program

          4. European countries undertook financing of Big Science in order to stop the "brain drain" to the United States

    D. The life of scientists and technologists

          1. Big Science supported many scientists and much specialized knowledge

          2. Specialization made teamwork, bureaucracy, and managers necessary

          3. Competition among scientists was often fierce

II. Toward a new society

    A. The expansion of science and technology contributed to economic growth, a rising standard of living, and substantial social change

    B. The changing class structure in Europe

          1. After 1945 the traditional class distinctions became less clear-cut, and society became more democratic

          2. Educational and employment opportunities made the middle class more open

              a. Talent and expertise became more important to success than inherited property or family connections

              b. The middle class grew greatly as entry became easier

          3. The rural working class shrank in size due to the mass exodus from the country

    C. Social security reforms and rising affluence

          1. Social security reforms reduced poverty, ill health, and poor housing

          2. These reforms promoted greater social and economic equality, but were costly

          3. Lower food costs and installment buying allowed for greater consumption of other goods — such as automobiles and household appliances

          4. Leisure and recreation, especially travel, became big business

    D. Renewed discontent and the student revolt

          1. Radical students claimed that increasing materialism was harmful and that postwar society was repressive and flawed

          2. The number of people entering European universities increased in the 1950s and 1960s

              a. Overcrowding resulted and a new "youth culture" emerged

              b. Many students believed they were not getting the kind of education they needed

              c. They were moralists and idealists who rejected consumerism

          3. With help from workers, student revolts over these issues occurred in the late 1960s and early 1970s

          4. The student rebellion reflected a disillusionment with materialism, technological society, and the Vietnam War

III. Women and the family

    A. Women's emancipation

          1. Women became better educated and more independent

2. The changing position of women in society altered the modern family

B. Marriage and motherhood

1. Since the Second World War, the trend has been toward earlier marriage and greater birth control within marriage
2. The birthrate in Western countries declined
3. Motherhood came to occupy a smaller portion of a woman's life than it used to
   a. The average woman's life expectancy increased from fifty years to seventy-five years between 1900 and 1970
   b. At the same time, most women were having their children when they were in their twenties
4. The age-old link between sexual intercourse and motherhood was severed by the development and use of birth control methods

C. Women at work

1. Women entered the labor market as full-time wage earners
2. Rising employment contributed to the growth of the women's liberation movement and the declining birthrate
3. Women came to understand that interruption of their careers to care for small children led to lower wages
4. The emotional aspects of marriage became more important, but the divorce rate kept moving up
5. The divorce rate rose dramatically — partly because of increased female economic independence

IV. Economic troubles in recent times

A. The reconstruction of society in the postwar years came to an abrupt halt in the early 1970s — largely because of the West's loss of control over oil prices and because of the fall of the monetary system

B. Money and oil

1. From 1944 to 1971 the world monetary order was based on the U.S. dollar
   a. The U.S. guarantee that the dollar could be cashed in for gold at $35 an ounce encouraged growth and monetary stability
   b. But U.S. overspending by 1971 caused a run on the dollar
   c. The ensuing abandonment of fixed rates made trade and investment insecure
2. The era of cheap oil (which had stimulated Western economic growth) came to an end in 1973
   a. Khadafy of Libya activated OPEC price increases
   b. The Yom Kippur War and OPEC oil embargos resulted in vast OPEC price rises

C. Inflation, debt, and unemployment

1. The world depression of the 1970s was pushed further by the Iranian revolution of 1978–1979

2. The crisis of unemployment and inflation hit western Europe harder than the United States
3. The crisis gave the Soviet Union leverage over energy-poor eastern Europe
4. International debt rose as rich and poor states borrowed for oil
5. Consumers borrowed as a hedge against inflation

D. Some social consequences
1. Optimism gave way to pessimism
2. Governments responded with extended benefits for the unemployed and the needy — thereby preserving political stability
3. Increased government spending without increased taxation led to budget deficits, increased debt, and inflation
4. Thatcher and Reagan represented a reaction against government spending and deficits
5. Big Science was cut, while many individuals adopted less indulgent lifestyles, and students became obsessed with jobs

## REVIEW QUESTIONS

Q-1. Why did science become Big Science in the postwar era? What is the purpose of Big Science?

Q-2. Why did the birthrate in Europe and the United States fall in the 1952–1979 era (see Figure 38.2 in the text)?

Q-3. Cite the evidence supporting the claim that the standard of living improved in North America and Europe. Has the *quality* of life improved as well?

Q-4. For the first time in history science and technology have been effectively joined on a massive scale. Explain why this happened and what the implications are.

Q-5. How has the rise of Big Science altered the lives of modern scientists?

Q-6. Some historians have argued that wars have actually promoted progress by speeding up technical change, while others have dismissed this idea. Analyze and discuss this in relation to the Second World War.

Q-7. What changes have taken place in the European class structure since the war? Does greater or less mobility exist? Has the distribution of income remained the same?

Q-8. What were the reasons for and outcome of the European student rebellions of the late 1960s?

Q-9. What changes in lifestyle for women have occurred in the past thirty or so years? Have these changes been beneficial to both men and women? Explain.

Q-10. What has happened to the fertility period of women to cause a greater need for birth control?

Q-11. How successful has modern science been in making a healthier society? Has the progress of medicine been oversold?

Q-12.   What are the seven habits that have been shown to be related to good health?

Q-13.   Discuss the causes of the worldwide economic crisis of the 1970s and 1980s. Could anything have been done to prevent it?

Q-14.   What were the social consequences of economic stagflation in the 1970s and 1980s?

## STUDY-REVIEW EXERCISES

*Define* each of the following key concepts and terms.

Big Science

scientific specialization

"stagflation"

"brain drain"

managerial class

social welfare reforms

women's emancipation/women's liberation movement

"consumer society"

antinuclear movement of the 1980s

*Explain* each of the following and give its significance.

Iranian Revolution of 1978–1979

development of radar

microwave transmission

large-scale entry of women into the labor force

post-Second World War explosion in university education

student protest of the 1960s

changes in women's fertility

population decline in Europe and America

decline of the European peasant class

1973 oil crisis

*Test your understanding of the chapter by answering the following questions.*

1.  Since 1945, the number of agricultural workers in Western Europe has *increased/ decreased*.
2.  In the past twenty years, European society has witnessed a fairly significant *rise/ fall* in the birthrate.
3.  Since the Second World War, the percentage of women who are full-time wage earners has *increased/decreased* sharply.
4.  The average European family today spends *more/less* of its income on food, as compared to a family living in the late nineteenth century.
5.  Welfare-state reforms in Britain since the Second World War have resulted in *greater/lesser* economic equality in that country.
6.  The trend since the 1940s has been *an increase/a decrease* in the cooperation between pure science and technology.
7.  Since 1945, European society has moved toward a *more/less* rigid class structure.
8.  It appears that the increase in economic independence among women has had *little/significant* effect on divorce and birth rates.
9.  The trend in Europe and the United States since 1945 has been toward *greater/ fewer* scientific bureaucracies.

## MULTIPLE-CHOICE QUESTIONS

1.  The close and lasting cooperation of pure science and applied technology began
    a.  during the Depression.
    b.  about 1900.
    c.  during World War Two.
    d.  during World War One.

2.  In eastern Europe today, most women
    a.  seldom work out of the home.

    b.   work until marriage.
    c.   are usually employed until retirement.
    d.   quit the work force after pregnancy.

3.  The welfare-state reforms of Europe have resulted in
    a.   little if any redistribution of national income.
    b.   slight redistribution of national income.
    c.   considerable redistribution of national income.
    d.   no changes in the standard of living.

4.  As a result of Big Science, the control that scientists have over their experimentation has
    a.   increased slightly.
    b.   decreased slightly.
    c.   increased significantly.
    d.   decreased significantly.

5.  Since about 1950 the number of European married women who work outside the home has
    a.   increased slightly.
    b.   decreased slightly.
    c.   increased significantly.
    d.   decreased significantly.

6.  The so-called European brain drain was the
    a.   loss of many scientists in the war.
    b.   move of many scientists to the United States.
    c.   lack of interest in science in society.
    d.   control of science by the state.

7.  The 1934 British air ministry experiments on air defense led to the development of
    a.   the atomic bomb.
    b.   the double helix.
    c.   jet aircraft.
    d.   radar.

8.  The famous 1939 letter to President Roosevelt that predicted the discovery of the atomic bomb was written by
    a.   Albert Einstein.
    b.   Ernest Rutherford.
    c.   General Marshall.
    d.   Winston Churchill.

9.  The country that took the lead in Big Science was
    a.   the Soviet Union.

b.  Germany.
c.  the United States.
d.  Britain.

10. The political party in Britain that took the lead in establishing a comprehensive national health system was the
    a.  Liberal party.
    b.  Conservative party.
    c.  Workers party.
    d.  Labour party.

11. The 1968 revolt in France that threatened de Gaulle's government was started by
    a.  industrial workers.
    b.  the Communist party.
    c.  students.
    d.  peasants.

12. The student radicalism in the late 1960s was inspired in part by the
    a.  Korean War.
    b.  Vietnam War.
    c.  Civil War.
    d.  Second World War.

13. The welfare-state legislation in Britain since World War Two resulted in
    a.  greater economic equality.
    b.  the disappearance of the aristocracy.
    c.  a dramatic rise in the birthrate.
    d.  total employment.

14. Since World War Two, the role of motherhood has occupied
    a.  more of women's time.
    b.  less of women's time.
    c.  neither more nor less of women's time.
    d.  increasing numbers of younger wives.

15. Desmond Bernal's book *The Social Function of Science* argues that
    a.  scientific research should remain free from government control and societal needs.
    b.  scientific research should be funded by the government depending on the social and political benefits expected from such research.
    c.  scientists are best suited to run the governments of the world.
    d.  scientific research should take place only within the confines of the university.

16. All but one of the following led directly to oil price increases in the 1970s.
    a.  The Yom Kippur War
    b.  The Vietnam War
    c.  OPEC embargoes
    d.  Khadafy's pressure on oil prices

17. The "misery index" indicates that the people who suffered most from the economic crisis of the 1970s and 1980s lived in
    a.  the United States.
    b.  Japan.
    c.  western Europe.
    d.  southeast Asia.

18. Only one of the following did not contribute to the economic crisis that began in the early 1970s.
    a.  Collapse of the world monetary system
    b.  War in the Middle East
    c.  Low birthrates in western Europe
    d.  Increase in oil prices

19. In 1973 the U.S. dollar
    a.  fell in value against most currencies.
    b.  rose in value against most currencies.
    c.  was placed on a fixed rate of exchange against other countries.
    d.  none of the above

20. The so-called Yom Kippur War began with
    a.  the British takeover of the Suez Canal.
    b.  the Israeli attack on Egypt.
    c.  the Egyptian and Syrian attack on Israel.
    d.  all of the above

21. The world's largest oil producer is
    a.  Syria.
    b.  Iran.
    c.  Egypt.
    d.  the Soviet Union.

22. Which of the following is true about the European job market since World War Two?
    a.  An increase in farm labor
    b.  A sharp increase in industrial labor

    c.  A decrease in white-collar and service jobs
    d.  A decrease in small businesses

23.  Big Science is characterized by which of the following?
    a.  Considerable emphasis on nonmilitary applications
    b.  A dramatic increase in private individual research
    c.  A reliance on government research grants
    d.  A distinctive split between pure science and technology

24.  Since World War Two, women have
    a.  become less independent.
    b.  married later.
    c.  practiced greater birth control.
    d.  had more children.

25.  Since the Second World War, scientists
    a.  have become less specialized.
    b.  have become subject to less government influence.
    c.  increasingly work together in teams.
    d.  have decreased in number.

26.  Which of the following is a trend since World War Two in European marriage and family practices?
    a.  Later marriage
    b.  Marriage for economic reasons
    c.  A rise in the birthrate
    d.  Less emphasis on motherhood

27.  Who was the brash American Ph.D. who wrote *The Double Helix* and desired fame and fortune through his scientific discovery?
    a.  James Watson
    b.  Ernest Rutherford
    c.  Francis Crick
    d.  John Desmond Bernal

28.  The economic stagflation experienced in the 1970s caused
    a.  governments to reduce social spending.
    b.  deficit spending by governments.
    c.  optimism.
    d.  a decrease in the number of bankruptcies.

## UNDERSTANDING HISTORY THROUGH READING AND THE ARTS

How has art reflected the ideals and trends in postwar society? The principal artists and the origins of their works are considered in E. Lucie-Smith, *Movements in Art Since 1945*\* (1986), while the most noteworthy art trends of the 1960s are discussed in *Pop Art*\* (1985) by L. Lippard et al. The danger of atomic war has fostered the production of a good number of films, including feature films such as *Dr. Strangelove*, *Fail-Safe*, and *Hiroshima, Mon Amour* and documentary films such as *The War Games* and *To Die, To Live*. An analysis of these and other films about nuclear war is found in a book by J. Shaheen, *Nuclear War Films* (1978). A good recent (1982) documentary about the effects of atomic testing in the 1950s is *Nick Mazacco: Biography of an Atomic Vet*.

## PROBLEMS FOR FURTHER INVESTIGATION

A number of women in the 1960s began writing about themselves and how they relate to the institutions of marriage, childbearing, and work and thereby contributed greatly to what became the women's movement of our day. Begin your investigation with the Frenchwoman S. De Beauvoir, *The Second Sex*\* (1953), and then the Australian G. Greer, *Sex and Destiny*\* (1985). Those who wish to compare the recent women's movement with earlier movements should turn to K. Rogers, *Feminism in Eighteenth Century England* (1982). On another liberation issue, the emergence of gay and lesbian minorities into urban politics is the subject of the Academy Award winning documentary film *The Life and Times of Harvey Milk* (1985); it was a PBS television presentation and is available on videotape.

   This chapter has suggested that a good number of problems have accompanied the changes in society since 1945. One of the most readable of the futurist books is R. Heilbroner's *An Inquiry into the Human Prospect*\* (1974). A world future dictated by technology is discussed in J. J. Servan-Schreiber, *The World Challenge* (1981), while the search for ethics in the age of technology is the subject of H. Jonas, *The Imperative of Responsibility*\* (1984), and R. Hardin et al., *Nuclear Deterrence*\* (1985), sketches out the positions of strategists and philosophers concerning a number of issues with regard to war and nuclear weapons. The problems and issues surrounding life in a British agricultural village in the 1960s are the subject of R. Blythe, *Akenfield*\* (1969).

\*Available in paperback.

# READING WITH UNDERSTANDING
## EXERCISE 6

## LEARNING HOW TO MAKE HISTORICAL COMPARISONS

An important part of studying history is learning how to *compare* two (or more) related historical developments. Such comparisons not only demonstrate a basic understanding of the two objects being compared, but also permit the student-historian to draw distinctions that indicate real insight.

For these reasons, "compare-and-contrast" questions have long been favorites of history professors, and they often appear on essay exams. Even when they do not, they are an excellent study device for synthesizing historical information and testing your understanding. Therefore, as the introductory essay suggests, *try to anticipate* what compare-and-contrast questions your instructor might ask. Then work up your own study outlines that summarize the points your essay answer would discuss and develop. The preparation of study outlines of course is also a useful preparation for essay questions that do not require you to compare and contrast.

### Exercise

Read the brief passage below. Reread it and underline or highlight it for main points. Now study the passage in terms of "compare and contrast." Prepare a brief outline (solely on the basis of this material) that will allow you to compare and contrast the Russian and German revolutions (of 1917-1919). After you have finished, compare your outline with the model on page F-3. Remember: the model provides a *good* answer, not the *only* answer.

The German Revolution of November 1918 resembled the Russian Revolution of March 1917. In both cases a genuine popular uprising toppled an authoritarian monarchy and established a liberal provisional republic. In both countries liberals and moderate socialists took control of the central government, while workers' and soldiers' councils formed a "countergovernment." In Germany, however, the moderate socialists won and the Lenin-like radical revolutionaries in the councils lost. In communist terms, the liberal, republican revolution in Germany in 1918 was only "half" a revolution: a "bourgeois" political revolution without a communist second installment. It was Russia without Lenin's Bolshevik triumph.

There were several reasons for the German outcome. The great majority of Marxian socialist leaders in the Social Democratic party were, as before the war, really pink and not red. They wanted to establish real political democracy and civil liberties, and they favored the gradual elimination of capitalism. They were also German nationalists, appalled by the prospect of civil war and revolutionary terror. Moreover, there was much less popular support among workers and soldiers for the extreme radicals than in Russia. Nor did the German peasantry, which already had most of the land, at least in western Germany, provide the elemental force that has driven all great modern revolutions, from the French to the Chinese.

Of crucial importance also was the fact that the moderate German Social Democrats, unlike Kerensky and company, accepted defeat and ended the war the day they took power. This act ended the decline in morale among soldiers and prevented the regular army with its conservative officer corps from disintegrating. When radicals headed by Karl Liebknecht and Rosa Luxemburg and their supporters in the councils tried to seize control of the government in Berlin in January, the moderate socialists called on the army to crush the uprising. Liebknecht and Luxemburg were arrested and then brutally murdered by army leaders. Finally, even if the moderate socialists had taken the Leninist path, it is very unlikely they would have succeeded. Civil war in Germany would certainly have followed, and the Allies, who were already occupying western Germany according to the terms of the armistice, would have marched on to Berlin and ruled Germany directly. Historians have often been unduly hard on Germany's moderate socialists.

## Comparison of Russian and German Revolutions (1917-1918)

*Similarities*

1. Both countries had genuine liberal revolutions.
   a. Russia—March 1917
   b. Germany—November 1918

2. In both countries moderate socialists took control.

*Differences*

1. Russia had a second, radical (Bolshevik) revolution; Germany did not.

2. In Germany workers and peasants gave radicals less support than in Russia.

3. In Germany the moderate Socialists stopped the war immediately and therefore the German army, unlike the Russian army, remained intact to put down radical uprisings.

# CHAPTER 39

## LIFE IN THE THIRD WORLD

## CHAPTER OBJECTIVES

After reading and studying this chapter you should be able to answer the following questions:

**Q-1.** How have the emerging nations of the Third World sought to escape from poverty? Have their efforts been successful?

**Q-2.** What has caused the prodigious growth of Third World cities, and what does this growth mean for their inhabitants?

**Q-3.** How do Third World thinkers and artists interpret their world and modern life before, during, and after foreign domination?

## CHAPTER SYNOPSIS

This chapter examines one of the most vexing and complex problems facing the world today — that of improvement of life in the Third World. The overall theme of the chapter is that, despite the enormous progress the Third World has made toward industrializing and modernizing, this progress has been uneven, has left serious imbalances, and has widened the gap between rich and poor. The term "Third World" is appropriate because it denotes a group of countries with certain common characteristics: all experienced foreign domination and a nationalist reaction, all are dominated by agricultural economies, and all are aware of their common poverty. As the chapter proceeds, it becomes clear that the Third World is united by the problems of how to successfully industrialize, control urbanization, and stop the population explosion.

It is difficult to understand the true dimensions of Third World poverty. Income statistics tend to overstate poverty levels because they do not account for the cheapness of basic necessities or the widespread reliance on noncash transactions. Hence poverty is best understood by looking at accounts of diet, housing, and public health services. Most Third World countries cannot provide minimal daily caloric requirements or meet the average diet of the rich nations of the Northern Hemisphere. It is a disappointing addition to this tragedy that, while the Third World countries have successfully contained certain killer diseases, a medical revolution has brought on a population explosion of an unprecedented size. The Third World population, which numbered about 1.7 billion in 1950, is expected to reach 5.2 billion by the year 2000. The primary cause of this is that while the medical revolution lowered the mortality rate, little was done to lower the birthrate — hence much of the progress made toward modernization and industrialization has been canceled by population increase.

Most Third World leaders saw industrialization as the way to modernize. In many ways, the Third World's first industrialization drive was a success: Industry grew and per capita income grew at record rates. The most popular route of those who dreamed of industrial greatness was that of a "mixed economy" — part socialist and part capitalist. India exemplifies this general trend, but it is in capitalist Taiwan and South Korea and in communist China that success is most notable. In South Korea and Taiwan, radical land reform, government encouragement of business, and considerable U.S. aid and multinational investment have laid the foundation for a growing and competitive market economy. China's land reform has been a major factor in its success in working out a balance between agriculture and industry.

Most Third World countries made a drastic mistake by neglecting to improve and modernize agriculture. By the late 1960s it was clear that Third World industrialization had not solved the puzzle of large-scale poverty, population explosion, and the need for agricultural self-sufficiency. A food crisis in India illustrates the world's nightmare visions of starvation and wars for survival. Agricultural development was avoided because it didn't hold the promise (or prestige) of industrialization and because the prerequisite land reform was unpopular with ruling elites. Besides, cheap food from America made paying attention to agriculture seem unnecessary. The Green Revolution of the 1960s changed all of this. The dramatic increase in agricultural production that followed made food self-sufficiency possible — although it appears that the Green Revolution works only in areas where peasants, and not big landlords, own the land. But like the medical revolution and industrialization, the Green Revolution has not lifted the landless peasants out of poverty.

It is the problem of urbanization without industrialization that has most affected the masses of the Third World. Half the world's city dwellers now live in Third World cities, which teem with makeshift squatter shantytowns. Runaway urban growth is an ever-present feature of Third World life. Rural poverty has pushed millions of people into already-crowded cities. Although most leaders and advisors either avoid them or hope to eliminate the shantytowns, overcrowding points to the fact that the gap between rich and poor in the Third World is monumental. There is no evidence, however, that any particular ideology — socialist, revolutionary, or capitalist — produces any more or less income inequality.

The great majority of urban dwellers are employed in low-paying and irregular industries, such as street selling and handicraft trades. Equally important, urban migration of men has fostered a new and more independent life for women, who have been left alone in the countryside. Meanwhile, education and mass communication have changed the ideas and aspirations of the masses. Unfortunately, although it is a path to government jobs and politics, education has failed to fulfill the hopes of the masses because it neglects the technical training that would allow them to move into modern agriculture and industry. At the same time, mass communication propagates the modern lifestyle and challenges old values. In this atmosphere of rootlessness, rising expectations, and poverty, members of a new school of writers point to the richness of Third World culture, hoping above all to reduce the loneliness and homelessness of its uprooted people.

## STUDY OUTLINE

I. Economic and social challenges in the Third World
  A. Third World peoples and leaders hoped that, with independence, they could fulfill the promises of a brighter future
    1. At first it was thought that the answer to rural poverty was rapid industrialization and "modernization"
    2. By the late 1960s, the failure of this program caused a shift in emphasis to rural development
  B. Defining the Third World and its poverty
    1. Despite some limitations, the concept "Third World" denotes a meaningful unity
      a. All the Third World has experienced foreign domination, a struggle for independence, and a common consciousness
      b. A large majority of Third World people live and work in agricultural settings
      c. Most Third World countries are poor and their average standard of living is low
    2. Understanding the poverty of the Third World is not easy
      a. A comparison of national income statistics often exaggerates Third World poverty
      b. Basic necessities are less costly in the Third World
      c. The statistics are often incomplete and do not account for noncash transactions
    3. "Poverty" means lack of food, unbalanced diet, poor housing, ill health, and scanty education

      a.   The health status of Asia and Latin America has been generally better than that of tropical Africa

      b.   Populations are overwhelmingly concentrated in the countryside as small farmers and landless laborers without basic skills and services

   4.   Mass poverty was a challenge to the leaders, who had promised that independence would bring improvement

C.  The medical revolution and the population explosion

   1.   A spectacular and ongoing medical revolution had come with independence

      a.   Modern methods of immunology and public health were adopted

      b.   The number of hospitals, doctors, and nurses increased

      c.   The recent trend is toward medical services for the countryside

   2.   This revolution has lowered the death rate and lengthened life expectancy

      a.   Child mortality declined

      b.   By 1980 life expectancy was between 40 and 64, whereas in developed countries it was about 71

   3.   This has accelerated population growth (see Figure 39.1)

      a.   The birthrate did not fall correspondingly

      b.   Malthus's conclusions have been revived and updated

      c.   Birth control and family planning are hindered by religious and cultural attitudes

D.  The race to industrialize, 1950–1970

   1.   Most Third World countries adopted the theory that European-style industrialization was the answer to their development

      a.   Much reliance was placed on state action and enterprise

      b.   The result for most was a "mixed economy" — part socialist, part capitalist

      c.   Heavy industry was promoted at the expense of agriculture

      d.   India's concentration on state planning of industry exemplifies these trends — including a neglect of agriculture and land reform

   2.   Nevertheless, this Third World industrialization drive was a success in many ways

      a.   Industrial growth exceeded population growth  and its pace was as rapid as in the pre-1914 United States

      b.   It stimulated an unprecedented growth in per capita income

      c.   The fastest growth was in the capitalist economies of South Korea, Taiwan, the Ivory Coast, Hong Kong, and Singapore

   3.   South Korea and Taiwan changed from typically underdeveloped nations into economic powers for several reasons

      a.   "Capitalist" land reform drew farmers into a market economy

  b.  Government encouraged business enterprise
  c.  U.S. aid and the multinationals encouraged growth
  d.  Some traditional culture was preserved, and political stability was maintained, but democracy suffered
4.  By the late 1960s it was clear that, for most countries, an economic miracle had not occurred and that industrialization had failed in important areas
  a.  The economic gap between rich and poor nations had widened
  b.  The main beneficiaries were not the rural masses
  c.  Industrialization failed to provide enough jobs
E.  Agricultural and village life
  1.  Since the late 1960s the limitations of industrialization have forced attention toward rural development and rural life
  2.  Why did Third World governments avoid agricultural issues?
    a.  Some saw agriculture as a mark of colonial servitude
    b.  Few saw how to improve peasant farming
    c.  Land reform was an unpopular issue in countries where powerful landlords prevailed
    d.  Free food from the West discouraged serious internal reform
  3.  Following the Indian food crisis of 1966–1967, fears of famine caused a shift of interest to Third World agriculture
    a.  The Green Revolution began in Mexico and then transformed agriculture in the Philippines, followed by India and China
    b.  Countries like India could feed their entire populations
    c.  This revolution appears to have brought profits to both large and small landowners
    d.  However, the landless or nearly landless people gained only slightly
    e.  The Green Revolution works best in countries with large peasant ownership
    f.  The Green Revolution has not been successful in Africa, and with the exception of Mexico, it has not worked in Latin America because of lack of peasant landownership
  4.  The Green Revolution, like the revolution in medicine and advances in industrialization, has not benefited the poorest groups in the Third World
II.  The growth of cities
A.  Urbanization in the Third World
  1.  Runaway urban growth is a feature of the Third World
    a.  Cities have grown rapidly, and the proportion of the total population living in the city has increased
    b.  Half the world's city dwellers live in Third World cities — which will be of staggering size by the year 2000

    2.  Cities have grown for many reasons
       a.  The rural population explosion and large landowning pattern (particularly in Latin America) have pushed masses of people to the cities
       b.  Many are pulled to the city by the hope of industrial employment
       c.  City life offers services and opportunities to break away from traditional rural society

B.  Overcrowding and shantytowns
    1.  Inadequate social services have made urban life difficult
    2.  Some governments have sought to limit and/or reverse migration to urban areas
    3.  Overcrowding, as in Singapore, has reached staggering proportions
       a.  Makeshift squatter settlements have sprung up overnight
       b.  These shantytowns house up to two-fifths of the urban populations
    4.  A debate exists over the worth of the shantytown environment
       a.  The "pessimists" stress the miseries of squatter life
       b.  The "optimists" point to worthwhile kinship ties and self-help fostered in the shantytowns
       c.  Some advise the government to help the squatters help themselves

C.  Rich and poor
    1.  The gap between rich and poor is monumental
       a.  Income distribution figures show inequality similar to that in pre-1914 Europe (see Figures 39.2 and 28.2)
       b.  The problem is not related to a country's ideological inclinations
    2.  The gap is greatest in urban areas
       a.  It is best seen in differences in housing: slums versus mansions with servants
       b.  A "modern" — Western — lifestyle is the byword of the urban elite
       c.  Education distinguishes the wealthy from the masses and is the road to government positions
       d.  The middle class is small and includes factory workers
       e.  The great urban majority work in traditional, low-paying, and irregular trades such as street selling

D.  Migration and the family
    1.  In Asia and Africa the great majority of migrants to the city are young men
       a.  This has had a great impact on traditional family life and the women left behind
       b.  The reasons for this pattern include the seasonal and temporary nature of urban work for many males
       c.  Also, kinship ties between city and original village encourage temporary migration by males

2. The consequences of this male out-migration have been mixed
   a. African and Asian women, once subordinates, became heads of households and embarked on the path to liberation
   b. Only children remain to help with the work
3. In Latin America, permanent migration of whole families is more typical
   a. This process has had less of an impact on women

III. Mass culture and contemporary thought in the Third World
   A. Education and mass communication
      1. Third World leaders and people view education as the avenue to jobs and economic development
         a. The number of young people in school has increased
         b. Still, compared to the rich countries, the percentage of children in school is low and the quality of education is mediocre
         c. The universities lack courses in technical education
         d. Because of "brain drain," many countries lose their best-educated people to the rich countries
         e. The educational system does not serve the needs of rural society
      2. Mass communication propagates modern lifestyles and challenges traditional values
   B. Interpreting the experiences of the emerging world
      1. Intellectuals and writers have responded differently to the search for meaning
         a. Some have merely followed a Western-style Marxist or capitalist line
         b. Others have broken with Western thought and values
         c. Fanon of Martinique argues that imperialist exploitation remains after independence
         d. He argues that the Third World provided Europe with its wealth
         e. Achebe argues that Africans must recognize and identify their native culture
         f. Achebe is critical of Third World leaders
         g. Naipaul criticizes Third World leaders and points to the plight of uprooted people
      2. These writers reflect the intellectual maturity and independence of many Third World writers

## REVIEW QUESTIONS

Q-1. Describe the level of poverty in the Third World. How well do statistics help us understand poverty?

Q-2.  What benefits and ill consequences did the so-called medical revolution bring to the Third World? Why did this revolution occur after independence was achieved?

Q-3.  Was European-style industrialization the solution for Third World underdevelopment? Discuss the strengths and weaknesses of Third World industrialization.

Q-4.  Describe the South Korea and Taiwan economic miracles.

Q-5.  What is a "mixed economy"? Why was it an attractive idea to the Third World countries?

Q-6.  Why did complacency with regard to Third World agriculture turn into a concern for agricultural reform? Where and under what circumstances has the Green Revolution worked best?

Q-7.  It has been said that, overall, the Green Revolution, the medical revolution, and industrialization represent large but uneven and unbalanced steps forward for the Third World. Explain.

Q-8.  Compare and contrast agricultural change in those regions with peasant landownership to those without peasant landownership.

Q-9.  Compared to the Western world, how rapidly are Third World cities growing? Why have Third World cities grown?

Q-10.  Which is the more convincing argument in the debate over the worth of the shantytowns — the pessimist or the optimist view?

Q-11.  How wide is the gap between the Third World rich and poor? How is this gap evidenced in contemporary Third World life?

Q-12.  Describe how urbanization has affected family patterns and female roles in Asia, Africa, and Latin America.

Q-13.  Discuss the impact of education and mass communication on Third World life.

Q-14.  What are the weaknesses of the Third World educational systems?

Q-15.  What are the principal ideas of the Third World writers Fanon, Achebe, and Naipaul?


## STUDY-REVIEW EXERCISES

*Define the following key concepts and terms.*

neo-Malthusian theory

Third World

Medical Revolution

mixed economy

Green Revolution

out-migration

"modern" lifestyle

"brain drain"

"bazaar economy"

shantytowns

*Identify each of the following.*

Frantz Fanon

Chinua Achebe

V. S. Naipaul

*Test your understanding of the chapter by answering the following questions.*

1. The so-called Third World *has/has not* been very successful in lowering its death rate.
2. Most Third World countries have experienced all *except* which one of the following? (a) foreign domination, (b) a struggle for independence, (c) populations that are overwhelmingly concentrated in poor cities, (d) sense of

   unity due to their awareness of their poverty. _____
3. The birthrate in the Third World has *declined/not declined*.
4. In the 1960s most Third World countries adopted the idea of a

   _____ economy, being part socialist and part capitalist.
5. For the most part, economic progress based on European-style industrialization *has/has not* worked for the Third World countries.
6. Which one of the following is *not true* about industrialization in the Third World? (a) It hardly benefited the rural masses. (b) It left societies vulnerable to food crises. (c) It provided more jobs than there were workers to fill them.

   (d) It was seen as more desirable than agricultural development. _____

7. The so-called Green Revolution works best in countries where (a) there is a small number of big landowners, (b) most of the land is peasant-owned.

   _____

8. Unlike in Asia and Africa, the migration pattern in Latin America *has/has not* encouraged the women's liberation movement.
9. Recent advice from the "optimists" to Third World politicians is that the shantytowns should be *eliminated/supported.*
10. In general, the educational system of the Third World lays primary stress on

   what kind of curriculum? (a) technical, (b) liberal arts. _____

## MULTIPLE-CHOICE QUESTIONS

1. Since gaining their independence, the populations of the Third World countries have
   a. increased dramatically.
   b. increased only slightly.
   c. decreased.
   d. not changed.

2. National income statistics, such as those collected by the United Nations to compare the standard of living of rich and poor nations, are
   a. misleading and promote distorted comparisons.
   b. reliable and helpful.
   c. reliable to estimate food and clothing only.
   d. the best indicator of poverty.

3. The health status of people in the Third World has been the lowest in
   a. Asia.
   b. Latin America.
   c. tropical Africa.
   d. India.

4. The main beneficiaries of Third World economic growth were the
   a. rural masses.
   b. poor.
   c. peasants.
   d. businessmen and the skilled and professional workers.

5. South Korea and Taiwan engineered an economic miracle by emphasizing
   a. socialist economic principles.

    b.  isolation from the world economy.
    c.  dynamic capitalism.
    d.  none of the above

6.  The Green Revolution
    a.  works best in economies where land is held by a few big landowners.
    b.  made many countries, such as India, food-sufficient.
    c.  failed in Mexico but succeeded in Bangladesh.
    d.  brought no benefits to small landowners.

7.  Fears of famine and food crisis in the Third World were partly a result of
    a.  the Green Revolution.
    b.  starvation in Mexico.
    c.  the failure of agricultural growth in Communist China.
    d.  near famine in India in 1966–1967.

8.  By the late 1960s it was clear that for most Third World countries,
    a.  industrialization had solved the problems of underdevelopment.
    b.  only a "mixed economy" would bring about industrialization.
    c.  industrialization had left them vulnerable to food shortages.
    d.  industrialization brought benefits to all segments of society.

9.  In Asia and Africa, the majority of the migrants to the cities have been
    a.  young men.
    b.  women.
    c.  families.
    d.  all of the above

10.  The major problem with Third World university education is that
    a.  it lacks students.
    b.  education is not recognized as important.
    c.  it does not have enough good teachers.
    d.  it fails to stress technical education.

11.  Frantz Fanon, the Martinique writer, sees Western influence in the Third World as
    a.  beneficial but short-lived.
    b.  exploitative even after independence.
    c.  important and beneficial because of its economic contributions.
    d.  irrelevant.

12.  Achebe argues that
    a.  European culture must be taught in Africa.

b.   European culture is the key to African identity.

c.   African culture was born out of European imperialism.

d.   African culture existed prior to the European invasions.

13.   Compared to the rich nations, the percentage of Third World children in school is

a.   about the same.

b.   higher.

c.   lower.

d.   higher in Asia, but lower in Latin America.

14.   The great majority of urban workers in the Third World work in

a.   factories.

b.   irregular trades such as street selling.

c.   professions.

d.   construction.

15.   The underlying message of Third World writers such as Achebe, Fancn, and Naipaul is that

a.   European domination brought benefits as well as damage.

b.   the colonial experience was a good way to break with tradition.

c.   real independence requires a break with Western culture.

d.   freedom can come only with industrialization.

16.   In the Third World, the gap between rich and poor

a.   is much less than in the industrialized West.

b.   has become much less since independence.

c.   is considerable and is similar to that in pre-World War One Europe.

d.   is about the same as that in the industrialized West.

17.   Which is true of Third World countries?

a.   Few have experienced foreign domination.

b.   All have experienced a decline in health services since independence.

c.   All have populations that are heavily rural.

d.   All are unaware of their poverty.

18.   The growth in Third World cities has been due to

a.   a rural population explosion.

b.   plentiful job opportunities in urban industry.

c.   rural people wanting to break away from traditional rural society.

d.   massive influxes of people from industrialized nations.

19.  Which of the following is considered a Third World "economic miracle"?
   a.   Kenya
   b.   Brazil
   c.   India
   d.   South Korea

20.  Paul Ehrlich, in his 1968 best-seller *The Population Bomb*, predicted that
   a.   the Third World would rise to destroy the West.
   b.   world death rates would increase dramatically.
   c.   Third World countries would catch up to industrialized nations by the year 2000.
   d.   massive immigration would occur from the Third World to the West.

21.  Probably the most substantial success of the Third World in the past thirty years is
   a.   the medical revolution.
   b.   stable political organization.
   c.   industrialization.
   d.   agricultural reform.

22.  The spraying of DDT in Southeast Asia has lowered the number of deaths due to
   a.   smallpox.
   b.   cholera.
   c.   bubonic plague.
   d.   malaria.

23.  The decline in the death rate of the Third World
   a.   has lengthened life expectancy.
   b.   accompanied a decline in the birthrate.
   c.   did not include a decline in infant mortality.
   d.   was not influenced by the medical revolution.

24.  A general rule of the Third World is a
   a.   capitalist economy.
   b.   mixed economy.
   c.   socialist economy.
   d.   barter economy.

25.  The Third World trend since the late 1960s has been to
   a.   deindustrialize.
   b.   institute massive land reforms.

    c.  coordinate rural development with industrialization.
    d.  deurbanize.

26.  The Green Revolution has been due in great part to
    a.  the work of Western plant scientists.
    b.  plentiful rainfall.
    c.  shifting global weather patterns.
    d.  the greenhouse effect.

27.  The Green Revolution's greatest successes have occurred in
    a.  Asia.
    b.  Latin America.
    c.  Africa.
    d.  Bangladesh.

28.  The "brain drain" affecting the Third World refers to
    a.  poor educational systems.
    b.  the disillusionment that rural workers have for education.
    c.  a lack of technical schools.
    d.  professionals educated in the West who do not return to their native countries.

## UNDERSTANDING HISTORY THROUGH READING AND THE ARTS

The lowest and poorest in history are hardly ever written about. A unique opportunity to understand life in the squalid shantytowns of Brazil (the *favelas*) is available in Carlina Maria De Jesus' book *Child of the Dark* (1962). Written on scraps of paper picked from gutters, this is a raw, primitive diary of a woman in the slums of São Paulo who fought daily for her survival and that of her three illegitimate children.

## PROBLEMS FOR FURTHER INVESTIGATION

Has land reform really helped the Third World poor? For the impact of land reform and agricultural policies on Third World countries see J. Powelson and R. Stock, *The Peasant Betrayal: Agriculture and Land Reform in the Third World* (1987), and on the issue of Third World poverty and food supply begin with F. M. Lappé and J. Collins, *Food First: Beyond the Myth of Scarcity** (1977).

*Available in paperback.

The puzzle of economic development is a difficult one, and it is subject to ever-changing analysis. One aspect of this puzzle has been the relationship between the Third World and the industrialized West and Japan. Those who are interested in this subject will want to read the latest book by Jean-Jacques Servan-Schreiber, *The World Challenge* (1982). Servan-Schreiber argues that the world's industrialized countries have a moral obligation to transfer their knowledge of advanced technology to the underdeveloped Third World.

A good place to begin, if you are interested in investigating the problem of population growth and how it relates to resources and production, is C. M. Cipolla, *The Economic History of World Population* (1974). This book has an excellent bibliography.

# CHAPTER 40

## ONE SMALL PLANET

## CHAPTER OBJECTIVES

After reading and studying this chapter you should be able to answer the following questions:

Q-1.  How is our planet organized politically?
Q-2.  How does the human race use its resources to meet its material needs?
Q-3.  What key ideas guide its behavior?
Q-4.  Is there hope for the planet's future?

## CHAPTER SYNOPSIS

The purpose of this chapter is to show how the modern world has become increasingly interdependent — at the very time when the global economic order generates a measure of animosity and the global political system threatens to destroy us all. The problem is that our great technological achievements have not been matched by any corresponding change in the way we humans govern ourselves. Hence the triumph of nationalism is one of the tragic results of human history. The United Nations has not been able to establish a global authority that transcends the sovereign and quarrelsome national states. The Security Council's ability to police the world remains theoretical and severely restricted. Instead, the United Nations affirms and reinforces the primacy of the national state. Although the Security Council has succeeded in quieting conflict between smaller states, it has become the victim of cold-war paralysis. The General Assembly, on the other hand, has become the sounding board for the Third World. The U.N. has made its greatest contribution in the area of its specialized agencies — such as world health, labor, trade, industrial development — responding to the Third World majority's successful expansion of the U.N.'s world mission.

The most striking and dangerous characteristics of our planet are its political complexity and its violence. The old Cold War hostilities remain very much alive. Nevertheless, the East-West blocs are less solid than they were. With the rise of middle, or regional, powers, such as Brazil, Nigeria, Iran, and India, which are intent on dominating their regions, the world is becoming increasingly multipolar. Hence we see not only a new plague of war, but a massive refugee problem that has left tens of millions homeless. Meanwhile, the East-West and multipolar drift to militarism has caused nuclear weapons to proliferate. The hopes of those who signed the nonproliferation treaty in 1968 have faded as the arms race surges ahead.

Ironically, alongside this increase in violence and political competition is a trend toward global interdependence — particularly in vital resources such as oil, air, and sea and in capital and technology. Here we see two major problems. First, a rapid growth in world population has placed great pressures on resources; second, an unequal distribution of world wealth threatens relations between the rich North and the poor South. Out of this, and encouraged by the OPEC oil coup, the Third World has gone some distance in the establishment of a "new international economic order" based on a more equitable distribution of the world's wealth. The author believes that our future lies in global collective bargaining, as the case of the international debt crisis in 1981 suggests, and not in international class war. To be sure, despite the harmful consequences brought on by the multinational corporations, the multinationals are a striking feature of global economic interdependence.

The ideas by which the human race lives have taken on a global unity as well. Europe's secular ideologies of liberalism, nationalism, Marxian socialism, and democracy have come to be shared by the rest of the world. Marxism and the concept of "modernization" in particular have come under attack and have undergone revision by intellectuals, such as the Yugoslav Djilas and the Russian Solzhenitsyn. Christianity has come under the spell of fundamentalism, as has the Islamic faith. At the same time, a whirlwind of mystical cults has accompanied a general global drift toward nonrational thought in popular literature and life.

## STUDY OUTLINE

I. World politics
  A. The human race has not matched its technological achievements with an effective global political organization — sovereign states still reign supreme
  B. Nation-states and the United Nations

1. Many Europeans and Americans have expressed disillusionment with the nation-state system; Toynbee believed that nationalism has upset the balance between humans and their habitat
2. The United Nations was founded in 1945 to maintain international peace and security
   a. A twelve-member Security Council was given the responsibility of maintaining world peace
   b. In practice, the Security Council's power is limited by the veto power of the Big Five
   c. The U.N. has reinforced the primacy of the national state
   d. The General Assembly is more of a Third World debating society than a law-making body
3. The U.N. also exists to solve international problems and promote human rights
4. Cold war politics has deadlocked the Security Council
   a. The General Assembly has assumed greater authority
   b. Here the Third World majority has stressed anti-Western issues
   c. The U.N. is often ignored, whereas most people identify with their own nation
   d. Yet the U.N. has established powerful international agencies — such as those promoting world health, agriculture, and industrial growth — to deal with global issues

C. Complexity and violence
   1. The old East-West cold war is still alive in the 1980s
   2. Tensions within the East-West blocs have weakened the superpowers — the U.S.S.R. and the United States
      a. China, Poland, and Afghanistan have challenged Soviet hegemony
      b. Western Europe has differed with the United States
   3. World politics has become "multipolar"
      a. New "middle powers" — such as Brazil, Mexico, Nigeria, Egypt, Israel, and Iran — have emerged
      b. Multipolar politics is regionalist, highly competitive, and violent
      c. Regional wars, such as in Lebanon and Cambodia, have destroyed entire countries
      d. A multitude of regional wars has created a serious world refugee problem

D. The arms race and nuclear proliferation
   1. Multipolar politics has encouraged militarism in countries such as Israel, South Africa, and Vietnam
   2. Many countries are developing nuclear weapon capacity
   3. Despite U.S. hopes for international control of atomic weapons, the Soviets built an atomic bomb

4.  Popular concern over nuclear fallout led to test ban and nonproliferation treaties
    a.  France, China, and India have disregarded the nonproliferation treaty
    b.  Part of this disregard was due to U.S. and USSR failures to move toward disarmament
    c.  The Soviet-U.S. nuclear arms race has speeded up since the failure of the United States to ratify the SALT II agreement
    d.  Fear of its neighbors has led powers such as India to "go nuclear"
    e.  It is possible that Israel, Iraq, South Africa, and Pakistan also have the bomb

II.  Global interdependence
  A.  While political and military competition between nations continues, nations find themselves increasingly dependent on one another in economic affairs, a fact that should promote peaceful cooperation
  B.  Pressure on vital resources
    1.  Predictions of a shortage of resources have led to doubts about unlimited growth
       a.  The 1970s pointed to the problems of population explosion, resource shortages, and pollution of the biosphere
       b.  OPEC price increases of 1973 caused much panic
       c.  Increased world demands have depleted much Third World resources and land — for example, overuse of land has caused the Sahara to advance southward
       d.  Many claim that the biosphere and the oceans are becoming poisoned
    2.  The greatest pressure on world resources comes from population explosion
       a.  Fortunately, birthrates have begun to fall in many Third World countries
       b.  Decline in child mortality, better living conditions, urbanization, and education encourage women to limit childbearing
       c.  Some state-run birth control programs, such as that in China, have succeeded
       d.  Elsewhere, as in India, the Muslim world, and the Americas, birth control is controversial and thus less successful
       e.  The prediction is that the present world population of 4 billion will not stabilize until it has hit 10–12 billion in about 2050
       f.  Some optimists argue that a more densely populated Earth can be supported
  C.  North-South relations
    1.  Many in the Third World (the "South") argue that the present international system is exploitive and needs to be reformed

      a.   They demand that a "new international economic order" be established

      b.   The "theory of dependency" argument claims that Third World "underdevelopment" is deliberate and permanent

   2.  The OPEC oil coup brought hope of greater world interdependence

      a.   The 1973–1974 coup brought the end to economic boom, and a massive global transfer of wealth occurred

      b.   The U.N. followed with a call for a "new international economic order"

      c.   The Program of Action and the Common Fund exist to give Third World countries greater control over their resources, to improve terms of exchange, and to reduce Third World debt

      d.   The United States and other nations have refused to agree to the new Law of the Sea

      e.   There are still sharp distinctions in terms of wealth and income

      f.   In reality, change will come through bargaining, not international class war

   3.  The international debt crisis illustrates North-South dependency

      a.   World recession has caused many Third World states to overborrow

      b.   U.S. banks have rescued Mexico and others from financial crisis

D.  The multinational corporations

   1.  Multinationals are huge business firms — such as IBM and Shell — that operate on a global, not national, basis

      a.   Supporters claim that multinationals will bring economic and technological unity to the world

      b.   Critics argue that multinationals are replacing nations

   2.  The multinationals emerged with the postwar economic revival

      a.   These firms applied new technologies and marketing techniques to industry

      b.   Since the late nineteenth century the United States has pioneered in mass production of standardized goods and developed advanced and innovative products

      c.   Firms learned how to treat the world as one big market

   3.  U.S. firms in oil and machinery led the way

      a.   This was known as "the American challenge" in Europe

      b.   They invested in Third World raw materials as well

      c.   By the 1970s the Japanese and European multinationals pushed into the game — and Japan's new economic power caused fear in the United States

   4.  The social consequences of the multinationals are great

      a.   They have created islands of wealth and consumerism in the Third World

      b.   Critics claim that multinationals, as they take over Third World industries, are a part of a growing neocolonialism

      c.   However, Third World governments have learned how to control and manipulate the multinationals

III.  Patterns of thought

    A.  Secular ideologies

       1.  Most secular ideologies — such as liberalism and nationalism — evolved out of the Enlightenment and then nineteenth-century Europe

          a.   The spread of secular ideology testifies to our global interdependence

       2.  Since 1945, Marxist ideology has been revised and criticized

          a.   New concepts, such as the idea of peasant revolution, have been injected into Marxism by Third World intellectuals

          b.   Yugoslavs claim that the Leninists and Stalinists have created a "new class" in history

          c.   Revel argued that communism has brought about totalitarianism rather than progressive socialism

       3.  Alternatives to traditional secular creeds have emerged

          a.   Sakharov advocates welfare capitalism and democratic socialism

          b.   Others argue that the best solution to human problems is internationalism

          c.   Solzhenitsyn, Heilbroner, and Schumacher typify the call for a return to a more simple life and alternative technologies

    B.  Religious belief: Christianity and Islam

       1.  Pope John Paul II exemplifies the surge of popular Christianity

          a.   He preaches a liberal social gospel along with conservative religious doctrines

          b.   Poland illustrates the strength of spiritualism in a communist country

       2.  Islam has also experienced a powerful resurgence

          a.   The trend among Muslim intellectuals after 1945 was to modernize Islam

          b.   Recently the swing has been a return to strict fundamentalism

          c.   Iran's revolution was in part an Islamic fundamentalist reaction to modernization

          d.   The Ayatollah Khomeini's Islamic Republic seeks a return to rule by the laws of the Qur'an

          e.   This antimodernism is based on Shi'ite Islamic beliefs

          f.   This fundamentalism has found popularity in every Muslim country

    C.  Searching for mystical experience

       1.  Meditation, mysticism, and a turn to the supernatural have become popular in industrialized societies

2. This illustrates the intellectual challenge from the non-Western world
   a. More people today are receptive to mysticism
   b. Heilbroner suggests that postindustrial people stress inner exploration rather than material accomplishment
   c. Thompson and others contend that the search for spiritualism will humanize our technological world

## REVIEW QUESTIONS

Q-1.  Why have some observers expressed disillusionment with nationalism and the nation-state system?

Q-2.  Describe the workings of the United Nations. Has it met its goals, and what have been its successes and weaknesses?

Q-3.  Explain how and why multipolar politics has made world affairs more complex and more violent.

Q-4.  Why has the world been thrown into a renewal of the arms race? What or who is to blame?

Q-5.  Why have countries such as India spent valuable resources on nuclear arms development?

Q-6.  Describe how the problem of resource shortages illustrates the interdependence of rich and poor nations.

Q-7.  How successful has been the worldwide attempt to limit population growth? Is overpopulation a serious problem?

Q-8.  Many people of the Third World argue that they are being exploited by the rich Northern nations. What is the basis of their argument? What do they seek with the so-called new international economic order?

Q-9.  Cite an argument for and an argument against the multinationals. Why did they emerge, and what have been the social consequences of their presence in Third World countries?

Q-10.  What is meant by "secular ideologies"? How has Marxism been revised and criticized in recent times?

Q-11.  What is religious fundamentalism, and how has it reinterpreted Christianity and Islam?

Q-12.  People today are more receptive to mysticism. Why? What forms does this take?

Q-13.  What effect has the Shi'ite Islamic faith had on Iranian society? On all of the Middle East?

## STUDY-REVIEW EXERCISES

*Define* the following key concepts and terms.

world population explosion

multipolar politics

proliferation of nuclear weapons

theory of dependency

new international economic order

Law of the Sea

religious fundamentalism

global interdependence

rich nations/poor nations

multinational corporations

*Identify* each of the following and give its significance.

OPEC

U.N. Security Council

United Nations

Afghanistan, 1978–1979

Vietnam's "boat people"

Somalia-Ethiopia War

Strategic Arms Limitation Treaty

international debt crisis of the 1980s

Andrei Sakharov

Milovan Djilas

United Nations "Common Fund"

Ayatollah Khomeini

Pope John Paul II

*Explain the basic ideas inherent in each of the following.*

Solzhenitsyn's "return to the earth" doctrine

Islamic fundamentalism

modern search for mystical experience

Sakharov's "convergence school"

Djilas's "a new class" interpretation of modern communism

Revel's idea of "phony" communist revolution

*Limits to Growth* study of 1972

*Test your understanding of the chapter by answering the following questions.*

1.  The trend in world politics has been toward *lesser/greater* gravitation of nations to the U.S. or Soviet camp.

2.  The _____ of the United Nations has the responsibility to maintain world peace, whereas the

    _____ has become an expression of Third World interests.
3.  Since the early 1980s, the population growth in the developed countries has *speeded up/slowed down*, while in poorer countries the birthrate has *speeded up/slowed down*.

4. It appears that Third World governments *have/have not* learned how to control and manipulate multinational corporations.
5. The trend in today's world is *toward/away from* nonrational, mystical experience.
6. The world trend since the SALT treaty of 1980 has been toward an *increase/decline* in the arms race.
7. The movement in global politics has been toward (a) East-West alignments,

   (b) multipolar alignments. _____


## MULTIPLE-CHOICE QUESTIONS

1. The goal of the "middle powers," which are making the world increasingly multipolar, is to
   a. increase their political and military prowess to the level of a Great Power.
   b. achieve economic independence for their region.
   c. dominate their region.
   d. form regional alliances strong enough to oppose the Great Powers.

2. The world's vast refugee problem has been aggravated largely by
   a. famine.
   b. disease epidemics.
   c. local wars and civil conflicts.
   d. natural disasters.

3. The first and second largest armies in the world are the Soviet and Chinese, respectively. Which of the following nations is in third place?
   a. United States
   b. Great Britain
   c. Vietnam
   d. France

4. Treaties have failed to halt the spread of nuclear weapons because
   a. the United States and Russia have ignored the treaties.
   b. smaller powers have been anxious to develop their own nuclear weapons.
   c. nations have feared their enemies more than nuclear weapons.
   d. all of the above

5. The text suggests that world population will stabilize in the mid-twenty-first century at
   a. 10 to 12 billion.

b.  6 to 8 billion.
c.  15 billion.
d.  none of the above

6.  Steps toward the establishment of the Third World's "new international economic order" are most likely to include
    a.  military action.
    b.  tariff wars.
    c.  global collective bargaining.
    d.  "soak the rich" taxes.

7.  It may be generally said of the Third World's debt to the West that
    a.  most of it can never be repaid.
    b.  additional loans are needed to prevent default.
    c.  its levels have dropped in recent years.
    d.  most nations are able to back their payments with gold.

8.  The trend among multinational corporations in Third World countries is for them to
    a.  behave exactly as they please.
    b.  treat natives as inferiors.
    c.  increasingly submit to local control.
    d.  become nationalized.

9.  Most of the more recent contributions to Marxist thought have come from
    a.  the Soviet Union.
    b.  the Third World.
    c.  eastern Europe.
    d.  intellectuals in western Europe.

10.  The Law of the Sea Treaty drawn up in the early 1980s
    a.  has been universally adopted.
    b.  is opposed by the Third World.
    c.  is supported by the Soviet bloc.
    d.  was opposed by the U.S. government.

11.  Most of the secular ideologies such as liberalism
    a.  are revivals of ancient ideas.
    b.  were products of twentieth-century thought.
    c.  originated in eighteenth- and nineteenth-century Europe.
    d.  are becoming less popular today.

12. Internationalists are
    a.  believers in the United Nations.
    b.  unpatriotic individuals.
    c.  in favor of world government.
    d.  in favor of creeping socialism.

13. Muslim fundamentalists believe
    a.  the Qur'an should be adapted to modern life.
    b.  the Qur'an should be taken literally.
    c.  in strict separation of church and state.
    d.  none of the above

14. It may be said of the Communist states that
    a.  they are still firmly under Soviet control.
    b.  there are real tensions among them.
    c.  the bloc is less solid than formerly.
    d.  both b and c

15. Many developing nations see defense spending as a way to
    a.  dominate their region.
    b.  induce economic development.
    c.  reduce unemployment.
    d.  spend surplus oil revenues.

16. European contributions to modern Marxist thought have been largely
    a.  economic theories.
    b.  agricultural models.
    c.  criticisms.
    d.  ignored.

17. Russia's Sakharov envisions the East and West meeting in some ideological
    middle ground. This is called
    a.  the cooperation theory.
    b.  convergence school.
    c.  détente.
    d.  none of the above

18. Philosopher William Thompson describes the search for mystical experiences
    as a
    a.  rejection of traditional religion.
    b.  mere fad.
    c.  defeat for scientific thought.
    d.  desire to humanize technology.

19. One problem with the study of futurology is that it
    a. is unduly pessimistic.
    b. has a low accuracy rate.
    c. sometimes represents predictions as certainties.
    d. is overly optimistic.

20. The Russian novelist Alexander Solzhenitsyn called on Soviet leaders to
    a. renounce Western technology.
    b. adopt population controls.
    c. adopt Western-style modernization and consumerism.
    d. renounce communism.

21. Ayatollah Khomeini's Islamic reform movement is founded on
    a. Westernization of Iran.
    b. support of the Shah.
    c. separation between church and state.
    d. a society based on religious fundamentalism.

22. Renowned British historian Arnold Toynbee argued in his book *Mankind and Mother Earth* that
    a. the national state is the truest form of government.
    b. global government is necessary to maintain peace on earth.
    c. overpopulation is inevitable.
    d. man is inherently evil.

23. What fraction of the earth's people are Muslim?
    a. One-half
    b. One-seventh
    c. One-twentieth
    d. One-fiftieth

24. Influential Yugoslav intellect Milovan Djilas has argued that
    a. Lenin contributed the most to Marxist thought.
    b. Trotsky was an ineffectual idealist.
    c. Stalin-type communism created a new class.
    d. the Marxist dialectic has lost its value.

25. Which of the following is considered a "middle power"?
    a. Burma
    b. Ecuador
    c. Brazil
    d. Botswana

26.  The second Strategic Arms Limitation Treaty
    a.  has failed to reduce the number of warheads.
    b.  was never ratified by the U.S. Senate.
    c.  called for reductions in stockpiles.
    d.  has succeeded in reducing the number of short-range missiles.

27.  In most countries, abortion is
    a.  free on demand.
    b.  outlawed because it is subversive to the state.
    c.  legal but expensive.
    d.  available but discouraged.

28.  Birthrates have remained much higher in Africa and South America than in Asia in recent years because in part
    a.  Asians are less virile.
    b.  Asian women are less fertile.
    c.  the sexual revolution never reached Asia.
    d.  contraception and abortion are controversial in Africa and South America.

## UNDERSTANDING HISTORY THROUGH READING AND THE ARTS

What have Russian intellectuals written about their own society? This chapter has discussed the views of a number of important Soviet writers. You can find further discussion of Sakharov's views in his book, *Progress, Coexistence, and Intellectual Freedom* (1970 edition), and Djilas's criticism of how the Marxist system works is found in his book, *The New Class* (1957).

What is the human prospect? In two of his books the renowned biologist René Dubos tells how humans are shaped by their environment and how we need to control the forces of urbanization and technology. His famous slogan "think globally, act locally" could well serve as a blueprint for ecological balance in nature and nations alike. The books are *So Human and Animal* (1968) and *Celebrations of Life* (1981).

## PROBLEMS FOR FURTHER INVESTIGATION

How the recent past has affected the present can be a rewarding and constructive study. Many research topics are suggested in two excellent periodicals. They are *Current History* and *History Today*, both of which specialize in looking at current world events from an historical perspective.

Those interested in pursuing the issue of the arms race and the possibility of nuclear war will want to begin with D. Halloway, *The Soviet Union and the Arms Race* (1983), and G. Kennan, *The Nuclear Delusion: Soviet-American Relations in the Atomic Age* (1982). A provocative look at the business of nuclear strategy in the 1950s and 1960s is *The Wizards of Armageddon* (1983) by F. Kaplan. An excellent way to pursue this chapter's look into the complexities of Polish-Soviet relations is to begin with *The Polish August* (1982) by N. Ascherson.

# ANSWERS TO OBJECTIVE QUESTIONS

## CHAPTER 15

*Provide approximate dates.*

1. 1348
2. 1309–1377
3. 1337–1453
4. 1414–1418
5. 1346
6. 1358
7. 1321

*Test your understanding.*

1. did not
2. bad
3. England, France
4. Lollards
5. economic
6. decrease

*Multiple-choice questions.*

1. d
2. d
3. a
4. a
5. b
6. d
7. c
8. b
9. b
10. c
11. c
12. d
13. a
14. a
15. b
16. c
17. d
18. c
19. a
20. a
21. d
22. c
23. c
24. b
25. b
26. b
27. b
28. c

## CHAPTER 16

*Test your understanding.*

1. Mansa Musa
2. *ghana*
3. Kilwa
4. (b)
5. Lake Texcoco,
   Tenochtitlan (Mexico City)
6. (b)
7. Huitzilopochtli
8. "black"

*Multiple-choice questions.*

| | | | |
|---|---|---|---|
| 1. c | 8. b | 15. b | 22. c |
| 2. a | 9. b | 16. d | 23. a |
| 3. c | 10. c | 17. b | 24. d |
| 4. c | 11. c | 18. d | 25. a |
| 5. c | 12. d | 19. c | 26. d |
| 6. b | 13. c | 20. a | 27. b |
| 7. c | 14. b | 21. a | 28. a |

## CHAPTER 17

*Test your understanding.*

1. Niccolo Machiavelli
2. less
3. increased
4. Thomas More
5. declined
6. is not
7. did
8. king
9. political
10. Martin Luther
11. Alexander VI
12. was
13. weaken
14. Protestant

*Multiple-choice questions.*

| | | | |
|---|---|---|---|
| 1. d | 9. d | 17. a | 25. b |
| 2. d | 10. d | 18. b | 26. a |
| 3. b | 11. c | 19. c | 27. c |
| 4. b | 12. b | 20. b | 28. c |
| 5. b | 13. b | 21. a | 29. b |
| 6. c | 14. b | 22. b | 30. c |
| 7. d | 15. b | 23. c | 31. a |
| 8. a | 16. a | 24. a | 32. c |

## CHAPTER 18

*Test your understanding.*

1. Thirty Years' War
2. Cortes
3. Las Casas
4. Edict of Nantes
5. sixteenth
6. Gustavus Adolphus
7. the United Provinces of the Netherlands
8. Amsterdam
9. Elizabeth I
10. skepticism
11. Charles V
12. Concordat of Bologna
13. Portugal

*Multiple-choice questions.*

| | | | |
|---|---|---|---|
| 1. b | 8. a | 15. c | 22. a |
| 2. d | 9. c | 16. c | 23. d |
| 3. d | 10. b | 17. c | 24. a |
| 4. b | 11. b | 18. a | 25. d |
| 5. a | 12. d | 19. c | 26. c |
| 6. b | 13. c | 20. b | 27. b |
| 7. c | 14. a | 21. a | 28. b |

## CHAPTER 19

*Test your understanding.*

| | | |
|---|---|---|
| 1. stadholder | 3. entered | 5. John Churchill |
| 2. Colbert | 4. disaster | 6. Laud |

*Multiple-choice questions.*

| | | | |
|---|---|---|---|
| 1. d | 8. d | 15. c | 22. c |
| 2. a | 9. c | 16. c | 23. a |
| 3. d | 10. b | 17. c | 24. a |
| 4. d | 11. a | 18. c | 25. c |
| 5. a | 12. c | 19. b | 26. a |
| 6. b | 13. c | 20. b | 27. d |
| 7. a | 14. a | 21. b | |

## CHAPTER 20

*Test your understanding.*

1. Peter the Great
2. Johann Sebastian Bach
3. increased
4. Suleiman the Magnificent
5. maintained
6. Frederick II (Great)
7. (1) 4  (2) 1  (3) 3  (4) 2  (5) 5  (6) 6
8. weaker

*Multiple-choice questions.*

| | | | |
|---|---|---|---|
| 1. d | 8. b | 15. a | 22. b |
| 2. c | 9. c | 16. b | 23. d |
| 3. a | 10. b | 17. a | 24. a |
| 4. c | 11. b | 18. d | 25. c |
| 5. d | 12. c | 19. d | 26. a |
| 6. b | 13. c | 20. d | 27. d |
| 7. a | 14. b | 21. b | 28. c |

# CHAPTER 21

*Test your understanding.*

1. water, earth
2. did not
3. motion
4. universal gravitation
5. philosophy
6. Portugal
7. was not
8. did not
9. skeptic
10. Newton
11. failed

*Multiple-choice questions.*

| | | | | | | | |
|---|---|---|---|---|---|---|---|
| 1. a | 8. b | 15. c | 22. b |
| 2. c | 9. a | 16. c | 23. d |
| 3. d | 10. a | 17. d | 24. a |
| 4. d | 11. a | 18. a | 25. c |
| 5. c | 12. b | 19. d | 26. d |
| 6. b | 13. a | 20. d | 27. a |
| 7. a | 14. b | 21. c | 28. a |

# CHAPTER 22

*Test your understanding.*

1. limited
2. was not
3. did
4. potato
5. longer
6. cowpox
7. the common people
8. Wesley

*Multiple-choice questions.*

| | | | | | | | |
|---|---|---|---|---|---|---|---|
| 1. b | 8. d | 15. b | 22. d |
| 2. d | 9. a | 16. b | 23. b |
| 3. b | 10. d | 17. a | 24. c |
| 4. c | 11. b | 18. b | 25. c |
| 5. b | 12. c | 19. d | 26. d |
| 6. a | 13. a | 20. a | 27. a |
| 7. b | 14. d | 21. a | 28. b |

# CHAPTER 23

*Test your understanding.*

1. Brazil
2. England
3. Muslim holy war
4. janissaries
5. Taj Mahal

*Multiple-choice questions.*

| | | | |
|---|---|---|---|
| 1. b | 8. c | 15. c | 22. d |
| 2. b | 9. d | 16. b | 23. b |
| 3. b | 10. b | 17. a | 24. d |
| 4. c | 11. a | 18. c | 25. a |
| 5. b | 12. a | 19. c | 26. c |
| 6. c | 13. b | 20. a | 27. a |
| 7. b | 14. d | 21. a | 28. b |

# CHAPTER 24

*Test your understanding.*

| | | |
|---|---|---|
| 1. Hung Wu | 3. was | 5. growth |
| 2. increased, more | 4. was | |

*Multiple-choice questions.*

| | | | |
|---|---|---|---|
| 1. d | 8. a | 15. b | 22. b |
| 2. b | 9. a | 16. c | 23. a |
| 3. c | 10. b | 17. b | 24. b |
| 4. c | 11. b | 18. a | 25. c |
| 5. a | 12. a | 19. b | 26. c |
| 6. b | 13. b | 20. d | 27. b |
| 7. a | 14. d | 21. a | 28. c |

# CHAPTER 25

*Test your understanding.*

| | | |
|---|---|---|
| 1. Trafalgar | 5. were not | 9. decrease |
| 2. an important | 6. Louis XVI | 10. victory |
| 3. Thomas Paine | 7. opposed | 11. military ruler |
| 4. Montesquieu | 8. Mountain | |

*Multiple-choice questions.*

| | | | |
|---|---|---|---|
| 1. c | 8. d | 15. b | 22. d |
| 2. d | 9. d | 16. d | 23. d |
| 3. d | 10. d | 17. d | 24. a |
| 4. a | 11. b | 18. c | 25. b |
| 5. d | 12. a | 19. b | 26. c |
| 6. c | 13. a | 20. d | 27. c |
| 7. a | 14. b | 21. c | 28. b |

# CHAPTER 26

*Test your understanding.*

1. 1780, textile
2. increased
3. James Watt
4. potatoes
5. Liverpool-Manchester, *Rocket*
6. decrease
7. Crystal Palace
8. increased
9. greater
10. *Zollverein*
11. decreased
12. factory, decrease

*Multiple-choice questions.*

1. d
2. b
3. d
4. b
5. b
6. b
7. b
8. a
9. b
10. a
11. a
12. c
13. c
14. a
15. d
16. a
17. a
18. b
19. a
20. b
21. d
22. c
23. c
24. b
25. c
26. c
27. c
28. c

# CHAPTER 27

*Test your understanding.*

1. defeat
2. Louis Napoleon
3. Eugène Delacroix
4. should not
5. Austrian
6. Johann Herder
7. Louis Blanc
8. competition, victory

*Multiple-choice questions.*

1. a
2. b
3. b
4. a
5. d
6. c
7. b
8. a
9. d
10. c
11. d
12. b
13. c
14. d
15. a
16. c
17. d
18. b
19. b
20. c
21. c
22. b
23. a
24. a
25. c
26. b
27. b
28. b

# CHAPTER 28

*Test your understanding.*

1. decreased
2. Bentham
3. antiseptic
4. 1890
5. improved
6. no change
7. labor aristocracy
8. rose
9. music halls
10. love
11. grow stronger
12. more
13. decreased

*Multiple-choice questions.*

1. a
2. b
3. a
4. c
5. d
6. a
7. d
8. b
9. a
10. c
11. a
12. c
13. c
14. c
15. b
16. b
17. b
18. a
19. b
20. c
21. b
22. a
23. a
24. c
25. b
26. c
27. d
28. a

# CHAPTER 29

*Test your understanding.*

1. approved
2. middle class
3. defeat, freedom
4. opposed
5. fell
6. Protestant, against
7. France

*Multiple-choice questions.*

1. b
2. b
3. c
4. d
5. b
6. c
7. c
8. c
9. b
10. c
11. c
12. b
13. c
14. d
15. a
16. b
17. b
18. c
19. d
20. c
21. b
22. c
23. c
24. b
25. d
26. a
27. a
28. d

# CHAPTER 30

*Test your understanding.*

1. (c)
2. (e)
3. (h)
4. (b)
5. (d)
6. (f)
7. (a)
8. (g)

*Multiple-choice questions.*

| | | | |
|---|---|---|---|
| 1. c | 8. a | 15. c | 22. b |
| 2. b | 9. a | 16. a | 23. c |
| 3. a | 10. b | 17. a | 24. b |
| 4. b | 11. c | 18. c | 25. d |
| 5. b | 12. b | 19. a | 26. d |
| 6. d | 13. a | 20. b | 27. d |
| 7. b | 14. b | 21. c | 28. a |

## CHAPTER 31

*Test your understanding.*

1. Creoles, peninsulares
2. encouraged
3. more
4. (a)
5. unfavorable
6. the United States, Britain
7. long, rare
8. (b)
9. two
10. Jacob Riis

*Multiple-choice questions.*

| | | | |
|---|---|---|---|
| 1. b | 9. d | 17. b | 25. d |
| 2. a | 10. b | 18. b | 26. b |
| 3. b | 11. c | 19. c | 27. b |
| 4. d | 12. a | 20. d | 28. b |
| 5. a | 13. d | 21. d | 29. c |
| 6. c | 14. b | 22. b | 30. c |
| 7. b | 15. b | 23. a | 31. c |
| 8. c | 16. d | 24. b | 32. b |

## CHAPTER 32

*Test your understanding.*

1. Belgium
2. Vladimir Lenin
3. June 28, 1914
4. Alexander Kerensky
5. Soviets
6. T. E. Lawrence
7. Brest-Litovsk
8. Bismarck
9. Black Hand

*Multiple-choice questions.*

| | | | |
|---|---|---|---|
| 1. c | 8. c | 15. a | 22. d |
| 2. a | 9. c | 16. b | 23. a |
| 3. c | 10. a | 17. a | 24. c |
| 4. c | 11. a | 18. a | 25. d |
| 5. c | 12. a | 19. c | 26. d |
| 6. d | 13. b | 20. b | 27. c |
| 7. b | 14. d | 21. a | 28. d |

# CHAPTER 33

*Test your understanding.*

| | | |
|---|---|---|
| 1. mandates | 4. in favor of | 7. less |
| 2. (c) | 5. France, Christian | 8. included in, |
| 3. accepted | 6. kibbutz | excluded from |

*Multiple-choice questions.*

| | | | |
|---|---|---|---|
| 1. d | 8. a | 15. c | 22. c |
| 2. b | 9. b | 16. d | 23. b |
| 3. a | 10. d | 17. c | 24. a |
| 4. b | 11. b | 18. d | 25. b |
| 5. a | 12. b | 19. a | 26. c |
| 6. a | 13. a | 20. a | 27. d |
| 7. c | 14. d | 21. b | 28. d |

# CHAPTER 34

*Test your understanding.*

| | |
|---|---|
| 1. were not | 3. discard |
| 2. Germany, Britain, France | 4. challenge |
| the United States | 5. J. M. Keynes |

*Multiple-choice questions.*

| | | | |
|---|---|---|---|
| 1. a | 8. a | 15. b | 22. a |
| 2. c | 9. a | 16. c | 23. c |
| 3. c | 10. d | 17. c | 24. a |
| 4. a | 11. c | 18. c | 25. b |
| 5. d | 12. c | 19. b | 26. c |
| 6. a | 13. d | 20. c | 27. d |
| 7. c | 14. c | 21. d | 28. d |

## CHAPTER 35

*Test your understanding.*

1. favored
2. refused
3. victory, disaster
4. right
5. do not
6. Benito Mussolini
7. was
8. Adolf Hitler
9. declined
10. pro-German
11. did not

*Multiple-choice questions.*

| | | | |
|---|---|---|---|
| 1. d | 8. c | 15. b | 22. c |
| 2. d | 9. c | 16. d | 23. a |
| 3. a | 10. c | 17. c | 24. b |
| 4. a | 11. c | 18. b | 25. b |
| 5. d | 12. a | 19. a | 26. a |
| 6. c | 13. d | 20. d | 27. d |
| 7. c | 14. c | 21. b | 28. d |

# CHAPTER 36

*Test your understanding.*

1. Marshall Plan
2. Warsaw Pact
3. Charles De Gaulle

*Multiple-choice questions.*

| | | | |
|---|---|---|---|
| 1. c | 8. b | 15. c | 22. c |
| 2. a | 9. b | 16. a | 23. a |
| 3. b | 10. d | 17. b | 24. a |
| 4. d | 11. b | 18. d | 25. d |
| 5. d | 12. d | 19. a | 26. d |
| 6. b | 13. b | 20. a | 27. a |
| 7. c | 14. c | 21. c | 28. c |

# CHAPTER 37

*Test your understanding.*

1. strengthened
2. did not
3. limiting
4. is
5. (b)
6. Jinnah, Pakistan, Bangladesh
7. did not
8. limiting
9. Achmed Sukarno

*Multiple-choice questions.*

| | | | |
|---|---|---|---|
| 1. b | 8. b | 15. b | 22. b |
| 2. c | 9. d | 16. d | 23. d |
| 3. a | 10. c | 17. d | 24. c |
| 4. a | 11. a | 18. b | 25. a |
| 5. c | 12. d | 19. c | 26. a |
| 6. a | 13. b | 20. a | 27. b |
| 7. d | 14. c | 21. b | 28. c |

# CHAPTER 38

*Test your understanding.*

| | | |
|---|---|---|
| 1. declined | 4. greater | 7. less |
| 2. fall | 5. greater | 8. limited |
| 3. increased | 6. an increase | 9. greater |

*Multiple-choice questions.*

| | | | |
|---|---|---|---|
| 1. c | 8. b | 15. b | 22. d |
| 2. c | 9. d | 16. b | 23. c |
| 3. c | 10. a | 17. d | 24. c |
| 4. d | 11. c | 18. c | 25. c |
| 5. c | 12. d | 19. a | 26. d |
| 6. d | 13. a | 20. c | 27. a |
| 7. d | 14. a | 21. d | 28. b |

# CHAPTER 39

*Test your understanding.*

| | | |
|---|---|---|
| 1. has | 5. has not | 8. has |
| 2. (c) | 6. (c) | 9. supported |
| 3. declined | 7. (b) | 10. (b) |
| 4. mixed | | |

*Multiple-choice questions.*

| | | | |
|---|---|---|---|
| 1. a | 8. c | 15. c | 22. d |
| 2. a | 9. a | 16. c | 23. a |
| 3. c | 10. d | 17. c | 24. b |
| 4. d | 11. b | 18. a | 25. c |
| 5. c | 12. d | 19. d | 26. a |
| 6. b | 13. c | 20. b | 27. a |
| 7. d | 14. b | 21. a | 28. d |

CHAPTER 40

*Test your understanding.*

1.  lesser
2.  Security Council,
    General Assembly
3.  slowed down,
    speeded up
4.  have
5.  toward
6.  increase
7.  (b)

*Multiple-choice questions.*

| | | | |
|---|---|---|---|
| 1. c | 8. c | 15. b | 22. b |
| 2. c | 9. b | 16. c | 23. b |
| 3. c | 10. d | 17. b | 24. c |
| 4. d | 11. c | 18. d | 25. c |
| 5. a | 12. c | 19. c | 26. b |
| 6. c | 13. b | 20. a | 27. a |
| 7. b | 14. d | 21. d | 28. d |